"As I see it, the chief duty of the historian is this: to see that virtue is placed on record, and that evil men and evil deeds have cause to fear judgment at the bar of posterity."—*Tacitus*

Tacitus was a formidable foe of tyranny: his histories express wrath at the imperial system, the corruption of court and city, and the decline of Roman virtue. As a historian he was concerned with the pathology of power—how it affects those who exercise it and those to whom it is applied; and his ability to analyze human emotions and penetrate character is that of a great literary artist.

The Annals centers on Rome, capital of the Empire, and on the frontiers, from 14 A.D. to 68 A.D. Tacitus tells what is happening in Britain (the famous rebellion of Queen Boudicca); in Africa and the East (the exploits of Germanicus); and, at the same time, at home in the decadent courts of the emperors. Powerful portraits emerge, not only of notables, but of a Roman centurion, a German chieftain, a minor political figure at Rome. With this remarkable translation by an eminent scholar, *The Annals* appear once more in a language as bold and brilliant as the immortal original.

Other Classical Writings in
MENTOR Editions

GREAT DIALOGUES OF PLATO,
translated by W. H. D. Rouse

A new translation into direct, forceful English of *The Republic* and other dialogues of the great philosopher of ancient Greece.   (#MQ672—95¢)

THE SATIRES OF JUVENAL,
translated with Introduction by Hubert Creekmore

All sixteen of Juvenal's mordant satires on the foibles of first-century Rome, newly translated by a poet and novelist.
                                                                                      (#MT535—75¢)

THE SATYRICON by Petronius,
translated by William Arrowsmith

A classic re-creation of Nero's pleasure-loving Rome by the cultured cynic, Petronius. In a brilliant new translation.
                                                                                      (#MP493—60¢)

GREEK HISTORICAL THOUGHT
edited by Arnold J. Toynbee

The eminent historian's brilliant translations of Greek historical writing from Homer to the age of Heraclius—a stimulating guide for our own times.   (#MP431—60¢)

The Annals of Tacitus

A New Translation by
D. R. DUDLEY

A MENTOR BOOK

Published by The New American Library, New York and Toronto
The New English Library Limited, London

FIRST PRINTING, OCTOBER, 1966

Library of Congress Catalog Card No.: 66–26534

MENTOR TRADEMARK REG. U.S. PAT. OFF. AND FOREIGN COUNTRIES
REGISTERED TRADEMARK—MARCA REGISTRADA
HECHO EN CHICAGO, U.S.A.

MENTOR BOOKS are published in the United States *by*
The New American Library of World Literature, Inc.
1301 Avenue of the Americas, New York, New York, 10019
in Canada *by The New American Library of Canada Limited,*
156 Front Street West, Toronto 1, Ontario,
in the United Kingdom *by The New English Library Limited,*
Barnard's Inn, Holborn, London, E.C. 1, England

PRINTED IN THE UNITED STATES OF AMERICA

LIST OF TABLES

LIST OF MAPS

LIST OF PLATES

INTRODUCTION

Tacitus' Life and Writings

Cornelius Tacitus, greatest of Roman historians, has put on record few details of himself—of his family, none. An inscription from Gallia Belgica names a Cornelius Tacitus as *procurator*, or imperial finance officer, in that province: this is almost certainly the historian's father. The family was probably of provincial origin from Gallia Narbonensis, though some have suggested north Italy.

The historian was born in 57 A.D. Nothing is known of his early life; a first-rate education can be deduced. The main outlines, at least, of his official career are clear. After holding the usual minor magistracies, he was raised in 78 A.D. to the patrician or highest grade of the Senate by Vespasian, that bourgeois Emperor whose origins were so like his own. He was praetor in 88, consul in 97, governor of Asia in 112–113 A.D. This leaves some gaps, and Sir Ronald Syme has suggested (1) a four-year command of a legion somewhere about 90 and (2) another provincial governorship, probably of one of the two German provinces, after the year 100. This latter post would be consistent with the interest and knowledge Tacitus displays in the history of the German frontiers, and indeed of the geography and peoples of unconquered Germany. Already famous as an orator in his forties, his great work as a historian belongs to the later years under Trajan and Hadrian. The date of his death is unknown, though it cannot be earlier than 118. There remain two other facts of consequence: first, his marriage in 77 A.D.

to Julia, daughter of Gnaeus Julius Agricola—an exceptionally close and happy partnership; second, his experience, at close quarters, of the Terror under Domitian—a traumatic experience which, as we shall see, affected his whole outlook as a historian.

His earliest literary work, the *Dialogus de Oratore*, was published about 80 A.D., and dealt with the problems presented by the decline in Roman oratory. A dialogue with four speakers, it already shows that gift for characterization for which the historian was to find such ample scope. It was followed by a long silence. Under a Domitian it was dangerous to write history, especially for a senator and a magistrate. With Nerva the frost broke. After the example of Sallust—whom he admired most of Roman historians—Tacitus wrote two historical monographs before working on a larger scale. Both appeared in 98 A.D. The *Agricola*, a tribute to his father-in-law, is at once a biography and a funeral oration. Agricola's career had culminated in his long term of office as governor of Britain (78–84 A.D.), with its grandiose but abortive design for the conquest of Caledonia. There is a brief disquisition on the ethnography and earlier history of Britain; then a description, in the highly stylized manner to be followed in the *Annals*, of Agricola's campaigns. The last chapter—a wonderful piece of rhythmic prose—is one of the finest things in all Latin literature. The *Germania* combines ethnography and geography in a study of Rome's most formidable enemies, the Germanic peoples who confronted her beyond the frontiers of the Rhine and the Danube. It draws heavily on secondhand material, especially the *Bellum Germaniae* of the elder Pliny—which Tacitus has not always bothered to bring up to date.

The major works, the *Histories* (published 104–109) and the *Annals* (published after 117), form a single grand historical design. The corpus of thirty books covers, between them, the period from the death of Augustus to the death of Domitian (14–96 A.D.). The *Histories* run from the death of Nero to the death of Domitian (69–96 A.D.), while the earlier period from the accession of Tiberius to the death of Nero is the subject of the *Annals*. Of the *Histories* there survive Books I–IV, and a part of V; of the *Annals*, I–VI (incomplete), parts of XI and XVI, and XII–XIV. Tacitus speaks of a history of reigns of Nerva and Trajan as a project reserved for his old age; it does not seem to have been carried out.

Tacitus' View of History

"As I see it, the chief duty of the historian is this: to see that virtue is placed on record, and that evil men and evil deeds have cause to fear judgment at the bar of posterity." This is the most explicit statement of Tacitus' view of the purpose of history: there are several others to the same effect. It will be seen at once how sharply it differs from what commonly passes as history in our own day. In the first place, it has a moral purpose. In the second, it is concerned, primarily, with individual persons and their characters, regarding these as the most important of the moving forces in history. Moreover, it is written as literature, and intended to be read aloud. Clio, in the ancient world, had as yet not parted company with her fellow Muses. To find a parallel, we should have to go back at least to the generation of Macaulay, before the writing of history had become the preserve of scholars. But it is, of course, the view that informs all the great historians of antiquity—certainly Herodotus, Livy, and Sallust. Thucydides, despite his aspirations to a "scientific" study of history, is not really an exception. Polybius may be, but only in so far as he cannot write in the grand manner. What gives the *Annals* their particular quality is not Tacitus' attitude to history, but his views of the Roman principate, and the highly wrought and individual style in which they are set forth.

Senator, historian, orator—the work draws on all three. As a senator, and a new man at that, he had the traditional regard for the old Republic, and an ingrained dislike of the principate. But he was a realist: the excesses of the "Stoic" opposition to Nero and Domitian moved him to admiration, not support. He had seen from the inside the working of the great imperial machine, and knew that it had come to stay. The real problem was to get a good man at the top—and a problem almost insoluble, because "absolute power corrupts absolutely." Like so many who have seen it at close quarters, Tacitus was fascinated with the workings of power. He is thus concerned to observe the reality of political power, as it cuts through the niceties of constitutional friction. But beyond that is the pathology of power, as it affects the men who exercise it and those to whom it is applied.

If Tacitus penetrates deep, he does so on a narrow front. He writes, primarily, for men of his own class and outlook. The narrative of the *Annals* has two poles: the capital of the Empire, and the frontiers. An analysis of the subjects treated in each chapter brings this out very clearly. Thus, for the first six books 55 percent is concerned with political affairs at Rome, 34 percent with the frontiers, 11 percent with other subjects. For Books XI–XVI the figures are: Rome 52 percent, frontiers 35 percent, other subjects 13 percent. Moreover, "politics of Rome" affords no wide selection of themes. The rise and fall of favorites, intrigues for the succession, palace scandals, treason, trials and their victims—it is, as Tacitus admits, a monotonous succession. But he has his answer; such are, in fact, the politics of despotism. Students of Kremlinology will be disposed to agree. Yet again, there is much more to the history of the Empire. Tacitus has little to say about the peaceful romanization of the provinces—the true glory of the *Pax Romana;* little on economics; almost nothing on cultural life. His digressions are indeed memorable, but they are isolated; they do not form any coherent pattern. Reading the *Annals,* one thinks of the revolving beam of some great lighthouse. It sweeps over and illuminates what lies in its path: beyond lie great areas of darkness.

It was Racine who called Tacitus the greatest of painters. He might with equal force have claimed him as a fellow tragedian. And, in the tradition of classical tragedy, Tacitus does not care for many actors on the stage. There is a careful choice of characters for treatment, vigorous pruning of detail, economy in the names of people and places. The rebellion of Boudicca in Britain (XIV, 29–39) will serve as an example. We are told the names of the governor of Britain, and of two procurators, the most important Roman officials concerned. Petilius Cerealis, who commanded the Ninth Legion in an unsuccessful battle, gets a mention, but not the place of his defeat nor the base to which he retreated. Poenius Postumus, camp commandant of the Second Legion, is named for his disastrous refusal to obey orders and subsequent suicide; the base in which he skulked is not given. The three cities captured by the Britons are noted by name, but not the place of the final battle. On the British side, only Boudicca and her husband Prasutagus are named: of their two daughters, the rape is recorded, but not the names. . . . In short, this major disaster, which spread over two years and must have involved at least a hundred thousand persons, yields the names of eight persons, four places, and two British tribes. But its dramatic possibilities are brilliantly exploited; these few chapters of Tacitus have been the raw material for more than one full-scale tragedy. The essence of Boudicca's rebellion is there, as the essence of the Dacian Wars is contained in that great contemporary work—so close in feeling to the *Annals*—the Column of Trajan.

The characters thus carefully selected are treated on a wide range of scale. Sometimes it is no more than a sketch, firmly but economically drawn, and at the moment of action—a Roman centurion, a German chieftain, a minor political figure at Rome. More important persons call for special notice: some of Tacitus' most memorable writing is found in such paragraphs. So with Poppaea Sabina as she enters, or Petronius Arbiter when he leaves the stage. Other characters, such as Corbulo, develop with the narrative, and receive a minimum of comment. There are group characters: the Roman army in victory, mutiny, and defeat: the Senate, no more than an echo of its former self, but never quite forgetting its past. For such major characters as Sejanus, Agrippina, or Germanicus, narrative and comment are on an ample scale, sometimes with the final tribute of an obituary. Above the rest, developing slowly and portentously over several books, tower those gigantic psychopaths, the Emperors. Claudius—uxorious, pedantic, and grotesque, with the odd appeal of those wholly devoid of dignity. Nero, the roistering young bully-boy with a taste for lechery and the arts, passing to the matricide and *folie de grandeur* of his later years. Above all, Tiberius—Tacitus' masterpiece, on which he lavished all his powers—the inscrutable countenance and the cold heart, the unwearying malevolence and the recondite lusts. In him Tacitus saw the archetype of the tyrant-Emperor, to which the sequel was Domitian. In his reign the law of treason was to unfold to an instrument of terror: then began that fearful system of spying and denunciation which so harassed the men of Tacitus' generation, reducing them all to silence, and sending the best of them to their graves. Tacitus' portrait of Tiberius is surely one of the most damaging indictments ever brought against a historical figure. So confident is Tacitus of having achieved his effect that he is generous in conceding his victim's good qualities. Many modern scholars have undertaken the vindication of Tiberius, and they have achieved notable success. They have shown that the Tacitean account proceeds from a settled bias, and employs every weapon in the armory of calumny. And yet, indelibly, the Tacitean image of Tiberius persists.

Style

No other writer of Latin prose—not even Cicero—deploys so effectively the full resources of the language. To read deeply and widely was part of the education of the Roman orator. There are in Tacitus many echoes of Virgil, Horace, Lucan, Lucretius, Ennius, and Livy, to name no more. Sallust, for his archaisms and contrived simplicity, was constantly before him as a model. But neither education nor reading could fashion the style of Tacitus into the unique thing it is. It was the product of many years of experiment, of a constant search for new words, a readiness to discard what had shown itself unsuitable. The periodic sentence, that majestic achievement of Ciceronian prose, is virtually abandoned. Constructions are chosen for impact and brevity, metaphors bold or deliberately harsh, adjectives painted in startling contrast. Full maturity is reached in the *Annals,* especially in the first six books. Intense, complex, subtle, and sustained, it belongs to Tacitus and to him alone—a weapon that none but its inventor could ever use.

Translator's Notes

All translators of Tacitus reach, sooner or later, the conviction that their task is impossible. They are right. From what has just been said, it must be clear that the full savor of his style is to be had only by those with a connoisseur's appreciation of

xiv

Latin prose. Most translators have therefore tried to reproduce at least one of the characteristics of Tacitean style—usually brevity, since that is the best known and the most readily assessed. Such was the chief aim of the great Italian translation of Davanzati (1637). Printed in parallel columns, translation and original run neck and neck through the chapters, with a triumphant dead heat at the end of each book. No such steeplechase is possible in the heavier going of the English tongue. It seems better to provide a base of good contemporary English, eschewing the colloquial and the transient, through which the historian at least may speak for himself. Thanks to the exhaustive analysis of Sir Ronald Syme (*Tacitus* XXVI, XXVII) the modern translator may hope to catch at least some notes of the stylist. Thus, I have consciously tried to reproduce Tacitus' wide range of synonyms for death: and I have taken the echoes of Virgil and Horace to license an occasional echo of Shakespeare or the Bible. One further point of style: although Tacitus is unflagging in sustaining the grand manner, he does not do so in a monotone, like that of French classical tragedy. He is a skilled and subtle parodist, and in his speeches we hear a wide range of voices, from the hoarse tone of the mob-orator Percennius (I: 17) to the childish whimper of Sejanus' little daughter being hurried off to her death (VI: Fr. 4). These effects Tacitus achieves with the lightest of touches. A few words, a phrase, are enough to score the text: a full interpretation can be brought out in recital or reading aloud. Lacking this resource, the translator is forced to a characterization more heavily stylized than in the original.

I have not thought it worthwhile to be consistent in the use of ancient or modern forms of place names, but a list of the most important places mentioned, and their modern equivalents, will be found on p. 405. I have also added a note on the Roman army of the first century A.D. The notes are in no sense a continuous commentary: they are restricted to the minimum that seemed necessary for an understanding of the narrative, or of the author.

The Annals of
Tacitus

BOOK I

1. The city of Rome was at first ruled by kings. Republican institutions and the consulship were established by Lucius Brutus. Dictatorships were assumed for an emergency: the powers of the Decemviri lasted no more than two years: those of the military tribunes were also short-lived.[1] Neither Cinna nor Sulla held long supremacy. The ascendancy of Pompey and Crassus soon passed to Caesar, as did the forces of Lepidus and Antony to Augustus. A world exhausted by civil war passed into his control, under the name of the principate.

Eminent historians have recounted the story of the old Republic in triumph and disaster. The times of Augustus, too, did not lack distinguished writers, until they were deterred by the mounting tide of adulation. The history of Tiberius, Gaius, Claudius, and Nero was, in their own lifetime, depicted in false colors through fear: after their deaths, raging hatred distorted the accounts. My purpose, then, is to deal briefly with Augustus, especially the end of his reign, and then to pass on to the principate of Tiberius and his successors. This I shall do without prejudice or partisanship, having no motives for either.[2]

2. After Brutus and Cassius were killed there were no more armies of the Republic. Sextus Pompeius was crushed in Sicily. Lepidus was deprived of his powers. Even Caesar's party had no leader save Octavian. He discarded the name of triumvir, bore himself as consul, and said that a tribune's powers were enough for him to protect the common people.

19

But when he had seduced the army by gifts, the common people by the provision of cheap food,[3] and everyone by the blandishments of peace, then little by little he began to enlarge his powers, to encroach on the proper functions of the Senate, the magistrates, and the laws. No one opposed him. Men of spirit had died on the battlefield, or in the proscriptions.[4] The remainder of the aristocracy were rewarded by wealth and position in proportion to their readiness to accept servitude. Having done well out of the revolution, they naturally preferred the existing security to the dangers and uncertainties of the old regime. The provinces showed no hostility to the new system. The rivalries of the contestants for power, the greed of republican governors, had made them distrustful of the rule of the Senate and people. They had derived no help from the laws, which were nullified by violence, intrigue, and, above all, by corruption.

3. As a support for his supremacy, Augustus made his sister's son, Claudius Marcellus,[5] high priest and aedile, despite his tender years. He also dignified Marcus Agrippa, of plebeian origin, but a fine general and his ally in victory, with two successive consulships. When Marcellus died, he took Agrippa as his son-in-law. His stepsons Tiberius Nero and Claudius Drusus were honored as victorious generals: this was when his own house was still intact. For he adopted Agrippa's sons, Gaius and Lucius, into the imperial family; even before they had ceased to be minors he was avid for them to receive the title of Princes of Youth, and to have consulships marked out for them, although he put on a show of reluctance. But Agrippa died; premature death or the intrigues of their stepmother Livia overtook Lucius as he was setting out for service in Spain, and then Gaius as he was returning, seriously wounded, from Armenia. Drusus was long dead. Tiberius was the only surviving stepson, and on him everything converged. He was made Augustus' son, shared his military command and tribunician powers, and was formally presented to all the armies. This was no longer, as before, the result of his mother's secret intrigues; it was done at her open request. She had so prevailed on the aging Augustus that he banished his only living grandson, Agrippa Postumus, to the island of Planasia. That young man was, it is true, void of any honorable accomplishment and of a brutish physique, but he had not been involved in any open scandal. But it was Germanicus, son of Drusus, whom the Emperor placed in command of the eight legions on the Rhine, and whose adoption by Tiberius he engineered. There was at this time a grown son of Tiberius (Drusus), but Augustus wished to buttress himself with all the support possible.

This was a period with no wars on hand except that against the Germans—a war undertaken not so much to extend the imperial frontiers nor for any worthwhile advantage, as to wipe out the disgrace of the army lost under Quintilius Varus.[6] At home there was tranquillity. The magistrates retained their titles. The young men had been born since the battle of Actium, most of the older generation during the civil wars. How many were left who could ever have seen the Republic?

4. So the state had been transformed, and the old free Roman character no longer existed. Equality among citizens had gone by the board: all awaited the Emperor's commands. There was no immediate danger, so long as Augustus retained his physical powers, and could support himself, the imperial house, and peace. But when he became advanced in age, and impaired by weakness, his approaching end brought hope of a change.

There was, in some circles, an idle discussion of freedom: most people dreaded war, though a few hoped for it. The great majority exchanged gossip, slanted this way and that, about the candidates for empire. Agrippa was a lout, embittered by his disgrace: neither in years nor in experience was he qualified for so gigantic an office. Tiberius was of mature age, and had proved himself in war. But he had all the ancestral haughtiness of the Claudian house, and had given many signs of a cruel disposition, though he tried to conceal them. Moreover, from his earliest years he had been reared in an imperial household: as a young man he had been loaded with triumphs and consulships; even those years in Rhodes—exile under the guise of retirement—had really been devoted to hatreds, dissimulation, and secret vice. Then there was his mother, with all her feminine excesses—"We shall be the slaves of a woman," men complained, "and of two youths, who will first burden down the state and then tear it in two between them!"

5. Amid these discussions, Augustus grew worse, and some suspected foul play by his wife. Indeed, there was a prevalent rumor that, only a few months earlier, Augustus, after taking a few people into his confidence, had gone with Fabius Maximus as his sole attendant to Planasia to see Agrippa. There had been a reconciliation, and so many tears on both sides that it seemed highly probable that Agrippa would be restored to favor in his grandfather's house. Maximus had told this to his wife Marcia; she had passed it on to Livia. This had come to Augustus' knowledge: when, soon after, Maximus died (suicide was never established), Marcia was heard to lament at the funeral that she had caused her husband's death. However that may be, Tiberius had only just reached Illyricum when he was recalled by a letter from his mother. It is uncertain whether he

found Augustus alive or dead when he got to Nola. The house and all the streets had been placed under strict guard by Livia. Hopeful bulletins were released, until the precautions dictated by the position had been taken. Then a single announcement proclaimed that Augustus had died, and that Tiberius now ruled.

DEATH OF AGRIPPA POSTUMUS

6. The first crime of the new reign was the murder of Agrippa Postumus. The soldier in charge was determined, Agrippa unarmed and unprepared, but the deed was performed with difficulty. Tiberius made no reference to it in the Senate. He gave it out that it had been done on his father's orders: that the officer left in charge had been given standing instructions not to delay over the murder of Agrippa, once Augustus was dead. There is no doubt that Augustus had complained loudly and often about the young man's character, and had induced the Senate to ratify his exile. But he had never steeled himself to murder any member of his house, nor was it credible that he should order the death of a grandson for the advantage of a stepson. A more likely reason would be that Tiberius, through fear, and Livia, with a stepmother's hatred, had hastened the end of the young man, whom they suspected and feared. The centurion announced, as soldiers do, that he had carried out his orders; Tiberius replied that he had given no orders, and that the matter must be answered for in the Senate.

When Sallustius Crispus, who had been privy to the plot and had sent instructions to the military tribune, learned of this, he was afraid that he would be produced as the person accused. If so, he would run an equal risk from truth or falsehood. He therefore warned Livia that the secrets of the palace, the advice of the Emperor's friends, and the faithful services of soldiers, were no matters for publicity. Tiberius must not undermine the principate by constant reference of business to the Senate. The essence of autocracy was that accounts would only balance if they had a single auditor.

7. But, in Rome, the consuls, the Senate, the knights, rushed headlong into servitude. The more illustrious, the more eager and hypocritical they were. To display joy at the death of an Emperor, or gloom at the succession of another, was equally untimely: countenances were carefully composed in a judicious blend of tears and relief, of grief and flattery. Sextus Pompeius and Sextus Appuleius, as consuls, were the first to take the oath

of allegiance to Tiberius. Then, in their presence, it was taken by Seius Strabo, commander of the Guard, and Gaius Turranius, in charge of the grain supply: next, the Senate, army, and people. Tiberius always acted through the consuls, as though it were still the era of the Republic, and he himself uncertain whether to rule or not. Even in the edict which called the senators together he only made use of his tribunician powers, which he had received from Augustus. Its terms were brief, and notably modest, announcing that he proposed to arrange for his parent's honors, that he would not leave the body, and that this was the sole public duty he meant to assume.

Yet, at the death of Augustus, Tiberius had issued the watchword to the Guard as its commander. He had bodyguards, armed attendants, and all the features of a court. Soldiers accompanied him to the Forum and to the Senate House. He sent dispatches to the army as though already in power. Only when addressing the Senate did he display hesitation. This was chiefly due to the fear that Germanicus, who had so many legions, besides a huge force of auxiliaries under his command, and was unanimously popular with the people, might prefer to possess himself of the throne rather than to wait for it. Besides, Tiberius deferred to public opinion far enough to prefer to seem the candidate chosen and summoned by the Senate, rather than the usurper smuggled to power by a dotard's adoption and the ambitions of his wife. Later, it was realized that his reluctance was assumed in order to expose the inclinations of the leaders of the state. What men said, how they looked, was distorted to some criminal significance—and stored for future use.

THE FUNERAL OF AUGUSTUS

8. On the first day of the Senate's session he allowed no business except the funeral of Augustus. The vestal virgins brought in the Emperor's will. It named Tiberius and Livia as his heirs, and adopted Livia into the Julian house. The grandchildren and great-grandchildren were all heirs of the second order, followed by the leaders of the state. Many of them he had hated, but here was an ostentatious claim for future glory. His legacies[7] were not beyond the scale of a private citizen, save a bequest of 43½ million sesterces to the state and to the people of Rome, 1,000 a head to soldiers in the Guard, 500 each to soldiers serving in Rome, 300 each to Roman citizens serving in the legions or auxiliary regiments.

There followed a debate on his funeral arrangements. The

most noteworthy speeches were those of Gallus Asinius, proposing that the funeral procession should pass through a triumphal arch, and of Lucius Arruntius, who wanted it to be preceded by the titles of the laws he had passed and the names of the peoples he had conquered. Messala Valerius further proposed that the oath of allegiance to Tiberius should be renewed every year. Tiberius asked him whether he himself had prompted this suggestion; Messala replied that it was his own idea, and that in matters of public interest he intended to use his own judgment and nobody else's, even if he risked causing offense. This was the only kind of flattery still left open. Then senators exclaimed that the body of Augustus should be borne to the funeral pyre on their shoulders Tiberius, with haughty condescension, refused. He also issued an edict warning the public against the same excessive enthusiasm that they had displayed at the funeral of Julius Caesar, lest they should insist that Augustus be cremated in the Forum rather than the Campus Martius,[8] his appointed resting place.

On the day of the funeral, troops were posted as though for security. This drew mockery from those who had witnessed or had heard from their parents of that occasion when slavery was in its salad days and there was an unsuccessful attempt to recover freedom. Then the attempted assassination of Caesar had seemed a fearful deed to some, but a glorious achievement to others. But now here was this aged princeps, after his long tenure of power, and with his heirs amply provided with resources against the state, and yet he needed a military guard to ensure a seemly burial!

9. Then followed much talk about the character of Augustus. Most people concentrated on such idle topics as the fact that the day when he first took up the sovereignty coincided with that of his death, that he died at Nola, in the same house and the same bedroom as his father Octavius. Attention was drawn to the number of his consulships—equal to those of Valerius Corvus and Gaius Marius put together—to the thirty-seven consecutive years during which he had held tribunician power, to his twenty-one salutes as victorious general, and to other aspects of his honors, whether repeated or novel.

Among the intelligent there was praise or criticism of his life in varying degree. Some maintained that filial duty and a national emergency which left no part for the laws to play had driven him to civil war—and this no decent method can ever begin or maintain. To avenge his father's murderers, he had had to make many concessions to Lepidus and to Antony. But when Lepidus grew indolent, and Antony deteriorated in de-

bauchery, the rule of a single man was the only possible remedy
for a country in turmoil. Even so, the regime set up was neither
a monarchy nor a dictatorship, but a principate. The Empire
was protected by the ocean, or by distant rivers: legions, fleets,
provinces formed a single system. There was the rule of law for
Roman citizens, decent treatment for the provincials. Rome
itself had been splendidly adorned. If a few instances of force
could be cited, it was to provide tranquillity for the majority.

10. Against this it was urged that piety toward his father
and the necessities of the state had only been put forward as
pretexts. Lust for power had led him to muster the veterans by
bribes, to raise a private army—though a mere boy—to seduce
the consuls' armies from their allegiance, and to feign support
for Sextus Pompeius. Then a senatorial decree enabled him to
assume the powers and rights of a praetor. Hirtius and Pansa
had been killed, whether by the enemy, or perhaps, in the case
of Pansa, by infecting his wound with poison, in that of Hirtius, by his own troops at the instigation of Octavian. He had
then taken over their troops: forced the Senate, against their
will, to make him consul: turned against the state the forces
he had been given to use against Antony. His proscriptions and
reassignments of lands had not even won the praise of those
who carried them out. Brutus and Cassius had, admittedly, met
their deaths because of a feud he had inherited from Caesar.
Even so, private vendettas must yield to the needs of the commonwealth. But he had deceived Sextus Pompeius by a false
peace, Lepidus by a false friendship. Antony had been trapped
by the treaties of Tarentum and Brundisium, and by marriage
with his sister: this treacherous relationship had cost him his
life. Peace had followed, certainly, but it was a bloody one—
the disasters of Lollius and Varus, the murders of Varro, Egnatius, Iullus.

Nor did criticism spare his private life. He had stolen Nero's
wife, then insulted the pontiffs by asking them whether it was
in order to marry her when she was pregnant. There had been
the gross extravagance of Vedius Pollio. Finally, Livia had been
a national disaster as a mother, a calamity to the house of
Caesar as a stepmother. There was no scope for the worship of
the gods, when Augustus wished to foster his own cult through
temples, divine effigies, and the service of flamens and priests.[9]
Even the selection of Tiberius as his successor had not been
prompted by affection or regard for the state. Once Augustus
had grasped his arrogance and cruelty, he sought glory for
himself by the worst of possible comparisons. And indeed, a
few years earlier, when Augustus had asked the Senate to re-

new Tiberius' powers as tribune, he had made certain references to his dress, deportment, and habits. Outwardly these were excuses; in reality, they were criticisms.

Augustus' funeral was duly held, and he was endowed by decree with a temple and divine worship.

THE OPENING OF THE REIGN OF TIBERIUS

11. Then all prayers turned to Tiberius. In the Senate, he had much to say about the size of the Empire, and his own moderation. Only the divine Augustus had been equipped with an intellect to handle such an undertaking. Invited by Augustus to take over a part of the burden, he had discovered by personal experience how difficult, how arduous it was to rule the world. Besides, a state containing so many illustrious men should not seek to impose every burden on the shoulders of one man; the joint efforts of several combined would more easily carry out the work of government. Such arguments were more lofty than convincing. Even when Tiberius was not dissembling, his words, by nature or habit, were ever hesitant and ambiguous. Here, where his whole object was to disguise his feelings completely, he was more involved than ever in obscurity and double-talk.

But the one fear of the senators was that they should show any sign of understanding him. There were tears, complaints, and prayers: appeals to heaven, to the statue of Augustus, to Tiberius himself. Then he ordered a document[10] to be produced and read. It was a detailed summary of the resources of the state. It listed the numbers of citizens and allies serving in the army, the size of the fleet, the number of client-kingdoms and provinces, the product of taxation, direct and indirect, the details of expenditure and of gifts. All this had been written out by Augustus in his own hand. He had further advised against extending the Empire beyond its present boundaries—whether from motives of fear or of jealousy.

12. At this point, while the Senate was lowering itself to the most servile forms of supplication, Tiberius happened to let fall the remark that, while he was unequal to the whole burden of the commonwealth, he would be willing to take charge of such part of it as might be committed to his care. Then Asinius Gallus said, "I ask you, Caesar, which part of the commonwealth you would choose to have committed to you." This unexpected question upset Tiberius, and for a while he was silent. Then he pulled himself together and replied that it ill

became his sense of modesty to select or reject any single aspect of a task which he would prefer to decline as a whole. Gallus realized by Tiberius' expression how deeply offended he was, but he went on, "The point of my question was not to separate what is of its nature indivisible, but to compel you, Caesar, to admit by your own argument that the commonwealth is a single body, and should be ruled by the mind of a single man." He added a eulogy of Augustus, and reminded Tiberius of his own triumphs in war, and of his splendid services to the state in peace for so many years. But this did nothing to appease Tiberius, who had long hated him for having married Vipsania, daughter of Agrippa, once Tiberius' own wife. This he regarded as conduct unbecoming a private citizen, and a persistence of the independent spirit of the father, Asinius Pollio.

13. Lucius Arruntius then spoke in the same terms as Gallus, and gave equal offense. Tiberius, it is true, had no long-standing grudge against him, but he was rich, in the public eye, of honorable attainments and equal reputation, and therefore suspected by the Emperor. Indeed, Augustus in the last discussions of his life had been reviewing the question of candidates for the offices of princeps—who might refuse it, who might want it though unequal to the task, and who again might both want it and be well qualified. He had pronounced Manius Lepidus as qualified, but likely to refuse, Gallus Asinius as avid for it, but too small a man, Lucius Arruntius as not unworthy, and likely to dare the attempt, if he had an opportunity. There is general agreement about the earlier names on this list, though some substitute Gnaeus Piso for Arruntius. All except Lepidus were destroyed by various charges manufactured by Tiberius. Even Quintus Haterius and Mamercus Scaurus touched a sore point in his suspicious mind—Haterius, when he said, "How much longer, Caesar, will you let us remain without a head of state?" Scaurus offended by saying that there was good hope that the Senate's prayers would not be in vain, because Tiberius had refrained from using his tribunician veto to block the consuls' proposals. He hit out at once at Haterius. Scaurus, with whom he was more deeply offended, he passed over in silence. Tired by the general uproar, he began to respond little by little to the entreaty of individuals, not to the point of openly admitting that he would assume supreme power, but to that of ceasing to deny—and being asked.

It is well known that when Haterius went to the Palatine to make his excuses, he found Tiberius at exercise and clasped his knees. This—or chance—caused Tiberius to stumble, and Haterius was almost killed by the guard. The danger of this distinguished man was to remain grave until he sought the help of Livia, and was rescued by her earnest entreaty.

14. On the Empress Livia,[11] too, the Senate showered much flattery. Some proposed that she be called "The Parent," others "The Mother" of her country; the majority favored adding the words "the Son of Julia" to Tiberius' titles. Tiberius said more than once that restraint should be shown in paying honors to women, and that he would use a like moderation in regard to any honors decreed to him. But, in fact, jealousy made him apprehensive; he felt that placing Livia on a pinnacle would lessen his own standing; consequently he even denied her a lictor, and forbade "an altar of adoption" or anything of that kind. But he sought proconsular power for Germanicus, sending a delegation to confer it on him, and to condole with him on the death of Augustus. That he did not seek the same powers for Drusus was due to the fact that Drusus was consul-designate, and in Rome. He nominated twelve candidates for the praetorship, the number customary under Augustus. When the Senate invited him to increase it, he took an oath that he would not do so.

15. This was the time when elections were first transferred from the Comitia to the Senate. Previously, although the Emperor's choice had determined the most important appointments, a few matters were still decided by the votes of the tribes. The people did not grumble at the loss of their rights, save for idle gossip; as for the Senate, it was quite content to be relieved from bribes and degrading canvassing. Tiberius showed moderation in commending no more than four names to be elected without canvassing or the possibility of rejection.

At this time the tribunes asked to be allowed to give games at their own expense in honor of Augustus. These were to be called "the Games of Augustus," and incorporated into the calendar. Permission was granted, but the treasury found the money. In the Circus the tribunes were allowed to wear triumphal robes, but forbidden to ride in chariots. Before long supervision of these games was transferred to the praetor concerned[12] with lawsuits between citizens and foreigners.

MUTINY ON THE DANUBE

16. Such was the state of affairs in Rome, when a mutiny broke out among the legions in Pannonia. No new cause had provoked it, but there was general unrest at the accession of a new Emperor, and the prospect of gain from civil war. Three

legions were encamped together in their summer quarters,[13] under the command of Junius Blaesus. Hearing of the death of Augustus, and the accession of Tiberius, he had canceled all fatigue duties as a sign of mourning—or of joy. From this moment the soldiers got out of hand: morale was relaxed; the most disloyal elements got a hearing; finally they set their minds on ease and idleness, despising discipline and toil.

In this camp was a certain Percennius, who had formerly led a claque in the theater,[14] but who was now a common soldier. He had a ready tongue, knew the intrigues of the theater, and how to raise a following. The soldiers were in doubt as to the conditions of service after Augustus' death: he would work on their minds in long conversations by night, or as the day ended. All the better elements moved away, and he soon had around him the scum of the army.

17. Before long there was a gang ripe for sedition, and he went among them, as though making a public speech. "Why," he asked, "obey a handful of centurions, and a number of tribunes smaller still, as though you were slaves? When will you ever have the courage to demand satisfaction, if not now, with a new Emperor, still insecure? You could approach him with words—or with arms! All these years you have been patient to the point of vice. You have served in the army for thirty or forty years, you are old men, and your bodies hacked away by wounds. Even discharge brings no end to your service. You are kept with the colors, still under canvas, still doing the same fatigues, though they give it another name.[15] Any who survive the long odds against them are sent to distant lands; under the name of a farm they get a muddy swamp or stony hillside.[16] In any case, the soldier's life is hard and unprofitable: his body and soul are valued at ten asses[17] a day. From that you have to pay for uniform, weapons, and lodging, give bribes to avoid the harshness of the centurions, or to buy yourself off duty. It is an endless round of blows and wounds, harsh winters, summers in the field, bloody battles, or a barren peace! There's only one remedy. We must enter the service on fixed conditions: pay, a denarius a day; discharge, after sixteen years; no service in the reserve; pay the men off in the camps where they've served. How about the Praetorian Guards, who get two denarii a day, and are sent home after sixteen years? Are their dangers greater than yours? I say nothing against guard duty in Rome: but we live among savages, we can look out from our quarters and see the enemy."

18. The crowd roared applause. They each had a grievance: one man the stripes of lashes, another his gray hairs, others old uniforms and ill-clad bodies. Their fury drove them to such a

pitch that they even talked of joining the three legions into one. But rivalry put an end to that: each man wanted his own legion to be first. So they tried another plan, and placed together the three eagles of the legions and the standards of the cohorts. Turf was piled up and a platform built, to make them more conspicuous. But as they were busy with this, Blaesus appeared. He reproached them, and tried to hold them back, man by man, shouting, "Better stain your hands with my blood! It's a lesser offense to kill your commander than to desert the Emperor! I will either keep my troops loyal and live, or be murdered to hasten your repentance!"

19. But they went on piling up the turf, and by now the platform was breast-high. At last, his persistence caused them to break off the work. With much eloquence Blaesus pleaded that the soldiers' demands should not be brought to the Emperor by rebellion and disorder. "In the old days," he said, "no troops ever put such requests to their generals: neither did you to Augustus. This is no time, as he enters on his principate, to load the Emperor with cares. But if you really intend, in time of peace, to embark on a course you never even contemplated as victors in the civil wars, why cast off your obedience? Why resort to a violence contrary to discipline itself, which is sacred? Choose your delegates. Let them present your demands in my presence." They all shouted that his own son, then a tribune, should fill this office. He must demand discharge for a man after sixteen years: when this was granted they would give him the rest of his instructions. When the young man had set out, some kind of discipline was restored. Even so, the troops plumed themselves at the thought that their commander's son was presenting their grievances. Disorder had brought results that good behavior would never have done.

20. Before the rebellion began, certain units had been sent to Nauportus to build roads, bridges, and the like duties. When they heard that there was rioting at the base, they tore down their standards and began to loot the nearest villages, and also Nauportus itself, a place the size of a municipality. Their centurions tried to check them, but met with jeers and insults, and finally with blows. Their special anger was directed against Aufidienus Rufus, the camp commandant. They took away his carriage, loaded him with equipment, and put him at the head of the column. With many jeers they asked him how he was enjoying the long marches and the heavy burdens. For Rufus had been a private, then centurion, and finally camp commandant. He had brought back the old tough methods: having long known severe toil himself, he was all the more hard-bitten because of what he had endured.

21. When these troops returned, rioting started again. The men broke loose, and plundered the countryside. To terrify the others, Blaesus picked out a few men who were loaded with plunder, had them flogged, and threw them into prison. Even at this point, the centurions and more reliable soldiers still obeyed their commander. But the prisoners struggled with their guards, clasped bystanders around the knees, called out the names of their comrades, or the century, cohort, or legion in which they served. The same fate, they warned, was in store for every single man. Especially did they revile the commander, calling the gods in witness, leaving nothing undone that could incite to pity and hatred, to fear and anger. All the troops made a rush, broke open the prison, and smashed the prisoners' chains. Deserters and condemned criminals were now mingled with the troops.

22. Now there was violence on a greater scale, and the rebellion had more ringleaders. A common soldier called Vibulenus was raised up on men's shoulders before the commander's tribunal. The troops were in disorder, hanging on his words. "You've brought back light and life to these innocent men," he shouted, "but who's to bring my brother back to life? Who's going to bring me my brother? The army in Germany sent him to you to talk about our common interests. Last night he was murdered—by gladiators, whom the general keeps under arms to destroy the serving soldier. Where's his body, Blaesus? Where have you thrown it? Even enemies don't begrudge a burial. Let me take my fill of embraces and tears, and then kill me! We've been murdered for no crime, but only for taking thought for the good of the legions: all I ask is that our comrades shall bury us!"

23. Weeping, beating his breast and face, he increased the general tension. Then he threw aside those holding him up, and cast himself headlong at the feet of one man after another. Such a tempest of hatred and anger did he arouse that some of the soldiers threw the gladiators from Blaesus' house into chains, some did the same to the rest of his household, and others rushed off to find the corpse. Had it not been soon known that no corpse was to be found, that the slaves under torture insisted that there had been no murder, and that, lastly, Vibulenus never had a brother, they were not far from murdering their own commander.

Even so, they drove the tribunes and the centurions out of the camp, plundered their baggage as they escaped, and lynched a centurion called Lucilius. This man had acquired, in soldier's language, the nickname of "Fetch-us-another!" because he would break his staff over a soldier's back and bellow for a second or a third. The other tribunes hid themselves for safety, except for Julius Clemens. He had a ready tongue, and they kept him to present their demands. Two legions, the Fourth and Fifteenth, were on the point of drawing their swords on each other, because the Fifteenth refused to give up a centurion called Sirpicus, whom the Fourth were determined to kill. But the men of the Ninth intervened, at first with prayers, and then, when these were rejected, with threats.

24. Tiberius was always inscrutable, and given to the supression of all bad news. But the reports of the mutiny caused him to dispatch Drusus, his son, and several prominent political leaders, together with two companies of the Praetorian Guard. Drusus was given no specific instructions, but was to act as the situation demanded. The cohorts were brought up to above establishment by the addition of picked men: the force was strengthened by the greater part of the Praetorian cavalry, and by a body of German troops,[18] then serving as bodyguards to the Emperor. At the same time Aelius Sejanus, commander of the Praetorian Guard, colleague of his father Strabo in that office, and a man of much influence with Tiberius, was sent to advise the young Drusus, and to make clear to the rest of the force what they stood to gain in rewards or punishments.

As Drusus approached, the legions made a show of duty by coming to meet him. But there was none of the customary joy, no glitter of decorations. They were slovenly of dress and dejected of bearing: under a parade of grief it came close to insolence.

25. As soon as Drusus had entered the ramparts, guards were posted on the gates; bands of soldiers carrying their arms occupied fixed parts of the camp. The rest surrounded the platform in a great multitude. There stood Drusus, asking for silence with a gesture. Whenever the soldiers looked at their own members, there was an uproar of angry cries: when they saw the Emperor's son they took alarm. There was a babel of confusion: loud shouts followed by sudden silence; as their emotions changed, they passed from fear to menace. At last the clamor died away. Drusus read the dispatches from the Emperor, which ran as follows: "The case of these brave legions, with whom I fought so many wars, is very dear to me. As soon as I have recovered from my personal grief, I shall put their requests to the Senate. Meanwhile, I have sent my son to grant whatever can be granted without further delay. All the rest must be referred to the Senate: it would be wrong to assume that they lack the power to show either indulgence or severity."

26. The meeting replied that the centurion Clemens had

their demands to put forward. These he presented: discharge
after sixteen years; bonuses on discharge, pay a denarius a
day; no retention of veterans with the colors. When Drusus
said these were matters for the Senate and his father, there was
an uproar. Why had he come, if he could neither raise their
pay nor lighten their burdens, nor do them any good at all?
Everyone had the power of ordering flogging or the death
sentence! It was an old habit of Tiberius to fob off the demands
of the soldiers by using the name of Augustus; now Drusus
was using the same trick. Would they never get anyone to
come to them save the sons of Emperors?[19] And it was a new
thing for their Emperor to refer the soldiers' rewards—and
only their rewards—to the Senate! Did he propose to consult
the Senate before executions or battles? Was it to be rewards
from despots, punishments without control?

27. Finally they streamed away from the platform, making
threatening gestures to any of the Praetorians who stood in
their way. This led to clashes, and the beginning of armed conflict. Their chief anger was directed against Gnaeus Lentulus.
Distinguished above the others in years and military experience, he was thought to have hardened Drusus' heart, and to
have been the first to reject "these insolent demands of the
men." Shortly afterward, he left the camp with Drusus, foreseeing danger and returning to the winter quarters. But they
surrounded him, asking, "Where are you going? To the Emperor, or to the Senate? There, too, are you going to speak
against the rights of the soldiers?" Then they rushed him,
hurling stones. Bleeding from the stones, and sure he was to
be killed, he was rescued by the main force which had come
with Drusus.

28. It was a night of menace, likely to end in violence. But
chance brought a respite, for in a clear sky the moon was
suddenly seen to grow dark. The soldiers, ignorant of science,
saw an omen of their present troubles in the eclipse of the
luminary. "Our plans will turn out well," they thought, "if
light and brightness are restored to the goddess." So they
clashed together bronze vessels and sounded the horns and
war trumpets. As she grew brighter or dimmer, they rejoiced
or despaired. Then clouds came up and covered her from
view: they thought she was lost in darkness. Minds that have
once given way to superstition are highly susceptible, and they
began to lament that it meant that their labors would be endless, that the gods themselves were turning from their crimes.

Drusus thought that the opportunity should not be lost but
that what chance had brought his way should be turned to wise
use. So he sent around the camp and summoned Clemens and

any other man of good conduct who could influence the mob. These men then went round among the sentries, the pickets, and the guards at the gates, now offering hopes, now using threats. "How much longer," they asked, "do we intend to hold the Emperor's son in durance? Where will this conflict end? Are we going to swear allegiance to Percennius and Vibulenus? Will Percennius and Vibulenus give us our pay, or our farms on discharge? Are they going to take over the Empire of the Roman people from Nero and Drusus? Why shouldn't we, the last to go wrong, be the first to repent? There is always delay over the redress of common grievances: private favors are paid as soon as they are earned."

This acted on their minds, and they had their mistrust of each other to split them, recruit from veteran, one legion from another. So, little by little, the sense of obedience returned. They left the gates, and replaced in their proper positions the standards which had been brought together at the start of the mutiny.

29. At dawn Drusus summoned a meeting. He was not a good speaker, but with innate dignity he reproached them for their past actions, and approved their present conduct. "Fears and threats," he said, "have no effect on me. Show yourselves obedient, let me hear your submission, and I will write to my father and ask him to receive your petitions without disfavor." At the soldiers' request a delegation was sent to Tiberius, consisting of the younger Blaesus, as before, Lucius Apronius, a knight serving in Drusus' cohort, and Justus Catonius, a centurion of the first class. Then there was a clash of opinion. Some were for waiting for the delegation to return, and for treating the soldiers kindly in the meantime; others favored stronger methods. "A mob," they said, "does nothing by half measures: you must terrorize them or dread them; overawe them once, and there's nothing to fear. While their minds are still swayed by superstition, let the general increase their fears by doing away with the ringleaders." Drusus was naturally disposed to harshness. Summoning Vibulenus and Percennius, he ordered them to be put to death. The usual account is that they were buried within the general's tent; though some say the bodies were thrown outside the ramparts to be on display.

30. Then all the ringleaders were hunted down. Some were found wandering outside the camp, and were struck down by centurions and soldiers of the Praetorian Guard. Some were given up by their own fellows as a proof of loyalty. An exceptionally early winter added to the soldiers' troubles. Heavy and continuous rains made it impossible for them to leave their tents, to meet together, even to keep the standards upright, for

these were blown down by gusts of wind or carried away by floods. And they still had hanging over them the fear of the wrath of heaven. They said that it was not for nothing that the stars had grown dim, the tempests had raged, in the face of their impiety. The only remedy for their disasters was to leave these unhallowed, polluted camps, to clear themselves by making atonement, and to return to their own winter quarters.

First the Eighth, then the Fifteenth, returned to base. The Ninth stood out waiting for letters from Tiberius, but then, isolated by the departure of the others, voluntarily anticipated the action they would soon have been forced to take. Since the situation was in hand for the present, Drusus went back to Rome without waiting for the return of the delegation.

MUTINY IN GERMANY

31. At this time, and for the same reasons, there were mutinies in the armies in Germany—even more violent, as the troops were more numerous. They had high hopes that Germanicus Caesar would be unable to tolerate another's rule, and would allow his legions to sweep everything before them by main force. There were then two armies on the Rhine. Caius Silius commanded that in Upper, Aulus Caecina in Lower, Germany. Supreme command was held by Germanicus, but he was then occupied with supervising the census in Gaul. Silius' troops watched with mixed feelings the rebellion that another army had begun. But in Lower Germany madness seized the troops, beginning with the Twenty-first and the Fifth legions, spreading to the First and the Twentieth. All these legions were stationed in the territory of the Ubii in the same summer camp, and now idle or employed on light duties only. When the death of Augustus was known, the mob of slaves, newly conscripted in Rome, unused to work and prone to insolence, played upon the simple minds of the rest. Now it was time, they argued, for the veterans to demand their discharge, for the younger men to get a rise in pay, and for everyone to clamor for relief from their hardships, and for vengeance on the cruelties of the centurions. This was not a case of a single man, like Percennius with the Pannonian legions, dealing with tired soldiers who looked over their shoulders at a more powerful army. This was sedition on a large scale; they proclaimed that Rome's fate lay in their hands, their victories extended the Empire, whose Emperors took from them their names.[20]

32. Caecina did nothing to forestall the rebellion: the general frenzy had broken his nerve. For, rabid with anger, the men drew their swords and fell on the centurions—those time-honored objects of a soldier's hatred, the first victims of any violence. They threw them down and flogged them, sixty strokes apiece, one for each centurion in the legion. Then the mutilated, bleeding, dying men were thrown out of the camp or into the Rhine.

Septimius broke away, reached the tribunal, and cast himself down at the commander's feet. Even there, they clamored for him so violently that he had to be yielded. Cassius Chaerea, known to later history for the murder of the Emperor Gaius, was then young and reckless: sword in hand, he fought his way through an armed mob. None of the tribunes, not even the camp commandant, could get a hearing. The men arranged patrols and sentry duties and whatever else was needed. Those with a deeper insight into the soldier's mind could clearly tell how far-reaching and unmanageable the revolt was from the fact there were not just a few scattered ringleaders. The men shared a unanimous passion, a unanimous sullenness, and maintained it so evenly that you would have thought them under a central control.

33. Meanwhile, as I said earlier, Germanicus was in Gaul on the census: there it was that he heard of the death of Augustus. He was married to that Emperor's granddaughter, Agrippina, and had several children by her. His own father was Drusus, Tiberius' brother, and he was a grandson of the Empress Livia. But both his grandmother and his uncle nourished secret hatred of him, all the stronger because it was unfair. For the older Drusus had still a place in the memories of the Roman people: if he had attained power, they thought, he would have restored the Republic. So they favored Germanicus, and placed the same hopes in him. For the young man bore himself as a private citizen and had a charming personality, very different from the haughty looks and ambiguous words of Tiberius. Besides, there were feminine jealousies. Livia had all a stepmother's hatred for Agrippina. Agrippina herself had a quick temper, but her chastity and her faithfulness to her husband enabled her to turn her stubbornness to good purpose.

34. As for Germanicus, the fact that he stood so close to supreme power only added to his loyalty to Tiberius. He took an oath of allegiance himself,[21] and administered it to his staff and to the states of the Belgae. But then he heard of the rebellion of the legions, and set out at once.

They met him outside the camp, eyes cast down as though

in remorse. But the moment he was inside the camp, complaints of various kinds were heard. Some, clutching his hand
as though to kiss it, put their fingers into their mouths to make
him touch their empty gums. Others showed bodies deformed
with age. At the meeting they crowded around him: he
ordered, "Form into your proper ranks!" "We can hear better
from where we are!" they replied. "Bring forward the standards," he commanded, "so that I can tell which unit is which."
The order was obeyed in a slovenly fashion. Then he began
with a tribute to Augustus, passing next to the victories and
triumphs of Tiberius, especially his splendid achievements in
Germany with these same legions. Next he praised the general
support shown by Italy, and the loyalty of the Gauls—nowhere was there opposition or discontent. All this they heard
in grim silence, or with occasional interruptions.

35. Next he turned to the rebellion. "Where is your sense
of obedience?" he asked. "What has happened to that old
soldierly discipline? What have you done to the tribunes and
the centurions?" They all bared their bodies, displaying the
scars of wounds or results of flogging. Shouting together, they
complained of having to bribe to get leave, of their wretched
pay, their hard toil, and (specifically) of making earthworks
and ditches, of fetching timber and fuel, and all the other
fatigue duties which are necessary—or are invented to prevent
slackness. The veterans, above all, roused an angry tumult.
"We've served for thirty years!" they shouted. "We're tired
and want relief before we drop dead at the same old drudgery!
End this heavy service, but don't leave us to starve!" Some
asked to be paid the legacies which Augustus had left them,
at the same time expressing support for Germanicus. "If you
want the Empire, sir," they said, "we're ready!" At this, he
leaped down from the tribunal as though contaminated. Their
weapons barred his way, and they threatened him if he did not
return. "Death is better than disloyalty!" he cried, drew his
sword, and pointed it at his own breast. The soldiers near him
seized his hand and wrenched it away. But, at the back of the
crowd, some men bunched together—and, incredible though
it sounds, even some in the front ranks—urged him to strike.
One man, Calusidius, drew his own sword and offered it, saying, "Take this, it's sharper!" But, angry as they were, the men
found this a brutal gesture and a sign of ill character. There
was a pause in which Germanicus' friends hurried him off to
his quarters.

36. Then they discussed remedial action. The soldiers were
reported as about to send a deputation to the army in Upper
Germany to bring them over: they were going to destroy the

town of the Ubii: then they would turn their hands, stained already with loot, to plundering the Gallic provinces. To add to their fears, the Germans knew all about the Roman rebellion, and would invade the moment the Rhine was left unguarded. If they armed auxiliaries and allies against the rebellious legions, it would mean civil war. Severity was risky, indulgence disgraceful: whether they gave the soldiers everything or nothing, the state was in danger. After discussing possible measures, they decided that a dispatch should be written in the name of the Emperor. It would give discharge to men of twenty years' service, and conditional release to men of sixteen years' service, who were to be kept with the colors, though their only duty would be to repel enemy invasion. The legacies would be paid in full, twice over.

37. The soldiers saw that this was an *ad hoc* improvisation, and demanded their concessions at once. Demobilization was hastily put into action through the tribunes, legacies were postponed for payment in the winter quarters. But the Fifth and the Twentieth would not leave until the amount due had been paid, in the summer camp, out of the traveling expenses of Germanicus and his staff. Caecina led the First and the Twentieth to the town of the Ubii—a disgraceful march indeed, for the money they had extorted from their general was conveyed together with the eagles and the standards. Germanicus left for the army in Upper Germany, and administered the oath of allegiance to the Second, Third, and Sixteenth legions, who took it without delay; the Fourteenth hesitated for a while. Then they were granted the concessions of pay and discharge, though they had not asked for them.

38. But there was a fresh attempt at mutiny among detachments of the disaffected legions who were acting as garrison among the Chauci. The execution on the spot of two soldiers soon stamped it out. This was done on the orders of Manius Ennius, camp commander: it was a salutary example, but not in accord with army regulations. Rebellion broke out again: he escaped and was discovered. Since his hiding place had been ineffective, he relied on boldness for a remedy. "You're not assaulting your camp commander," he cried, "but Germanicus, your general, Tiberius, your Emperor!" Then, silencing all opposition, he took up the standard, pointed it to the Rhine, and shouting, "Anyone who falls out will be treated as a deserter!" he led them back to winter quarters—still disaffected, but not daring to act.

39. Meanwhile the deputation from the Senate reached Germanicus at Ara Ubiorum. Two legions—i.e., the First and the Twentieth—were there, also the veterans, newly discharged

but still with the colors. These men were alarmed, beside themselves with guilty conscience about their past actions, and
apprehensive that the delegation from the Senate was going to
nullify the gains they had won by sedition. A crowd must have
a scapegoat, even a bogus one. So they attacked the leader of
the delegation, Lucius Munatius Plancus, an ex-consul, accus-
ing him of stirring the Senate to action against them. In the
dead of night they burst into Germanicus' quarters to demand
their standard, which was being kept there; crowding around
the door and blocking the gates, they forced the Emperor's
son to get up from bed and hand over the standard, under
threat of death. Then, roaming the streets, they met the delegates, who had heard the uproar and were making their way
to Germanicus. They insulted and were on the point of killing
them—Plancus above all. His rank made it impossible for
him to retreat; his only refuge in the hour of danger was the
camp of the First Legion. Then he clasped the eagles and the
standards, and tried to put himself under their protection. But
if the standard-bearer Calpurnius had not averted the final
act, there would have been an event rare even between
enemies: an envoy of the Roman people, in a Roman camp,
would have shed his blood on the altars of the gods. When day
at last dawned, and when general and soldiers could see the
facts for what they were, Germanicus entered the camp, sent
for Plancus, and placed him on the tribunal. Then he in-
veighed against this disastrous outbreak of violence, saying
that it was heaven's anger, not the soldiers', which had broken
out afresh; he explained why the delegates had come, and
spoke in solemn but eloquent terms about the rights of delegates, the serious, unmerited danger in which Plancus had
been placed, and the disgrace the legion had brought upon
itself. The soldiers were not so much pacified as cowed, and
he got the delegates away with an escort of auxiliary cavalry.

40. At this fearful period there was general criticism of
Germanicus for not going to Upper Germany, where the
troops were loyal and could be used against the rebels. Discharge, bribes, and soft policies generally had done more than
enough harm. If he counted his own life cheap, why keep his
little son and his pregnant wife among men who had gone
berserk and outraged every human right? He could restore
them, at least, to the Emperor and to Rome. Germanicus
hesitated because of his wife's opposition: she proclaimed
herself Augustus' granddaughter, she would show her breed-
ing in the face of danger! At long last, weeping and clasping
in his arms his pregnant wife and their little boy, he insisted
that she should leave. So they set out, a pitiable group of

women—the general's wife, a refugee, clasping her baby son to her bosom; around her, weeping, the wives of his friends, forced out with her, and equally distraught. Those who stayed were no less affected.

41. This was no successful Caesar, in his own camp. This was how a captured city would appear: the tears and groans caused the very soldiers to look and listen. They came out of their tents. "What is that noise of weeping? What disaster does it mean? These noble ladies—and no centurion to escort them: no soldiers: none of the escort due to the wife of the commander-in-chief! And they're going to the Treviri, going to trust themselves to foreigners!" The men felt ashamed and pity seized them when they thought of Agrippina's father, of her grandfather Augustus, her father-in-law Drusus. She had been a faithful wife and a good mother. Then there was her little boy, born in the camp, brought up with soldiers as his playmates; "Little Boots" (Caligula) was their nickname for him, because to win popularity he was often shod in a miniature pair of common army boots. But jealousy of the Treviri was what really swayed them. Some of them ran up to Agrippina, begging and beseeching, "Come back to us! Stay here!" —others going to Germanicus himself.

42. Still sore with grief and anger, he addressed them as they crowded around: "My wife and child are no dearer to me than my father (the Emperor) and my country. But he has his dignity to protect him, as the other armies protect Rome and its Empire. I would gladly have sacrificed my wife and children for your glory. Now I am removing them far out of reach of your lunacy. Whatever crime is impending shall glut itself on my blood, lest the murder of Augustus' great-grandson and Tiberius' daughter-in-law should make you more guilty yet! In these last days, is there any crime or outrage at which you have stopped short? Words fail me to describe this gathering. 'Soldiers'—is that a word to use of men who besiege in arms their Emperor's son within their own ramparts? 'Citizens'— inappropriate for those who trample on the authority of the Senate! Rights due to enemies, the immunity of ambassadors, the very rights of nations, you have scorned them all. The deified Julius Caesar quelled a mutiny with a single word. 'Quirites'* he called them, when they would not take the oath. The deified Augustus could terrify the legions who had fought at Actium with his very appearance and gaze. I am scarcely their equal, as yet, but I am their descendant: it would be a strange and scandalous thing if the troops of Spain or

* Civilians.

Syria flouted my authority. But here are the First and Twentieth legions, one which got its colors from Tiberius, the other
which fought so many battles with him, and won so many
honors! A fine return you make to your old commander! Is
this the news I am to report to the Emperor, who hears nothing
but good from all the provinces? His own recruits, his own
veterans, are dissatisfied, demanding release and bonuses. They
—and they alone—are murdering their centurions, expelling
the tribunes, arresting their generals, drenching the very camp
and the river in blood! And I am a prisoner, begging for my
life among men who hate me.

43. "My friends showed little foresight in snatching my
sword, that first day of the meeting, when I was ready to
thrust it into my breast! The man who proffered his was a
truer friend. I should have died then, ignorant of so many
crimes committed by my own troops. You could have found a
commander who might have left my murder unavenged, but
who would have had vengeance for Quintilius Varus and the
three lost legions! Heaven forbid that the glory of rescuing
Rome and conquering the German tribes should go to the
Belgae, though they are ready to do it. Augustus, I call on your
spirit in heaven! My father, Nero Drusus, your image and
your memory live among these soldiers! Shame and glory are
returning to their minds: let them wash away this stain, and
turn their anger to the destruction of foreign foes, not citizens!
And you, soldiers—your hearts are changed, I see it in your
faces. Do you want to respect the delegates, obey the Emperor, give me back my wife and child? Very well, quit the
company of the rebels: hand them over: that will prove your
repentance, and bind you to loyalty."

44. They admitted the justice of his reproaches. Begging
for mercy, they urged him to punish the guilty, forgive those
who had forgotten their duty, and lead them against the enemy.
"Call the lady back, sir," they said, "and our little playmate:
don't let him be a hostage with the Gauls!" The request for
Agrippina he refused, since winter was near and her time was
coming upon her. But Caligula should return: the rest was up
to them. They were changed men. They rushed off and
dragged the ringleaders in chains before Gaius Caetronius,
commander of the First Legion. Judgment and execution were
carried out in this way on each and every one: The legions
stood around, swords drawn; the condemned man was displayed on the rostrum by a tribune; if they shouted "Guilty!"
he was executed there and then. The soldiers rejoiced in the
slaughter, as though it purged them of their guilt. Germanicus

did nothing to stop it, although he had given no orders for it. At least the resentment caused by this brutality would fall on those who carried it out.

What had been done with the legions was applied to the veterans still with the colors. Then they were sent to Raetia, ostensibly for the defense of that province against a threatened attack by the Suebi, in reality to snap their link with those camps of evil memory, notorious alike for the enormity of the crimes there committed, and for the harshness with which they had been punished. Next he revised the list of centurions. Summoned by their commander, the centurions gave their name, rank, and place of origin: then they recited the number of years of service, their battle record, and any decorations they held. If the tribunes and soldiers spoke well of their efficiency and good record, they kept their commission; if they concurred in labeling them corrupt or cruel, they were discharged with ignominy.

45. Immediate difficulties had been resolved. But another intractable problem was the disaffection of the Fifth and Twenty-first legions, in winter quarters at Vetera, sixty miles distant. They had set the rebellion afoot: its worst crimes were their doing; undeterred by any feelings of repentance or by the punishment of their fellow soldiers, their anger was still rumbling. So Germanicus got ready a task force, a flotilla, and a contingent of auxiliaries, ready to reduce them by arms if they would not obey his orders.

46. At Rome the disturbances in Germany were announced before the outcome of those in Pannonia was reported. There was panic and a general criticism of Tiberius. He was making a mock of the Senate and people, unarmed and unprotected as they were, by all this pretense of delay; the soldiers, meanwhile, were in revolt, and two half-grown boys, lacking full authority, could not bring them to heel. He should have gone himself, and shown them the full majesty of an Emperor: they would soon give way, confronted by a prince of his long experience, vested with supreme power to reward and to punish. Augustus in his old age had paid so many visits to Germany: was it to be borne that Tiberius, still in the prime of life, should sit in the Senate, chopping logic with the senators? Rome's subservience was well provided for: now was the time to mollify the minds of the soldiers, and induce them to accept peace.

47. Tiberius remained deaf to these arguments. Nothing swayed his fixed purpose not to quit the capital or place himself and the state in danger. His difficulties were numerous and

varied. The German army was the stronger, the Pannonian nearer; the former was supported by the resources of Gaul, the latter was closer to Italy. To which should preference be given? And would the slight further inflame the one placed second? Through Drusus and Germanicus he could keep simultaneous contact with both, and retain his dignity as well, always more effective at a distance. The young princes could quite properly refer certain matters to their father, and he could himself negotiate with, or break, those who withstood Germanicus and Drusus. But if they spurned the Emperor, what other resource was left? Still, as though on the brink of departure, he chose a staff, prepared equipment, and fitted out ships. Soon he was able to plead the approach of winter and the pressure of business—excuses which deceived the intelligent for a time, the mob for a while longer, and the provinces for longer still.

48. Germanicus had now concentrated his forces and was ready to take vengeance on the mutineers. But he decided to pause for a while to see if they would profit from the example of the other legions. He therefore sent dispatches to Caecina in these terms: "I am coming with a strong force. Unless you give the agitators the punishment they deserve, I shall use indiscriminate massacre." At a secret meeting, Caecina read these words to the standard-bearers, the men in charge of the eagles, and other reliable elements. "Let us redeem the whole army from disgrace, and ourselves from death," he urged. "In peace, you can consider cases on their merits: in war innocent and guilty are slaughtered alike." They then approached other men thought to be trustworthy, and found that the greater part of the two legions remained loyal. The generals fixed the time to bring into force the plan decided upon—to put to the sword every possible revolutionary and criminal. At the signal, they burst into the soldiers' quarters and butchered them unawares. Only those in the secret knew why the slaughter had started, and when it would end.

49. This was civil war of a kind wholly without precedent. There were no battles, no opposing armies. Messmates who had shared the same quarters were splitting into parties, taking up arms. Shrieks, weapons, bloodshed, were obvious: the reasons for them mysterious: the outcome at the mercy of chance. Some of the loyalists, too, were killed, for the rebels took up arms as soon as they realized for whom the attack was meant. No general or tribune was there to control the slaughter; *carte blanche* was given to the mob, they could glut themselves with vengeance. It was later that Germanicus entered the camp.

Bursting into tears, he exclaimed, "This is no remedy—this is a massacre!" Then he ordered the bodies to be burned.

The troops were still restless, and eager to be led against the enemy, in atonement for their madness. Only wounds won in battle, and displayed on their guilty breasts, could appease the shades of their slaughtered fellows. Germanicus supported their zeal. A bridge was thrown across the Rhine, and over it he led a force of 12,000 legionaries and twenty-six infantry and eight cavalry squadrons of auxiliaries, whose loyalty had been unaffected in the rebellion.

50. The Germans had been in high spirits—and close to the frontier—so long as the Romans were pinned down, first by mourning for Augustus and secondly by the outbreak of the rebellion. But now the Roman commander made a forced march through the Caesian Forest to the line begun by Tiberius. Here he pitched his camp: his front and rear protected by earthworks, the flanks by palisades. Dark forests lay ahead, and a choice of routes. One was short and familiar, the other longer, unexplored, and consequently unguarded by the enemy. The longer route was chosen, and they pressed on with all speed. For scouts had announced that this was to be a festal night among the Germans, devoted to banquets and ceremonies. Caecina was ordered to go ahead with the light-armed troops and clear a passage through the forests: the legions followed some little way behind. A starry night was in their favor: they reached the villages of the Marsi and surrounded them with pickets. The Germans were in bed or sprawled over their tables; no watch was kept. Carelessness and confusion reigned: they had no thought of war. Yet, if it was peace, it was the peace of crapulousness and exhaustion.

51. To spread devastation further, Germanicus divided the eager legionaries into four columns; for fifty miles around the earth was laid waste with fire and sword. Neither age nor sex was spared: sacred shrines were destroyed along with the dwellings of men. The temple of Tanfana, the holy place of that district, was razed to the ground. No casualties were suffered by our men: their victims were half-asleep, unarmed, or stragglers. But the massacre roused the Bructeri, Tubantes, and Usipetes, who blocked the forests through which the Roman army would return. Germanicus found this out, and prepared for march or battle. The van was formed by part of the cavalry and the auxiliary cohorts; next came the First Legion; the baggage was in the middle, with the Twenty-first guarding its left flank and the Fifth its right. The Twentieth Legion protected their rear, and behind them came the rest of

the auxiliary forces. The enemy made no move until the columns were stretched out in the forest. Then, with a light assault on the front and flanks, they made their main effort against the rear guard. The massed German troops threw our light-armed cohorts into confusion. Then Germanicus rode up to the Twentieth and shouted, "Here's your chance to wipe out the rebellion! Forward, soldiers! Turn your shame into glory!" Burning with anger, the troops made a single charge, pushed the enemy into the open, and cut them to pieces. Meanwhile, the head of the column had emerged from the forest and fortified the camp. The rest of the journey was without incident. Encouraged by the recent action, the troops had forgotten the past. So they returned to winter quarters.

EVENTS IN ROME

52. The news of this action brought to Tiberius both joy and anxiety. The rebellion was over; that was good. But it was a bad thing that Germanicus had sought to gain the favor of the troops by the concessions about money and discharge: and so was the glory he had won in war. Still, his achievements were repeated to the Senate, and the Emperor praised his valor —but all in such high-flown language that it was hard to believe these were his real feelings. A shorter speech about Drusus and the end of the rebellion in Pannonia carried greater conviction. All the concessions made by Germanicus were extended to the Pannonian armies.

DEATH OF JULIA

53. In this same year Julia died. Her father Augustus had banished her for immorality, first to Pandateria, then to the city of Rhegium, on the straits by Sicily. While Lucius and Gaius Caesar were still living she had been married to Tiberius, and she had despised him as her inferior: this, above all, was the reason for Tiberius' retirement to Rhodes. When he became Emperor she was still banished in disgrace, and her last hopes went with the death of Agrippa Postumus. Tiberius left her to die by slow starvation, confident that her long banishment would allow her murder to pass undetected.

His cruelty to Sempronius Gracchus arose from a similar

cause. Of a noble family, shrewd wit, and untimely eloquence, this man had debauched Julia while she was still the wife of Marcus Agrippa. His lusts did not end there: when she was transferred to Tiberius this pertinacious adulterer made her recalcitrant and offensive to her new husband. Indeed, letters which she sent to Augustus complaining about Tiberius were thought to have been drafted by Gracchus. So, banished to Cercina, an island off the coast of Africa, he endured fourteen years of exile. Now soldiers were sent to kill him. They found him on a headland, waiting, but not for good news. He asked for a brief delay in order to send a letter with his last instructions to his wife Alliaria. Then he offered his neck to the assassins. The resolution with which he met his end was not unworthy of the name of the Sempronii, which he had disgraced in his life. Some accounts say that the soldiers came, not from Rome, but from Lucius Asprenas, governor of Africa, and that this was done on Tiberius' instructions, in the vain hope that the odium would fall on Asprenas and not on himself.

54. The same year saw the adoption of new religious ceremonies, for a new order of Companions of Augustus was set up. This was modeled on the Companions of Titus, set up by Titus Tatius to preserve the rites of the Sabines. Twenty-one Companions were chosen by lot from among the leading men in Rome; Tiberius, Drusus, Claudius, and Germanicus were added to their number. The first celebration of the Augustan Games saw a riot caused by rivalry among the ballet dancers. Augustus had shown indulgence to spectacles of that kind, because of Maecenas' passion for the dancer Bathyllus. Nor did he himself disdain such amusements, and he thought it a mark of democracy to share the pleasures of the people. Far other was the bent of Tiberius' character, but the people had been indulged for so many years that he did not yet venture to turn them to more serious things.

15 A.D. Consuls Drusus Caesar and Gaius Norbanus

EVENTS IN GERMANY

55. In the consulship of Drusus Caesar and Gaius Norbanus a triumph was awarded to Germanicus, though the war was still unfinished. His main effort he was reserving for the summer, but at the beginning of spring he made a sudden attack on the Chatti. The hope was that the enemy could be split between Arminius and Segestes—distinguished, the one for treachery, the other for loyalty, to Rome.[22] Arminius was the great agitator of Germany. Segestes had given many warnings of seditious plots. At the time of the last banquet before they took up arms, he had advised Varus to arrest himself, Arminius, and the other chiefs; the common people would make no war when their chiefs were out of the way, and later on he would be able to sort out the innocent and the guilty. But Varus fell a victim to fate and to the power of Arminius. Segestes was dragged into the struggle by the common feeling among his people, but he remained hostile to Arminius. A personal grudge embittered their quarrel, for Arminius had carried off his daughter, already promised to another man. So father-in-law hated son-in-law, and ties which strengthen the bond between friends here served to inflame animosity between enemies.

56. So Germanicus gave Caecina four legions, five thousand auxiliaries, and levies hastily raised from among German tribes on our side of the Rhine. He himself commanded the same number of legions, with twice as many auxiliaries, and established a fort on the Taunus range in a place earlier fortified by his father. Then, with his light-armed troops, he swooped down on the Chatti, leaving Lucius Apronius to guard the roads and bridges. A long drought (most unusual in that climate) and half-empty rivers had enabled him to push on unimpeded, though he feared storms and floods on his return. So suddenly did he fall on the Chatti that he butchered or took prisoner all of feeble age or sex. The young warriors swam the

river Eder and tried to stop the Romans from building a bridge; arrows and artillery fire drove them off. Then followed abortive negotiations for peace. A few came over to Germanicus; the rest dispersed to the forests, leaving their villages and towns. Germanicus burned Mattium, their chief town, ravaged the open country, and withdrew to the Rhine. The enemy did not dare to attack his rear guard, as they usually do when they retire through cunning rather than for fear. The Cherusci had been minded to help the Chatti, but the rapid movements of Caecina deterred them. When the Marsi ventured an attack, they were successfully driven away.

57. Soon after this envoys arrived from Segestes, demanding protection from his own countrymen, who were besieging him. Arminius was more influential with them, because he favored war: among barbarians, the readier a man's boldness, the greater weight he will carry and the more he will be trusted in times of trouble. Segestes had included his own son, Segimund, in the deputation. But the young man had a conscience which caused him to hesitate. For, in the year of the rebellion in Germany, though he held an office of priest at the Altar of the Ubii,[23] he had torn off his sacred fillets and gone over to the rebels. Still, in the hope of finding pardon from the Romans, he took his father's messages; he met with a kindly reception and was sent with a guard to the Gallic bank of the river.

Germanicus found it worthwhile to retrace his steps and attack the besiegers. Segestes was rescued, with a great number of his kindred and dependents. Among them were women of high rank, including that daughter of Segestes who was now the wife of Arminius. She was of her husband's, rather than her father's, temper. She shed no tears and made no plea for mercy: she folded her hands over her bosom, and looked down upon her pregnant womb. Some trophies of the disaster to Varus were also brought in; they had been assigned as booty to many of those who now surrendered.

58. There, too, stood Segestes, huge of frame, free from fear because he had been a loyal ally to Rome. He spoke as follows: "This is not the first day on which I have shown my loyalty and good faith to the Roman people. The deified Augustus gave me Roman citizenship; from that day onward I have chosen my friends and enemies in terms of your interests. This through no hatred of my own country (and in any case, traitors are hateful, even to those they aid) but because I thought the interests of Romans and Germans were one and the same, and because I preferred peace to war. So I denounced Arminius—who had raped my daughter and broken his

treaty with you—to Varus, who then commanded your army. But Varus was idle: knowing how little protection there was in the laws, I begged him to arrest myself, Arminius, and the other conspirators. I call that night to witness; I wish I had not survived it! The sequel calls for tears rather than excuses. I imprisoned Arminius, in chains; he and his faction did the same to me. Now, meeting you for the first time, let me make it clear that I prefer the old state to the new, peace to restlessness. I want no reward: I am anxious to clear myself of treachery. Also, I am a suitable conciliator for the people of Germany: if they prefer repentance to destruction I ask forgiveness for my son's youthful error. For my daughter, I admit I brought her here against her will. You must decide whether she shall be treated as my daughter, or as one bearing a child to Arminius."

Germanicus made a kindly reply. Safety was promised to his children and kindred, and for Segestes himself, residence in the old province.[24] Then Germanicus withdrew his army, and was awarded the title of "Imperator" by Tiberius. Arminius' wife gave birth to a male child. This boy was brought to Ravenna. I shall tell later how ironic was the fate that befell him.[25]

59. The news that Segestes had surrendered and had been well received was welcome to those who wanted peace, but distasteful to the war party. Arminius was violent by nature; now he was inflamed to madness by the capture of his wife and the subjection to slavery of her unborn son. He rushed around among the Cherusci, calling for war against Segestes and Germanicus. His taunts were unrestrained. "A fine father! a great Imperator, a brave army, whose combined forces have captured one weak woman! I slaughtered three legions and their generals: I fought, not by treachery and against pregnant women, but openly against armed men. In the groves of Germany you can still see the Roman eagles which I hung up before our country's gods! Let Segestes dwell on the shore of slavery: let his son resume his priesthood—for a human being! True Germans will never forgive themselves if they see the rods and fasces and toga between the Rhine and the Elbe! Other people may know nothing of the Roman Empire, of its punishments and its taxes: we have swept all that away. The deified Augustus, and Tiberius whom he chose, have gone forever—don't be afraid of a youthful general and a mutinous army! If you love your country, your ancestors, and your old freedom, rather than tyrants and new colonies, don't follow Segestes to infamy and slavery—follow Arminius to freedom and glory!"

60. This roused not only the Cherusci, but also neighboring

tribes. Inguiomerus, an uncle of Arminius, and for long in good standing with the Romans, joined the cause. This added to Germanicus' fears. To prevent war swelling to a single head, he created a diversion by sending Caecina with forty auxiliary units through the territory of the Bructeri to the river Ems, while Albinovanus Pedo took a force of cavalry through the lands of the Frisii. Germanicus embarked four legions and sailed across the lakes.[26] The rendezvous for infantry, horse, and fleet was on the Ems. The Chauci offered help, and were taken into the expeditionary force. The Bructeri began a scorched-earth policy, but were dispersed by Lucius Stertinius with a light-armed force sent out by order of Germanicus. Between slaughter and booty, they found the eagle of the Nineteenth Legion, lost with Varus. The whole force was now taken to the farthest bounds of the Bructeri, and all the land between the Ems and the Lippe laid waste. They were here close to the Teutoburgian Forest, where the remains of Varus and the three legions were reported to be lying, unburied.

61. The commander was now seized with a desire to pay the last honors to the fallen soldiers and their general. No man with him but was overcome with pity when he thought of friends and relations, of the chances of battle and of the lot of man. Caecina was sent ahead to reconnoiter the pathless forests, and to provide bridges and causeways over the deep marshes with their treacherous expanse.

So they trod that unhallowed ground of evil memory and hideous aspect. There was the camp of Varus, its wide expanse and its headquarters testifying to the work of three legions. Next a half-ruined earthwork and a shallow ditch showed where the last survivors had gathered. In the middle of the battlefield bones lay white, scattered where the men had fled, piled up where they had made a stand. By them were broken weapons, horses' limbs, skulls fixed to tree trunks. In the groves hard by were the barbarians' altars, where the tribunes and senior centurions had been sacrificed as victims. The survivors of the disaster, who had escaped from the battle or from captivity, showed where the generals had fallen, where the eagles had been seized. "Here was where Varus got his first wound: over there he died by his own hand. That was the mound from which Arminius made his speech; here were the gibbets and pits for the prisoners; thus in his insolence did he mock our eagles and standards!"

62. So a Roman army, six years after the disaster, came to this place and buried the bones of the men of three legions. No one knew whether he was casting earth over his own kindred, or those of another. All were regarded as kinsmen, all as blood-

brothers: their anger was against the enemy; fury mingled with sorrow as they worked at the task of burial. Germanicus laid the first turf on the funeral mound—an offering to the dead and a solace to the living. This was ill received by Tiberius—perhaps because he construed all Germanicus' actions in the worst sense. Or perhaps he felt that the sight of so many un-buried corpses would diminish the troops' eagerness for battle, and make the enemy appear too formidable. Again, he may have thought that a general associated with the augurs and their ancient rites did wrong to pollute himself by touching the dead.[27]

63. Germanicus followed Arminius, who had withdrawn to the wilderness. As soon as he got a chance, he ordered the cavalry to press forward and seize the flat ground occupied by the enemy. Arminius first ordered his men to fall back in close order to the forests. Then he wheeled around and a force hidden in the woods was given the signal to charge. This new attack threw the Roman cavalry into disorder; reserve battalions sent into action were shattered by the retreating columns and added to the panic. Gradually they were being forced back onto marshy ground, well known to the victorious Germans, but dangerous to those unfamiliar with it. But then Germanicus sent up the legions in battle order, thus alarming the enemy and heartening our troops. The battle ended on equal terms.

When the army had been withdrawn to the Ems, he used a fleet to transport the legions in the same way that he had brought them. Part of the cavalry were ordered to seek the Rhine along the shores of the ocean. Caecina, at the head of his own troops, was using known routes in his withdrawal, but his instructions were to get past the Long Bridges[28] as soon as possible. These formed a narrow trackway over an immense marsh; they were the work of Lucius Domitius. All the rest was marshland, treacherous with peat bogs, and broken up by streams. Around it lay sloping forests, now filled with Arminius' men. Using shortcuts and forced marches, they had got ahead of the Roman army, impeded as it was by its baggage and arms. Caecina's problem was how to repair the broken-down old causeway and keep off the enemy while so doing. He decided to camp on the spot, so that repairs and fighting could be started in parallel.

64. The barbarians kept up pressure on front and flank, trying to break through our pickets and attack the working party. Workers and fighters united to make a fearful uproar. Now everything told against the Romans; the ground was no more than a deep morass, treacherous to stand on, slippery for

movement. Their breastplates burdened down their bodies; they could not throw their javelins standing in water. But the Cherusci were used to battles in the bog. Big, tall men, with huge spears, they could wound at long range. The legions were beginning to waver when night delivered them from a battle that was going badly.

Success made the Germans tireless. They took no thought for sleep; diverting the streams that rose among the hills to the low ground, they flooded it out, destroyed what our soldiers had been able to accomplish, and left it all to be done over again. But Caecina had spent forty years in the army as soldier and as general: he had known triumph and disaster, and he kept his nerve. As he planned the next step, he thought the only thing to do was to keep the enemy in the forest until his own wounded and the more heavily laden part of his forces had gone on ahead. For between the high ground and the marshes there was an open space, enough for the mounting of a thin line of battle. So the legions were posted, the Fifth on the right flank, the Twenty-first on the left, the First to escort the marching column, the Twentieth to ward off pursuit.

65. It was a night of turmoil and of contrasts. The Germans spent it in feasting, with joyous song and fierce cries which filled the low-lying valleys and echoed through the forests. On the Roman side were flickering campfires, snatches of talk, the men lying by the ramparts or wandering among the tents, sleepless rather than watchful. The general had a fearful dream. He saw Quintilius Varus, blood-boltered and rising up from the fen: the specter called and beckoned him, but he refused: it stretched out its hand to touch him, but he thrust it away.

At daybreak the legions on the flank—whether through fear or obstinacy—left their positions and occupied firmer ground beyond the swamps. Arminius had a clear run, but he did not attack at once. He saw that the Roman heavy equipment was bogged down in the mud and ditches, and that the troops around it were in disarray. Units were out of position; as usual in such conditions, men were quick to look after themselves and slow to obey orders. Then he ordered the Germans to bear down on them, shouting, "Here's another Varus, and more legions in the trap!" Then with a picked force he cut clear through the column, taking care to wound the horses first. They slipped in their own blood and in the slimy bog, threw their riders, scattered everything in their path, and trampled on the fallen. Around the eagles the situation was desperate. The color-bearers could neither carry them for the shower of missiles nor plant them in the muddy ground. When

Caecina tried to rally the line, his horse was stabbed under him and he was surrounded, but the First Legion came to his support. Here the enemy's greed was a help: leaving off killing, they made for loot. As evening drew on, the legions struggled out onto solid ground. But this was not the end of their miseries. There were earthworks to be built, soil to be collected; most of their implements for moving earth and cutting sods had been lost. The soldiers had no tents, the wounded no dressings. As they divided up rations that were stained with mud and blood, the soldiers spoke bitterly of the deadly darkness, of the one day which remained for so many thousands of men.

66. A horse broke its tether, careered around in panic at the noise, and carried confusion among those who met it. Such an alarm was caused by this among those who thought the Germans had broken in that they rushed in a body to the gates, especially to the main gateway, farthest from the enemy and handy for escape. Caecina found out that the panic was groundless. But neither his authority, nor entreaties, nor bodily force, would hold the men back. So he threw himself down in the gateway, and blocked it that way; the men at least lacked the gall to go out over the general's body. Meanwhile tribunes and centurions spread the news that it was a false alarm.

67. Then Caecina summoned the men to his headquarters and said, "Men, you must keep quiet and listen to me. This is an emergency. Our only hope is to fight our way out. But we must fight to a plan: you must keep inside the defenses until the enemy comes up to storm them. At that moment, we break out at all points, and keep going till we reach the Rhine! But if you retreat there are more forests, deeper bogs, and a bloody enemy still before you. Victory will bring honor and glory." He spoke of their dear ones at home, of all their battle honors; nothing was said of reverses. Then, starting with his own, he divided up the horses of the staff and generals among the best fighters, making no distinction of rank. These would make the first charge; the infantry would follow.

68. Hope, greed, and divisions among the chiefs caused almost equal disturbance to the Germans. Arminius was for allowing the Romans to come out, and then trapping them on difficult, marshy ground. Inguiomerus favored a bolder plan, of the type barbarians enjoy—surrounding the camp, so that it could be stormed, with more prisoners and richer booty. So, at daybreak they filled in the ditches, threw down hurdles, and rushed forward. When they grasped the top of the palisade, few soldiers lined it, and these seemed paralyzed with fear. But as they were entangled with the defenses the signal was given;

there was a blare of trumpets and war horns. Shouting and charging, the Romans poured upon the rear of the Germans. "Here are no swamps or forests," they shouted, "only a fair field and an open fight!" The enemy had been counting on the easy slaughter of a few ill-armed men. Now the blast of trumpets and the flash of arms fell on them with the greater impact because they were unexpected; they went down to defeat, as ill prepared to meet reverses as they had been greedy of success. Arminius got away unscathed. Inguiomerus quitted the field badly wounded. The brute mass of the German infantry were slaughtered, so long as daylight and the fury of our men lasted. At length, as night fell, the legions reentered their camp. They had more wounds than ever, and no less hunger. And yet they had everything—strength, health, abundance—in the possession of victory.

69. Meanwhile, the rumor spread that the army had been cut off, and that a hostile German army was marching on Gaul. There were some who would not have shrunk from the disgrace of destroying the bridge across the Rhine, had not Agrippina prevented it. This noble-hearted lady played a general's part through these days, dispensing food and dressings to the needy and wounded with her own hands. Pliny,[29] who wrote the story of the German wars, says that she stood at the bridgehead to praise and thank the legions as they came into camp. This deeply impressed Tiberius, who felt that something must lie behind it. All this attention to the army was not for use against a foreign foe. What was left for the generals to do, when a woman inspects the camps, takes the salute by the standards, and even plans to distribute awards! Surely it showed ambition enough to dress the general's son in a private's uniform and parade him around as "Prince Little Boots"! Agrippina counted for more with the army than the generals or the commanders. She, a woman, had quelled a mutiny when the Emperor's name was of no avail. All this was enlarged and heightened by Sejanus. He knew Tiberius' nature, and made a long-term investment in hatred; the Emperor would store it away and bring it out later with interest accrued.

70. To return to Germanicus. He ordered Publius Vitellius to take back overland two of the legions which had been brought by ship, the Second and the Fourteenth.[30] This was to allow the flotilla to ride more easily in shallow water, and ground less heavily when the tide ebbed. The first stages of Vitellius' journey were easy, being over firm ground, where the tide did not rise high. But later there was a gale from the north, and that at the time of the autumnal equinox, the worst period for Atlantic storms. In the surge the marching column lost its

footing and was swept away. The whole land was flooded—sea, shore, and fields all looked alike. There was no telling firm ground from treacherous, shallows from deep water. The men were knocked down by the waves and sucked away by the undertow: baggage, mules, and lifeless bodies floated around and bumped up against each other. Companies could not be kept together; some men were in the water up to their chests, others to their necks. Sometimes the ground beneath would give and they would be thrown different ways and go under. The waves were an enemy against whom they could not rally and encourage each other. Brave men and cowards, the sensible and the rash, good plans and bad, were in like case. The fury of the storm swept all away.

At long last Vitellius struggled out onto higher ground, and the column followed. They passed the night without any necessities, with no fire, and, many of them, naked and wounded. They were as badly off as men in a city beleaguered by enemies: indeed, such men can profit from an honorable death; these had nothing but an ignominious end before them. But dawn brought back dry land; they reached the river where Germanicus was waiting with his fleet. Then the legions were embarked. A rumor had got about that they were all drowned; none believed them safe until they saw Germanicus and the army back at base.

71. By now Stertinius, who had been sent to receive the submission of Segimerus, brother of Segestes, had brought that chieftain and his son to the city of the Ubii. They were both granted a pardon, Segestes without difficulty; in the case of the son there were reserves, since he was said to have insulted the corpse of Varus. There was now a competition between Gaul, Spain, and Italy to make good the losses of the army, each offering to supply arms, horses, and money as available. Praising their public spirit, Germanicus took only arms and horses for use in action. Compensation to the soldiers he paid from his own purse. To erase by kindness all memory of the disaster, he visited the wounded and praised their deeds. Inspecting their wounds, he would cheer one man by hope, another by commendation. From them all, by his affability, and the interest he took in them, he won greater loyalty for himself, and greater zeal for battle.

THE LAW OF TREASON

72. This year triumphal decorations[31] were awarded to Aulus Caecina, Lucius Apronius, and Gaius Silius for victories won in the German wars. The people often hailed Tiberius with the title "Father of His Country," but he declined it. Though the Senate approved taking the oath to observe his enactments, he refused to allow it. "All human affairs," he would say, "are uncertain; the more I have, the more slippery the ground on which I stand." But this did nothing to gain him credit for a republican outlook. For he revived the law of treason: it had indeed been known under that name in the old Republic, but applied to other offenses—betrayal of an army, for example, or rousing the people to sedition, or bad administration of the commonwealth—that tended to derogate from the dignity of the Roman people. It was concerned solely with deeds; words went unpunished. Augustus was the first to bring the investigation of libelous writings under this heading; prompted by the impertinence of Cassius Severus, author of notorious libels against prominent men and women. Later Tiberius, in answer to the inquiry of the praetor Pompeius Macer as to whether charges of treason should be brought before the courts, replied that the laws must be enforced. He, too, had been embittered by anonymous verses, attacking his cruelty and arrogance, and his bad relations with his mother.

73. It is worthwhile to record the first tentative proceedings against Falanius and Rubrius, knights of modest means. They illustrate very well how this iniquitous procedure began, and how cleverly it was handled by Tiberius. For it began stealthily. Then it was suppressed; finally it burst into flames and destroyed everything. Falanius was accused of having enrolled a certain Cassius, an actor and a male prostitute, among the priests of Augustus who were maintained in all the great houses on the lines of the priestly colleges, and further, with having disposed of a statue of Augustus when he sold his gardens. Rubrius was said to have violated the divinity of Augustus by perjury. When Tiberius heard of the charges he wrote to the consuls, to the effect that Augustus had not been translated to heaven with the object of ruining Roman citizens. The actor Cassius, and others of his profession, had taken part in the shows which his mother had organized in honor of Augustus: there was nothing sacrilegious in including the statues, or those of other gods, in the sale of house or garden properties. The perjury charge was to

be judged as though it were Jupiter whose name had been taken in vain: the gods must look after their own injuries.[32]

74. Shortly after this, Granius Marcellus, governor of Bithynia, was arraigned by his own finance officer, Caepio Crispinus, on a charge of treason, seconded by Romanus Hispo. This Caepio entered on a course of life which the injustices of the times and the outrageous conduct of contemporaries were to render infamous. Moody, obscure, and ambitious, he wormed his way into the Emperor's confidence by anonymous denunciations. Soon everyone of standing was imperiled: he had influence with one man but was hated by all the rest. Following his precedent, others rose from beggary to wealth, and brought catastrophe on their fellow citizens and finally on themselves.

The allegation against Marcellus was that he had repeated scandalous stories about Tiberius. It was a charge that could not be refuted, for the prosecutor had attributed to the defendant details of the most odious of the Emperor's vices. These things were true; therefore men believed that they had been said. Hispo added that Marcellus had put a statue of his own above that of the Caesars, and that on another statue he had knocked off the head of Augustus and substituted one of Tiberius.

The Emperor was furious. Forgetting his usual taciturnity, he announced that he intended to vote openly and under oath in this case, and that everyone else would have to do the same. But there still remained some vestiges of our dying freedom, and so Gnaeus Piso said, "I would ask you, Sire: when are you going to vote? If first, you set me an example to follow: if last, I am afraid that I may, unintentionally, disagree with you." Tiberius was really shaken. His previous outburst had been unrestrained; now he swallowed the rebuff and allowed Marcellus to be acquitted on the charge of treason. The charges of embezzlement were then referred to the appropriate court.

75. Senatorial investigations were not enough for Tiberius. He would sit in the law courts—on the edge of the platform, so as not to oust the praetor from his seat. His presence sustained many suits against pressure and intrigue from powerful quarters. But though he was acting in the interests of truth, the effect was to diminish freedom.

At this period, the senator Pius Aurelius complained that his house had been undermined by the construction of a public road and an aqueduct, and appealed to the Senate. Treasury officials resisted the claim. But the Emperor came to his help and paid him the value of his house; indeed, he never minded laying out money in a good cause, a virtue he retained long after he had shed all others. When Propertius Celer, an ex-praetor, asked permission to resign from the Senate on grounds of poverty, he made him a grant of one million sesterces, after ascertaining that his indigence was hereditary. Others tried the same approach, but were ordered to prove their case to the Senate. His anxiety to be strict made even his honorable actions seem harsh. As a result, others endured their poverty in silence rather than receive relief in the glare of publicity.

OTHER EVENTS OF THE YEAR

76. This same year, the Tiber, swollen by continuous rains, flooded the lower parts of the city. When the floods receded there was great loss of life and damage to property. Asinius Gallus proposed consulting the Sibylline books. Tiberius—with his passion for obscurity in all things, human and divine—refused. But he entrusted to Ateius Capito and Lucius Arruntius the task of devising ways of controlling the river. Achaea and Macedonia had begged for relief from their burdens of taxation, and it was decided for the time being to remove them from the list of senatorial provinces and entrust them to imperial administration.

Drusus served as president of a gladiatorial display given in his own name and that of his brother Germanicus. He showed a passion for bloodshed—worthless blood though it was—which the people thought ill-omened, and which Tiberius is said to have reproved. There are various theories as to why Tiberius took no share in the games himself. Some allege his dislike of crowds, others his gloomy temperament and reluctance to be compared with Augustus, who attended and enjoyed them. I can hardly credit that his motive was to make a public exhibition of his son's sadism, and to win him popular disfavor, though that view has been advanced.

77. Riots in the theater, which had begun the previous year, now took a turn for the worse. There were fatal casualties, not merely among civilians, but to soldiers and a centurion. An officer of the Guards was seriously wounded trying to protect officials from insult and put down disorders among the spectators. The Senate took up the whole matter, and a motion was put forward to give the praetors the power to flog actors. The tribune Haterius Agrippa interposed his veto and was strongly attacked by Asinius Gallus. Tiberius said nothing; he allowed the Senate some semblance of freedom. But the veto stood, for the deified Augustus had given a ruling that actors were exempt

from corporal punishment, and Tiberius thought it sacrilege to go counter to what he had said. But a number of measures were passed to restrict their salaries and control the hysteria of their followers. The most important of those were: no senator should enter an actor's house; no Roman knight should escort them in public; no shows were to be held except in a theater. Any spectator misbehaving could be punished with exile by the praetors.

78. The people of Spain petitioned for a temple to Augustus to be built in the colony of Tarragona. Permission was granted, and this served as a general precedent for the provinces. The people complained about the 1 percent purchase tax which had been imposed since the civil war, but Tiberius said that the military treasury relied on this source of income;[33] also, that the country would be unable to support itself unless the period of military service was fixed at twenty years. So the untimely concession of discharge after sixteen years, granted during the mutinies, was henceforth canceled.

79. Then Arruntius and Ateius reported back to the Senate on the problem of flood control. They proposed that the streams and lakes which fed the Tiber should be diverted. Deputations from the municipalities and cities were then given a hearing. The Florentines objected to a proposal that the Chiana should be diverted from its natural channel into the Arno, which would be disastrous for them. A very similar case was stated by the people of Interamna. A proposal to divert the river Nar into small channels would ruin the best agricultural land in Italy. Reate strongly objected to a plan for damming the Veline Lake at its outlet into the Nar, saying this could cause floods in the neighborhood. Nature, they said, had acted in the best interests of mankind in assigning to each river its own mouth, its own course, its proper source, and its appropriate limits. They must also have regard to the religious cults of their cities, which had founded rites and sacred groves and altars in honor of their native rivers. Indeed, Father Tiber himself would object to flowing with diminished grandeur, deprived of his attendant streams. The representations of the cities, or religious scruples, or possibly engineering difficulties, caused the Senate to adopt the resolution of Gnaeus Calpurnius Piso that "no action be taken."

80. Poppaeus Sabinus was continued in office as governor of Moesia, and Achaea and Macedonia were added to his command. Here was another characteristic of Tiberius, to prolong commands and, often, to retain men in military and other posts until the very end of their life. Various reasons are alleged for this: some saying he disliked new business and preferred to keep a decision on a permanent basis once it was made: others

that jealousy induced him to keep the spoils of office in a few hands only. Others suppose that his own cleverness impaled him on the horns of a dilemma; he did not hunt out exceptional merit, but again he disliked vice. From outstandingly good governors he had to fear rivalry, from outstandingly bad, public scandal. Indeed, his procrastination in these matters reached such a pitch that he even assigned provinces to men whom he had not the slightest intention of allowing to leave Rome.[34]

81. I cannot make any firm statement about elections to the consulship, either at the beginning of Tiberius' reign or at any other period. Accounts are hopelessly confused, both in historical sources and in the Emperor's speeches. Sometimes he would suppress the candidates' names, but supply details of their family, career, and military service that would make it clear who they were. At others he would suppress even this information, and merely warn them not to disturb the elections by canvassing, promising his own support for this purpose. Very frequently he would declare that the names forwarded to the consuls were the only nominations received. It was open to others to come forward, if they thought their standing or achievement qualified them to do so. That sounded impressive, but in fact it was verbiage, if not trickery. The more ample the cloak of liberty which seemed to be spread about them, the more catastrophic the plunge to servitude they were soon to take.

BOOK II

16 A.D. Consuls Sisenna Statilius Taurus and Lucius Scribonius Libo

THE EASTERN PROBLEM

1. In this year there were disturbances throughout the kingdoms of the East and the Roman provinces. Trouble began with the Parthians. They had asked for a king from Rome, and received him: now, though he was of the blood of the Arsacids, they despised him as a foreigner. This king was Vonones, whom Phraates had sent as a hostage to Augustus. Phraates had defeated Roman armies and generals, but had always been punctiliously respectful toward Augustus, and had sent some of his offspring[1] to Rome to strengthen bonds of friendship—not so much, to be sure, through fear of us as through doubts about the loyalty of his own countrymen.

2. Following the death of Phraates and the monarchs who succeeded him in palace quarrels, the leaders of the Parthian state sent a deputation to Rome to summon Vonones, the eldest of Phraates' sons. Augustus took this as a tribute to himself, and lent financial help. The Parthians received Vonones with much joy—as usual at the outset of a reign. But then they began to feel themselves disgraced. "We have gone to another world," they said, "to find a king, and we have got one infected with the sophistication of our enemies. The throne of the Arsacids is being handled and bandied about as though it were one of the Roman provinces! Where is the glory we won through butchering Crassus and expelling Antony if one of Augustus' possessions, inured to years of slavery, now rules in Parthia?" Their aversion was increased by Vonones' character,

which marked him off from the habits of his ancestors. He seldom hunted, took little interest in horses, was carried in a litter in his progress through cities, and despised the traditional Parthian banquets. Mockery was also directed at his Greek favorites, and his way of keeping even ordinary domestic utensils under lock and key. He was most accessible and of an affable disposition, but such qualities were unknown to the Parthians, who looked on them as a strange new vice. Since these were alien to their own customs, they hated Vonones as much for his good qualities as for his bad.

3. So Artabanus, of the blood of the Arsacids and reared among the Dahae,[2] was summoned. In the first battle he was defeated, but mustering another army, he gained the throne. The defeated Vonones found refuge in Armenia, where the throne was then vacant. Lying between the Roman and Parthian empires, Armenia was at that time hostile to us because of the criminal conduct of Antony. He had lured the king of Armenia, Artavasdes, into his power with a show of friendship, then imprisoned him and finally put him to death. His father's memory made his son Artaxias unfriendly to us, and he relied on Parthian protection for himself and his kingdom. But the treachery of his kinsfolk caused the death of Artaxias, after which Augustus gave Tigranes as king to the Armenians, and Tiberius Nero conducted him to his kingdom. The reign of Tigranes did not last long, nor did that of his children, although following the oriental custom they were united in matrimony as well as power.[3]

4. After this, and at the command of Augustus, another Artavasdes was set up, only to be ejected, with some misfortunes to our arms. Then Gaius Caesar was appointed to settle affairs in Armenia. He crowned Ariobarzanes, a Median by birth, but acceptable to the Armenians because of his physical beauty and high intelligence. When Ariobarzanes met an accidental death they would have nothing to do with his descendants. For a while they sampled the rule of a queen, Erato, but that did not last long. Finally, irresolute, disorganized, and masterless rather than enjoying freedom, the Armenians placed the refugee Vonones on the throne. But Artabanus became a menace: Vonones could command little support from the Armenians, and help from us would mean a Parthian war. So the governor of Syria, Creticus, sent for him and kept him under guard, allowing him the title and full royal state. How Vonones intrigued to escape from this degrading position I shall recount in its proper place.

WAR IN GERMANY

5. Tiberius was by no means displeased with this turn of events in the East. It gave an excuse for transferring Germanicus from the legions he knew so well and putting him in a new provincial command, with its attendant risks of disaster and treachery. As for Germanicus, his own soldiers' increased measure of devotion, and the Emperor's disfavor, were alike motives for seeking a speedy victory. He therefore began to plan his campaigns, and to review his successes and failures in the past two years. His evaluation was as follows: "In pitched battles and on level ground we can defeat the Germans. Factors in their favor are forests, swamps, the short summers, and the early winters. Our own men are worse affected by long marches and loss of weapons than by casualties. The supply of horses from the Gallic provinces is drying up. Our long supply trains are exposed to ambush, and hard to protect. But if I approach by sea, an element familiar to us and unknown to the enemy, then I can set an earlier date for the attack and bring up the legions and their supplies simultaneously. The cavalry and their horses will be fresh; conveyed along the coast and up the river channels, they can be disembarked in the very heart of Germany."

6. Such was the plan he adopted. The census in Gaul was entrusted to Publius Vitellius and Gaius Antius: Silius, Anteius, and Caecina supervised the construction of a flotilla. A thousand ships were thought to be adequate, and their construction was pushed ahead. Some were of shallow draught, pointed bow and stern, and broad-beamed to withstand heavy seas. Others were flat-bottomed to allow grounding. Most of them were equipped with steering oars on either side, to allow of quick movement forward or backward. Many had decks for the transport of artillery, horses, and supplies. They were easy to sail, their oars gave them a turn of speed, and the keenness of their complement made them impressive and formidable. They were to assemble at the Island of the Batavi, where good landing facilities made it possible to embark troops, take on board supplies, and carry the war into the enemy's country. The river Rhine flows in a single channel (or is broken by small islands only) up to this point, but it separates into two rivers, as it were, when it reaches the land of the Batavi. The German channel preserves its name and its rapid current until it joins the Atlantic. But the Gallic channel is broader and more

placid—this is the arm called the "Vahala" by the natives;[4] then it again changes its name to the Meuse and discharges through a huge estuary into the same ocean.

7. As the ships were being assembled, Germanicus sent Silius with a light-armed force to raid the Chatti. Hearing that the fort on the Lippe was under siege, he himself took six legions to its rescue. But sudden rains made it impossible for Silius to do more than capture the wife and daughter of Arpus, chief of the Chatti. Germanicus failed to engage the besiegers, who scattered at his approach; earlier, they had destroyed the mound so recently erected as a memorial to the legions of Varus, and also the old altar in honor of Drusus. The mound Germanicus decided not to restore, but the altar was rebuilt, and there was a funeral parade, with the legions, to the memory of Drusus. Then a new chain of fortifications secured the whole country between Fort Aliso and the Rhine.

8. By now the fleet had mustered. The supply ships were sent on ahead, the legionaries and allies taken aboard the vessels assigned to them. As he entered the waterway known as the "Canal of Drusus," Germanicus addressed a prayer to his father. "Look with favor," he begged, "on a project so like your own; with your example and your memory be behind me in thought and action." Then he made a successful voyage through the lagoons into the ocean, and as far as the mouth of the river Ems. He left the fleet on the left bank of that river. This was a mistake. Since the troops had to operate on the right bank, he would have done better either to sail farther upstream, or to disembark on the right bank. As a result, several days were lost over the building of a bridge. The cavalry and the legions passed the first tidal marshes, before the waters rose, in good order. But the rest of the column, containing the allies and some Batavian troops, tried to show their contempt for the waters and their skill in swimming. They were thrown into confusion and lost men by drowning.

While Germanicus was setting out his camp, news came of a rebellion of the Ampsivarii in his rear. Stertinius, sent with a force of cavalry and light-armed troops, punished their disloyalty with fire and slaughter.

THE ENCOUNTER WITH ARMINIUS

9. The river Weser now ran between the Romans and the Cherusci.[5] Arminius stood on its bank, and with him the other chieftains. He asked whether Germanicus had come, and was

told that he was there. Then he asked to speak with his brother. Now this brother Flavus was with the Roman army; he had distinguished himself by his loyalty, and a few years earlier had lost an eye while serving under Tiberius. Permission being granted, Flavus came forward to the bank, and was greeted by Arminius. Sending away his own bodyguards, Arminius requested that the bowmen on our side of the river should be withdrawn. When this was done he asked, "Where did you get that ugly wound on the face?" Flavus named the place and the battle. "And what reward did they pay you for it?" was the rejoinder. Flavus then recounted his increased pay, the torque, crown, and other military decorations he had received. "The wages of slavery," jeered Arminius, "and cut-rate!"

10. Then began a dispute in good round terms. Flavus spoke of the glory of Rome, the immense resources of the Emperor, the heavy penalties visited on the conquered, the clemency that awaited surrender—even Arminius' wife and child had been received in a friendly fashion. Arminius spoke of their country's claims, ancestral freedom, the household gods of Germany and of their mother, who added her prayers to his. "Come back, man," he said "to your kith and kin, and to your own people: be their leader, not their betrayer!" Then they passed to an exchange of insults, and it would have come to fighting, river or no river, had not Stertinius rushed up and held Flavus back, though he was full of anger and shouting for arms and a horse. There on the other bank was Arminius, threatening and challenging to a fight: some of his words were in Latin, for he had once commanded a force of native auxiliaries in the Roman army.

11. The next day the Germans stood in battle order across the Weser. Thinking that it was military madness to risk the legions unless there were bridges and a force to guard them, Germanicus dispatched the cavalry across the river by the fords. They were commanded by Stertinius and Aemilius, a centurion of the first grade. To split the enemy forces, they crossed at widely separated points. Chariovalda, leader of the Batavi, dashed across where the stream ran fastest. The Cherusci feigned flight, and lured them on to flat ground surrounded by forests. Then they collected together, rushed out from every side, beat down resistance, followed the Batavi as they gave way, and finally bunched them up into a ball and assailed them fiercely from long range and short. Chariovalda held his position for some time in the face of this savage assault; at last, urging his men to keep together and force their way out, he made for the thickest of the fighting. Here his horse was killed under him, and he went down under a shower of

weapons, many of the chieftains at his side. The rest escaped from danger either through their own efforts, or thanks to the cavalry brought to their aid by Stertinius and Aemilius.

THE BATTLE OF IDISTAVISO

12. Information brought in by a deserter warned Germanicus that Arminius had chosen the ground for a battle: other tribes too had gathered in the forest sacred to Hercules,[6] and they were going to venture a night attack on the camp. The information seemed trustworthy, and indeed the German campfires could be seen; scouts who crept up closer reported hearing the whinnying of horses, and all the noise of a huge, undisciplined host. Now that the hour of the decisive battle was at hand, Germanicus thought it wise to test the feelings of the common soldier. But how to discover the authentic mood of the troops? "Tribunes and centurions," he argued, "report what sounds good rather than what is true; freedmen are still slaves at heart, my friends are sure to flatter me. If I call an assembly, the majority will only echo the sentiments of the few. The best way to explore their minds is when they are at mess: here, private and unguarded, soldiers reveal their real hopes and fears."

13. So, at nightfall, he left the general's tent by a secret path, unknown to the sentries. With one companion, and throwing an animal's skin over his shoulders, he passed along the camp roads, halted at the tents—and learned how high his reputation stood. Some spoke of their general's noble birth, others of his physical beauty; all agreed about his endurance, his charm of manner, the level temper he kept in jest or earnest. "We must butcher these traitors, these peace-breakers, for glory and revenge!"

It so happened that one of the enemy, who knew Latin, rode his horse up to the lines and in a loud voice promised in the name of Arminius to reward deserters with wives and lands and a hundred sesterces a day for the duration of the war. This roused the soldiers to fury. "Just wait for daylight!" they shouted. "Let's have the battle! We'll take the Germans' lands for ourselves, and rape their women! We accept the omen. It's the German lands and women that shall be our booty!" About midnight there was an attack on the camp, but no discharge of missiles. Units were thickly posted at the outworks, and they left no loophole unguarded.

14. That same night brought Germanicus a dream of good import. He thought that as he was sacrificing, some of the vic-

tim's blood fell on his purple-bordered robe; thereupon he received a clean one from the Empress's hands. The omen encouraged him, and the auspices confirmed it. He therefore called a meeting of the troops, to explain to them the plans he had made and the tactics which were best suited to the impending battle. "It's not only on level ground that we have the advantage," he said. "If we use our heads we can profit from the forests and rough country. The enemy have huge shields and long spears that can't be handled so easily among the tree trunks and undergrowth as the spears and swords and close-fitting armor of the Romans. Let them have it thick and fast, smash their faces with your shield-bosses! These Germans don't have breastplates and helmets. Their shields aren't made of iron and leather, but only of woven osier twigs, or painted boards of no thickness. The front rank have spears, after a fashion, the others short pikes or sharpened staves. They're ugly to look at, and they're good enough for a short charge. But they can't take wounds, they've no sense of shame: they run away without thinking of their general. Cowards in defeat, they disregard human and divine law in the hour of victory. If you're really tired of traveling and seafaring, this battlefield is where you can stop! The Elbe is nearer than the Rhine, and there's no more fighting in prospect. I am treading in my father's and my uncle's footsteps; place me as a conqueror where they stood, and there's an end of the war!"

15. The general's speech roused the men to enthusiasm, and the signal was given for battle. Arminius and the other German chieftains did not fail to harangue their men, tribe by tribe. "These are the men," they said, "who had the best turn of speed in Varus' army. They chose mutiny rather than a battle! Some of them have backs lashed with stripes, others are maimed by storms and gales. They're exposing themselves again to a furious enemy: heaven is against them, they have no hopes left. How did they get here? In ships, over the pathless ocean, where no one could stop them and turn them back again. Ships and oars won't be any good to them, once we've got to fighting, and they're beaten! Remind yourselves of Roman greed, cruelty, and arrogance! What else can we do, except to keep our freedom, or die before it turns to slavery!"

16. This inflamed their spirits. They called for battle and were led to a plain called Idistaviso. This takes the form of an irregular crescent between the hills and the Weser, as the river banks recede or the spurs of the hills advance toward it. In the rear was the forest, the branches high from the ground, and devoid of undergrowth.[7] The plain and the forest fringes were held by the barbarians: the Cherusci alone were posted

on the heights, so they could charge down on the Romans once they were locked in battle. The Roman order of battle was as follows: in the van the German and Gallic auxiliaries: behind them the foot-archers: then Germanicus with four legions, two cohorts of the Praetorian Guard, and a picked force of cavalry; then in due order another four legions, the light-armed troops, the mounted archers, and the other auxiliary units. A general alert was in force, each man ready to pass from marching to battle order.

17. When he saw the bands of the Cherusci, whose boldness had caused them to rush forward, he ordered our best cavalry to attack them on the flank. Stertinius with the other cavalry units was ordered to surround them and attack them from the rear. Germanicus would come at the right moment. Meanwhile the general saw the most propitious of all auguries, for eight eagles flew toward the forest and went into it. "Forward, men!" he shouted. "Follow the Roman birds, the guardian spirits of the legions!" The infantry went forward to the assault, and the cavalry that had been sent ahead fell on the enemy flank and rear. A strange spectacle followed—two enemy forces retreating in opposite directions, those in the forest seeking the plain, those from the plain streaming back into the forest! Between the two the Cherusci were dislodged from the hills, though Arminius did all he could to rally them by voice, by example, and by showing his wounds. He bore down on the archers, and would have got out that way, had not the Raetian, Gallic, and Vindelic units blocked his path with their standards. But with a great leap, and thanks to the speed of his horse, he burst through, having smeared his face with his own blood to escape recognition. Some accounts say that he was recognized by the Chauci serving in the Roman army, and that they let him escape. The same courage—or the same deceit—saved Inguiomerus. The rest were butchered far and wide. Many tried to swim the Weser, but a hail of weapons or the force of the current accounted for them, or (later) the throng of runaways and the collapse of the bank. Some disgraced themselves by climbing trees and hiding among the branches. But archers were brought up to pick them off in sport: or the trees were thrown down and they were dashed to the ground.

18. It was a great victory, and our casualties were light. From the fifth hour of the day till nightfall the slaughter of the enemy went on. For ten miles the ground was covered with German corpses and weapons. Among the booty were chains that they had brought along, confident of the outcome, for the Romans. The soldiers saluted Tiberius as "Imperator" on the field of battle: a mound was built, and arms were piled

up in the form of a trophy on which the names of the conquered tribes were inscribed.

THE BATTLE IN THE FOREST

19. The sight of this trophy did more to arouse grief and fury among the Germans than all their wounds, disasters, and losses. They had been getting ready to leave their own territory and withdraw across the Elbe, but now they flew to arms and demanded battle. Chiefs and people, young and old, made sudden, violent attacks on the Roman column. Finally they selected a place enclosed by forests and a river, where the flat ground was narrow and swampy. The forests themselves were surrounded by a deep morass on all sides save one, where the Angrivarii had built a broad earthwork to divide their lands from the Cherusci. On this earthwork the German infantry were stationed. The cavalry were in the forest, under cover, ready to fall on the Romans from the rear as soon as they entered.

20. But these dispositions were known to Germanicus in full detail. He understood the enemy's plans and positions, what they showed and what they concealed, and was ready to turn their cleverness to their own destruction. To Seius Tubero, one of the legionary commanders, he assigned the cavalry and the plain. The infantry battle order was such that some were to advance into the forest, where the approach was over level ground, and others were to scale the earthwork. He himself undertook the difficult assignment, leaving the rest to the legionary commanders. Those advancing across level ground easily reached their objectives in the forest. But scaling the earthwork was like trying to climb a wall, and these troops were seriously harassed by blows from above. Germanicus saw that at close quarters the odds would be heavy against him, so the legions withdrew a short distance and slingers and hurlers were advanced to discharge their missiles and dislodge the enemy. The artillery fired javelins: the more the defenders exposed themselves, the more readily were they wounded and borne down. Once the earthwork was captured, Germanicus himself at the head of the Praetorian cohort led a charge into the forest. There bitter hand-to-hand fighting began. The enemy had the swamp behind him, the Romans the river or the mountains. Both could only fight it out where they were. Valor was their only hope, victory the only way to safety.

21. The Germans matched us in fighting spirit, but their

tactics and their weapons told against them. With great numbers crowded in a narrow space, they could not thrust out their huge spears and recover them. They could not exploit their quickness of limb, nor charge, compelled as they were to fight a stationary battle. But the Romans, holding their shields close to their chests, and grasping their swords firmly by the hilt, struck savagely at the huge limbs and unguarded faces of the Germans, and hacked their way forward over heaps of enemy dead.

The endless dangers he had faced had unnerved Arminius, or else he was handicapped by his recent wound, for he was below his usual form in battle. Inguiomerus was everywhere: in his case it was bad luck rather than lack of courage that afflicted him. On the Roman side, Germanicus took off his helmet so that he could be clearly recognized. "Keep up the pressure!" he shouted. "Kill them off, we don't want prisoners! Wipe out the whole race, that's the only way to finish the war!" Finally, when day was far advanced, he withdrew one legion from action to make a camp. The others glutted themselves with enemy blood until night fell. The cavalry action ended in a stalemate.[8]

22. At a formal parade, Germanicus congratulated the troops on their victory. A heap of arms was piled with the proud inscription: THIS MONUMENT WAS DEDICATED TO MARS AND JUPITER AND THE DEIFIED AUGUSTUS BY THE ARMY OF TIBERIUS CAESAR AFTER THE CONQUEST OF ALL THE TRIBES BETWEEN THE RHINE AND THE ELBE. Of himself he said nothing. This may have been through fear of jealousy, or he may have felt that it was enough to know what he had done. Soon he sent Stertinius to attack the Angrivarii, unless they promptly surrendered. In fact, they offered unconditional surrender, and received full pardon for all their misdeeds.

THE GREAT STORM

23. By now summer was far advanced, and certain legions were sent back overland to winter quarters. The bulk of them, however, Germanicus embarked on shipboard, sailing down the Ems to the Atlantic. It was a calm sea at first, broken only by the thousand ships as they proceeded, rowing or under sail. But soon came a burst of hail from a black bank of clouds, accompanied by sudden squalls from every direction, which

cut off visibility and impeded steering. The soldiers became panic-stricken. Ignorant of the perils of the sea, they got in the way of the sailors, tried clumsily to help, and interfered with the routine of the skilled navigators. Then everything, wind and wave alike, gave place to a great southerly gale, drawing its strength from an endless belt of storm clouds, born in the waterlogged lands and deep rivers of Germany, and striking more chill because of the nearness of the frozen North. Ships were overwhelmed, driven far out to sea, or onto islands with sheer cliffs or hidden shoals.[9] Scarcely had these dangers been avoided when the tide turned, to set in the same direction as the gale. Now the anchors would not hold: they could not bail out as the waves burst in: horses, mules, baggage, arms, were cast overboard to lighten the hulls as waves dashed over the side, or water seeped through the joints.

24. The Atlantic is the stormiest of all seas, the climate of Germany the foulest in the world. Here, then, was disaster on a new and unprecedented scale. On one side were the shores of enemy country, on the other seas so wide and deep that this is thought to be the last, landless ocean. Some of the ships were sunk: more were cast away in far, uninhabited islands, where the troops either starved to death or ate the bodies of the horses washed up with them. Germanicus' warship was the only one to make a landfall in the territory of the Chauci. All those days and nights he spent on the cliffs and headlands, reproaching himself as responsible for this dreadful disaster. It was as much as his friends could do to stop him from throwing himself into the sea. At long last, the waters flowed back, the winds turned favorable, and the ships came limping in. Some were short of rowers, others used garments for sails, still others were being towed by ships in better case. These were hastily patched up and sent off to search the islands. In this way, most of the troops were rescued. Many, too, were returned by the Angrivarii, recently surrendered, who ransomed them from the inland tribes. Some had even been driven ashore in Britain, and were sent back by the petty kings of that island. As they came in from their far adventures they had marvels to tell: fearful hurricanes, strange birds, sea monsters half human, half animal. All these they had seen or imagined in their fears.

25. Reports that the fleet was lost raised the Germans' hopes, and Germanicus had to take measures to suppress them. He sent Gaius Silius with thirty thousand infantry and three thousand cavalry to attack the Chatti, while he himself led a still more powerful force against the Marsi. Their chief, Mallovendus, had recently surrendered, and had revealed that

in a neighboring grove one of Varus' eagles lay buried, and only lightly guarded. At once a force was sent for a frontal attack on the enemy, and another to form a digging party to their rear. Both accomplished their mission. Thus encouraged, Germanicus made a deep penetration, ravaging and destroying an enemy who seldom dared to stand his ground, or if he did, was immediately routed. Prisoners revealed how thoroughly the Germans were demoralized. "These Romans," they said, "are invincible, proof against every disaster. They have lost their fleet and their weapons, the shores are strewn with the bodies of their men and horses. But still they come to the attack, with no less courage and fierceness than before—and in numbers that seem greater than ever!"

WITHDRAWAL OF GERMANICUS

26. Then the troops were led back to winter quarters, glad to have counterbalanced the disasters of the storm by this successful campaign. Germanicus displayed much generosity, settling in full all claims for losses that were presented. He was confident that the enemy were wavering, and beginning to think of suing for peace; one more summer in the field, and the war could be wound up. But he kept getting letters from Tiberius advising him to return and celebrate the triumph already voted. "We have had enough," said the Emperor, "of successes and disasters. You have won great victories, but you must also remember what the winds and waves have done —through no fault of the general—to cause grievous and heavy loss. I was sent into Germany by Augustus nine times, and I achieved more by diplomacy than war. That was how the Sugambri surrendered, how the Suebi and King Maroboduus were induced to keep the peace. As for the Cherusci and the other bellicose tribes, the vengeance of Rome has been duly provided for; now we can leave them to quarrel among themselves." Germanicus asked for one more year to bring his plans to fruition. Tiberius applied heavier pressure by offering the young prince—who never sought to push himself forward —a second consulship, but one whose duties he would have to discharge in person. He adduced further arguments. "If it is necessary to prolong the war, you must leave your brother Drusus the raw material for glory. There are now no enemies except in Germany: that is where he must win the name of 'Imperator' and gain the wreath of victory." Germanicus hesitated no longer, though he saw clearly that these arguments

were fictitious, and that he was being deprived, through jealousy, of the honors he had won.

ROME. THE CASE OF LIBO DRUSUS

27. At about this period, Libo Drusus, a member of the family of the Scribonii, was accused of plotting treason. I shall set the beginning, course, and issue of this affair, as a first instance of practices which for many years gnawed at the vitals of the commonwealth. Firmius Catus, a senator and a close friend of Libo's, induced that fatuous young man, easily led into folly, to take an interest in the forecasts of astrologers, the rites of fortunetellers, and the interpretation of dreams. He reminded Libo that he was the great-grandson of Pompey, the grandnephew of that Scribonia who had once been the wife of Augustus, and thus a cousin of the Caesars, and that his house was full of ancestral images; he encouraged him in indulgence and in debt, and shared both his dissipation and his financial embarrassment. The object of all this was to accumulate evidence against him.

28. When he had enough witnesses—and indeed the evidence of slaves in corroboration—he sought a private interview with the Emperor. He laid bare the charges, named the accused; a certain Flaccus Vescularius, a Roman knight better known to Tiberius, acted as go-between. Tiberius received the information but declined the interview, pointing out, however, that this same Flaccus could still be used for communication. Meanwhile he made Libo praetor, and asked him to dine. Not a jot did his expression alter, his voice betrayed no emotion; he was a consummate dissimulator of anger. He could have put an end to all Libo's words and actions; he preferred to know them.

But then a certain Junius, whom Libo had approached to raise the spirits of the dead, laid information with Fulcinius Trio. Trio ranked high among informers, and was eager to win an evil reputation. He pounced on the defendant at once, went to the consuls, and demanded that the affair be investigated by the Senate. The Senate was indeed summoned, the notice of meeting proclaiming that they were to deliberate on a matter of high and terrible import.

29. Meanwhile Libo dressed himself in mourning, and with an escort of ladies of rank paid calls on the houses of the great, seeking the support of his wife's relatives in his hour of danger. All refused him. They found different excuses, but

were actuated by the same fears. On the day of the Senate meeting he was so prostrate with nervousness and ill-health—though some say his physical symptoms were feigned—that he was carried in a litter to the door of the Senate House. Leaning on his brother for support, he stretched out his arms toward Tiberius and begged for mercy. There was a blank response. Then the Emperor, in a neutral tone of voice so as not to appear either to exaggerate or to lessen the charges, read the accusation and the names of the accusers.

30. Besides Trio and Catus, Fonteius Agrippa and Gaius Vibius entered themselves as accusers. There was much competition between them as to who should deliver the principal speech against the defendant. They failed to reach agreement among themselves, and Libo had no one to act for him. Vibius therefore announced that he would bring forward the indictments, one by one.[10] He then produced some really silly charges—among them, that Libo had inquired whether he would ever be wealthy enough to pave the Appian Way with coin all the way to Brundisium. There were other things of the same kind, stupid and meaningless, or, looked at in another way, pathetic. But in one of the indictments the prosecutor professed to find mysterious symbols entered in the handwriting of Libo against the names of members of the imperial house. Libo denied that he had written them. But slaves identified the handwriting, and it was agreed to question them under torture. Now there was an ancient senatorial resolution which forbade the interrogation of slaves when their masters were charged with capital offenses. But Tiberius was ingenious at finding legal innovations. He ordered these slaves to be sold one by one to a treasury agent, so that the interrogation of Libo's slaves could proceed without infringing the decree of the Senate!

The defendant therefore asked for a day's postponement. He went home and, through the agency of his friend Publius Quirinius, made his final appeal to the Emperor.

31. The reply was that the appeal should go to the Senate. Meanwhile Libo's house was put under military guard. Such a racket did the soldiers raise in the forecourt of his house, so audible and conspicuous was their presence, that Libo became distracted at the very dinner party which he had planned as his last worldly pleasure. Grasping slaves by the right hand, he called for someone to dispatch him, and thrust forward a sword. They started back in horror, and knocked over the lamp that had been placed on the table. In this darkness—for him, the darkness of the grave—Libo stabbed himself twice in the

belly, and fell groaning. Freedmen ran up, and the soldiers, seeing that he was dead, withdrew.

The Senate, however, showed no loss of energy in pressing on with his trial. Tiberius solemnly declared that he would have asked for him to be pardoned, however guilty, but for this untimely suicide.

32. His property was divided up among the accusers, and honorary praetorship conferred on those of them who were in the Senate. Then Cotta Messalinus proposed that the effigy of Libo should not follow his posterity in procession to the grave;[11] Gnaeus Lentulus, that none of the Scribonii should bear the name of Drusus. On the motion of Pomponius Flaccus a public thanksgiving was decreed. Gifts to Jupiter, Mars, and Concord, and a declaration that the Ides of September, the day of Libo's suicide, should be a public holiday, were approved from a motion proposed by Lucius Piso and Gallus Asinius and Papius Mutilus and Lucius Apronius. Their motions, and the servility they displayed, I have set down as showing that this evil is of long standing in the state. A senatorial decree was passed to expel astrologers and magicians from Italy. One of them, Lucius Pituanius, was thrown from the Tarpeian Rock; another, Publius Marcius, was decapitated by the consuls according to the ancient ritual, to the blare of trumpets outside the Porta Esquilina.[12]

ROME. A DEBATE ON LUXURY

33. The next time the Senate was in session Quintus Haterius, an ex-consul, and Octavius Fronto, an ex-praetor, spoke at length on the subject of luxury. A decree was passed forbidding the use of solid gold plate for private dinner parties, and also that effeminate custom, the wearing of silk garments by the male sex. Fronto went very much further, and asked for the setting of limits on the use of silver plate, furniture, and household slaves—for it was still a custom of the Senate to allow members, in declaring their opinion, to bring forward any proposals they thought in the public interest. Asinius Gallus put the opposite point of view. "With the growth of the Empire," he said, "private fortunes have also increased. There is nothing new in this; it has a respectable antiquity. Money had one value in the time of the Fabricii, and quite another in that of the Scipios. The yardstick is the condition of the state. When the state was poor, the private standard of living was frugal; when it reached its present degree of affluence, per-

sonal fortunes, in some cases, have risen to match. In matters of household, furniture, plate, and all consumer goods, the index of excess or moderation is the owner's means. If distinctive scales of wealth have been laid down for senators and for knights, that does not mean they are different kinds of people. It simply means that, just as they take precedence over others in their seats in the theater, in their rank, and in their privileges, so they are to have the same priority in what conduces to mental relaxation and bodily health. Surely it cannot be maintained that men of higher station, who have to shoulder more anxieties and run more risks, should also lack means of compensation for these cares?"

These were fine phrases, though in fact they were an argument for vice. But an audience who shared his outlook lent them ready assent. Tiberius wound up the debate by saying that this was not an opportune time to employ the censor's powers, but, if the situation called for it, he would not hesitate to apply remedial measures.

ROME. THE CONDUCT OF LUCIUS PISO

34. During this debate Lucius Piso, after an attack on political intrigues, legal corruption, and the savagery of prosecutors threatening to take up cases, declared that he would withdraw from Rome and live in some secluded country retreat for the future. On this note he left the Senate House. The Emperor was most perturbed: he left nothing undone that kind words could do to induce Piso to change his mind, and asked his relatives to use their influence to stop his departure.

This same Piso shortly afterward gave a notable example of independence of mind and temper when he summoned to court Urgulania, a lady who seemed raised above the law because of her friendship with the Empress. But Urgulania took no notice of his summons: instead, she was carried in her litter to the palace. He stood his ground, although the Empress complained that this was an insult and affront to her own dignity. Tiberius thought he owed it to his mother, in common politeness, to appear before the praetor and support Urgulania. He left the palace, ordering his guards to follow at a distance. He could be seen walking through the crowd, perfectly at ease, and chatting on various subjects to pass the time. Piso was implored by his friends to desist, but in vain: finally the Empress ordered that the sum in dispute should be paid. Piso emerged with credit from the incident, and the Emperor gained in popularity. But Urgulania continued to enjoy an excessive influence in the state. Summoned as a witness in a case being tried before the Senate, she did not bother to come, and a praetor was sent to take her evidence in her own house. Yet an ancient custom required that even a vestal virgin, when summoned to appear, must give her evidence in open court.

ROME. DEBATES IN THE SENATE

35. I should not mention the issue of the vacation that year, had not the opposite views expressed on that subject by Piso and by Asinius Gallus made it worth while to do so. The Emperor had intimated that he would be away from Rome: Piso thought this an additional argument for proceeding with business. "If the Senate and knights can discharge their functions in the Emperor's absence," he declared, "it is a credit to the state." Gallus had been forestalled by Piso in this show of independence. He maintained that it was not in accord with the dignity of the Roman people to proceed in the absence of the personal control of the Emperor. The crowd of Italians, and the influx of visitors from the provinces, should await his return. Tiberius listened in silence as the argument developed. The decision was to adjourn.

36. But Gallus did have one open clash with the Emperor. He proposed that magistrates should be elected five years in advance; that commanders of legions who had not held the praetorship should be praetors-designate from the date of the proposal; and that the Emperor should nominate future candidates for each year. This was obviously a far-reaching proposal, whose implications struck at the hidden principles of autocratic rule. Tiberius handled it as though it were intended to increase his powers. "I could not undertake," he declared, "to make or to postpone so many promotions. Even making them for a year at a time it is scarcely possible to avoid giving offense, though a near hope can console a present disappointment. But what resentment is likely to be aroused in those who see their claims deferred for more than five years! How can we forecast a man's attitude, connections, and fortune so far ahead? Men elected one year in advance are likely to become arrogant; what if they can plume themselves on office for five years ahead? It will mean the quintuplication of magistracies. It will also invalidate the laws which prescribe definite timetables for candidates canvassing for office, and for seeking and holding office."

This speech was favorably received: but its effect was to maintain the Emperor's grip on power.

37. Certain senators were given gifts of money. The more surprising, then, that he dealt so summarily with the plea of Marcus Hortalus, a young man of good family and obviously devoid of means. This Hortalus was a descendant of the orator Hortensius, and had received a grant of one million sesterces from Augustus on condition that he should marry and have children, to prevent so distinguished a family from dying out.

So his four children were standing at the door of the Senate House when Hortalus rose to speak. They were meeting in the palace: Hortalus kept turning to the statue of Augustus, also to that of Hortensius, where it stood among the great orators. "Gentlemen," he said, "you see how many these children are and how young. They have been brought up not by any wish of mine, but by the Emperor's command; my ancestors had deserved a posterity. In these changed times, I have been unable to win or acquire any money or popular favor, or even eloquence, the ancestral property of our house. I was perfectly content that my slender means should not disgrace me nor burden others. At the Emperor's command I took a wife. Behold the result—a progeny which springs from all these consuls and dictators! I say this, not in vainglory, but to win your sympathy. Under your rule, Caesar, they will attain whatever offices you wish. Meanwhile save the great-grandsons of Hortensius, the protégés of Augustus, from becoming paupers!"

38. Seeing the Senate favorably inclined, Tiberius immediately put in an objection. "If," said he, "every pauper comes here demanding money for his children, we shall never satisfy individual claims, and the treasury will be exhausted. Though our ancestors allowed senators to digress from the subject under discussion and bring forward opinions on matters of public interest, this was not for the object of allowing us to serve our private ends and increase our own fortunes. Such matters must be invidious to the Senate and the Emperor, whether the requests are granted or refused. This is not a request, but a demand, quite unforeseen, wholly out of place. The Senate is assembled for the discussion of other business, and a member rises and embarrasses it with a recital of the number of his children and their ages! I am involved in the same kind of pressure, and he tries to batter down the doors of the treasury. If we empty it by favoritism, we shall have to replenish it by crime. The late Emperor gave you money, Hortalus, but under no constraint, and with no obligation to maintain the supply. Energy will falter, idleness be fostered, if no one relies

on his own hopes and fears, but waits expectantly for money from others, without bestirring himself. Such men are a disgrace to themselves and a burden to us." These and similar sentiments—apart from those who applaud all the sayings of princes, good or bad—were received in silence or with suppressed mutterings. Seeing this, Tiberius paused for a while, then said he had given his reply to Hortalus. But, with the approval of the Senate, he would be ready to grant his male children 200,000 sesterces each. Other members expressed gratitude. Hortalus said nothing. He may have been panic-stricken, or he may have retained his ancestral dignity, even in humble circumstances. Tiberius took no further interest in him, though the house of Hortensius soon sank to degrading poverty.

ROME. THE PLOT OF CLEMENS

39. In this same year the audacity of a slave could have brought the state low with disturbances and civil strife, had not prompt steps been taken to check it. When the death of Augustus was announced, a certain Clemens, slave of Agrippa Postumus, conceived the idea of going to Planasia, smuggling away Agrippa by violence or stealth, and taking him to the armies of Germanicus. This was assuredly no servile plan. But the slowness of a freighter hindered the design: the murder of Agrippa was accomplished. Clemens now turned to a bolder and riskier course. Stealing Agrippa's ashes, he landed at Cosa, a promontory on the coast of Etruria. Now he hid himself and let his hair and beard grow long—for in looks and age he bore some resemblance to his master. Then, through suitable confederates in the plot, the story was circulated that Agrippa was still alive. As always with forbidden news, this was at first done by secret conversations. Then rumors were spread, and found ready belief from the lunatic fringe, or from agitators eager to promote a revolution. Clemens himself paid visits to the neighboring cities by night, never showing himself openly nor staying long in the same place. Truth thrives on publicity and delay, falsehood on haste and uncertainty. So he either left a place as soon as he became too well known, or went to another before anyone had heard of him.

40. Meanwhile the whole of Italy heard the report that the gods had preserved Agrippa. It was believed in Rome; when Clemens reached Ostia there was a huge crowd to greet him.

Secret gatherings of his supporters were held in the city. Tiberius was uncertain and distraught. Should he use troops to suppress his own slave, or should he leave it to time itself to deflate the credulity of the public? He alternated between fear and shame, between the feeling that no precautions should be omitted, and the reflection that one should not be afraid of everything. Finally, he handed the matter over to Sallustius Crispus, who chose two of his dependents (or, as some say, two soldiers) and instructed them to approach Clemens, pretend to be in the plot, and offer money, help, and a share in the danger. They carried this out to the letter. Then, waiting for a night when he was off his guard, they took along an adequate force, bound and gagged Clemens, and hauled him off to the palace. When Tiberius asked him, "And how did you turn yourself into Agrippa?" he replied, "The same way you turned yourself into Caesar." Nothing would induce him to betray his accomplices. Tiberius did not dare to execute him publicly; orders were given to dispatch him in a secret part of the palace, and to remove the corpse in dead secrecy. Many of the Emperor's own household, and also senators and knights, are said to have contributed funds and advice to the conspiracy; yet there was no investigation.

OTHER EVENTS OF THE YEAR

41. At the end of the year an arch was dedicated close to the temple of Saturn, to commemorate the recovery of the eagles of Varus under the leadership of Germanicus and the auspices of Tiberius.

A temple to Fors Fortuna was dedicated on the banks of the Tiber in the gardens which the dictator Julius Caesar had bequeathed to the Roman people. A chapel of the Gens Julia and a statue of the deified Augustus were consecrated at Bovillae.

17 A.D. Consuls Gaius Caelius Rufus and Lucius Pomponius Flaccus

ROME. THE TRIUMPH OF GERMANICUS

On the twenty-sixth of May Germanicus celebrated his triumph over the Cherusci, the Chatti, the Angrivarii, and all other peoples as far as the Elbe. Spoils and captives were displayed, pictures of mountains, rivers, and battles carried in the procession. The war he had been prevented from finishing was, for this purpose, regarded as finished. The handsome person of the commander, the five children who loaded his chariot, riveted the gaze of every spectator. Secret apprehension filled them as they thought how little good the favor of the people had brought his father Drusus, how his uncle, Marcellus, the universal popular favorite, had been cut down in the flower of his youth. Brief and unlucky, they thought, are the loves of the Roman people.

42. In the name of Germanicus, Tiberius made a donation of three hundred sesterces apiece to the common people, and named himself as colleague to Germanicus in his consulship. None believed that this was a mark of genuine affection; and Tiberius decided to get rid of him, though by an honorable excuse. He soon found grounds for this, or, rather, availed himself of what chance put in his way. King Archelaus had ruled in Cappadocia for fifty years. Tiberius detested him, for when he was at Rhodes, Archelaus had never shown him any mark of respect. This omission was in no way due to arrogance on Archelaus' part: it was deliberate. Confidants of Augustus had warned him, when Gaius Caesar stood high in favor and had been sent on a tour of inspection to the East, that it was dangerous to be on friendly terms with Tiberius. But when the line of the Caesars came to an end and Tiberius was on the throne, Archelaus was drawn from his lair by means of letters written by the Empress. She did not conceal her son's hostility, but held out a hope of pardon if he came to Rome to beg for it. Archelaus failed to detect the trap—or feared violence if he seemed to understand it. He hastened

to Rome, found Tiberius inexorable, and was soon on trial before the Senate. He was exhausted, not by the charges, which were spurious, but by old age and anxiety. Kings do not like being treated on equal terms, much less as inferiors. So, whether due to natural causes or suicide, his span of life came to an end. His kingdom became a province, and Tiberius announced that the revenues would make possible a reduction of the 1 per cent sales tax, which was to be fixed at ½ per cent in future.

At the same time the death of Antiochus, king of Commagene, and Philopator, king of Cilicia, left their kingdoms in confusion, for the larger party favored Roman rule, the others rule by a native king. Moreover, the provinces of Syria and Judaea, exhausted by their burdens, asked that their taxes be reduced.

GERMANICUS IN THE EAST

43. Tiberius raised these matters in the Senate, as also the state of affairs in Armenia, which I mentioned earlier.[13] "Only the wisdom of Germanicus," he said, "can provide a settlement: I am getting on in years; Drusus is not sufficiently mature." So the Senate entrusted to Germanicus these overseas provinces, granting him a *maius imperium* superior to those of all provincial governors, senatorial or imperial. But Tiberius had removed Creticus Silanus from Syria: he was closely connected with Germanicus through the engagement of his daughter to Germanicus' eldest son, Nero Caesar. In his place he appointed Gnaeus Piso.

Piso was a hot-tempered, insubordinate man, his intransigence inherited from his father. During the civil war this latter had energetically helped the republican party against Caesar when their fortunes revived in Africa, then he supported Brutus and Cassius. Allowed to return to Rome, he did not seek public office, but eventually he was begged by Augustus to take the consulship, and consented. Besides the temper derived from his father, Gnaeus Piso was further fired by the wealth and high lineage of his wife Plancina. He would scarcely yield precedence to Tiberius; Tiberius' sons he despised as far beneath him. He never doubted that the object of his appointment in Syria was to keep Germanicus under control. Indeed, there are those who maintain that he was given secret instructions by Tiberius personally: certainly Livia advised Plancina, from a very feminine desire to persecute Agrippina.

For the court was distracted and divided by unspoken partisanship for either Drusus or Germanicus. Tiberius favored Drusus, son of his own blood. But the hostility of his uncle won most people for Germanicus, who was, besides, of much better family on his mother's side, being the grandson of Mark Antony and the great-nephew of Augustus. Drusus' great-grandfather, the Roman knight Pomponius Atticus, seemed out of place among the statues of the Claudii. Then again, the fertility and good name of Germanicus' wife Agrippina gave her precedence over the younger Livilla, wife of Drusus. But the brothers themselves preserved the most cordial relations, wholly unaffected by the intrigues of their supporters.

GERMANY. ARMINIUS AND MAROBODUUS

44. Soon after this, Drusus was sent to Illyricum to gain military experience and win the loyalty of an army. Tiberius thought that army life was better for the young man than the dissipations of the capital, and indeed that he himself would be safer if both the young princes had troops at their command. The excuse, however, was the request of the Suebi for aid against the Cherusci. The departure of the Romans and the withdrawal of threats from abroad had led these two nations, from the bellicosity natural to their country, and their own rivalry, to turn their swords against each other. They were well matched, both the nations themselves and their leaders. But Maroboduus bore the name of "king," distasteful to the people, whereas Arminius and his struggle for freedom had popular approval.

45. As a result, not merely the Cherusci and their allies, the old soldiers of Arminius, were engaged in the war, but that chief even gained support by the defection from Maroboduus to himself of Suebian tribes, namely the Semnones and the Langobardi. These would have guaranteed his superiority had not Inguiomerus led a force of his own retainers over to join Maroboduus. The sole reason for this was that Inguiomerus, the older man, could not bear to serve under his young nephew. So the armies formed up for battle, and hopes ran high on either side. This was no longer the old Germanic warfare, of scattered charges and disorderly bands. They had learned much in the long struggle against Rome—to follow the standard, to place reserves, to obey the commands of a general. Arminius had reviewed, on horseback, his entire army.

As he came up to each division, he asserted that they had recovered their freedom and had massacred Roman legions, and that in fact many of them carried Roman spoils and weapons. "This Maroboduus," he cried, "is a runaway! He never risked a battle, but skulked in the depths of the Hercynian forest! Later he sued for peace with Rome by presents and deputations. He is a traitor, the agent of the Roman Emperor! We ought to crush him with the same resolution we showed in killing Quintilius Varus. Remember all the battles we fought, and how in the end the Romans were driven out—a clear proof of who won the war!"

46. Maroboduus also boasted of his own deeds and abused his enemy. Holding the arm of Inguiomerus, he exclaimed, "Here is the man who represents all the glory of the Cherusci, the author of all their victories! Arminius is a lunatic. Ignorant of warfare, he takes on himself the credit for the defeat by treachery of three legions that had lost their way, and their unsuspecting commander! His victory has cost Germany dear, and has brought disgrace to himself, for his wife and child are still prisoners in Roman hands. When Tiberius attacked me with twelve legions, I preserved German honor unimpaired. We parted on equal terms. Now we have the choice—and I am not ashamed of it—of a new war against the Romans or a peace without bloodshed."

Besides these speeches, the two armies had reasons of their own to encourage them to battle. The Cherusci and the Langobardi had their glorious past and the freedom they had retained; on the other side there was the hope of extending their empire. Seldom has there been so great a clash nor a battle so bitterly contested. On both sides the right wings were driven in. While the warriors were waiting for the battle to be renewed, Maroboduus withdrew his camp to the hills, an acknowledgment of defeat. Deserters gradually weakened him so much that he retreated to his own territory among the Marcomanni, and sent ambassadors to Tiberius to ask for help. The reply was that he had no right to request Roman help against the Cherusci, since he had not assisted the Romans in any way when they were engaged with the same enemy. But, as I have said, Drusus was sent to secure peace on the frontiers.

THE GREAT ASIAN EARTHQUAKE

47. In the same year twelve great cities of Asia were destroyed by an earthquake. It happened at night, which made the disaster all the more terrible and unexpected. The usual means of safety in such a calamity—rushing out into the open—proved of no avail, since fugitives were swallowed up by fissures which opened in the ground. Accounts say that enormous mountains subsided, plains became steep slopes, fire flashed among the ruins. Sardis seemed worst hit, and attracted most sympathy. The Emperor made them a grant of ten million sesterces, together with a remission for five years of all taxes, whether due to the public or to the imperial treasury. Magnesia-by-Sipylus was the next worst affected, and was so treated in compensation. Remission from direct taxation was authorized for Temnos, Philadelphia, Aegeae, Apollonis, the Mosteni, the Macedonians of Hyrcania, Hierocaesarea, Myrina, Cyme, and Tmolus. It was also decided to send a member of the Senate to assess the damage and provide remedial measures. Marcus Ateius, an ex-praetor, was chosen, for the governor of Asia was an ex-consul, and there was some danger of rivalry and obstruction arising if the two men were of equal rank.

ROME. TIBERIUS' GENEROSITY

48. This public munificence of the Emperor's was augmented by an equally striking instance of private generosity. A wealthy lady, Aemilia Musa, died intestate, and the imperial treasury claimed her estate. But Tiberius transferred it to Marcus Aemilius Lepidus, who was connected with her family. Again, on the death of the wealthy Roman knight Pantuleius, when he was named heir to half the estate, Tiberius handed the whole legacy to Marcus Servilius, when it was discovered that the latter had been named in an earlier will of undoubted authenticity. He explained that in both cases, the money was needed by the family, to maintain its rank. Indeed, he refused to accept any bequest which he had not earned by friendship: he would have nothing to do with strangers, or with those who named the Emperor as heir because of family quarrels.

But, although he relieved cases of honorable distress, he punished those who had bankrupted themselves through extravagance or improper conduct. Thus Vibidius Virro, Marius Nepos, Appius Appianus, Cornelius Sulla, and Quintus Vitellius were expelled from the Senate, or allowed to resign.

TEMPLES RESTORED

49. At this period he dedicated a number of temples whose repair Augustus had ordered because they were damaged by fire or age. For example, that to Liber, Libera, and Ceres near the Circus Maximus, originally dedicated by the dictator Aulus Postumius, that to Flora, in the same district, built by Lucius and Marcus Publicius as aediles, also the temple of Janus, near the vegetable market, built by that Gaius Duilius who won the first Roman victory at sea and celebrated a naval triumph over the Carthaginians. Germanicus consecrated a Temple of Hope which had been vowed by Aulus Atilius in the same war.

THE LAW OF TREASON

50. Meanwhile the law of treason was coming to ripeness. Even Appuleia Varilla, the niece of Augustus' sister, was charged under it: she was accused of having slandered the deified Augustus, also Tiberius and his mother, and, being a relative of Augustus, of having committed adultery. It was decided that the Lex Julia covered the charge of adultery. Tiberius pressed for a distinction between the charges under the law of treason: condemnation was called for, if she had indeed profaned the name of Augustus; the remarks alleged to have been made about himself he did not wish to see investigated. The consul then asked him what procedure he wished to see followed regarding the slanders against his mother; he made no reply. At the next meeting of the Senate, however, he requested, in her name, that no slanders against her, however worded, should be made into a charge. The charge of treason against Appuleia was therefore dismissed. On that of adultery he deprecated the severer penalties, suggesting that her relatives should follow the traditional custom and remove her more than two hundred miles from Rome. Her lover, Manlius, was banned from Italy and Africa.

51. There was a dispute about who should succeed the praetor Vipstanus Gallus, recently deceased. Germanicus and Drusus (both being then in Rome) supported Haterius Agrippa, a relative of Germanicus: but a majority opinion believed that the question of the number of children a candidate possessed should decide the day, as the law enjoined. Tiberius was delighted to find the Senate split between his sons and the law. The law—obviously—was the loser, but not immediately, and by a narrow margin, and that is how laws had formerly been overruled, even at a time when they stood for something.

AFRICA. THE REBELLION OF TACFARINAS

52. In the same year war broke out in Africa, where the enemy forces were led by Tacfarinas. He was a Numidian, who had served as an auxiliary in the Roman army, deserted, and collected together a band of nomads and robbers for booty and plunder. But then he marshaled them, in military fashion, into infantry and cavalry units; soon he was no longer a brigand chief but the leader of the Musulamii. They were a powerful tribe, living on the edge of the African desert, a district where there was as yet no urban life: he took up arms and dragged with him the neighboring tribe of the Mauri, under their chief Mazippa. The army was divided into two: Tacfarinas took an élite with Roman weapons and kept them in camp to be trained in obedience and tactics; Mazippa with the light-armed forces spread fire and murder and brigandage far and wide. They forced the Cinithii, a considerable people, to join the confederacy. But then Furius Camillus, governor of Africa, concentrated the legion and all his auxiliary units and led them against the enemy. His was a small force, compared with the numbers of the Numidians and Mauri, but his one anxiety was that they should not evade battle. The African hope of victory lured them to their own defeat. The legion was posted in the center, with two auxiliary cavalry squadrons on the wings. Tacfarinas accepted the challenge, and the Numidians were put to flight. So, after many years, the family of the Furii once more won military distinction. After the great Camillus,[14] who restored Rome, and his son, other families had won the general's laurels; moreover, the Camillus of this context was thought to be no soldier. The more readily, then, did Tiberius praise his achievements to the Senate. They awarded him the ornaments of a triumph, and he lived so modestly that it was not fatal to him.

18 A.D. Consuls Tiberius Caesar Augustus III, Germanicus Caesar II

GERMANICUS IN THE EAST

53. Next year, Tiberius held his third consulship, Germanicus his second. Germanicus took office in Nicopolis, a city in Achaea, which he had reached by way of the Illyrian coast, after visiting his brother Drusus in Dalmatia. In both the Adriatic and the Ionian seas he had encountered bad weather, so he spent a few days at Nicopolis to allow his ship to refit. There he saw the gulf where the great battle of Actium had been won, the spoils dedicated by Augustus, the camp of Antony—all evoking memories of his ancestors. For, as I have said, Augustus was his great-uncle, Antony his grandfather; and these lands had many associations of joy and sorrow. Thence he went to Athens: to that ancient city and ally he made the concession of appearing with only one lictor.[15] The Greeks provided him with a most elaborate reception, and by reciting the words and deeds of their ancestors in the distant past lent a certain impressiveness to their adulation.

54. After visiting Euboea, he sailed to Lesbos, and here Agrippina gave birth to Julia, the youngest of her children. Then, skirting the province of Asia, he reached Perinthus and Byzantium, cities of Thrace, and passed by way of the straits into the Black Sea. He was enthusiastic in visiting ancient and historic sites: he also restored provinces distressed by internal strife or the excesses of Roman magistrates. On his return he tried to visit the shrines of Samothrace, but was prevented by northerly gales. So he visited Troy, venerable for the many vicissitudes of fortune and for the origins of Rome. Then, again coasting along the shores of Asia, he landed at Colophon to visit the oracle of Apollo at Claros.[16] There is no priestess there, as at Delphi, but a priest, usually from Miletus, and chosen from certain families. He simply hears the name and number of those consulting the oracle; then he enters a cave, drinks the water of a hidden spring, and, although generally ignorant of letters or poetry, produces

responses in verse on any subjects the consultant may have
in mind. The story goes that he prophesied—in riddles, as is
usual with oracles—that Germanicus' death would not be long
delayed.

PISO IN THE EAST

55. Piso lost no time in setting about his designs. He made
a violent descent on Athens, alarming that people with a
brutal speech. Indirectly, he criticized Germanicus, saying that
he had praised in indulgent terms out of keeping with the dignity of Rome, a people no longer true Athenians (now extinct
from their many disasters) but the scum of the earth. They
had backed Mithridates against Sulla, Antony against the
deified Augustus. His reproaches delved far back into Athenian
history, including failures against the Macedonians and injustices to their own countrymen. He had, indeed, a private
grudge against the Athenians for their refusal to release at his
request a certain Theophilus, condemned by the Areopagus
on a charge of forgery.

Then he made a sea passage by the short route through
the Cyclades and caught up with Germanicus at Rhodes.
Germanicus was well aware of Piso's attacks on him, but his
kindness was such that, when a storm endangered Piso, so
that the death of an enemy might well have been ascribed to
chance, he sent ships to rescue him. Piso was not mollified in
the slightest. Delaying no more than a day, he left Germanicus
and reached Syria ahead of him.

The moment he reached the army in Syria he began dis-
tributing his gifts and bribes to the men in the ranks. Centurions of long service and the stricter tribunes were removed
and replaced by his own creatures, or by notorious bad characters. There was idleness in the camp, riotous behavior in
the cities; troops wandered round the countryside out of control; corruption reached such a point that Piso received the
sobriquet "father of the army." Plancina, too, went beyond
the proprieties usually observed by ladies. She attended exercises and maneuvers, and slandered Agrippina and Germanicus. Even some of the better soldiers were so foolish as to
support her, for the rumor had got abroad that all this was
not out of line with the Emperor's wishes. Germanicus knew
what was going on, but his immediate care was to be first in
Armenia.

THE PROBLEM OF ARMENIA

56. Geography and the character of that people have long made it an unreliable country. It has a long frontier with the Roman provinces: it also stretches inland as far as Media.[17] Placed between two world empires, it has frequently been on bad terms with both, hating Rome, jealous of Parthia. At that time it had no king, owing to the removal of Vonones. Popular support inclined to Zeno, son of the king of Pontus, Polemo. From early childhood he had copied Armenian manners and customs: his fondness for hunting, feasting, and other barbarian amusements had won him the favor of high and low. So, in the city of Artaxata, with the approval of the nobles and in the presence of a vast multitude, Germanicus bestowed on him the royal insignia. Then his subjects did homage to him as King Artaxias, a title he took from the name of the capital.

Next Cappadocia was organized as a province,[18] and Quintus Veranius became its governor. A reduction was made in the taxes which the native monarchs had imposed, to encourage better hopes of Roman rule. Quintus Servius was appointed to Commagene, then placed under the rule of praetors for the first time.

SYRIA. GERMANICUS AND PISO

57. The affairs of the allies had now been placed on a satisfactory footing. But this was no comfort to Germanicus, who was still harassed by the insolence of Piso. Ordered to bring some of the legions to Armenia, or send them in charge of his son, Piso had done neither. But at last the two men met, at Cyrrus, headquarters of the Tenth Legion. Both took pains with their demeanor, Piso to show no fear, Germanicus to display no threats—he was, as I have said, of a generous disposition. But his friends were well versed in whipping up illfeeling, and they produced a great variety of charges, true or false, against Piso himself, Plancina, and their sons. Only a few close friends were present at their interview. Germanicus spoke first, with barely concealed anger: Piso replied with a mixture of apology and insolence. They parted open enemies. After this, Piso seldom sat on the tribunal with Germanicus;

if he did he looked sulky and was obviously critical. At a banquet given by the king of Nabataea, when heavy gold crowns were given to Germanicus and Agrippina, and lighter ones to Piso and the other Romans, he was heard to remark that this feast was for the son of the Roman Emperor, not of a king of Parthia. He thrust his crown aside, with much grumbling about extravagance—irritating for Germanicus, though he endured it.

58. Meanwhile envoys had arrived from Artabanus, king of Parthia. They had been sent to remind Germanicus of the friendship and alliance between the two empires, and to seek a renewal of their pledges. In honor of Germanicus the Parthian king was willing to come as far as the bank of the Euphrates. He now requested that Vonones should not be kept in custody in Syria, for the agents of the latter, working at short range, were inciting the tribal nobles to rebellion. Germanicus in reply spoke with due solemnity about the alliance of Rome and Parthia, and with suitable modesty about the king's coming, and the honor done to himself. Vonones was removed to Pompeiopolis, a city on the coast of Cilicia. This was done not merely at the request of the Parthian monarch, but as a blow to Piso, whom Vonones had courted by many attentions, and by showering gifts on Plancina.

19 A.D. Consuls Marcus Junius Silanus and Lucius Norbanus Balbus

GERMANICUS IN EGYPT

59.[19] In this year Germanicus paid a visit to Egypt to see its antiquities. The reason given, however, was to look into the affairs of that province: opening the public granaries,[20] he reduced the price of grain. He won popular regard in many ways: by dismissing his military escort, by wearing only sandals on his feet, and by dressing in Greek costume. This was in imitation of Publius Scipio Africanus, who is said to have done the same in Sicily at the height of the Second Punic War.[21] Tiberius gently criticized his dress and behavior, but objected in the strongest terms to his breach of Augustus' injunctions against entering Egypt without the permission of the Emperor. For, among the other fundamental rules of the principate, Augustus had jealously guarded that which forbade Roman senators or wealthy knights from visiting Egypt without permission. That province he kept isolated, lest anyone should be able to threaten Italy with famine by holding—even with feeble forces against huge armies—a country that contained key positions by land and sea.[22]

60. Germanicus was ignorant of the criticism of his visit when he began his journey up the Nile. He started from the city of Canopus. This was founded by Spartans who buried there their steersman Canopus, when Menelaus, returning to Greece, had been driven off his course onto the Libyan coast. Thence he visited the nearest mouth of the Nile, sacred to Hercules: the natives claimed that the original and genuine Hercules was born in their country, though many later strong men took his name. Next he inspected the vast remains of ancient Thebes. There, reared on great piles of masonry, inscriptions in Egyptian writing proclaim its former magnificence. One of the senior priests, requested to interpret the language of his forefathers, explained how Egypt had once possessed 700,000 men of military age. With this army, King Ramses[23] had conquered Libya, Ethiopia, Media, Persia, Bactria and Scythia, and all the lands inhabited by Syrians, Armenians, and Cappadocians, reaching as far as Bithynia on one shore of Asia Minor, and Lycia on the other. There could still be read the list of tributes assessed on the conquered lands, the payments of gold and silver, the numbers of weapons and horses, the gifts to the temples of ivory and incense, and all the quantities of grain and raw materials paid by each several nation. The total was as impressive as the revenue now raised by the arbitrary rule of Parthia or the power of Rome.

61. Other marvels, too, were there for Germanicus to see—notable among them, the stone statue of Memnon, which gives a singing note when struck by the sun's rays at dawn; the Pyramids, huge as mountains, built amid the pathless, shifting sands of the desert by the wealth and rivalry of kings; the lakes dug out of the earth to receive the Nile's overflow: elsewhere, the river's gorges, with depths no line can plumb. At last he came to Elephantine and Syene, once the farthest bounds of the Roman Empire, which now extends to the Persian Gulf.[24]

GERMANY. THE END OF MAROBODUUS

62. While Germanicus during this summer busied himself

with the affairs of several provinces, Drusus won no little credit by provoking disorders in Germany, so that he might give the final push to the power of Maroboduus, already broken. Among the Gotones was a young chief called Catualda, whom Maroboduus had once expelled, and who now sought his revenge in the latter's time of trouble. He invaded the territory of the Marcomanni with a powerful force, seduced some of their leaders to form an alliance with him, and broke into the seat of royal power and the fortress close by it. Here was found the booty earlier won by the Suebi: here, too, camp followers and traders from the Roman provinces. First, a commercial treaty, then the profit motive, finally forgetfulness of their own land, had induced each man of this company to leave his own country and settle in that of an enemy.

63. Maroboduus was now completely deserted. His only resource was to throw himself on the mercy of the Emperor. Crossing the Danube, the northern boundary of the province of Noricum, he wrote to Tiberius. He did not use the language of an exile or suppliant, but rather wrote in terms of his former prosperity. "I was once," he said, "a great king, and many nations sought me as their guest; but I preferred the friendship of Rome." Tiberius replied that he should have a safe and honorable refuge in Italy, if he chose to remain there; if he wished to go elsewhere, he could depart as freely as he had come. But in his speech to the Senate he took the line that Philip had not posed so great a threat to Athens, nor Pyrrhus and Antiochus to the Roman people. There is still extant a speech of his on the subject of the greatness of Maroboduus, the fierce spirit of the peoples over whom he ruled, the menace of such an enemy so close to Italy, and his own cleverness in bringing him low. Maroboduus was kept at Ravenna, so that the Suebi could be threatened with his restoration if they got out of hand. In fact, he did not leave Italy for eighteen years, and in his old age his reputation dwindled because of this immoderate clinging to life.[25] The same fate overtook Catualda, and a like refuge in Roman territory. For shortly afterward he was driven out by the Hermunduri, under the leadership of Vibilius, was received as a refugee, and sent to Forum Julii, a colony in Gallia Narbonensis. The followers of these two kings were settled beyond the Danube between the rivers Marus and Cusus, under the rule of Vannius, of the tribe of the Quadi, to avoid disturbances from their being brought into peaceful provinces.

THRACE. THE END OF RHESCUPORIS

64. News came in at this time that Artaxias had been made king of Armenia by Germanicus. The Senate therefore decreed an ovation for Germanicus and Drusus. Triumphal arches were erected flanking the temple of Mars the Avenger,[26] and the statues of the two Caesars displayed. Tiberius was better pleased at having achieved peace by diplomacy than he would have been by a military victory. He next proceeded to use guile against Rhescuporis, king of Thrace. Rhoemetalces had formerly been king over the whole nation, but on his death Augustus had assigned part of Thrace to his brother Rhescuporis, and the rest to his son Cotys. This award had given the cultivated territory, the cities, and the area adjacent to Greece to Cotys, the rugged, unsubdued territory bordering on enemy country to Rhescuporis. The kings' characters suited the lands they ruled. Cotys was genial and civilized, Rhescuporis savage, grasping, and unwilling to share the kingdom. At first a false amity prevailed. Then Rhescuporis began to encroach, to trespass on the portion of Cotys, and to resort to violence when a protest was made. This he did cautiously so long as Augustus lived, since that Emperor had effected the division of the kingdom and would be likely to punish a breach of the agreement. But when he heard that there was a new Emperor in Rome, he began to provoke war by sending out armed plunderers and demolishing forts.

65. Tiberius was always disturbed by the upsetting of an agreement once made. He chose a centurion to warn the kings not to resort to force. Cotys at once dismissed the troops he had assembled. Rhescuporis, in a show of reasonableness, asked for a conference; for, he said, they could easily settle their differences by discussion. Place and time were fixed, then terms were readily agreed upon, since Cotys was accommodating and Rhescuporis treacherous in all points, so that mutual concessions were soon reached. Rhescuporis then gave a feast, ostensibly to ratify the treaty. Feasting and drinking went on far into the night; then, when Cotys was off his guard he was thrown into chains. When he realized how he had been tricked, he appealed to the sacred right of kings, to the common gods of their family, and to the laws of hospitality. But now Rhescuporis had the whole of Thrace in his grip. In a letter to Tiberius he protested that there had been a plot against him, but he had forestalled its author: meanwhile, he strengthened his own

forces, cavalry and infantry, on the pretext of impending war against the Bastarnae and Scythians. Tiberius wrote a mild reply: if there was no bad faith, he could rely on his own innocence. But neither Tiberius nor the Senate could determine the rights and wrongs of the case without an investigation. Rhescuporis must therefore give up Cotys, come to Rome, and let Cotys take on the odium of being under a criminal charge.

66. This letter was sent by Latinius Pandusa, governor of Moesia, together with soldiers who would escort Cotys to Thrace. Rhescuporis was torn between fear and rage. In the end he thought it better to be accused of a crime he had committed, rather than one he had merely planned: so he killed Cotys and gave it out that the death was due to suicide. But Tiberius had resolved on his policy, and he did not change it. Pandusa, whom Rhescuporis accused of having been prejudiced against him, died, and Pomponius Flaccus was appointed governor of Moesia: he was a veteran soldier, and a close friend of the king, and thus all the better qualified to betray him.

67. Flaccus crossed into Thrace, made lavish promises, and induced the king to enter the Roman defenses—though when Rhescuporis bethought himself of his crimes, he saw reasons to hesitate. A strong guard was placed around him, ostensibly as a mark of honor. Tribunes and centurions employed advice and persuasion: the farther they advanced from Thrace, the more obvious became his arrest: when at last they entered Rome, Rhescuporis knew that he was trapped.

He was accused in the Senate by the widow of Cotys, and condemned to detention far from his kingdom. Thrace was then divided between his son Rhoemetalces—who was known to have opposed his father's policy—and the children of Cotys. Since these latter were minors, the ex-praetor Trebellenus Rufus was appointed as regent for their part of the kingdom. The precedent here was the dispatch of Marcus Lepidus to Egypt to protect the children of Ptolemy IV Philopator. Rhescuporis was sent to Alexandria and there killed during an "attempted escape"—whether genuine or not.

THE END OF VONONES

68. At about this time Vonones, whose removal to Cilicia I have already mentioned, bribed his guards and tried to escape, first to Armenia, then to the Albani, the Heniochi, and his kinsman the king of Scythia. Pretending that he was going hunting, he moved away from the coast to the pathless woods. Then the

speed of his horse took him to the river Pyramus; but the inhabitants had heard of his escape and broken down the bridge, and there was no ford. So he was intercepted on the bank by Vibius Fronto, commander of a cavalry squadron. Shortly afterward, he was stabbed to death—apparently in a fit of anger—by Remmius, a veteran recalled to the colors. This man had previously been his guard, a fact which reinforced the suspicion that he had been privy to the escape, and had murdered Vonones to prevent this from leaking out.

SYRIA. THE DEATH OF GERMANICUS

69. When Germanicus returned from Egypt, it was to find that all the orders he had given, both military and civilian, had been canceled or reversed. For this he bitterly reproached Piso, and received an answer in terms equally uncompromising. Then Piso decided to leave Syria: but Germanicus fell ill. On hearing of his recovery, and the payment of vows made for his health, Piso sent lictors to drive away the sacrificial victims, break up the preparations for sacrifice, and disperse the rejoicing people of Antioch. Then he returned to Seleucia, waiting to see the issue of Germanicus' illness, which had once more affected him. It was a terrible disease, made worse by the belief that Piso had poisoned him. For under the floor and behind the walls of his house were found parts of corpses, disinterred from their graves, magic formulas, incantations, the name of Germanicus written on tablets of lead, charred, blood-stained human ashes, and other objects of sorcery which are supposed to devote souls to the powers of darkness. At the same time the messengers sent by Piso were accused of spying out the symptoms of his malady.

70. All this aroused Germanicus to anger, no less than to fear. If his threshold was to be besieged, his last breath to be gasped out under the eyes of his enemy, what would happen to his unhappy wife, to his young children? Poison, it seemed, was too slow: Piso was in urgent haste for the sole command of the province and the army. But Germanicus was not yet helpless, nor should the murderer long profit from his crime. He therefore wrote a letter, explicitly renouncing friendship with Piso:[27] many accounts say that he ordered him out of the province. Piso at once set sail; but cruised slowly so that he could quickly return if Germanicus died and he was able to reenter Syria.

71. For a time Germanicus had hopes of recovery. But then he grew weaker, and the end was at hand. To his friends around his bed he spoke as follows: "If this were a natural end,

I could justly reproach heaven for snatching me by an early
death from my parents, my children, and my country. As it is,
I am undone by the criminal deeds of Piso and Plancina. My
last prayers I leave in your hearts. Tell my father and my
brother of the agonies I have suffered, of the treacheries that
gave me a dreadful death to crown an unhappy life. My relatives, those who shared my hopes, even those who envied me,
will surely lament that one who knew such prosperity, and
survived so many wars, has fallen to a woman's treachery!

"You will be able to lay a complaint to the Senate, to invoke
the laws. The chief duty of a friend is, not to follow the dead
with idle laments, but to remember his wishes, to carry out his
instructions. Even strangers will weep for Germanicus: you
must avenge me, if it is me you love, and not my fortunes!
Show the Roman people the granddaughter of Augustus, my
wife; recite to them the names of our six children. Their sympathy will go to the accusers. Any story of criminal orders
given to Piso will seem incredible—or unforgivable!" His
friends grasped the dying man's right hand and swore that they
would give their lives rather than renounce vengeance.

72. Then he turned to his wife. He begged her—by her
memory of him, by their children—to temper her proud spirit,
to bow to cruel fortune. When she got back to Rome, let her
cast away ambition, and not provoke the jealousy of those who
had more power than herself. This was said openly: privately
he is said to have revealed to her the grounds for distrusting
Tiberius. Shortly afterward, his life ended, to the great grief of
the province and all surrounding peoples. Foreign countries and
their kings mourned for his kindness to allies, his clemency
toward enemies. To see him or hear him inspired reverence.
Standing so high in power, he had retained dignity and
grandeur, but was wholly free from jealousy or pride.

SYRIA. FUNERAL OF GERMANICUS

73. There was no procession of ancestral effigies at his
funeral, but it was notable for the tributes paid to his virtues.
Indeed, there were those who drew a parallel with the death of
Alexander the Great, citing the appearance, age, and manner
of death of Germanicus, and also the place, not far from that
where Alexander died.[28] For they were both handsome, of
high birth, not much more than thirty years of age, and done
to death by the treachery of their own people in a foreign land.
But Germanicus had been kind to his friends and restrained in

his pleasures; he had married one wife only, and all his children were legitimate. Nor was his military record inferior, though he lacked Alexander's dash; he had won many victories in Germany, but had been prevented from completing the conquest. Had he been in supreme command, had he possessed the name and powers of a king, he would have matched Alexander's glory in war just as surely as he excelled him in mercy, self-control, and all other good qualities. Before his body was cremated, it was displayed naked in the Forum of Antioch, where it was to be interred. It is not established whether it bore marks of poison: on this topic opposite conclusions were reached, according to whether people's prejudices inclined them to sympathy for Germanicus or support for Piso.

74. A conference now took place between all the Emperor's representatives, and other senators in the province. Its object was to decide who should be the governor of Syria. Apart from Vibius Marsus and Gnaeus Sentius, there was little competition; but there was a long debate over their claims. Finally Marsus withdrew in favor of Sentius, who was his senior, and who pressed his case more vigorously. Sentius then dispatched to Rome a woman who was a notorious poisoner and an intimate of Plancina, Martina by name. This was at the instance of Vitellius, Quintus Veranius, and others, who began drawing up charges and a bill of indictment as though the defendants had already been named.[29]

75. By now Agrippina was prostrate with grief and illness. But she could not endure anything that stood in the way of vengeance, and she took ship with her children and the ashes of Germanicus. Universal sympathy went out to this great lady, whose high marriage had once won her the respect and admiration of crowds. Now she bore in her bosom her husband's ashes; she had no certainty of being able to avenge him, her own future was uncertain, and her fecundity was now untimely because it exposed her all the more to fortune's blows.

THE CONDUCT OF PISO

Meanwhile, the news of Germanicus' death reached Piso at Cos. He received it with undisguised pleasure. Sacrificial victims were slain, temples visited. His own joy was unconfined: still more that of Plancina, who for the first time since the death of her sister put off her mourning and appeared in all her finery.

76. Now centurions began to stream in to Piso, bringing assurances of the loyalty of the legions, and urging him to re-

turn to the province, now without a ruler, from which he had been unlawfully expelled. When he asked for advice on a course of action, his son Marcus said, "I think you should go to Rome at once. So far you have done nothing that cannot be remedied. Unsupported suspicion and idle gossip are nothing to be feared. Your quarrel with Germanicus may bring you unpopularity, but not punishment. Your enemies have deprived you of the province, and that is as far as they will go. If you go back to Syria and Sentius resists, it will mean civil war. In such a case, you will lose the support of the centurions and soldiers: they keep the memory of their general fresh in their minds, and their loyalty to Caesar is what really counts with them."

77. But one of his closest friends, Domitius Celer, took an opposite line. "Use your opportunity," he advised. "You are the governor of Syria, not Sentius. You have the fasces, the legal power, the command of the legions. If there is any opposition brewing, who has a better right to take up arms than the man who is the Emperor's representative, and who carried his personal instructions? Even rumors need time to grow stale: even the innocent are apt to be overwhelmed when prejudice is fresh. But if you control the army and husband your strength, events may take a turn for the better in ways we cannot now foresee. Besides, why rush to Rome, and find that your arrival coincides with that of Germanicus' ashes? The tears of Agrippina, the unthinking mob, will sweep you away on a mere rumor, before you have been given a hearing, or prepared a defense! As it is, the Empress knows what you have done, the Emperor supports you, though secretly. Those who most publicly bewail the death of Germanicus are those who derive most pleasure from it."

78. It did not take much to convert Piso to this course, ready as he was for dangerous policies. In dispatches to Tiberius he charged Germanicus with luxury and arrogance, saying that he himself had been expelled to make possible a revolution: now, however, he was back in his command in the same spirit of loyalty in which he had held it. Meanwhile, he placed Domitius Celer on board a ship, with instructions to sail direct to Syria, avoiding coasts and islands. The deserters who came in were organized into companies, camp followers were armed, and a draft of recruits on its way to Syria intercepted as he crossed to the mainland. He also wrote to the kings of Cilicia for support: his son Marcus, though he had advised against making war, was energetic in preparing for it.

79. As they coasted along Lycia and Pamphylia, they fell in with the squadron of ships taking Agrippina to Rome. With bad blood on both sides, they got ready to fight: but later mutual

fear restricted them to an exchange of abuse. Marsus Vibius commanded Piso to go to Rome to plead his case. Piso retorted that he would do this as soon as the praetor in charge of cases of poisoning appointed a date and named the parties.

Meanwhile Domitius had reached Laodicea in Syria. He made for the headquarters of the Sixth Legion, thinking that legion the likeliest sympathizer with his plans for revolution, but its commanding officer, Pacuvius, forestalled him. Sentius informed Piso of this in a letter, and warned him not to try to seduce the army with his agents, nor harass the province by war. Then he collected together all men loyal to the memory of Germanicus or hostile to his enemies. He warned them of the attack impending on the majesty of the Emperor and the state itself, and placed himself at the head of a powerful force, ready to go into action.

80. Though Piso's plans, so far, had gone badly, he took the safest course now open, and threw himself into the fortress of Celenderis. What with deserters, the new recruits, his own slaves and those of Plancina, and the reinforcements sent by the kings of Cilicia, he could muster a force equivalent to perhaps one legion. He proclaimed that he was the Emperor's representative, and that he was being kept out of his province, not by the legions (who had invited him back), but by Sentius, whose criminal charges covered personal hostility. "Stand in line," he said. "The soldiers will never fight when they see Piso, whom they call 'Father!' If it is a question of rights, mine is the better case: if it comes to arms, I am not helpless."

Then he drew up his troops in front of the fortifications, on a steep precipitous hill bounded on its other flanks by the sea. Against him were the veterans, in companies and reserves. They were the better troops: but the rough ground favored Piso, though neither the hopes nor the spirits nor the rustic weapons of his troops were a match for the other side. When battle was joined, the result was only in doubt until the Roman troops had reached the plateau; then the Cilicians fled to the safety of the fortress.

81. Meanwhile Piso made an unsuccessful attack on the fleet which was blockading the coast. Returning, he showed himself on the walls of the fort, beating his breast, calling individuals by name, offering bribes and inciting to mutiny. His only success was to cause the standard-bearer of the Sixth Legion to desert and to bring over the standard.

At this point Sentius gave orders for the trumpets to sound for action. A mound was thrown up, scaling ladders planted on it, and picked men launched to the attack, covered by spears, stones, and firebrands hurled by the artillery. At long last Piso's stubbornness gave way, and he asked to be allowed to stay on in the fortress, disarmed, while the question of the governorship of Syria was referred to the Emperor. These terms were not accepted: he was granted safe conduct and a passage to Rome—no more.

82. At Rome, when the news of Germanicus' illness became public property (exaggerated, as with all news from afar) there was an outburst of grief, anger, and complaint. "This," they said, "is the reason for sending Germanicus to a far country, for making Piso governor of Syria. This is the purport of all those secret conversations between Augusta and Plancina! What our fathers said when Drusus died is perfectly true: rulers begrudge their sons' popularity with the people. Germanicus and Drusus have both been brought down because they were planning to bring freedom back to the Roman people, with equal rights for all."

This public rumor was so aggravated by the announcement of Germanicus' death that, before there could be any official notice or resolution of the Senate, all business was suspended, the courts adjourned, and the great houses went into mourning. There was nothing but silent lamentation—and that no mere parade of sorrow. Men wore the usual trappings of bereavement, but the sorrow in their hearts was deep and real.

Some traders who had left Syria before Germanicus died brought more reassuring news about his condition. It was immediately believed, immediately publicized. As men met together it was uncritically repeated; suitably embellished, the joyful news was spread over a wider audience. People rushed through the streets, besieged the doors of the temples. Night only increased their credulity, affirmation grew bolder in the dark. Tiberius did nothing to check the rumor, leaving the lapse of time to do its work. So the grief of the populace was as though they had lost Germanicus for the second time.

83. Every mark of honor that affection or ingenuity could prescribe was granted to Germanicus. His name was inserted in the Salian hymn.[30] Magistrates' chairs, garlanded with oak leaves, were placed in his honor at meetings of the priests of Augustus. An ivory statue of him headed the procession in the Circus. His posts as priest and augur were reserved for members of the Julian house. Triumphal arches were set up in Rome, on the banks of the Rhine, and on Mount Amanus in Syria, with inscriptions relating his achievements and proclaiming that he had died for his country. There was a cenotaph at Antioch, where he was cremated, and a tribunal at Epidaphne, where he had breathed his last. It would be difficult to enumerate all the statues in his honor, and all the places where they

were set up. But when the Senate proposed an immense shield, of solid gold, among the statues of the great orators, Tiberius insisted that it should be of the usual material and the standard size. "Rank," he said, "is not to be made the criterion of eloquence: Germanicus will be suitably honored if he has a place among the great orators of old." The knights ordered that one of their blocks of seats in the theater—that for juniors—should bear the name of Germanicus: his effigy was to be carried at the head of their procession in the parade on the fifteenth of July. Many of these tributes are still rendered but some were dropped, either immediately or in the course of time.

84. While grief for Germanicus was still fresh, his sister Livilla, wife of Drusus, gave birth to twin boys. This happy event, rare even in humble homes, raised the enthusiasm of the Emperor to such a pitch that he boasted to the Senate that never had twin sons been born to a father of such rank in the state. Thus everything—even the products of chance—was turned to his own glorification. But the people, at a time like this, saw in it a cause for grief. That Drusus' family should be increased seemed yet another blow to that of Germanicus.

EVENTS IN ROME

85. In this same year the Senate took active steps to suppress female immorality, forbidding any woman whose grandfather, father, or husband held the rank of Roman knight to take up the profession of prostitution. A woman called Vistilia, born of a family in which the praetorship had been held, had actually registered with the aediles a notice that her services were available. In the time of our ancestors this was an accepted custom; they thought that the public admission of an infamous life was punishment enough for these amoral creatures. But now Titidius Labeo, Vistilia's husband, was called upon to explain why, his wife having admitted her misconduct, he had failed to avail himself of the remedy provided by the law. His plea was that the sixty days allowed him for consideration had not yet expired. It was therefore decided to proceed against Vistilia only, and she was exiled to the island of Seriphos.

Action was also taken on the expulsion of those who adhered to Egyptian and Jewish cults. A resolution of the Senate decreed that four thousand descendants of freedmen, of military age and infected with these superstitions, should be sent to suppress banditry in Sardinia. If they fell victim to the climate, they would be little loss. The rest would have to renounce their abominable practices by a given date, or else leave Italy.

86. The Emperor next reported that a vestal virgin would have to be chosen to replace Occia, who had presided over that order with unblemished sanctity for fifty-seven years. Fonteius Agrippa and Domitius Pollio were thanked for vying with each other in offering their daughters to the service of the state. Pollio's daughter was selected, solely on the grounds that her mother had remained faithful in her marriage; for Agrippa had disgraced his family by a divorce. The unsuccessful girl received a dowry of one million sesterces as a consolation.

87. The people complained bitterly of the outrageous cost of grain. Tiberius fixed a retail price, promising compensation to the dealers at the rate of two sesterces a bushel. He was offered the title of "Father of His Country" for this, but rejected it, as on previous occasions.[31] He sternly rebuked people who spoke of his "divine" occupations, and who called him "master." Speech was indeed constrained and hazardous under an Emperor who dreaded freedom and loathed flattery.

88. I find in historians of this period who are also senators[32] that a letter was read in the Senate from Adgandestrius, a chieftain of the Chatti, offering to kill Arminius if poison could be provided for the assignment. The reply was that the Roman people took vengeance on its enemies in open battle, not by fraud and treachery. With this proud reply Tiberius set himself by the side of the generals of old, who had refused to poison King Pyrrhus, and had revealed the plan to him. But the withdrawal of the Romans and the fall of Maroboduus led Arminius to aim at royal power. His fellow countrymen opposed him in the name of freedom: war broke out and was waged with varying fortunes: at last he perished by the treachery of his kinsmen. There can be no doubt that he was the liberator of Germany. He fought against the Roman people not, as did other kings and generals, in the early days of their power, but at the height of their imperial glory. He lost battles but never a campaign. He lived for thirty-seven years, and knew twelve years of power. To this day he lives in the songs of the barbarians. Greek historians know nothing of him—their admiration is kept for what is Greek. We Romans undervalue him; while we belaud antiquity, we take too little thought for the history of modern times.

BOOK III

20 A.D. Consuls M. Valerius Messalla, M. Aurelius Cotta

ROME. THE OBSEQUIES OF GERMANICUS

1. Winter though it was, Agrippina pressed on with her voyage without pause. Only when she reached Corcyra, the island opposite to the coast of Calabria, did she halt for a few days to compose her mind: her grief had overwhelmed her, and she did not know how to bear it. At the news of her approach there gathered together at Brundisium—the port which she could most quickly and easily reach—family friends, many officers who had served under Germanicus, and also many strangers from the neighboring towns. Some thought it their duty to the Emperor; the majority followed their example. As soon as the fleet hove in sight, the harbor, the foreshore, the very walls and houses, if they offered a good view seaward, were crowded with mourners. They asked themselves whether they should receive Agrippina as she landed in dead silence, or with some phrase of greeting. They had still to decide what course was appropriate when the fleet drew in—no brisk rowing as usual, but every one with a set expression of grief. Then, with her two children, holding the funeral urn, her eyes cast down, Agrippina left the ship. A loud groan went up from all. Friends or strangers, men or women, their laments were indistinguishable: save only that those who had sailed with Agrippina were exhausted with sorrow; those who had newly come to meet her displayed it more openly.

2. Tiberius had sent two companies of the Guards, and had ordered the magistrates of Apulia, Calabria, and Campania to

discharge their duties in honor of his son. So the ashes were borne on the shoulders of tribunes and centurions. Ahead were the standards, undecorated, the fasces reversed. As they passed through the colonies, the common people wore mourning, the knights formal dress: each city, as its resources allowed, burned garments, spices, and other funeral offerings. Even from towns not on the route people came to offer up victims and altars to the spirits of the dead, to show their grief by tears and lamentations. Drusus came as far as Tarracina, with his brother Claudius and those of Germanicus' children who were at Rome. The consuls Marcus Valerius and Marcus Aurelius (now in office), the Senate, and a large part of the Roman people crowded the roads, in scattered groups and weeping bitterly. There was no flattery of Tiberius in this; all knew he was hard put to it to hide his joy at the death of Germanicus.

3. Tiberius and the Empress Livia did not appear in public. They may have thought it beneath their dignity to mourn openly, or they may have feared that with all eyes upon them their hypocrisy would be known for what it was. Nor can I find, either from historians or the daily *Gazette*,[1] that his mother Antonia played any prominent part, though in addition to Agrippina, Drusus, and Claudius, his other relatives are mentioned by name. Perhaps ill health prevented her, or perhaps her mind was so bowed down with sorrow that she could not bear to see the evidence of her loss before her eyes. A more likely explanation, however, is that Tiberius and the Empress Livia, who did not leave the palace, forbade her to do so. It could thus appear that their sorrows were equal, and that the mother was setting the example for the uncle and grandmother.

4. On the day when the remains were taken to the Mausoleum of Augustus, there was now a widespread silence, now a confused uproar of grief. The streets of Rome were crowded. Torches blazed in the Campus Martius. Soldiers under arms, magistrates without their badge of office, the people mustered in their tribes—all proclaimed that Rome had fallen, that hope had gone. So ready and so open was their talk that they seemed to have forgotten their rulers. But what struck Tiberius most forcibly was the universal popularity of Agrippina. "The glory of her country," they called her, "the one true descendant of Augustus, the only genuine pattern of old-fashioned virtue." Turning their gaze to heaven, they prayed that her children might live to survive their wicked enemies.

5. Some comment was aroused by the absence of the ceremonies of a state funeral, and comparisons were drawn with the splendid tribute paid by Augustus to Germanicus' father, Nero Drusus.[2] In the depth of winter, the Emperor had gone

in person to Ticinum; he had never left the corpse, and accompanied it into Rome. The effigies of the Claudii and Julii surrounded the bier. There was public mourning in the Forum, a eulogy from the Rostra—everything, in fact, that ancient custom or modern invention could prescribe. Germanicus had not even been accorded the honors due to any noble. Granted that it was necessary to cremate his body in a foreign land because of the long journey—all the more reason to pay at a later stage the honors that chance had earlier denied him. "His brother," men said, "made a journey of one day; his uncle could not even go to meet him at the city gate. Where are the features tradition demands, the waxen effigy at the head of the bier, carefully rehearsed poems to honor his virtues, a funeral oration, the tears that at least provide a semblance of grief?"

6. All this was known to Tiberius. To put an end to public discussion, he published an edict in these terms: "Many noble Romans have died for their country: none has ever been mourned with such heartfelt sorrow. This is honorable to all and has my approval; but limits must be observed. Great princes and an imperial people have other standards than those which suit modest homes and petty states. When sorrow was fresh, your mourning was appropriate, and your very grief a source of comfort. But now we must recapture that firmness of mind in thrusting aside sorrow which Julius Caesar showed when he lost his only daughter, or Augustus when bereaved of his two grandsons. I need not cite ancient instances to show how the Roman people have endured with steadiness the loss of armies, the death of generals, the complete destruction of noble families. Princes die, the commonwealth endures. Resume your business; resume—for the Megalesian Games are due—resume your very pleasures.[3]

7. So they came out of mourning and went about their business. Drusus set off for the army in Illyricum. Every heart was set on exacting vengeance on Piso. There were frequent complaints that he was enjoying the pleasures of a tourist among the beauties of Asia and Greece, and craftily using delay to undermine the evidence of his guilt. It was, for example, common knowledge that Gnaeus Sentius[4] had sent on the notorious poisoner Martina. She died suddenly at Brundisium. Poison was found in a lock of her hair: her body displayed no signs of suicide.

8. Piso had sent his son ahead of him to Rome, with instructions to soothe the Emperor; meanwhile he himself paid a visit to Drusus, expecting from him not the hostile reaction of one who had lost a brother, but the more complacent attitude of one who had seen a rival removed. To show himself unpreju-

diced, Tiberius received the younger Piso graciously, and gave him the lavish presents usually accorded to the sons of great families. Drusus said to the elder Piso that, if the rumors current were true, his anger would exceed all other; but he hoped they were idle inventions, and that no one would be ruined by the death of Germanicus. This was said publicly: he avoided any private interview. Obviously it was said on Tiberius' instructions: the young man was usually artless and natural: here he was employing all an old man's cunning.

9. After crossing the Adriatic, Piso landed at Ancona. Then he passed through Picenum and down the Via Flaminia,[5] overtaking a legion on its way from Pannonia to Rome, and to an eventual posting in Africa. Rumor has it that he frequently displayed himself to these troops on the march. To avoid suspicion —or because cowards are always changing their plans—he set out from Narnia to sail first down the Nar and then the Tiber. The anger of the people was increased by the way in which he landed by the Mausoleum of Augustus, in broad daylight and when the banks were crowded with people. A great train of clients followed Piso, and Plancina had her woman friends; they all looked very cheerful as they passed on their way. His unpopularity was heightened because his house, close to the Forum, was gaily decorated. There were banquets and dinner parties, and all so conspicuous that they could not be hidden.

ROME. TRIAL AND DEATH OF PISO

10. On the next day, Fulcinius Trio asked the consuls to allow him to prosecute Piso. To this Vitellius, Veranius, and other members of Germanicus' staff objected, saying that Trio had no standing in the matter, and that they themselves, not in the role of accusers, but as witnesses and collectors of evidence, would submit the instructions of Germanicus. Trio thereupon abandoned his claim to be the prosecutor on this charge, but did succeed in winning permission to attack Piso's earlier career. Then Tiberius was asked to take over the investigation. Piso had no objection to this, for he was afraid of prejudice on the part of the Senate and people. Tiberius, he knew, was in a position to ignore gossip, and was moreover involved in his mother's intrigues. Truth and willful misrepresentation were more easily distinguished if there was only a single judge; bias and enmity would prevail if there were many. Tiberius was very well aware what a grave problem this investigation would present, and how his character was being assailed by rumor. So,

with a few of his intimates as assessors, he gave a hearing to the accusers' charges and the submissions of the defendant. Then he remitted the whole case to be tried before the Senate.

11. Meanwhile Drusus returned from Illyricum and entered Rome. The Senate had awarded him an ovation for bringing in Maroboduus and for his other successes of the previous summer,[6] but he chose to postpone it. After this, Piso approached Lucius Arruntius, Publius Vinicius, Asinius Gallus, Aeserninus Marcellus, and Sextus Pompeius to plead in his defense. All found some excuse to decline. But Manius Lepidus, Lucius Piso, and Livineius Regulus came to his aid. The entire city was agog to see how loyal the friends of Germanicus would prove themselves, how the defendant would put his case, whether Tiberius would manage to suppress and conceal his feelings. Never had the Roman people been more excited; never had there been so much covert criticism, such unvoiced suspicion, of the Emperor.

12. When the Senate met, Tiberius made a speech of carefully phrased impartiality. "Piso," he said, "was my father's friend and had been his representative. I appointed him as Germanicus' helper in the East, and this was approved by the Senate. Unprejudiced inquiry must determine whether he embittered the young prince with recalcitrance and disobedience, and then rejoiced at his death, or whether he murdered him. If," he went on, "Piso as governor exceeded the bounds of his office, if he failed in obedience to his commander, if he rejoiced in his death—and my loss—then I shall bear him hatred and ban him from my house. But I shall avenge my personal wrongs without calling on the power of an Emperor. But if murder is proved against him—and murder must be punished whatever the rank of the victim—then you must give to the children of Germanicus, and to us who are his parents, the satisfaction of the vengeance that is our due. There is yet another matter that you must determine. Did Piso rouse his troops to mutiny and rebellion? Did he win their support by bribery? Did he try to recover his province by force? Or are these exaggerated charges, invented by the prosecution? I have cause to be annoyed by their excess of zeal. What was the point of stripping his body and exposing it to the public gaze, and of allowing the rumors of his death by poison to circulate even among foreigners, if this matter is still undecided and *sub judice?* I weep for my son and shall ever weep for him. But I intend to allow the defendant every means of establishing his own innocence, or the unfairness of Germanicus, if such there was. My instructions to you are that you are not to regard accusations as proven simply because my personal sorrow is involved in this case. If kinship

or friendship prompts Piso's defenders, let them act with all the zeal and eloquence they can command to help him in his hour of peril. Let the prosecution display zeal and energy to the same degree. In one respect only will we allow Germanicus more than the law concedes, and that is that the inquiry into his death shall be held in the Senate House rather than the Forum. Let all other aspects of the case show the same scrupulousness. Drusus' tears, my grief, are wholly irrelevant—as are the slanders people are concocting against us."[7]

13. Next the prosecution was granted two days, and the defense—after an interval of six days—was allowed three. Trio began with an old story of little import about Piso's intrigues and corruption as governor of Spain. If the defendant could clear himself of the more recent charges, this would not harm him. Equally, conviction on the graver charges would mean that its refutation would not clear him. Then followed Servalus, Veranius, and Vitellius. All spoke with much vigor, and Vitellius with much eloquence. The accusation was that his hatred of Germanicus and desire for revolution had led Piso to seduce the loyalty of the soldiers, allowing them to get out of order and plunder the provincials. So far had this gone that the riffraff called him "the Father of the Legions." But against all loyal elements, and especially the friends and staff of Germanicus, his conduct had been harsh. Finally, he had used witchcraft and poison to kill Germanicus: then after abominable rites and practices on his part and Plancina's, he had used force against the state. Only defeat in battle made possible his prosecution.

14. The defense faltered badly on several points: bribery of the troops, the abandonment of the province to the whims of every scoundrel, even insults against the commander, had to be admitted. But the charge of poisoning, and that alone, was met with an adequate defense. The prosecution failed to establish that, at a dinner party given by Germanicus, Piso, his immediate neighbor, had poisoned his food with his own hands. It seemed absurd to suggest that he could have done this before so many eyewitnesses and in the presence of another man's slaves—indeed, under the very gaze of Germanicus himself. Piso offered his own slaves to the torture and demanded that it should be applied to the waiters.

But his judges, for different reasons, hardened their hearts. Tiberius resented the attack on the province, the Senate refused to believe that Germanicus had died a natural death. . . .[8] A request for the production of private correspondence was refused by both Tiberius and Piso. Outside the Senate House the voice of the people made itself heard: they proclaimed that they would lynch Piso if the Senate failed to do its job. Piso's statues were dragged to the Gemonian Stairs[9] and would have been smashed to pieces if they had not been saved and replaced on the Emperor's instructions. Piso was hurried to a litter and escorted home by a tribune of the Guard. Opinions differed as to whether his function was to protect the prisoner or to carry out his execution.

15. The same hatred pursued Plancina, but a higher influence was exerted on her behalf, and it was uncertain how far, in her case, Tiberius would dare to go. She swore to share Piso's fortunes so long as his hopes were uncertain, and to perish with him, if need be. But then the secret entreaties of the Empress Livia procured her a pardon: little by little she began to detach herself from her husband, to separate her defense from his. Piso took this as a portent of doom. He doubted whether it was worthwhile going on, but his sons persuaded him to steel his resolution and enter the Senate House once more. The prosecution attacked again, senators spoke fiercely against him, nothing but hostility and insult came his way. The most alarming feature was the implacable, unemotional bearing of Tiberius, whom he saw to be absolutely resolved to give way to no human feeling. He returned home, wrote a few notes as though preparing his defense for tomorrow, signed the letter, and gave it to a freedman. Then he bathed and dined as usual. When the night was far gone and his wife had left the bedroom, he ordered the doors to be locked. At dawn he was found dead, his throat cut. On the floor was a sword.

16. I recall hearing older men speak of a document which was often seen in Piso's hands, though he never made it public. His friends, however, proclaimed that it was a letter from Tiberius conveying his instructions about Germanicus. Piso had intended to produce this in the Senate to show the guilt of Tiberius, but had been tricked out of doing so by a promise from Sejanus that was never kept. They also said that he did not commit suicide but had been dispatched by an assassin. I cannot confirm either of these statements, but I think it my duty to reveal what was being said by men still alive when I was young.[10] In the Senate, Tiberius assumed an expression of grief, complaining that the manner of Piso's death increased his own unpopularity. He repeatedly cross-questioned Piso's son[11] to discover how his father had spent his last day and night. The young man answered most of his questions cautiously, but over certain details he was rather unguarded. Then Tiberius produced and read some notes of Piso's, couched in the following terms: "The plot concocted by my enemies, the odium aroused by this false accusation, have brought me down and left no place where my simple innocence can survive. I call heaven to

witness, Caesar, that I have always been loyal to you, and dutiful to your mother. I beg you to look after my sons. Gnaeus had no part in my conduct, good or bad, since he was in Rome all the while. Marcus advised me against returning to Syria—would that I had given way to my son, rather than he to his old father! Since he is innocent, the more fervently do I beg that he shall not have to pay the penalty for my wrongdoing. By forty-five years of loyal service, by the joint consulship with yourself which your father, the divine Augustus, thought fit to bestow upon me, by our personal friendship, I beseech you to spare the life of my unhappy son. This is my last request." There was no mention of Plancina.

17. Tiberius thereupon absolved the younger Piso from any guilt for his share in the civil war; he had entered it on instructions from his father that a son could not disobey. At the same time he referred with sorrow to the fall of this noble house, and to the end of Piso, deserved though it may have been. Then, with a mixture of shame and dishonor, he mentioned Plancina, emphasizing Livia's plea for mercy on her behalf. This added fuel to the private resentment felt toward her by all decent persons. "So," they said, "the grandmother receives the murderess of her grandson, interviews her, snatches her from the Senate! Only Germanicus lacks the protection we have offered to all. Vitellius and Veranius voiced the grief felt for him. Tiberius and Livia have spoken for Plancina. Let her now exercise her skill and her poisons on Agrippina and the children—she has proved that they work! This excellent grandmother and uncle may as well drain the blood of Germanicus' unhappy house to the last drop."

Two days were spent on this farce of an investigation: Tiberius urging Piso's sons to defend their mother. Prosecutors and witnesses followed each other, but there was no evidence for the defense, and pity began to supersede hatred for Plancina. When the consul, Aurelius Cotta, was asked to speak first[12] (for if the Emperor presided even magistrates had to declare their opinion), he proposed that Piso's name should be expunged from the official records, that half his estate should be confiscated, and the other half given to Gnaeus Piso if he changed his first name. Marcus should be expelled from the Senate, receive a grant of five million sesterces, and be banished from Rome for ten years. Plancina should receive an amnesty because of the intercession of the Empress Livia.

18. The Emperor mitigated these proposals in several respects. There was no erasure of Piso's name from the official records: this had not been done in the case of Mark Antony, who took up arms against the state, nor of Jullus Antonius, who

polluted the household of Augustus. Marcus Piso was not degraded, and was allowed to inherit his patrimony. As I have repeatedly mentioned, Tiberius was not addicted to avarice, and was disposed to be lenient through shame at the acquittal of Plancina. When Valerius Messalinus suggested a golden statue in the temple of Mars the Avenger, and Caecina Severus an altar of vengeance, Tiberius vetoed the proposals. Such tributes, he said, should be rendered when they had won victories over a foreign foe; domestic calamities should be veiled in private mourning. Messalinus had also proposed that Tiberius, the Empress, the younger Antonia, Agrippina, and Drusus should be publicly thanked for avenging Germanicus. Claudius was not mentioned. In the Senate Lucius Asprenas asked Messalinus whether the omission was deliberate: only then was Claudius' name included. The more I reflect on history, ancient or modern, the more obvious it becomes that all human affairs are pervaded by irony. Whether in public opinion, his own hopes, or the respect felt for him, the most unlikely candidate for the principate was precisely the man whom fortune was keeping up her sleeve.[13]

19. A few days later Tiberius proposed in the Senate that Vitellius, Veranius, and Servaeus should be elected to the priesthood. He promised to support Fulcinius for office but warned him not to allow his eloquence to become unduly vehement. So ended the process of avenging the death of Germanicus. It has been very variously recounted, not only by contemporaries but in later generations. Obscurity always surrounds great issues. Some people are ready to take on trust what is only hearsay; others falsify the truth; the passing of time amplifies both kinds of distortion.

Drusus left Rome to take up his command, and reentered it for his ovation.[14] A few days later his mother Vipsania died, the only one of Agrippa's children to come to a natural end. All the others died on the field of battle, or among allegations of poison or starvation.

AFRICA. THE WAR WITH TACFARINAS

20. The same year Tacfarinas—whose defeat at the hands of Camillus in the previous summer[15] I have already recounted —renewed the war in Africa. At first he carried out isolated raids and avoided reprisals by his speed of movement. Then he began to plunder villages and carry off heavy booty; finally he besieged a Roman cohort near the river Pagyda. The fortress

was commanded by Decrius, an active soldier with battle experience, who considered the siege a disgrace. He called on his men to go out and fight in the open, drawing them up in formation outside the fort. The first charge scattered the cohort. Decrius rushed into the rain of missiles to stop the rout, cursing the standard-bearers for allowing Roman soldiers to run from a disorderly pack of deserters. He was wounded, but although his eye was pierced he kept his face to the enemy and continued to fight until he was killed, abandoned by his men.

21. When Lucius Apronius, who succeeded Camillus,[16] learned of this he was much more concerned with the loss of face to Rome than with the success of the enemy. He revived the old custom—obsolete in these days—of selecting by lot every tenth man in the cohort and flogging him to death. This severity had a tonic effect. A detachment of veterans, no more than five hundred strong, routed these same forces of Tacfarinas when they attacked a town called Thala. It was in this battle that a private soldier, Rufus Helvius, won the decoration for saving the life of a Roman citizen. Apronius gave him the collar and spear; Tiberius added the Oaken Garland, affecting displeasure that this had not already been granted by Apronius, who was competent to do so. Tacfarinas, seeing his Numidians demoralized and disinclined for sieges, waged guerrilla warfare. When he was pressed, he would retreat; then he would attack again in the rear. So long as these tactics were maintained, the African leader made fools of the tired and irritated Roman forces. But finally he made for the coast, his movements impeded by all the booty he had collected, and did not move far from a stationary base. Then Apronius Caesianus, the governor's son, with a force of cavalry and auxiliary cohorts, reinforced by the most mobile troops of the two legions, defeated the Numidians in battle and drove them into the desert.

ROME. SCANDALS AMONG THE ARISTOCRACY

22. This same year Aemilia Lepida, who besides her membership in the great house of the Aemilii counted both Sulla and Pompey among her ancestors, was denounced on a charge of having falsely claimed to have borne a son to Publius Quirinius, a childless old millionaire. There were other charges of poisoning, adultery, and consulting astrologers about horoscopes of the imperial family. Her brother Manius Lepidus appeared for the defense. After the decree of divorce had been pronounced,[17] Quirinius had shown such rancor against her as

to win her some sympathy, guilty and depraved though she was. It was almost impossible to make out Tiberius' real feelings in this trial, such an extraordinary alternation—or mixture—of anger and clemency did he display. He began by begging the Senate not to investigate the charge of treason; then he induced the ex-consul, Marcus Servilius, and other witnesses to come forward with precisely the kind of evidence he had seemed to wish to exclude. He also handed over to the consuls slaves of Lepida who were under the guard of soldiers, but refused to allow them to be questioned on any matter relating to his house. Drusus, the consul-designate, was excused the necessity of stating his opinion first. Some took this as a non-dictatorial gesture, for it meant that the others would not have to agree with Drusus. Others read it as savagery: for only a verdict of guilty would induce such a withdrawal.[18]

23. There was an exhibition of games during the trial. Lepida entered the theater, with a group of noble ladies, and with tears and prayers invoked her ancestors, especially Pompey, whose memorials and statues were plainly to be seen.[19] The crowd was moved to compassion and sympathy, and violently abused Quirinius—a dirty, low-class, childless old man who was being preferred to a lady who had been the destined wife of Lucius Caesar, the daughter-in-law of Augustus himself. But then her slaves were tortured, and her misconduct revealed. On the proposal of Rubellius Blandus she was made an outlaw;[20] this penalty was upheld by Drusus, though others were for milder measures. Then Scaurus, to whom she had borne a son, managed to avert the confiscation of her estate. At this stage Tiberius announced his discovery from Quirinius' slaves that Lepida had tried to poison their master.

24. Within a short space of time the Calpurnii had lost Piso, the Aemilii Lepida. But these calamities among the houses of the great were counterbalanced by the return of Decimus Silanus to the Junii. I shall briefly recount the story. The Emperor Augustus had been notably fortunate in all his public dealings, but his private life was calamitous because of the immorality of his daughter and grandchild.[21] He expelled them both from Rome; their lovers were visited by banishment or death. Misbehavior between men and women—an everyday offense—he described by the high-sounding terms of sacrilege and treason. This led him far from the tolerance our ancestors had displayed, and even that embodied in his own legislation. I intend to record the fates of other victims of this period, if I complete my present plans and am spared for future labors. Decimus Silanus had been one of the younger Julia's lovers,

but his conduct went unpunished, except that he lost the friendship of Augustus. He knew this was tantamount to exile, and it was not until the reign of Tiberius that he ventured to appeal to the Senate and the Emperor. This he did through his brother Marcus Silanus, a powerful advocate because of his eloquence and high birth. While Marcus was thanking the Senate, Tiberius interrupted him to say that he too shared the pleasure of his brother's return from his long journey—a perfectly legitimate one, because he had not been expelled by the Senate, nor by the law. But he, personally, fully maintained his father's dislike of Silanus, whose return in no way altered the wishes of Augustus. Silanus stayed in Rome from then on, but was excluded from public office.

AN EXCURSUS ON THE ORIGINS OF CIVIL LAW

25. Next there was a proposal to modify the Lex Papia Poppaea. This had been introduced by Augustus in his last years to strengthen the "Julian Laws" which he had promoted to increase the penalties against celibacy, and to win revenue for the treasury. But it did not succeed in stimulating marriage and the bringing up of children—childlessness had too many attractions. What it did do was to endanger increasing numbers of people, since there were informers in every household, ready to do damage by their interpretations of the law. Once immorality had been the danger; now it was legalism.

I am tempted at this point to discuss in more detail the origins of law and the means whereby we have been brought into the present complex and endless labyrinth of legislation.[22]

26. Primitive man knew no lusts, was innocent of crimes or wrongdoing, and had no need of the law and its penalties. He needed no rewards, since good deeds were done for their own sake. Since he never had any wrong desires, there was no need for the sanction of fear. But when men ceased to be equal, self-seeking and violence took the place of moderation and decency. Despotism followed and in many countries has become permanent.[23] But some communities—others at once or when they wearied of the rule of kings—preferred to set up laws. The first laws were simple, the work of simple men. The most famous of these are the code of Crete, the work of Minos; of Sparta, that of Lycurgus; and at Athens, that of Solon, a more elaborate and sophisticated system. At Rome, Romulus ruled as an autocrat; then Numa introduced a religious code, to

which Tullus Hostilius and Ancus made additions. But the chief Roman legislator was Servius Tullius:[24] even kings obeyed his code.

27. After the expulsion of the Tarquins, the Roman people frequently opposed the aristocratic faction in the name of freedom and unity. The Council of Ten, drawing on every custom of good repute from whatever source, drew up the Twelve Tables. This was the last instance of equitable legislation.[25] Later laws—apart from those aimed at specific criminal offenses—were usually the product of party strife, and their object was to acquire unconstitutional power, to expel distinguished citizens, or to achieve other, and no less reprehensible, aims.[26]

Hence the rise of demagogues like the Gracchi, Saturninus, and also of Drusus,[27] whose bribery was on the Senate's behalf. Thus the Italians were bribed with promises, then checked by the tribunes' veto. Even during the Social War and the civil wars that followed, there was the same spate of conflicting legislation. Then Sulla became dictator, and abrogated or reversed earlier legislation, to add a great deal of his own. There was a breathing space, but not for long. Disorder returned when the bills of M. Aemilius Lepidus restored to the tribunes the old powers of stirring up trouble with the people. After this, legislation was no longer for the public good, but for private interests. Corruption was at its zenith, legislation incessant.

28. Then Pompey was granted his third consulship, and asked to reform public life. But his remedies were worse than the abuses themselves; the laws he promoted he broke in his own person. He ruled by the sword, and perished by the sword. From then on, there was for twenty years neither law nor morality. Crime paid, and went scatheless, decency led to destruction. At long last, in his sixth consulship,[28] Caesar Augustus felt secure in his power, and canceled what he had enacted in his days as triumvir. The measures he passed introduced us to peace—and the principate.

Then the screw was tightened. There were spies and a system of rewards: under the Lex Papia Poppaea, any withdrawal from the privileges of parenthood meant ceding vacant estates to the universal parent—the state.[29] These informers wormed their way ever more deeply into society at Rome, and indeed throughout Italy and wherever there were Roman citizens. Many lost their status, and there was universal panic. But then Tiberius appointed a commission, consisting of five ex-consuls, five ex-praetors, and an equal number of ordinary senators, chosen by lot. It slashed through many legal complexities, and for a time afforded a measure of relief.

ROME. OTHER EVENTS OF THE YEAR

29. At this time, Nero Caesar, one of Germanicus' children, reached his first manhood. Tiberius recommended to the Senate that he should be excused from holding the minor office of the viginitvirate,[30] and allowed to enter for the quaestorship, five years earlier than the normal age. This caused amusement. Tiberius alleged that at Augustus' request similar exemption had been granted to himself and his brother. But even then, I am sure, there must have been those who secretly mocked at such "requests": though at that time the vaulting power of the Caesars was in its early stages, and the custom of our ancestors was still in view. Again, there was a closer connection between grandfather and grandson than between stepfather and stepson.[31] Nero was also granted the priesthood; on the first day of his public appearance there was a distribution of gifts to the people. The people rejoiced to see a son of Germanicus growing to manhood: their joy was increased by the marriage of Nero to Julia, the daughter of Drusus. But pleasure in this event was matched by the dismay felt for the plan for an engagement between Claudius' son and the daughter of Sejanus. This was regarded as polluting the nobility of the imperial house, and of inflating Sejanus even beyond the inordinate ambitions with which he was credited.

OBITUARIES OF THE YEAR

30. Two notable men died at the end of the year—Lucius Volusius and Sallustius Crispus. The ancient family of Volusius had never before held an office higher than the praetorship: he brought it the consulship. Exercising the powers of a censor to select men for the Boards of Ten from among the knights, he accumulated the huge fortune for which his house became conspicuous. Crispus was a knight by origin, but had been adopted by the distinguished Roman historian Gaius Sallustius,[32] whose sister was Crispus' grandmother. This would have given him easy access to a public career, but he chose rather to emulate the example of Maecenas. So, though he did not enjoy senatorial rank, his influence exceeded that

of many who had held the consulship or won triumphs. There was none of the traditional simplicity about him; indeed, he carried elegance and refinement to the point of opulence and the brink of decadence. Underneath, though, was an intellect fully equal to great affairs, and all the keener for an outward display of indolence and sloth. While Maecenas lived, Crispus held second place to him as a confidential adviser to the Emperor: after his death, Crispus' influence was paramount. He was in the secret of the murder of Agrippa Postumus. But in his old age his intimacy with the Emperor was apparent rather than real. So it had been with Maecenas: fate sees to it that these relationships seldom last—or perhaps satiety comes on either when one party has given all it can or the other has no more to ask.

21 A.D. Consuls Tiberius Caesar Augustus IV and Drusus Caesar II

31. This year was marked by the consulships of father and son, Tiberius' fourth, Drusus' second term in that office. Three years earlier Tiberius had partnered Germanicus: but the uncle had derived little pleasure from the association, and in any case the bond was not so close. Early in the year the Emperor withdrew to Campania, ostensibly for reasons of health, and as the first step to prolonged and unbroken absence, possibly also to allow Drusus to discharge the consul's duties single-handed in the absence of his father. The young prince had a chance to win favor by a trifling matter which grew to a great contest. Domitius Corbulo (I), an ex-praetor, complained in the Senate that the young noble Lucius Sulla had refused to give up his seat to him at a display of gladiators. Age, ancestral custom, and the support of the older generation favored the claims of Corbulo, but Mamercus Scaurus, Lucius Arruntius, and other friends of Sulla used their influence on his behalf. There was an exchange of speeches, and several references to the strict decrees by which our ancestors had curbed the disrespect of young men. In the end, Drusus spoke in terms calculated to soothe ruffled feelings, and Sulla's apolo-

gies were conveyed to Corbulo by Mamercus Scaurus, who was Sulla's uncle and stepfather, and one of the most eloquent orators of the age.

This same Corbulo made repeated complaints of the unusable condition of many Italian roads, through the frauds of contractors and the slackness of the authorities. He gladly undertook to prosecute on this issue: the subsequent convictions and forced sales caused loss of reputations and bankruptcy to individuals quite out of proportion to any gain to the public.

AFRICA

32. Shortly after this Tiberius sent letters to the Senate to report another attack on Africa by Tacfarinas. He requested that they should choose a governor of Africa of military experience, and active enough to undertake a campaign. Sextus Pompeius (II) seized this chance of giving public expression to his dislike of Marcus Lepidus, criticizing him as idle, bankrupt, and a disgrace to his ancestors, and demanding that he should be debarred from the ballot for the governorship of Africa, and of Asia as well. The Senate demurred. They thought Lepidus easygoing rather than idle, and felt that his inherited poverty, and the way in which he had sustained his rank without reproach, should count as a merit rather than the reverse. So he was elected to Asia, and it was agreed that the Emperor should choose for the African vacancy.

ROME. A DEBATE ON GOVERNORS' WIVES

33. In the course of the debate Severus Caecina proposed that governors proceeding to their provinces should not be accompanied by their wives. He prefaced this with repeated declarations that he was on perfectly good terms with his own wife, who had borne him six children. "But," he said, "I have practiced at home what I now propose in public: in more than thirty years of provincial service I have never allowed her to leave Italy. There were good reasons for the old rule forbidding wives to be taken to provinces or abroad. The presence of women stimulates extravagance in peace, timidity in war. It makes a Roman army look like a barbarian migration. The female sex is not only weak and unable to endure hardship, but, given encouragement, cruel, avaricious, and greedy

for power. They become familiar with private soldiers, and have centurions eating out of their hands. Only recently a woman conducted the parades of cohorts, the maneuvers of the legions! Think how charges of corruption against officials usually direct most of their accusations against the wives. The moment they enter a province they attract its worst elements; they undertake business, and conduct intrigues. Then escorts are doubled, there are two centers of power—and the most extravagant and outrageous orders are those that emanate from the women. Once they were restrained by the Oppian Laws and by other legislation; now they have cast off their chains and dominate our homes, public business, the army itself!"

34. This speech won little support. There were frequent interruptions, claiming that the proposal was out of order, and that Caecina was wholly unfit to undertake the censor's role in so great a matter. Then Valerius Messalinus, in whom some semblance persisted of the oratory of his father Valerius Messala, spoke in reply. "We have changed for the better many of the stricter institutions of our ancestors, and it has been good to do so. Rome is not beset, as formerly, by enemies at the gate; the provinces are no longer hostile. We make a few concessions, nowadays, to women's needs: but they do not damage their husbands' households, still less burden the provincials. For the rest, women share their husband's lot, and in peacetime there is nothing to prevent them. In war, I agree, we must shed our load, but when our labors are over, is it not better to relax with our wives? We are told that some women have succumbed to greed for power or wealth. What of it? Have not magistrates, and many of them, shown themselves influenced by all kinds of undesirable appetites—but we do not leave provinces ungoverned. Husbands have often been corrupted by their wives' wickedness—but are all bachelors blameless? The Oppian Laws were passed because the state of the nation made them necessary: later, there were relaxations and alleviations, as the situation required. Do not let us disguise our own abdication under other names. If a woman transgresses, it is her husband's fault. But it would be a bad thing to allow the feebleness of one or two husbands to deprive us all of our wives' companionship in good times and in bad. It would mean abandoning the weaker sex to its own extravagance, to the lusts of other men. Even when the husband is there to play the watchdog, it is hard to keep a marriage intact! What is to happen when there is a kind of divorce, prolonged over several years? In correcting scandals elsewhere, it would be well to bear in mind the immorality rife in Rome."

Drusus spoke briefly about his own marriage. "Princes have to undertake long tours to distant parts of the Empire. Think of Augustus' many journeys to the East and West, always with Livia by his side! I have been to Illyricum, and, if the public needs require, shall undertake other journeys. But I shall do so in a very grudging spirit if you intend to separate me from my dear wife, mother of all our children." So the proposal of Caecina was shelved.

35. The next day the Senate was in session, there was a letter from Tiberius, indirectly criticizing the senators for referring so many decisions to him. He named Manius Lepidus and Junius Blaesus as candidates for the governorship of Africa. Both then addressed the Senate. Lepidus' chief concern was to get himself excused: he urged medical grounds, the tender years of his children, and a daughter due to be married. He thus conveyed, without openly saying it, that Blaesus was the uncle of Sejanus, and so above competition. Blaesus made a pretense of renunciation, but did not maintain it like Lepidus, and was elected among the plaudits of his toadies.

36. Next a practice was denounced which was giving rise to much private discontent. For a pernicious custom had grown up whereby riffraff of all kinds were using the opportunity of insulting their betters and then escaping punishment by clasping a statue of the Emperor. Indeed, even slaves and freedmen had used threatening words and gestures against their patrons or masters. This led Gaius Cestius to make a speech to the effect that while princes were undoubtedly like the gods, nonetheless the gods only responded to just petitions. The Capitol and the other temples of Rome were not to be regarded as an asylum to which men could resort as an aid to criminal conduct. "It means the end of law," he said, "when Annia Rufilla, whom I convicted of fraud, is able to insult and threaten me in the Forum, by the very threshold of the Curia, and I dare not proceed to law against her because she clings to the statue of the Emperor." Others were able to quote similar cases, some of them far more serious. The Senate begged Drusus to impose exemplary punishment; he sent for Annia Rufilla, condemned her, and ordered her to be committed to the public prison.

37. Then two Roman knights, Considius Aequus and Caelius Cursor, who had falsely laid a charge of treason against the praetor Magius Caecilianus, were punished by senatorial decree at the request of Tiberius. Drusus' reputation gained from these two occasions. Living in Rome, mixing in society, and hearing what people felt, he seemed able to

mitigate the secretive plans of Tiberius. Even his extravagance was not held against him; for it was thought better for him to devote his days to his building schemes and his nights to carousing, rather than live the bleak and solitary life of Tiberius, with its gloomy vigilance and evil intentions.

38. But Tiberius was indefatigable, and so were the denouncers. Ancharius Priscus had denounced the governor of Crete, Caesius Cordus, for extortion. There was a further charge of treason, the usual makeweight at that time for every prosecution. When one of the leading men in Macedonia, Antistius Vetus, was acquitted of adultery, Tiberius reproached the judges, and ordered a retrial on a count of treason. For Antistius was said to have had seditious dealings with Rhescuporis, when he took up arms against us after the murder of his brother Cotys. As a result, Antistius was banished, and it was enjoined that he should be imprisoned in an island inaccessible from Macedonia or Thrace.

EVENTS IN THRACE

Now that Thrace was divided between Rhoemetalces and the children of Cotys—for whom Trebellenus Rufus was regent because they were minors—that country was in disorder. Unfamiliar with Roman rule, the people criticized Rhoemetalces no less than Trebellenus, for not avenging their wrongs. Three powerful tribes, the Coelaletae, Odrysae, and Dii, took up arms. But their leaders did not join forces and were all of low standing: hence a serious outbreak of war was avoided. Some plundered their own neighborhood, others crossed the Haemus mountains to rouse the distant tribes to arms. The most numerous and powerful body laid siege to the king in the city of Philippopolis, the foundation of Philip of Macedon.

39. As soon as Publius Vellaeus, the nearest Roman commander, heard of this, he sent auxiliary cavalry and infantry into action against the marauders and those trying to pick up recruits. He himself led the main infantry force to raise the siege. Success attended him at all points. The plunderers were annihilated, the besieging forces started quarreling among themselves, and the royal army made a timely sortie as the legion came up. One could scarcely name it a battle or an engagement: rather was it a massacre of ill-armed stragglers, brought about without loss to us.

GAUL. THE REBELLION OF FLORUS AND SACROVIR

40. This was the year in which the states of Gaul, distracted by the burden of their debts, broke out into rebellion. The most energetic leaders of the rising were Julius Florus among the Treveri, and Julius Sacrovir among the Aedui.[33] Both were of high rank: their ancestors' services to Rome had earned them Roman citizenship at a time when that was a rare privilege, accorded only to merit. At secret conclaves they attached to themselves the most desperate elements and those driven to rebellion by poverty or the fear engendered by their crimes. They then agreed that Florus should rouse the Belgic peoples, Sacrovir the nearest Gallic tribes. At meetings held in public and private they delivered harangues about the unending tribute, the unrelenting burden of interest, and the cruelty and arrogance of the Roman administration. "The Roman army," they said, "is mutinous at the news of Germanicus' death. Now is a splendid time to regain our freedom. Only consider how Gaul flourishes, while Italy is in decay, the Roman mob is untrained to arms, the whole strength of the armies is non-Italian."[34]

41. Virtually every state of Gaul was affected by the seeds of this rebellion, but it first came to a head among the Andecavi and Turoni.[35] Acilius Aviola, governor of Gallia Lugdunensis, brought the Andecavi to heel with the unit which garrisoned Lyons. The same Aviola also suppressed the Turoni with a legionary force sent by his colleague, the governor of Lower Germany. It was aided by Gallic chieftains whose object in offering help was to conceal their treacherous intentions for production at a more opportune time. Indeed, Sacrovir himself was conspicuous, fighting in the Roman ranks with his head uncovered. This was said to be a display of valor; prisoners suggested that it was to identify him, and to insure that he would not be shot at. This was reported to Tiberius, but he took no action: his indecision strengthened the rebellion.

42. Meanwhile Florus pressed on with his designs. He tried to induce a cavalry regiment, raised among the Treveri but trained by Roman instructors, to begin the war by a massacre of Roman businessmen. A few of the soldiers listened to him; most remained loyal. But a crowd of debtors and bondsmen did take up arms, and took refuge in the forests of the Ardennes. There they were blockaded by legionary

forces, sent from opposite directions by the governors of the two German provinces, Visellius and Gaius Silius. A Gaul called Julius Indus was sent ahead with a picked body of troops from the states of the Treveri. He was at odds with Florus, and thus all the more ready to undertake his mission. Florus' followers were still an undisciplined mob, and Indus scattered them. But Florus escaped to inaccessible retreats and cheated the victors. But at last, seeing his escape route blocked by Roman troops, he killed himself. So ended the rebellion among the Treveri.

43. The rebellion of the Aedui was on a more massive scale, for they were a wealthier people, and there were no forces near at hand to suppress them. Sacrovir's forces seized Augustodunum, the capital city, where the sons of Gallic chieftains were being educated in the liberal arts.[36] Using them as hostages, he joined their parents and kinsmen to his cause. At the same time he distributed among them weapons which had been manufactured in secret. His forces amounted to forty thousand men: one-fifth of these were armed as legionaries; the rest had hunting spears, butcher's knives, and the like. There were also some slaves training to be gladiators. These wore a complete covering of iron armor, known as *cruppellarii* or "Iron Men";[37] they were impervious to blows, though ill suited to the attack. These forces were increased by volunteers from neighboring states, which had not openly joined the rebellion. Moreover, the Roman generals were quarreling, since each claimed to be in command of operations; finally, the feeble and aged Visellius yielded to the active Gaius Silius.

44. At Rome the report was that not merely the Treveri and Aedui, but all the sixty-four states of Gaul, were in revolt. The Germans had joined them, Spain was wavering—as usual, rumor had exaggerated everything. Loyal citizens were grieved by the danger to the state, but there were many opponents of the regime who longed for change and welcomed even a threat to their own safety. There was much criticism of Tiberius for wasting his time over accusers' reports in the face of this grave rebellion. "Is Sacrovir," they asked, "going to appear before the Senate on a charge of treason? Here are the men who are going to put paid to all these bloodthirsty letters from the Emperor: war is a welcome relief from the horrors of peace!" But Tiberius affected, more than ever, an air of unconcern. He stayed where he was, his countenance unmoved, the daily round unchanged. So impenetrable was his reserve; or perhaps he knew that

the rebellion was on a modest scale, though exaggerated by rumor.

45. Meanwhile Silius advanced with his two legions, sending on his auxiliary troops, and laid waste the territory of the Sequani, neighbors of the Aedui, and their partners in rebellion. Then he made a forced march to Augustodunum. The standard-bearers vied with one another to force the pace, and the soldiers refused the usual halts and rests at night: once they met the enemy and saw him face to face, they felt, the victory was as good as won. Twelve miles from the city, the forces of Sacrovir were seen occupying open ground. The Iron Men were in the center, the properly equipped units on the wings, the worse-armed elements in the rear. On a splendid horse Sacrovir went around among the chiefs, reminding the Gauls of their ancient glories and of all the defeats they had inflicted on the Romans. Victory would bring them freedom and honor, defeat a slavery more intolerable than before.

46. It was a short speech, and did nothing to cheer his men. The legions were approaching in battle array. The Gallic townsmen were disorganized and lacked combat experience: they did not know how to use their eyes and ears. Silius knew that victory was assured and a speech of encouragement superfluous. Nonetheless he spoke. "What an insult," he shouted, "for the conquerors of Germany to have to fight against Gauls! One infantry unit wiped up the Turoni, one cavalry squadron the Treveri. In this army, a few troops shattered the Sequani! These Aedui are rich, vicious, and unfit for combat. Show them up for what they are! When they start to run, spare their lives." A great roar of cheering went up: the cavalry surrounded the enemy and the infantry assaulted his front. For a little while the Iron Men caused delay, as their armor-plating resisted our javelins and swords. But then the troops picked up axes and spades, and went at them and their armor as though demolishing a wall. Others knocked over these immobile lumps with poles and pitchforks: unable to heave themselves upright, they were left for dead. Sacrovir first fled to Augustodunum, and then, fearing betrayal, made for a farmhouse with his faithful followers. There he committed suicide, and his followers killed each other. The farm was set alight over them and all their bodies destroyed.

47. Then and then only did Tiberius write to the Senate to announce that the war was begun—and finished. He neither suppressed nor exaggerated the truth, but claimed that victory had been gained through the loyalty and courage of his representatives and by his own policies. He then went on to explain why neither he nor Drusus had gone to the seat of

war. In so great an empire, it was not fitting for its rulers, merely because trouble broke out in one city or another, to leave the capital, where the reins of government were held. Now, when his going could not be ascribed to panic, he intended to investigate the situation and find a settlement. The Senate decreed thank-offerings, prayers for his safe return, and other honors of the kind. Cornelius Dolabella, seeking to outbid everyone in an absurd competition in flattery, proposed that the Emperor should receive an ovation when he entered Rome from Campania. This drew a letter from Tiberius. His fame, he said, did not stand so low that, after conquering so many warlike nations, after winning—and declining—so many triumphs in his early manhood, he felt the need in his old age of the empty glory of a stroll through the suburbs.

48. At this time, he asked the Senate to accord a public funeral to Sulpicius Quirinius. This man had no connection with the ancient and noble family of the Sulpicii. He came from bourgeois stock in Lanuvium, but he was a good general, and a distinguished record of service under Augustus had won him the consulship and an honorary triumph for capturing the fortresses of the Homonadenses in Cilicia. Later he was appointed adviser to Gaius Caesar in Armenia. He had paid court to Tiberius in his retirement at Rhodes, as the Emperor declared in the Senate, praising the attention shown to himself and blaming Marcus Lollius as the person responsible for the perverse and contentious behavior of Gaius. Others, however, had no happy memories of Quirinius. He had persecuted Lepida, as I have said, and he was an avaricious old man who wielded more power than he should.

49. At the end of the year the knight Clutorius Priscus was attacked by an informer. He had written a well-known poem, lamenting the death of Germanicus, and received an honorarium from Tiberius. Now it was said that he had written a second poem during an illness of Drusus, hoping that, if he died, the publication would be still more lucrative. This poem he had been conceited enough to read aloud in the house of Publius Petronius, and in the presence of his mother-in-law, Vitellia, and many other ladies of rank. When the informer went into action, the other women were frightened into giving evidence. Vitellia steadfastly denied that she had heard anything. But the hostile evidence carried the greater conviction, and on the proposal of the consul-designate, Haterius Agrippa, sentence of death was passed.

50. Marcus Lepidus opposed the motion in these terms: "If, gentlemen, our sole consideration is the disgraceful re-

marks of Clutorius Priscus—which have defiled both him and
his audience—then prison, hanging, or even the tortures reserved for slaves, are all too good for him. But though vice
and crime have no limits, still the Emperor's clemency and
your own precedents, ancient and modern, prescribe some
moderation in the penalty and cure. Folly is not the same
thing as crime, nor words as deeds. What we need is a resolution that will not leave his crime unpunished, while leaving
us no regrets either for leniency or undue severity. I have
often heard Tiberius complain of suicides, as depriving him
of the prerogative of mercy. Clutorius is, as yet, alive; his
survival will not endanger the state, and his death will point
no moral. His writings are pretentious and silly, but they are
trifling and unlikely to last. No serious danger is to be appre-
hended from someone who betrays himself, not to win the
minds of men, but to impress a group of silly women. So, let
him leave Rome, go into exile, and have his property confiscated. I propose this as if he stood convicted under the law
of treason."

51. Rubellius Blandus, alone of the men of consular rank,
supported Lepidus. The rest voted for the resolution of Haterius Agrippa. Clutorius was imprisoned and executed without
delay. With his usual tortuosity, Tiberius reprimanded the
Senate for their action. He praised their dutifulness in so
sternly punishing even this minor offense, but complained of
the overhasty action against mere verbal indiscretions. He
praised Lepidus, but he did not censure Haterius Agrippa.
The Senate therefore passed a motion prescribing that their
resolutions should not be reported to the treasury for nine
days, and that criminals should not be executed during this
period. But the Senate had no power to reconsider a verdict,
nor did the interval of time usually cause Tiberius to show
leniency.

22 A.D. Consuls Gaius Sulpicius, Decimus Haterius

52. This year was one of peace in foreign affairs. At Rome, however, there was disquiet over the possibility of a vigorous drive against the prevailing luxury, which had gone beyond all measure in the squandering of money. A good deal of it, although serious, could be concealed by not divulging prices. But expenditure on the belly and its gluttony was discussed with such publicity that it was felt that stern measures could be looked for from an Emperor as parsimonious as Tiberius.

First Gaius Bibulus, then the other aediles, complained that the sumptuary laws were being disregarded, that there was a daily increase in the prices of foodstuffs on the black market, and that nothing but severe measures could remedy the situation. The matter was brought up in the Senate, but without debate they referred it to the Emperor.

Tiberius had long had private doubts as to whether it was practicable to hold in check such immoderate appetites. An attempt at restraint might even be harmful, for it would be undignified to start measures which could not be maintained, or maintained only by the humiliation and disgrace of men of prominence. He therefore wrote to the Senate a letter whose substance was as follows:[38]

53. "Members of the Senate, on all other matters it may be proper for me to be asked, and to express, my opinions in your House. But on the matter you now refer to me, I should prefer to turn a blind eye. If I do not, and you point out to me the anxious faces of senators whose extravagance renders them liable to punishment, I am afraid I might see them, and so catch them out. Perhaps our energetic aediles should have had a word with me first. I might well have advised against taking any action against evils so deep-rooted and of such long standing—for by so doing we only reveal ourself as powerless to deal with them. But they have done their duty as I expect all magistrates to do. For me, however, silence is

unbecoming, speech inconvenient. I am neither aedile nor praetor nor consul. People expect something altogether grander and more impressive from the Emperor—they all take credit to themselves for their good deeds, but make one man the scapegoat for all their failings. And if I have to get back to the old standards of simplicity, where do I start? With the enormous mansions and their polyglot hordes of slaves? With their heavy gold and silver plate, their masterpieces of painting and sculpture? With men's clothes—undistinguishable from women's—or with that special feature of feminine extravagance, the transfer of Roman currency to foreign, often hostile nations, for the purchase of jewelry?

54. "I am well aware that there is much criticism of these things when people meet together, and demands for their regulation. But if a law were passed and penalties prescribed, these very critics would complain that the country was being ruined, that all citizens of distinction were being menaced, and that everyone was open to persecution. When you have chronic bodily ailments that have become exacerbated by time, you can make no headway but by drastic and violent measures: equally, feverish disorders of the mind can be assuaged only by remedies no less hectic than the passions which produced them. All the laws of our ancestors, now forgotten, all the enactments of the divine Augustus (now contemptuously disregarded, a more serious matter still), have done little more than to ensure that extravagance should flourish. If a man desires what is not yet forbidden, he may fear punishment when it is; but once he does with impunity what is prohibited, there's an end of fear or shame. But on what was the old frugality founded? On self-control from every man, and on the fact that we were all citizens of one city. Our domination of Italy brought us few temptations—but our wars of conquest taught us to be prodigal of other people's money, the civil wars of our own.

"The matter the aediles have brought before us is unimportant—even, if you look at our other problems, insignificant! No one brings up the fact that Italy is dependent on other countries, that the very life of the Roman people is daily at the hazard of wind and wave. If the resources of the provinces did not come to the aid of both masters and slaves, and augment the product of our lands, these parks and mansions of ours would hardly feed us. This, gentlemen of the Senate, is the task the Emperor has taken on his shoulders, this is what will bring the state to disaster if it is neglected. For our other troubles, what is needed is a change of heart: shame could restrain us; their necessity, the poor; their satiety, the rich.

"If any of the magistrates possesses the requisite strictness and energy, I shall thank him for it, and gladly transfer to him a part of my burdens. But if they want to denounce vices and thereby earn themselves credit, and then leave to me the ill will they have provoked—then I must plainly intimate to you, gentlemen, that I, too, am not eager to make enemies. Where the state requires it, I shall not shun unpopularity, harsh and unfair as it generally is. But I have good reason to avoid it in cases where it is useless and unprofitable to you or myself."

55. When the letter had been given a hearing, the aediles were allowed to let the matter drop. But this vice of gourmandizing, which in the hundred years between the battle of Actium and the principate of Galba reached such fantastic proportions, has gradually gone out of fashion. The reasons merit consideration. Rich and noble families of the highest standing were once brought low by this cult of extravagance. For in these days it was possible to court—and be courted by—the people, our allies, even foreign monarchs. The more splendid a man's wealth, palace, and style of living, the greater stood his reputation and the more clients he would attract. But then came the reign of terror. A great reputation brought ruin; those who survived learned to be more discreet. Then, too, there was the flood of new men from the municipalities and colonies—even from the provinces—into the Senate. They brought with them their own simpler tastes. Good fortune or their own merits often made them wealthy in later life, but they still kept their earlier habits.[39] Vespasian, especially, marked a return to a stricter economy, with his own old-fashioned way of dress and behavior. Respect for the Emperor and a desire to follow his lead then became more effective than the fear of legal penalties. Indeed, it may well be that there is a kind of cycle in human affairs, and that morals alternate as do the seasons. Ancient times were not always better: our generation too has produced many examples of honorable and civilized behavior for posterity to copy. One must hope that this praiseworthy competition with our ancestors may long endure.

ROME. THE ELEVATION OF DRUSUS

56. By checking the growing power of the informers, Tiberius had won credit for moderation. This prompted a letter

to the Senate asking them to confer on Drusus the "authority of a tribune." This term was invented by Augustus as a designation of supreme rank when he wished to avoid titles like "king" or "dictator," yet needed something to set him visibly above all other holders of power. Later he chose Marcus Agrippa to share this authority, and, when Agrippa died, Tiberius Nero. His object was to designate his successor, and at the same time to bridle the vaulting ambition in others. He knew he could rely on Tiberius' modesty, and his own primacy.

Following this example, Tiberius now brought Drusus to the supreme power: while Germanicus lived he did not take a decision between them. His letter began by invoking the help of the gods, so that the country might benefit from his proposals. It then went on to a plain, unvarnished account of the young man's character. He was married, had three children, and was now at the age when the divine Augustus had summoned himself (Tiberius) to these responsibilities. There was nothing premature about Drusus' elevation. He had quelled rebellions, victoriously ended wars: having held a triumph and twice been consul, he would now be a partner in a task he knew very well.

57. The senators had foreseen this request and had time to polish up their flattery. But they produced nothing new—statues of Caesars, altars to the gods, temples, triumphal arches, all the hackneyed honors. Marcus Silanus, however, sought to honor the tribunician authority by derogating from that of the consuls; his proposal was that all public and private monuments should henceforth be dated by bearing the names, not of the consuls, but of the holders of tribunician power. Quintus Haterius then moved that the resolution passed that day be recorded in letters of gold in the Senate House. This degrading obsequiousness was met with mockery, especially as he was so old that it could only bring him dishonor.

58. At this period Junius Blaesus was continued in office as governor of Africa. Servius Maluginensis, the high priest[40] of Jupiter, asked for the governorship of Asia. He claimed that it was commonly but wrongly believed that holders of his post could not leave Italy: in fact, their legal position coincided with that of the high priests of Mars and Quirinus. If these men held governorships of provinces, why not the high priests of Jupiter? No popular legislation forbade it, the book of religious ceremonies held nothing to the contrary. Ordinary priests had often presided over ceremonies if the high priest of Jupiter were incapacitated by illness or public duty. Moreover, after the violent death of Cornelius Merula, that post had been unfilled for seventy-five years. If it could be unoccupied for so long without detriment to the public ceremonies, how readily

could it support the one year's absence of a provincial governor! At one time, the Pontifex Maximus used to deny governorships to high priests because of personal rivalries. Now they had a Pontifex Maximus who, thanks to the will of heaven, was also the first of mankind, far above rivalry, envy, or personal considerations.

59. But the augur Lentulus and others spoke against the proposal, and it was decided to obtain the views of the Pontifex Maximus, the Emperor. Tiberius postponed any consideration of the problem of the powers of the chief priest of Jupiter. Meanwhile he wrote to the Senate to curtail some of the ceremonies proposed for Drusus' elevation to tribunician power. He singled out for criticism the proposal about the gold letters, as being arrogant and not in accord with ancestral custom. Letters from Drusus were also read before the Senate. Composed in a vein of modesty, they achieved the contrary effect. "Has the rot really gone so far," asked the senators, "that a young man who has received such honors cannot pay his respects to the gods of Rome, enter the Senate, or assume the auspices of office on his native soil? Is he at war, then, or detained in some distant land? Not at all, he is making a leisurely tour of the lakes and coasts of Campania. This is the first lesson his father has taught him—a fine beginning for the future ruler of the world! The Emperor is elderly, he might shrink from the public gaze and plead his weariness and the labors he has passed. But what is to detain Drusus—except conceit?"

THE SANCTUARIES OF ASIA

60. Tiberius had reinforced the power of his principate, but he permitted the Senate a shadow of their old prerogatives when he asked them to investigate a number of petitions from the provinces. Throughout the cities of Greece, a dangerous practice was growing up of allowing criminals to escape punishment by claiming rights of asylum. The temples were full of slaves with criminal records; debtors were availing themselves of sanctuary to cheat their creditors; even men sentenced on capital charges were admitted. No power availed to put down riots among communities that claimed to be protecting religious observance but were really protecting crime. It was therefore decided to ask the cities to produce their charters and send their representatives to Rome.

A few cities, whose claims lacked legality, voluntarily abandoned their rights. But many persisted, relying on cults of high

antiquity or good service done to Rome. And a noble sight it
was, on that day, to see the Senate engaged on the investigation of privileges granted by our ancestors, treaties made with
allies, charters conferred by monarchs who had lived before
the days of Roman power, and indeed the very cults of the
gods themselves: moreover, the Senate was at liberty, as in
former times, to confirm or revoke.

61. The first delegation was that of Ephesus. Their claim
was that Apollo and Diana were not born at Delos, as the popular belief asserted: there was at Ephesus a river Cenchrius, a
grove Ortygia, where Latona, come to her time, had borne these
two divinities, leaning on an olive tree (the tree still survived).
The grove had been consecrated by the will of the gods: there
Apollo had evaded the anger of Jupiter after the slaughter of
the Cyclopes. Later Father Liber,[41] after his victory in battle,
had pardoned the suppliant Amazons as they begged for mercy
at the altar. The sanctity of the temple had been augmented by
permission of Hercules, during his rule of Lydia. Its privileges
had not been lost under the sway of the Persians, and they had
later been respected both by the Macedonians and by ourselves.

62. Next came the turn of Magnesia-by-the-Maeander.
They recounted the decrees of Lucius Scipio and Lucius Sulla
rewarding them for loyalty and courage against Antiochus III
of Syria and Mithridates of Pontus respectively. They had decreed that there should be inviolable sanctuary in the temple
of Diana Leucophryne. Then Alexandria Aphrodisias and
Stratoniceia produced decrees of the dictator Julius Caesar,
citing their long-standing adherence to his cause, and also a
more recent commendation from Augustus. This last praised
them for the unswerving allegiance to Rome they had maintained in the face of a Parthian invasion. Alexandria Aphrodisias was anxious to protect the cult of Venus, Stratoniceia
that of Jupiter and Diana of the Crossroads.[42] Hierocaesarea
adduced claims that went farther into the past. Their temple of
the Persian Diana[43] had been founded in the reign of Cyrus the
Great: they were able to quote the fact that Perpenna, Isauri-
cus, and many other Roman generals had recognized the sanctity, not merely of the temple, but of an area two miles around
it. They were followed by the people of Cyprus claiming on
behalf of three shrines: the Paphian Venus, founded by
Aërias; Venus of Amathus, founded by his son of that name:
Jupiter of Salamis, which Teucer founded as he fled from his
father, Telamon.

63. Embassies from other cities were also heard. But they
were so numerous, and partisanship ran so high, that the Senate

began to weary of the matter. They therefore instructed the consuls to investigate the charters and, in cases where a flaw appeared, to report back to the Senate. The consuls' report approved the cases I have quoted, and also confirmed the rights of asylum in the temple of Aesculapius at Pergamum. All other claims, however, were ruled out because they went back too far into antiquity. For example, Smyrna claimed that an oracle of Apollo had started its temple of Venus Stratonicis; Tenos also cited him as calling for a statue and temple of Neptune. The people of Sardis were, comparatively, modernists—their temple was the gift of Alexander the Great; Miletus cited Darius with equal confidence. The temples in these cities were to Diana and Apollo. The Cretans claimed for a statue of the divine Augustus.

Decrees of the Senate were worded in terms of great respect, but they imposed limits. It was ordained that inscriptions should be set up in letters of bronze as a record, and also as a warning not to let religious rites serve to disguise undue rivalry between the cities.

64. At about this time the Empress Livia fell dangerously ill, and Tiberius had to hasten back to Rome. Mother and son now lived on excellent terms—or else they kept their hatreds to themselves. A little earlier, dedicating a statue of Augustus in the Theater of Marcellus, Livia had caused Tiberius' name to be written after her own. This Tiberius was supposed to have resented as an insult to the dignity of the Emperor—but he suppressed his feelings and stored them in his memory. But now the Senate decreed thanksgivings and major games, to be organized by the pontifices, the augurs, the Board of Fifteen for Religious Ceremonies, the Board of Seven for Solemn Banquets, and the Companions of Augustus, all acting jointly. Lucius Apronius further proposed that the fetiales should preside at the games. This was opposed by the Emperor, who cited precedents to define the functions of the various priesthoods. The fetiales, he said, had never enjoyed such standing. The Companions of Augustus had only been included because their priesthood specifically related to the family on whose behalf vows were being offered.

65. It is no part of my plan to record all decrees of the Senate, unless they were particularly honorable, or scandalous to an unusual degree. The proper function of history, as I conceive it, is to insure that merits are not passed over, and that base words and deeds will have occasion to fear the judgment of posterity.[44] But in truth this was a thoroughly corrupt period, deeply tainted by servility. It was not merely the greatest figures who had to protect themselves by obsequiousness; all

the ex-consuls, most of the ex-praetors, many even of ¹
nary senators, all rose to their feet in a competition to ₘ
base and saponaceous proposals. It is on record that whenever
Tiberius left the Senate House he would exclaim (in Greek)
"Men ready to be slaves!" He was no friend of civil liberty, but
even he found such a degree of self-abasement intolerable.

THE CASE OF JUNIUS SILANUS

66. From this point, sycophancy gradually changed into
persecution. Gaius Junius Silanus, governor of Asia, was accused by the provincials of extortion. He was also attacked by
the ex-consul, Mamercus Scaurus, the praetor Junius Otho, and
the aedile Bruttedius Niger, for sacrilege against Augustus and
treason against Tiberius. Mamercus cited a number of ancient
precedents, among them the attacks on Lucius Cotta by Scipio
Africanus, on Servius Galba by Cato the Censor, and on
Publius Rutilius by Marcus Scaurus. But it was not crimes of
this sort that drew down the vengeance of Scipio and Cato, nor
of the famous Scaurus, whom this Mamercus, his grandson and
a disgrace to his family, was now dishonoring by his shameful
activities! Junius Otho had once kept an elementary school: he
owed his position as senator to the influence of Sejanus, and
his origins, obscure as they were, were dishonored by his
shameless endeavors. As for Bruttedius, he was a person of
culture and attainments, and might have won the highest office,
could he have steered a straight course. But he was a man in
a hurry: he wanted to outstrip first his equals, then his superiors, finally his own expectations. Impatience was his downfall,
as it has been of many good men who have spurned the slow,
safe course of promotion for honors won before their time.

67. The list of Silanus' accusers also included Gallius Publi-
cola, his quaestor, and Marcus Paconius, a member of his staff.
It was quite clear that the defendant had been guilty of brutality and extortion. But he was trapped in a situation that
might have ruined even an innocent man—so many senators
were against him, and the most eloquent orators of Asia, specially selected for the purpose, were for the prosecution. Silanus was conducting his own case, and he was no speaker. He
was handicapped by that nervousness which weakens even the
most practiced eloquence. Tiberius made no attempt to temper
his looks or his words, and repeatedly joined in the cross-
examination. Silanus had no chance to rebut or evade: indeed
he had to make some confession, lest the Emperor should seem

to ask in vain. A treasury agent purchased his slaves to permit of their being examined under torture. None of his friends could help him in his extremity as the charges of treason were pressed: this was the chain that bound to silence. So Silanus asked for a brief adjournment, and then gave up his defense. He did, however, write a letter to Tiberius of mixed entreaty and reproach.

68. Tiberius thought a precedent was needed to justify the action he had planned against Silanus. He therefore produced a letter of the deified Augustus about Volesus Messala, a former governor of Asia, together with the Senate's decision in that case, and ordered them to be read aloud. Then he asked Lucius Calpurnius Piso to express his views. Piso began with a long disquisition on the imperial clemency, but went on to propose that Silanus should be outlawed and banished to Gyara. This won general support, though Gnaeus Lentulus suggested that the property Silanus had inherited from his mother, who was of the Atian family,[45] should be separated from the rest of the estate and granted to her son. To this suggestion Tiberius agreed.

69. As a refinement of sycophancy, Cornelius Dolabella included in a denunciation of Gaius Silanus' character a proposal that no person of scandalous life and reputation should take part in the draw for provincial governorships. The laws, he urged, punished offenses: but how much better for the allies, and kinder for the offenders, to prevent offenses from occurring? Tiberius spoke strongly against this suggestion. "I know," he said, "the rumors about Silanus, but we must not take action on rumors. Provincial governors often falsify expectations entertained of them, whether for good or bad: the challenge of high office is a spur to some, an obstacle to others. The Emperor cannot be expected to inform himself of everything, nor must he become involved in the intrigues which are not his. The law takes account of what has been done, precisely because the future is uncertain. That is why our ancestors determined that punishment should follow the crime. It was a wise ruling, and has always commanded acceptance: do not subvert it. Emperors carry burdens enough; and they do not lack for power. The laws are diminished when arbitrary authority holds sway. Where the laws allow of action, one should not employ the imperial prerogative." An effort to please was rare enough in Tiberius, and it was warmly welcomed. Moreover, he knew how to temper justice with mercy, so long as his personal feelings were not involved. So he concluded by saying that Gyara was a bleak and uncivilized place: as a concession to the Junian house, and to a former senator, Silanus

should be allowed to live instead in Cythnus. This, he added, was the request of Silanus' sister, Torquata, a vestal virgin of the old, untainted sanctity. The proposal was agreed to without debate.

CONDEMNATION OF CAESIUS CORDUS

70. The complaint of the people of Cyrene was taken next. On the prosecution of Ancharius Priscus, Caesius Cordus was convicted of extortion. Lucius Ennius, a Roman knight, was charged with having melted down an effigy of the Emperor for silver plate, but Tiberius refused to allow his name to be entered on the list of defendants. In a show of independence, Ateius Capito opposed him publicly. The senators, he declared, must not be deprived of the right to take action, nor should offenses of such magnitude enjoy immunity. The Emperor was known to be slow to resent his own injuries, but this must not extend to indulgence to antisocial actions. Tiberius understood very well that more lay behind this than was openly expressed, and maintained his veto. Capito's disgrace was all the more flagrant because of his eminence in religious and civil law, and it compromised both his high office and his personal distinction.

SOME RELIGIOUS ISSUES

71. Next arose a religious problem. Where was the vow to be discharged which the equestrian order had offered to Fortuna Equestris for the recovery of the Augusta? Though there were many temples of Fortuna in Rome, none were of that dedication. But it was reported that there was at Antium a temple so designated. Moreover, all cults, temples, and divine effigies in Italy were under the jurisdiction of Roman law. So the gift was deposited at Antium. Since religious questions were under debate, the Emperor produced his deferred judgment in the case of Servius Maluginensis, high priest of Jupiter. He caused to be read an ordinance of the pontifices enjoining that, if the high priest of Jupiter were incapacitated by illness, he could at the discretion of the Pontifex Maximus be away for a period of more than two nights, provided that it did not include days of public sacrifice, nor take place more than twice in the same year. This ruling had been passed in the principate of Augustus. It made it quite clear that an absence for a year

and a provincial governorship were inadmissible for high priests of Jupiter. He cited, too, the veto which the Pontifex Maximus Lucius Metellus had passed on Aulus Postumius. So the province of Asia was allotted to the ex-consul next in seniority to Servius Maluginensis.

ROME. FAMOUS BUILDINGS REPAIRED

72. At this period Marcus Aemilius Lepidus asked the Senate to allow him to embellish and repair the Basilica of Paulus, the building which commemorated the Aemilian family.[46] It was a period when public munificence was still in vogue: indeed, Augustus had permitted Taurus, Philippus, and Balbus to use spoils won from the enemy, or their own ample means, to beautify Rome and gratify posterity. In this tradition Lepidus, though himself of modest means, refurbished the great memorial of his house. Tiberius himself undertook to restore the Theater of Pompeius, destroyed by an accidental fire. None of the family were wealthy enough for the undertaking, but the name of Pompeius was allowed to remain. He warmly thanked Sejanus for the labor and vigilance which had confined the damage of this serious conflagration to the loss of a single building. The Senate commissioned a statue of Sejanus to be put up in the Theater of Pompeius. Again, when Tiberius, a little later, awarded an honorary triumph to Junius Blaesus, he emphasized that this was a compliment to his nephew, Sejanus. Yet Blaesus had thoroughly earned the distinction by his own achievements.

AFRICA. TACFARINAS AGAIN

73. Tacfarinas, though often defeated, had always been able to draw fresh forces from the interior. He had now become so insolent that he actually sent envoys to Tiberius, demanding, on the threat of an otherwise endless war, lands for himself and his army. No other insult to the Roman people or himself ever infuriated Tiberius so much as that this deserter and brigand should behave like a belligerent.

Even when Spartacus had defeated consular armies and was freely ravaging Italy, he had not been allowed to make his own conditions of surrender, although the state itself was reeling under the terrible wars with Sertorius and Mithridates. Now at the very pinnacle of Roman power, was this bandit Tacfarinas to be bought off by peace and a grant of lands? Blaesus was therefore entrusted with the task of inducing the rest of Tacfarinas' followers to put down their arms by promise of an amnesty. Every means was to be used to lay their leader by the heels. Many surrendered in the hope of pardon: Tacfarinas was then attacked by the use of his own methods.

74. His force had always been weaker in numbers, but better at brigandage: it had operated in several bands to avoid battle and seek to entrap the enemy. Blaesus therefore organized three columns, operating on three lines of advance. Cornelius Scipio, commander of a legion, blocked the route by which a raid could be made on Leptis, followed by a retreat to the country of the Garamantes. On the other flank, a force under the command of Blaesus' son protected the people of Cirta against incursions. The governor himself and picked troops were in the center. Forts and blockhouses were sited to cramp and restrict the enemy. Wherever they moved there was a Roman army, in front, on the flank, even in the rear. These tactics caused the enemy heavy casualties and prisoners.

Then Blaesus split each of his three columns into smaller units, commanded by centurions tried and proved in battle. Usually, when summer was over, the troops were withdrawn and stationed in winter quarters in the old province of Africa. Blaesus abandoned this plan, and set up a line of forts as prescribed for the opening phases of a campaign. Then, with mobile forces of troops trained in desert fighting, he forced Tacfarinas to change and go on changing his encampments. At last, having captured Tacfarinas' brother, he withdrew—prematurely, as it turned out, for our allies, since enemy forces were still strong enough to renew the war. Tiberius, however, regarded the war as at an end, and allowed Blaesus to be saluted as "Imperator" by his legions. This honor was by tradition granted to generals by the free acclamation of their victorious troops. It could be held by several generals at the same time, who enjoyed no precedence over the others. Augustus had granted the title in several cases. Its award by Tiberius to Blaesus was the last.

ROME. OBITUARIES OF THE YEAR

75. Distinguished men who died that year included Asinius Salonius, grandson of Marcus Agrippa and Asinius Pollio, half-brother of Drusus, and fiancé of a granddaughter of

Tiberius. Also Ateius Capito, whom I have previously mentioned, the outstanding jurist of his day. His grandfather had been one of Sulla's centurions, and his father had never risen higher than praetor. Augustus had made him consul before the statutory age to allow him to outrank another distinguished jurist, Antistius Labeo. That single generation produced those two great civil geniuses: but Labeo, who never compromised his independence, had the more honorable reputation, whereas Capito's servility gave him more authority with the Emperor. That Labeo never got beyond the praetorship earned him credit from the obvious injustice of it: Capito's consulship won him hatred and dislike.

76. Sixty-four years after the battle of Philippi, Junia, niece of Cato, wife of Cassius, sister of Brutus, passed away. Her will caused much public comment. She had been very rich, and she mentioned most leading members of the aristocracy in terms of respect, but not the Emperor. Tiberius took this very well. He did not prohibit a laudatory oration from the Rostra, nor the other features of a solemn funeral. The effigies of twenty leading families headed the funeral procession; the Manlii, the Quinctii, and others no less distinguished. But the effigies of Cassius and Brutus outshone them all—because they were not on public display.

BOOK IV

23 A.D. Consuls Gaius Asinius Pollio and Gaius Antistius Vetus

1. This year was for Tiberius the ninth of public stability and domestic good fortune—for he reckoned the death of Germanicus on the credit side. But suddenly fortune shattered this state of affairs. Tiberius became cruel, or entrusted power to cruel men. The root and cause of the change sprang from Aelius Sejanus, commander of the Guard. Earlier, I spoke of his influence; now I must explain his origins, character, and criminal attempt at usurpation. He was born at Volsinii, and his father, Seius Sejanus, was a Roman knight. In his early years he attached himself to Gaius Caesar, the grandson of Augustus, and there was a rumor that he sold his person to the lusts of the rich and depraved Apicius. Later, he used his talents on Tiberius to such effect that that Emperor, so inscrutable to others, showed himself frank and outspoken toward Sejanus. This was not due to low cunning: in that quality Tiberius was his master. Rather was it the anger of heaven against the Roman state, to which Sejanus' career, and his fall, were equally calamitous.[1] He combined physical energy and audacity of mind: keeping his own secrets, he was prone to traduce others. In him were blended servility and arrogance: behind a mask of modesty there was an unbridled appetite for power. Hence his extravagance and luxury. Hence too—even more in evidence—his untiring activity. Aimed at the throne, this is as dangerous as excess.

2. Earlier, the commander of the Guard had wielded little

influence, but Sejanus concentrated in a single camp the units that had been scattered about the city, so that orders could be given out simultaneously, and the men would gain in self-confidence, and be more formidable to others, by being so obviously numerous and conspicuous. To be quartered in small units, he would say, meant laxity of discipline: in a sudden emergency, united action would be more effective: morale would profit by their removal from the fleshpots of the city. When the camp[2] was built, he gradually wormed his way into the troops' favor by visiting them, and calling them by name. Tribunes and centurions were appointed by him personally. Nor did he neglect to court the ambitions of the senators. High office and provincial governorships went to his favorites. Tiberius indulged him to such an extent that not only in private conversation, but in speeches to the Senate and dispatches to the people he called him "the partner of my labors."[3] He allowed honors to be paid to statues of Sejanus in the theaters and fora of Rome, and at the headquarters of the legions.

3. But a well-stocked imperial house, with the Emperor's son in the vigor of youth, and grandsons grown to manhood, stood in the path of his ambitions. It would be hazardous to assassinate them all, and simultaneously: subtlety called for a timetable of crimes. So Sejanus decided to follow devious methods and to begin with Drusus, against whom he bore a fresh grudge. For Drusus had little use for rivals, and a hot temper: when a chance quarrel had broken out, he had raised his hand against Sejanus and, meeting resistance, punched him in the face. Surveying every possibility, Sejanus concluded that his readiest course was to seduce Drusus' wife, Livilla, the sister of Germanicus. She had been plain in her girlhood but was now one of the beauties of the day. Pretending to be passionately in love, Sejanus seduced her. Having gained his first criminal objective, he went on—and a woman who has parted with her virtue will stick at nothing—to tempt her with offers of marriage, of sharing the Empire, and of murdering her husband. So this princess, the grandniece of Augustus, the daughter-in-law of Tiberius, the mother of Drusus' children, disgraced herself, her ancestors, and her posterity in an intrigue with a provincial adulterer.[4] For risk and infamy, she sacrificed honor and position. Her physician and friend, Eudemus, was let into the secret; professional reasons gave him ready access to her in private. Sejanus sent away his own wife, Apicata, who had borne him three children, lest she should offend his mistress. But the enormity of the crime he

had in mind led to alarms, postponements, and (sometimes) confusion of plans.

4. At the beginning of the year Drusus, the son of Germanicus, assumed the toga, and the Senate decreed to him the same honors that had been granted to his brother Nero. Tiberius spoke in warm commendation of his own son Drusus' friendly and paternal feelings for the children of Germanicus. And indeed Drusus (although brotherly affection and a high position do not go well together) was thought to be well disposed to the young men, or, at least, not to dislike them.

At this time the old plan—so often produced—of a tour of the provinces by Tiberius, was once more revived. The Emperor pointed out that there were very many veterans whose discharge was due, and that the armies would have to be brought up to strength by conscription. Voluntary recruiting had fallen off: even when it existed, the old discipline and bravery were no longer in evidence, since voluntary enlistment appealed only to rogues and vagabonds. He then briefly enumerated the legions and the provinces which they defended. In this I propose to follow him, setting out the Roman armed forces and the client-kings at a time when the Empire was so much smaller than it is now.[5]

ADMINISTRATION OF THE EMPIRE

5. A fleet guarded Italy on either shore, based at Misenum and Ravenna. The southern coasts of Gaul were protected by the warships Augustus had captured at Actium; fully manned, they were stationed at Forum Julii. The main concentration of force—eight legions—was on the Rhine, available as required against Gaul or Germany. Three legions were posted in Spain, whose conquest had only recently been completed.[6] King Juba ruled Mauretania as a gift from the Roman people. The rest of Africa was held by two legions, and a like force was stationed in Egypt. All that vast extent of country from western Syria to the river Euphrates was controlled by four legions: client-kings such as those of Albania and Iberia were protected by Roman power against other empires. Rhoemetalces and the children of Cotys ruled Thrace. The banks of the Danube were protected by two legions in Pannonia, two in Moesia. A further two legions were in reserve in Dalmatia, whence they could quickly move if an emergency arose in

Italy. Rome, however, had forces of its own in the three urban cohorts and the nine cohorts of the Imperial Guard. These were largely recruited from Etruria, Umbria, the old lands of Latium, or the earliest Roman colonies.[7] Besides these, at suitable points in the provinces our allies provided warships, cavalry regiments, and infantry, in all hardly inferior in strength to the Roman legions. To list them, however, I found to be something indeterminate: for their numbers and postings varied from time to time as circumstances required, now rising to a peak and again falling away.

6. But I think it would be germane to consider other aspects of the public administration thus far in the reign, since this was the year Tiberius' principate took a decisive turn for the worse. Firstly, then, public business, and the most important private lawsuits, were handled in the Senate. The leading senators enjoyed freedom of speech, and lapses into servility were corrected by the Emperor. In conferring office he took account of high ancestry, military distinction, or eminence in the arts of peace: it was clearly apparent that the best candidates were chosen. The consulship and the praetorship retained their prestige: the lower magistrates exercised the functions of their office. Aside from the law of treason, the laws were worthily administered.

Levies of grain, indirect taxes, and the other items of public revenue were collected by companies of Roman knights.[8] The imperial estates were entrusted to carefully selected agents, some of whom were known to the Emperor only by repute.[9] Once chosen, they were kept in office, often continuing in the same employment far into old age. There was some public distress from the high price of food, but here the Emperor was not to blame. He left undone nothing that money or energy could achieve against bad harvests or stormy seas. He saw to it that the provinces did not suffer from new imposts, and that the existing ones were not made more burdensome by cruelty or avarice on the part of the magistrates: physical punishments and confiscations of property there were none. He kept few estates in Italy; his slaves were inconspicuous; a few freedmen provided his household staff. Any dispute with a private individual was taken to the courts.

7. This tenor of administration was maintained—not in any gracious fashion but after Tiberius' usual grim and even terrifying manner—until the death of Drusus led to a change. So long as Drusus lived, it had remained in force: in the early stages of his power Sejanus wanted to gain reputation for liberal policy. Moreover, he had reason to fear an avenger who never bothered to conceal his hatred, who was loud in

complaints that the Emperor looked elsewhere for a coadjutor while his son still lived. And how long before this coadjutor became a colleague? It was the first steps to power that presented difficulties: establish yourself, and supporters and partisans are readily found. "Sejanus has already built this praetorian camp on his own initiative: the soldiers are at his disposal. His statue is in the Theater of Pompeius: the grandsons of the Drusi will be his grandsons.[10] We shall have to appeal to his self-restraint from now on, and hope that his ambition will be sated." Drusus spoke in this vein often and in public. As for his confidences, they were betrayed by his faithless wife.

DEATH OF DRUSUS

8. The need for haste was clear to Sejanus, and he selected a poison which, given in small doses, might be made to look like a natural illness. It was administered to Drusus by the eunuch Lygdus;[11] this came out eight years later. Through all the period of Drusus' illness, and even between his death and the funeral, Tiberius attended the Senate. He may have felt no anxiety, or he may have wished to stage a display of fortitude. When the consuls took their seats on the ordinary benches as a token of mourning, he sharply rebuked them, reminding them of their dignity and office. When the senators wept, he fought down his own grief and addressed them with words of comfort. "I know very well," he said, "that I am open to criticism in coming to the Senate when my bereavement is so recent. Mourners can hardly bear to hear the consolations of their kinsmen, or to look upon the light of day. We must not condemn them for weakness, but I have sought a more powerful remedy by throwing myself into the arms of our country." Then he went on to speak in moving terms of the extreme old age of Livia,[12] of the raw youth of his grandsons, and his own declining years. He asked that Germanicus' children, the sole comfort of his present distresses, should be brought into the Senate House. The consuls went out, spoke kindly to the boys, brought them in, and placed them before Tiberius. Taking them by the hand, he said, "Members of the Senate, when their father died, I entrusted these boys to their uncle. He had children of his own, but I begged him to rear them and cherish them as if they were his blood, and, for the sake of the future, to mold them after his own pattern. Now that Drusus is gone I address the same plea to you. I beg you, gentlemen, by our

country and our country's gods, adopt and guide these boys,
the great-grandchildren of Augustus, the heirs of a noble line.
Fulfill my office, and your own. Nero and Drusus, these senators will be your parents. Born as you are, it matters to our
country whether you fare well or ill."

9. General grief followed his words, and prayers for a
happy issue; if he had stopped there, he would have filled his
hearers' minds with pity and with pride. But he went on to
speak of stale and empty issues—the restoration of the Republic, the consuls (or someone else) to take over the government in his place. All this cast doubt on what he had said
with sincerity and meaning. The same honors which had been
granted to Germanicus were now voted to Drusus, with the
additions to be expected of a second round of adulation. It
was a splendid funeral, notable for the long procession of
effigies. Among them were Aeneas, founder of the Julian
house, the kings of Alba, the Sabine nobility with Attus
Clausus, and the effigies of the Claudii, following in long array.

10. My account of the death of Drusus has been based on
the consensus of the best authorities. But there is another
story I ought not to omit—widely believed at the time, and
even now not wholly extinct. It tells how Sejanus, having already seduced Livilla, went on to seduce the eunuch Lygdus.
His youth and beauty endeared him to Drusus and he had
become one of his confidants. The conspirators are said to
have reached agreement on a time and place for giving the
poison. But Sejanus was reckless enough to change the whole
plan. Secretly denouncing Drusus of a plot to poison Tiberius,
he warned the Emperor not to drink from the first cup that
would be put before him when he dined with his son. This
was the trap, and the old man fell into it. At the dinner table
he passed his cup to Drusus. Unsuspecting, Drusus eagerly
drained it—thereby increasing the suspicion against himself.
Fear and shame, they allege, made him claim for himself the
death he had planned for his father.

11. This rumor was widespread at the time, but it is found
in no good authority. Moreover, it can be refuted at once.[13]
What man of common sense—let alone Tiberius, with all his
experience of affairs—would kill his own son, with his own
hand, leaving the case unheard, and giving himself no chance
to alter his mind? Surely he would have tortured the man who
supplied the poison, to find out whose orders he was following. Accustomed as he was to use prevarication and delay in
dealing with strangers, would he not have employed them with
his only son, a young man never before convicted of wrong-
doing? But Sejanus was thought capable of any crime, and

the Emperor was foolishly indulgent to him. Both were so loathed that even this fantastic and unlikely tale was believed. Rumor is always prodigal of horrors when princes die. In any case, the real story of the crime was divulged by Apicata, wife of Sejanus, and confirmed, under torture, by Eudemus and Lygdus. No historian has ever been so hostile to Tiberius as to charge him with this crime, though they may have investigated all his other misdeeds and laid them at his door. My object in mentioning and rebutting this canard has been to show by a striking instance the falseness of idle rumors. I do beg all my readers not to prefer mere hearsay—however popular and sensational—to the plain truth, without embroidery.

PLOTS AGAINST AGRIPPINA

12. When Tiberius delivered the funeral speech for his son from the Rostra, the Senate and people, by dress and demeanor, made a show of grief. But it was outward rather than sincere. In their hearts they rejoiced at the reviving fortunes of the house of Germanicus. Yet this new tide of popularity—and Agrippina's failure to keep her hopes to herself—merely precipitated their downfall. Sejanus had seen that Drusus' death brought neither vengeance to his murderers nor grief to the public, and his criminal recklessness was yet further inflated. He had gained his first objectives, and now began to consider how to remove the children of Germanicus, since they were now next in line for the throne.

But he could hardly poison all three. Their servants could not be bribed, neither could Agrippina be seduced. The best hope was to play on her rebelliousness, the dislike the Empress Livia had long felt toward her, and the recent complicity of Livilla in his plans. These could be used with Tiberius to imply that Agrippina, proud of her offspring, and supported by popular favor, was aiming at the throne. He found accomplished calumniators to foster these rumors, among them—a selection of his own—a certain Julius Postumus. Through an affair with Mutilia Prisca, this man had become an intimate of the Empress, and a ready tool for Sejanus. For Prisca enjoyed great credit with the old lady, and could easily inflame her naturally jealous temperament to the point of a break with her grandson's wife, Agrippina. Even Agrippina's closest friends were beguiled into exciting her unruly ambitions by talk of treason.

13. Meanwhile Tiberius continued to play his full part in public affairs. His work brought him consolation, and he continued to try legal cases and to handle petitions from the provinces. On his proposal, the Senate granted remission of taxes for three years to the cities of Cibyra in Asia and Aegium in Achaea, which had been destroyed by earthquakes. Vibius Serenus, governor of Further Spain, was convicted of violence, and banished to the island of Amorgos because of his criminal behavior. Carsidius Sacerdos was accused of having supplied grain to Tacfarinas, a public enemy, but he was acquitted. Gaius Sempronius Gracchus was implicated in the charge. As a baby he had been taken by his father to the island of Cercina to share his exile. There he had grown up among the exiled criminals, men of no education. Petty trade of some sort in Africa and Syria had won him a livelihood, but he did not escape the dangers of high rank. Had not Aelius Lamia and Lucius Apronius, governors of Africa, protected him as an innocent person, he would have fallen a victim to his father's ruin and his own high but unlucky name.

14. This same year brought embassies from two Greek cities. The people of Samos sought confirmation for the ancient right of asylum in the temple of Juno, as did those of Cos for the temple of Aesculapius.[14] The Samian case rested on a decree of the Amphictyonic Council, supreme arbiter of Greek affairs when, after the foundation of cities throughout Asia, the Greeks ruled its coasts. The Coan claim yielded nothing on the score of antiquity, and there was a further claim of a local nature, for when King Mithridates massacred Roman citizens throughout Asia and the islands, the temple of Aesculapius had been thrown open to them as a refuge. Next, since the praetors had often complained, but to no purpose, about the insolence of actors, the Emperor now at last took the matter to the Senate. "These ballet dancers," he said, "cause public disorder and private immorality. That old popular favorite, the Oscan farce, has now become so vicious and depraved that it needs the authority of the Senate to suppress it." The dancers were then banished from Italy.[15]

15. This year brought Tiberius two bereavements—the death of one of Drusus' twin sons, and the loss of an old friend. This was Lucilius Longus, who had stood by him in good days and in bad, and had been the only senator to ac-

company him in his retirement[16] to Rhodes. So, parvenu though he was, Longus was accorded, by a decree of the Senate, a state funeral, and a statue in the Forum of Augustus.[17] The Senate, indeed, still handled all public business. Thus, when Lucilius Capito, the Emperor's agent in Asia, was prosecuted by the province, Tiberius declared with much emphasis, "I restricted his authority to my own slaves and personal revenue. If he has exercised the powers of a governor, or made use of troops, he has exceeded his instructions. The Senate should hear the provincials' case." They did, and Capito was condemned. On this account and for the condemnation of Gaius Silanus, a year earlier, the cities of Asia voted a temple in honor of Tiberius, Livia, and the Senate. Permission was granted. Nero expressed the thanks of the provincials to the Senate and to his grandfather. His audience listened to him with pleasure: the memory of Germanicus was still fresh, and they saw him again and heard his voice in the young man. Nero had the modesty and grace that befit a prince, qualities which seemed still more appealing because they knew the danger he stood in from the hatred of Sejanus.

16. About this time Tiberius spoke in the Senate[18] of the choice of a high priest of Jupiter to replace Servius Maluginensis, deceased, and of the need for introducing amendments to the law. The old custom was to name three candidates, of noble birth and from parents married by the ceremony of confarreatio,[19] and to select from these. But the custom of confarreatio had fallen into disuse in all but a few cases, and so the field was more restricted than it used to be. He adduced several reasons for the change, notably that neither men nor women were now interested in the old rites, which moreover introduced difficulties of practice which they were anxious to avoid. Moreover, when a person became a high priest, he passed out of his father's control, while his wife passed into that of the high priest.[20] A decree of the Senate, or a new law, was called for: Augustus had set the example of mitigating some of the rigors of the old traditions to suit modern requirements. There was a discussion of the religious issues involved, and it was decided to make no change in the office of high priest, but a law was passed making the wife of a high priest subordinate to her husband for ceremonial purposes, while enjoying the same legal rights as other women in other respects. Then the son of Maluginensis was chosen to succeed his father. To add to the dignity of the priesthood and to serve as an inducement for persons to undertake these burdens, a grant of two million sesterces was voted for the vestal virgin Cornelia on being admitted to replace Scantia.

It was further decreed that Livia should sit among the vestal virgins when she attended the theater.

24 A.D. Consuls Servius Cornelius Cethegus and L. Visellius Varro

17. At the beginning of the year the pontifices—and the other priests following their example—included the names of Nero and Drusus in the public prayers offered up for the health of the Emperor. They were prompted not so much by affection for the young princes as by flattery: but too much flattery, in a degenerate society, may be as dangerous as too little. For Tiberius had never been overfriendly to the house of Germanicus, and on this occasion he could not endure that these youths should be placed on a par with his own venerable years. So the pontifices got a peremptory summons and the question, "Did you do this in answer to Agrippina's entreaties, or to her threats?" They replied that they took responsibility. Most of them were men of the highest rank, or Tiberius' relatives, and they got off with a light rebuke. But later, in a speech to the Senate, the Emperor delivered a warning against anyone who sought "to arouse ambition in these impressionable young minds by granting them honors before their time." Sejanus had pressed him to this, declaring, "The country is divided as though by a civil war: there are those who assert that they belong to Agrippina's party and there will be more if there are no countermeasures; the only cure for the growing discontent is to make a sharp example of one or two of the ringleaders."

THE CASE OF GAIUS SILIUS

18. This prompted an attack on Gaius Silius and Titius Sabinus. Both were endangered by their friendship with Germanicus. It was also fatal to Silius to have held a great com-

mand for seven years, to have won triumphal honors in
Germany, and to have been the conqueror of Sacrovir. The
greater his fall, the more alarm it would spread among the
others. Moreover, there were many who thought he added to
his own disfavor by lack of tact. He boasted unduly that his
troops had remained loyal while others turned to mutiny. "If
my legions had wanted to make a move," he would say,
"Tiberius' government wouldn't have lasted long!" The Emperor saw this as derogatory to his own position: benefits on
that scale he could never repay. And, in general, the good
services of others are tolerable only so long as they can be
reciprocated: pass this limit, and the dividend is not gratitude
but hatred.

19. Sosia Galla, Silius' wife, had also incurred the Emperor's disfavor because of her friendship with Agrippina. It
was therefore decided that Sabinus could wait, for this was
the couple that must be destroyed. The consul, Varro, was let
loose upon them, and under pretext of a paternal feud satisfied Sejanus' hatred at the cost of his own dishonor. The defendant asked for a brief delay, until his accuser should vacate
his consulship. Tiberius refused. Magistrates had the right of
proceeding against private individuals. The consul's powers
must not be impaired; it rested on his vigilance "to see that
the state came to no harm." This dressing of new tyranny in
archaic phrases was very typical of Tiberius.[21]

So there was much reciting of formulas to summon the
Senate, as though Silius were really being tried by due process
of law, or Varro a consul—or, indeed, Rome a Republic! The
defendant said nothing, or, if he tried to defend himself, made
no secret of whose enmity was oppressing him. The charges
against him were that he had known of the conspiracy of
Sacrovir but had failed to take action, that he had disgraced
his victory by avarice, and that his wife had shared his guilt.
They could not clear themselves on the charge of avarice, but
the whole case was conducted as though the charge were
treason. Silius forestalled an inevitable condemnation by
suicide.

20. There followed, nonetheless, a savage onslaught on his
estate. The provincial taxpayers got no redress; indeed, they
had not asked for any. But generous gifts by Augustus were
revoked, and every single claim of the imperial treasury was
pressed. This was the first time Tiberius had gone to such
lengths against another man's property. Sosia was exiled on
the proposal of Asinius Gallus, who moved that half of the
estate should be confiscated, and half passed to the children.
To counter this, Lepidus proposed a quarter for the accusers,

as the law allowed, and the remainder for the children. I have found this same Lepidus in those evil days to have been a wise and weighty man: he often succeeded in altering for the better the harsh actions of the sycophants. Moreover, he must have had discretion, for he never lost his influence and friendship with Tiberius. This leads me to doubt whether it is by fate and the destiny of our birth (as in other matters) that some encounter the sweet aspect of princes, and others their ruin. May there not be some scope for our own judgment to find a safe course, free from vaulting ambition and from hazard, and avoiding either dangerous intrigues or dishonorable parasitism? Messalinus Cotta, the equal of Lepidus in rank but very different in character, induced the Senate to pass a decree that magistrates in the provinces, though guiltless and not involved in the guilt of others, should nonetheless have to answer for their wives' misdoings as though for their own.

THE CASE OF PISO

21. A case was then opened against Calpurnius Piso, a man of high birth and independence of mind. I have told earlier how he openly proclaimed in the Senate that he was leaving Rome because of the machinations of his enemies; also how he had dared to brave the influence of Livia and drag Urgulania before the courts from her refuge in the palace. Tiberius took this equably at the time: but his was a mind that brooded over his wrongs; though the shock might have died away, the memory remained vivid. So Quintus Granius accused Piso of uttering treasonable remarks in private, adding to the charge that he kept poison in his house, and wore a sword when entering the Senate. This last charge was passed over as too atrocious to deserve credit. But on the others, and they were many, he was ordered to stand trial. His death— and how timely it was—meant that the case was never heard. The Senate also considered the case of Cassius Severus, who had been banished. He was a man of lowly origin and evil life, but an effective speaker. He had pursued so many enmities that the Senate, on oath, had banished him to Crete: even there, the same practices had earned him such a crop of hatreds, new and old, that he was stripped of his property, "deprived of fire and water,"[22] and left to end his days on the barren rocks of Seriphos.

PLAUTIUS SILVANUS

22. At this time the praetor Plautius Silvanus, for reasons unknown, killed his wife by throwing her down from an upper story. Taken before the Emperor by his father-in-law Apronius, he told a confused tale: he himself had barely roused from sleep; he did not know what was going on; his wife had killed herself . . . Tiberius at once went to the house, inspected the bedroom, and discovered indications that the woman had put up a struggle and been dragged to her death. The matter was referred to the Senate; but when a panel had been sworn, Urgulania, grandmother of Silvanus, sent her grandson a dagger. This was at once taken as a hint from the Emperor, conveyed through Urgulania's friendship with Livia. Silvanus, having first tried to kill himself with a sword, caused his veins to be opened. Later his first wife, Numantina, was acquitted on a charge of having caused her husband's madness through spells and philters.

AFRICA AND TACFARINAS

23. This same year saw the Roman people, at long last, delivered from the war with the Numidian Tacfarinas. Earlier, the Roman generals had ceased pursuing the enemy as soon as they thought they had done enough to earn triumphal honors. By now there were three laureled statues in Rome, and Tacfarinas still harried Africa. He was getting help from Mauretania, where King Ptolemy, the son of Juba, was youthful and indolent. Men were glad to escape his freedmen and their servile tyranny by going off to fight. Then, too, the king of the Garamantes received his stolen goods and helped his depredations; though he did not invade with an army, he sent light-armed guerrilla bands, who came from so far that their numbers were exaggerated. From the province of Africa, the penniless and desperate flocked to his standard, all the more readily because Tiberius—as though no enemy were left in Africa after the successes of Blaesus—had recalled the Ninth Legion. The governor, Dolabella, had not ventured to try to keep it, for he had more regard for the orders of Tiberius than for the hazards of war.

24. Tacfarinas had spread the rumor that other peoples

were attacking the Roman Empire, and that the Romans were gradually evacuating Africa. Those who remained could be overwhelmed if all who preferred freedom to slavery would join in the attack. His army reinforced, he pitched camp and besieged the city of Thubuscum. But Dolabella concentrated all his forces; using the terror of the Roman name, and the fact that the Numidians could never stand up to an infantry battle, he was able to raise the siege at the first attempt, and to fortify selected positions. Then the chieftains of the Musulamii who were working for rebellion were executed. The several expeditions which had already been undertaken against Tacfarinas had made it clear that it was impossible to catch a mobile enemy with a single heavily armed force. Dolabella therefore enlisted the help of Ptolemy and his subjects, and organized four columns under the command of Roman generals or military tribunes. Hand-picked Mauretanian officers led raiding parties: Dolabella had the general direction of all units.

25. News soon came in that the Numidians had encamped in a derelict fort called Auzea, which they had previously burned. It was a strong position because of the vast forests by which it was surrounded. But Dolabella at once launched a force of infantry and cavalry regiments in attack, keeping their objective secret. At dawn with the blast of trumpets and fierce cries of battle, they fell upon the barbarians, who were still half asleep. The Numidian horses were tethered, or grazing far afield. The Roman infantry was concentrated, the cavalry was properly disposed, all preparations for battle were complete. But on the enemy side there was universal neglect—no weapons, no order, no battle plan. Like sheep they were butchered or dragged to captivity. The Roman soldiers were infuriated by the toils they had had to undergo in search of an enemy who always refused to stand and fight. At last they could glut themselves with blood and vengeance. They spread the word through the ranks to make for Tacfarinas, whom they knew well after so many clashes; only by killing him could they end the war. Tacfarinas' bodyguard fell around him, his son was taken prisoner, and the Romans surrounded him on all sides. He rushed on their spears, and avoided captivity by a death which cost us many casualties. That brought hostilities to a close.

26. Tiberius refused Dolabella's request for triumphal honors. This was done to please Sejanus, and to avoid eclipsing the glory of Sejanus' uncle, Blaesus. This denial did nothing for Blaesus, and added to the reputation of Dolabella: with a smaller army he had managed to capture important prison-

ers, kill the enemy leader, and round off the campaign. He brought with him a deputation from the Garamantes, a spectacle rare in Rome. The tribe had been deeply disturbed by the death of Tacfarinas, but thinking themselves innocent, had sent to make peace with the Roman people. The services of Ptolemy in the war were duly recognized, and an ancient custom was revived: to do him honor, a senator was sent to convey an ivory scepter and a triumphal toga, as in the days of the Republic, and to salute him as king, ally, and friend of the Roman people.

ITALY. AN ABORTIVE SLAVE REBELLION

27. This same summer chance cut short a slave rebellion which was brewing in Italy. It was led by a certain Titus Curtisius, a former soldier of the Praetorian Guard. He began by holding secret meetings at Brundisium and in the neighboring towns. The next stage was to publish leaflets, openly calling on the country people from the remote hill pastures, and their half-savage slaves, to strike a blow for freedom.[23] But, as though by the intervention of heaven, three warships on patrol for the benefit of traders in the Adriatic put into harbor. Also in the district was the quaestor Cutius Lupus, who had charge of the ancient office of controller of the pasture lands. He disposed the men from the ships at strategic points and utterly shattered the rebellion in its earliest stages. Tiberius then hastily dispatched a strong force under the command of the tribune Staius, who conveyed the chief rebel and the other ringleaders to Rome. The city was in a state of alarm, due to the ever-increasing numbers of slaves, and the constantly shrinking total of freeborn citizens.

ROME. THE CASE OF THE SERENI

28. This same year produced a most dreadful instance of wretchedness and malignity. Two men came before the Senate. Both were called Vibius Serenus: the father was the defendant, the son his prosecutor. The father had been dragged back from exile, in a state of misery and squalor: now he was cast into chains, and his own son accused him. Spruce of dress and eager of countenance, the young man combined the roles of informer and prosecuting counsel. His father, he said, had

plotted against the Emperor, and sent agents to stir up rebellion in Gaul. Funds for this purpose had been given by the ex-praetor Caecilius Cornutus. Cornutus, worn out with anxiety, and thinking that prosecution was tantamount to a death sentence, killed himself. But the defendant did not lose heart. Shaking his fetters at his son, he called on the gods to avenge him. "Take me back into exile," he shouted, "where such things are unknown—and see that my son is punished in the end!" He stoutly maintained that Cornutus was innocent, though the false accusation had thrown him into a panic. "That will soon be seen," he said, "if you can find the others. You can't suppose I planned to murder the Emperor and start a revolution with only one accomplice?"

29. The prosecutor then denounced Gnaeus Lentulus and Seius Tubero. This was highly embarrassing for Tiberius. They were leading citizens and his personal friends: Lentulus was in extreme old age, and Tubero in bad health. They were at once freed from the charge. But the father's slaves were tortured, and their evidence weakened the case for the prosecution. By now the son's crimes had unhinged his reason. Terrified by popular threats, dreading prison or the Tarpeian Rock or the fearful punishment of a parricide,[24] he fled from Rome. But he was summoned back from Ravenna, and forced to proceed with the prosecution. Tiberius made no secret about a long-standing grudge he harbored against the elder Serenus. For, after the condemnation of Libo, Serenus had addressed a letter to Tiberius complaining that everyone's zeal had been rewarded except his own. He enlarged on this in terms much too impertinent for that arrogant ear, so quick to take offense. The Emperor paid him back eight years later. Even though the evidence of the slaves under torture had been unsatisfactory, he was able to find charges that related to the intervening years.

30. Senators then voted for the ancient punishment against Serenus, but Tiberius, to avoid ill-feeling, vetoed it. Then Asinius Gallus proposed that he should be exiled on Gyara or Donusa. This too he rejected, pointing out that those islands were both waterless. "If we grant a man's life," he said, "we must allow him the means of life." So Serenus was sent back to Amorgos. The suicide of Cornutus led to a proposal that the prosecution should not be granted a reward in cases where a man accused of treason killed himself before sentence was pronounced. It would have been carried, but the Emperor spoke sharply and with unusual openness in support of the accusers: "The law will be brought into contempt," he said, "and the country undone. Better cancel the laws than remove

their watchdogs!" So the informers, a class of men bred for the ruin of the state, and never checked by any form of punishment, received incentives to productivity.

ROME. THE CASE OF COMINIUS

31. But a modicum of relief was allowed to intrude into this endless round of tragedy. Gaius Cominius, a Roman knight, was found guilty of publishing a libelous poem about the Emperor. Tiberius acceded to the prayers of his brother (a senator) and pardoned him. This made all the more remarkable Tiberius' standing preference for harsh measures, knowing as he did a better way, and the reputation to be won by mercy. When he erred, it was not through lack of insight— not that there is any need of supernatural powers to decide whether the joy expressed at the acts of sovereigns is true or feigned. And indeed, although normally he spoke from a script and appeared to express himself with a struggle, Tiberius' own diction was easy and effortless in his lenient intervals.

THE CASE OF SUILLIUS

But when Publius Suillius, who had been a quaestor with Germanicus, was banished from Italy on a charge of having received a bribe during a lawsuit, Tiberius proposed the harsher punishment of deportation to an island, and did so with such heat that he took an oath to testify that it was in the public interest. At the time this was coldly received, but the behavior of Suillius on his return put it in a better light. For the next generation knew him as a powerful favorite, making long and profitable use of the friendship of the Emperor Claudius, but never to any good end. A similar penalty was inflicted on the senator Catus Firmius, who had falsely accused his own sister of treason. I have recounted how this same Catus entrapped Libo, and then turned informer to ruin him. Tiberius remembered this, and spoke against banishment, though on another pretext; he did not oppose expulsion from the Senate.

32. I am very conscious that a good deal of what I have related—and still have to relate—can only seem trivial, unworthy of being set on record.[25] But it would be wrong of anyone to set this book of mine alongside the earlier histories of the Roman people. Then, the historians were dealing with

great wars, cities captured, kings routed and taken prisoner. In internal affairs, they had the disputes of consuls and tribunes, land laws and grain laws, the struggle between the orders—all themes of ample scope. I labor in a narrow field, and shall reap no glory. Mine is the theme of a peace unbroken (save for petty wars), of a distressful country, and of an Emperor caring nothing about enlarging the Empire. Still, a certain profit is to be had from a close scrutiny of these petty events, unimportant though they seem at first sight. It is often from such as these that great issues arise.

33. All nations and cities must be held either by the people, by the aristocracy, or by a single man. Blends and compounds of these forms of government are easy to commend but hard to establish; if established, they seldom last. When the people held power, or under the sway of the aristocracy, it was worthwhile to study mob psychology, and how to control and guide it; or again, to have a thorough insight into the minds of the Senate and the nobility. This was how men gained the reputation for being wise, for understanding the spirit of the age. Now that conditions have changed, and public affairs at Rome are virtually under the control of one man, there is some point in the inquiry and report I have to offer. Few men have the intelligence to discern the good from the bad, the expedient from the harmful: most have to learn these lessons from the experience of others. Profit, then, it may afford; pleasure it can hardly give. Descriptions of new countries, the shifts of fortune in great battles, the deaths of famous generals—these are what grip a reader's mind, and bring him recreation. I have to recall harsh edicts, prosecution following on prosecution, false friendships, the ruin of innocent men, trials all ending in the same way. It is a plethora of monotony, and the reader can only balk. Again, criticism tends to spare the writer of ancient history; no one cares whether we praise the Roman or the Carthaginian armies more eagerly. But there are many descendants alive of those who suffered punishment or disgrace under Tiberius. Even when the families have died out, you will find men who regard an attack on vices which resemble their own as an attack launched against themselves. Glory and virtue arouse enmity; where the contrast is too obvious they seem to imply a rebuke. But to my theme.

25 A.D. Consuls Cornelius Cossus and Marcus Asinius Agrippa

34. This year saw the prosecution of Cremutius Cordus. The charge was a new one, then brought for the first time, for he was accused of having published a historical work in which Brutus was praised, and Cassius called "the last of the Romans." His prosecutors were Satrius Secundus and Pinarius Natta, clients of Sejanus. This, and the fact that Tiberius heard the defense with a scowl on his face, was fatal to the defendant. Having resolved to die, Cremutius Cordus spoke as follows: "Members of the Senate, it is my words that are under attack: I am innocent in deeds. Even my words were not directed against the Emperor, or his father, to whom the law of treason relates. I am accused of having praised Brutus and Cassius. Many have written their histories, none without commendation. Titus Livius, most eloquent and most trustworthy of historians, spoke of Gnaeus Pompeius in such terms that Augustus dubbed him 'Pompey's partisan'—yet their friendship was unaffected.[26] Scipio, Afranius, nay, Brutus and Cassius themselves, he wrote of as men of honor, not as bandits and parricides, as they are called nowadays. In the writings of Asinius Pollio they have a noble memorial; Messala Corvinus spoke of Cassius as 'my leader.' Both historians kept their wealth and honors to the end of their days. Marcus Cicero praised Cato to the skies. What was Caesar's answer, dictator though he was? To write an 'Anti-Cato,' as though appealing to a jury! The letters of Antonius, the speeches of Brutus, are full of abuse of Augustus, abuse false and fictitious: the poems of Bibaculus and Catullus contain many insults against Caesar.[27] Both the deified Julius and the deified Augustus tolerated the poets and spared their works. I hardly know whether to praise them more for their moderation or for their wisdom. Overlook an insult and it fades away: resent it, and you seem to admit its truth.

35. "I say nothing of the Greeks. With them not merely

159

liberty but license went unchecked; if there was any punishment, it was words for words. There has always been the utmost freedom to speak of those whom death has placed beyond the reach of favor or prejudice. Are Cassius and Brutus under arms on the field of Philippi, while I harangue the people to civil war? No, they are in their graves these seventy years; but as they are known from their statues, which even the victor has spared, so they still have a place in the records of history. Posterity accords every man the honor he deserves; if I am now to be condemned, men will remember me as they remember Brutus and Cassius." Then he left the Senate House, and starved himself to death. The Senate decreed that his books should be burned by the aediles, but they were hidden, and published later, and they survive. The more can one deride the fatuousness of those who suppose that a little brief authority can be used to quench the memory of generations yet to come. To attack genius is to fan the light of its authority to a brighter glow. Foreign tyrants and Roman imitators of their bloodiness achieve nothing but fame for their victims and disgrace for themselves.[28]

36. The whole of that year was such an uninterrupted round of prosecutions that on the very day of the Latin Festival, when the new city prefect, Drusus, was about to inaugurate his office, Calpurnius Salvianus came forward with an accusation against Sextus Marius. This drew a rebuke from the Emperor, and caused Salvianus to be sent into exile.

The inhabitants of Cyzicus were charged with negligence in maintaining the cult of Augustus,[29] also of using violence against Roman citizens. They lost their independence, which they had won in the war against Mithridates, when their own bravery, as much as the help of Lucullus, had enabled them to beat off a siege. Fonteius Capito, a former governor of Asia, was acquitted on charges of corruption. It appears that these had been falsely leveled against him by Vibius Serenus. Not that this damaged Serenus; indeed, the public hatred even served to protect him. The more unscrupulous a prosecutor was, the more unassailable his position. Only the humblest and least successful practitioners were ever brought to book.

37. It was at this time that the province of Further Spain sent a deputation to request that it should be allowed to erect a temple in honor of Tiberius and his mother, as had been done in Asia. Now Tiberius had always been steadfast in rejecting compliments, and he thought this a useful opportunity to refute gossip that he was becoming ambitious. He therefore addressed the Senate in some such terms as these:[30] "I am aware, gentlemen, that some have found me infirm of purpose in not refus-

ing the cities of Asia when they came before me with a like request. Hence I must vindicate my silence on that occasion and reveal my policy for the future. The deified Augustus did not refuse to allow a temple to be built at Pergamum in honor of himself and the city of Rome. I regard every deed and word of his as having the force of law, and was all the readier to follow the example he had sanctioned because my own cult was to be linked with a worship of the Senate. One such instance may be pardonable: to have my statue worshiped along with the gods in every province would be overweening arrogance. Moreover, the worship paid to Augustus will be diluted if there is indiscriminate flattery.

38. "I know myself, gentlemen, to be but mortal: the office I discharge is the office of a man. I am well content to occupy the first place among men, and to that I call you to witness, and ask posterity to remember. They will do justice in full measure to my memory if they pronounce me worthy of my ancestors, mindful of your interests, resolute in danger, and not afraid of unpopularity in the public service. Let these be my temples in your hearts, let these be my noblest and most lasting monuments. For if the memory of posterity turns to hatred, then memorials of stone are but neglected sepulchers. So I call our allies, the citizens of Rome, and the gods to witness to these prayers. May heaven grant me to the end of my days a peaceful mind, and a knowledge of what is due to gods and men. May the citizens of this Empire remember in kindly fashion, when I am gone, my deeds and my reputation."

In this verdict he persisted, rejecting, even in private conversation, any worship for himself. Some judged it modesty; others, self-distrust; and others argued that it showed a lack of spirit. "All the best of mankind," they averred, "have had lofty ambitions. So it was that Hercules and Liber among the Greeks, Quirinus and Augustus among ourselves, have won their way to heaven. The hopes of Augustus are more admirable than the doubts of Tiberius. A prince has everything else from the start, but a good reputation with posterity must be constantly worked for. To despise glory is to despise virtue."

MARRIAGE PLANS OF SEJANUS

39. Sejanus was by now unbalanced by too great success, and by the unbridled ambition of a woman, for Livilla was forever badgering him about the marriage which he had promised her. So he sent a memorandum to the Emperor: it was the

custom to put things in writing for him, even when he was in Rome. The gist of it was as follows:[31] "The indulgence of your father Augustus, and your own graciousness on many occasions, have accustomed me to bringing my hopes and prayers to the ears of my prince as readily as to those of the gods. I do not seek the glittering prizes, now or ever. I should much prefer to watch and work for the Emperor's well-being, like any common soldier. Yet I have gained the greatest of honors: I am thought worthy of marrying into the imperial family. This is whence my hopes arise. I have heard that Augustus, when thinking of his daughter's marriage, brought under review men of knightly rank. If, therefore, there is any question of a husband for Livilla, keep it in mind that your friend would gain only honor from the connection. I do not wish to lay down the burdens that have been imposed on me: if I can strengthen my house against the malignity of Agrippina, if I can afford protection of my children, that will be enough. If I can live my span of life under such an Emperor as yourself, I shall be satisfied and more."

40. Tiberius replied by praising Sejanus for his loyalty, and recounting—briefly—the honors he had given him, and asking for time to review the whole matter afresh. Then he returned a second answer. "Other people," he said, "only have to look to their personal interests: princes are placed otherwise, and must think first of the opinion of the public. So I have not used the stock answer—though it would have been easy—that Livilla can decide for herself whether to marry again after Drusus' death, or to go on living in his household, or that she has a mother and grandmother who can more readily advise her than I could do. I am going to be frank. First, Agrippina's enmity. If Livilla marries it will add fuel to the fire; indeed, it will split the imperial household in two. Even now, there is no containing these feminine rivalries, and they involve my grandsons in their contentions. What if this marriage intensifies the jealousy? You are mistaken, Sejanus, if you think you will be able to remain in your present position, nor will Livilla, the wife first of Gaius Caesar and then of Drusus, be content to grow old at the side of a Roman knight. Suppose I allowed it—do you think it would satisfy those who have seen her brother, her father, and our ancestors fill the highest offices of the state? You say you wish to retain your present status. But those officials and political leaders who force their way in upon you and consult you in everything are openly complaining, even now, that you have risen far above the proper status for a Roman knight, and have far surpassed the heights climbed

by any of my father's friends. They envy you, and their criticism reaches out to me.

"You say that Augustus seriously considered marrying his
daughter to a Roman knight. Is it so very surprising that, distracted as he was by so many cares, and clearly foreseeing on
what an eminence such a marriage would set a son-in-law, he
though of Gaius Proculeius and others noted for their lives of
retirement, men not involved in public affairs? If we are to
take account of Augustus' hesitations, the significant thing is
that he actually bestowed his daughter first on Agrippa, and
then on me.

"I have spoken openly, as your friend. I shall not oppose
what you and Livilla have decided. But I have schemes of my
own, additional ties to link you with me more closely. I say
nothing of them now. All I shall say is this: your qualities,
your devotion to me, render nothing beyond your reach. In
due course, I shall disclose them either to the Senate or the
people."

41. Sejanus took fright, not merely for his marriage, but on
graver issues. He wrote begging Tiberius to discount suspicion,
and disregard rumors and the enmity which was growing
against him. But it would diminish his power to shut out the
constant stream of visitors, while to admit them would be to
give a stick for his critics to use against him. So he turned his
mind toward persuading Tiberius to settle his residence in some
attractive place far away from Rome. Such a course would offer
many advantages. He could control, or largely control, audiences, and also letters to the Emperor, which would be conveyed by soldiers of the Guard. Then, as Tiberius settled into
old age and surrendered to the charms of his retreat, he would
be all the more ready to delegate official business. Meanwhile,
as Sejanus' crowds of visitors decreased, so would his unpopularity; by cutting down on the trappings, he would increase
the realities of power. So little by little he began to enlarge on
the tiresomeness of life in Rome, the swarms of people, the
crowds of petitioners, and to expatiate on the blessings of peace
and solitude, free from annoyances and intrigues, where one
could concentrate on essential business.

42. Tiberius was hesitating, but the trial of the able and
well-known Votienus Montanus made him the more anxious to
avoid meetings of the Senate. For there could be heard, both
with embarrassing frequency and to his face, remarks about
him which were both true and vexatious. For Votienus was
charged with making insulting remarks against the Emperor,
and one of the witnesses, the soldier Aemilius, repeated the
slander in all its details in his anxiety to prove the case. The

senators protested, but he went on obstinately. Tiberius was forced to hear the insults with which he was assailed in private, and was so shocked that he exclaimed, "I must clear myself, either now, or during the trial!" The prayers of his friends, and a general spate of flattery, barely sufficed to appease him. Votienus was convicted on a charge of treason. Tiberius seemed actually eager to substantiate his bad reputation for harshness to defendants. A lady called Aquilia, convicted of adultery with Varius Ligus, was punished by exile, though the consul-designate Lentulus Gaetulicus had only brought the prosecution under the Julian Law.[32] Apidius Merula was struck off the senatorial register for failing to swear obedience to the acts of the deified Augustus.

THE TEMPLE OF DIANA, AND OTHER PETITIONS

43. Then a hearing was given to deputations from Sparta and Messene about the right to the temple of Diana-in-the-Marshes. The Spartan case was that it had been consecrated by their ancestors and in their territory, and they cited historical sources and poems to that effect. But then it had been taken from them by Philip (II) of Macedon in the course of a war; later it was restored by judgments of Caesar and of Mark Antony. The Messenian claim rested on the ancient division of the Peloponnesus among the descendants of Hercules: their king had got the territory of Denthalia, in which the shrine stands. This fact was attested by inscriptions in bronze and marble. If poetry and historical sources were to be used as records, they had more and better on their side. The judgment of King Philip was not an act of arbitrary power, but based on the facts of the case: it had been confirmed by King Antigonus and by the general Lucius Mummius: the people of Miletus, called in as arbitrators, had made the same award: so recently, had the governor of Achaea, Atidius Geminus. Judgment was given for the Messenians.

The people of Segesta appealed for the restoration of the temple of Venus on Mt. Eryx, now in ruins with the passing of time. They recited the well-known story of its origin,[33] and Tiberius, delighted with the legend, undertook to pay for the restoration as a relative of the founder.

Next a petition of the people of Massilia came before the House. The example of Publius Rutilius served as a precedent, for he had been exiled from Rome and admitted to citizenship by Smyrna.[34] Following this, Vulcacius Moschus, exiled from

Rome and admitted to Massilia, had left his property to the Massilian state as though to his own country.

DEATHS OF THE YEAR

44. Among the distinguished men to die that year were Gnaeus Lentulus and Lucius Domitius. Lentulus had been consul, and won triumphal honors over the Getae; he had further won respect for the patient endurance of poverty, then for great wealth, honorably acquired and used with moderation. Domitius was the son of a father renowned in the civil wars: he had fought first for Antony, then for Octavian. His grandfather had died on the field of Pharsalus, on the republican side. Domitius himself had been chosen as the husband of the younger Antonia, Octavia's daughter.[35] He had led an army across the Elbe and made a deeper penetration into Germany than any of his predecessors.[36] For this he was awarded triumphal honors.

Another death was that of Lucius Antonius, of a famous but ill-omened house. His father, Jullus Antonius, had been put to death for adultery with Julia. Lucius was only a boy at the time, but Augustus, his great-uncle, sent him to Massilia, where his exile could be disguised as following his studies. But the Senate decreed him a public funeral, and he was buried in the mausoleum of the Octavii.

ATROCIOUS AFFAIR IN SPAIN

45. In this year a terrible crime was committed in Nearer Spain by a member of the uncivilized tribe of the Termestini. As the governor of the province, Lucius Piso, was traveling unescorted—for it was a time of peace—this man attacked him and murdered him with a single blow. He got away through the speed of his horse: then, reaching wooded country, he turned it loose and eluded pursuit in the steep, pathless terrain. But not for long. The horse was captured, and taken around the villages until they found who its owner was. He was arrested and tortured to make him give the names of his associates. But he called out loudly in his native language that it was useless to torture him—his partners could stand by and watch him, no smart or pain would ever drag the truth out of him. And the very next day, when they led him out to be tor-

tured again, he broke away from his guards, dashed his head against a rock, and expired immediately. The death of Piso was attributed to treachery on the part of the Termestini: it seems that he was redressing a misprision of public funds in a more stringent fashion than the barbarians could tolerate.

26 A.D.   Consuls Gnaeus Cornelius Lentulus Gaetulicus and Gaius Calvisius Sabinus

DISORDERS IN THRACE

46. In this year an honorary triumph was awarded to Poppaeus Sabinus for the losses inflicted on certain Thracian tribes. These peoples were mountaineers, accustomed to living hard, and violent in action. This disposition caused them to revolt, as also their objection to a system of conscription which took all their best warriors for the Roman auxiliary forces. Even their own kings they only obeyed when they felt like it. If they sent any contingents, it was under their own chieftains, and to be employed only in fighting their neighbors. Now the rumor was that their warriors were to be split up, mixed with other tribes, and sent to different places overseas.

But, before taking up arms, they sent a deputation to stress their loyalty and friendship to Rome. This would be maintained, so long as fresh burdens were not laid upon them. But if they were to be treated as conquered and enslaved, then they had weapons, young warriors, and the spirit to choose liberty or death. They pointed to their hill forts, perched on crags, where they had sent their parents and wives, and they threatened war—onerous, bitter, and bloody.

47. Sabinus returned a mild answer, while he was mustering his forces. But when Pompeius Labeo had joined him with a legion from Moesia, and King Rhoemetalces had sent native troops who remained loyal, he joined these to his own forces and marched against the foe. They were holding the wooded gorges, but when some of them rashly showed themselves on the open mountainside, the Roman commander attacked and scattered them. The barbarian casualties were not heavy, since they could easily withdraw. He therefore set up a fortified

camp, and occupied it with a strong force. His position was on a long, narrow, level mountain plateau which stretched to the nearest enemy fortress. This had a numerous garrison of Thracians, both fully armed and irregulars. Its bolder warriors were dancing and shouting before the ramparts (their tribal custom), and a picked body of archers were sent against them. They did very well at long range, inflicting numerous wounds without casualties to themselves. Then they got too close, and a sudden sortie drove them back upon a Sigambrian cohort, placed in support because they were always ready to encounter danger—and were a match for the enemy in dancing and the clashing of arms.

48. Then he moved his camp closer to the enemy. The loyal Thracians I mentioned earlier were left behind in the older fortifications, with free license to ravage, burn, and loot. A condition was, however, that looting must stop at nightfall, and that a safe and vigilant night be spent within the ramparts. For a while they obeyed this order; then they got reckless on booty and revelry. They failed to stand guard, gave themselves up to banquets and carousals, and stretched out on the ground, overcome with alcohol and sleep. The enemy observed their slackness. They organized two assault parties, one to attack the Thracian freebooters, and the other to assault the Roman camp. They did not expect to capture it, but hoped that in the noise and hail of weapons the Roman soldiers would be too concerned with their own danger to notice the other battle. They deliberately chose a night attack, to add to the alarm. The attack on the legionary rampart soon broke down. But the Thracian auxiliaries, lying by the ramparts or wandering about outside them, were thrown into panic by a single charge. They were slaughtered mercilessly—the more so because they were regarded as deserters and traitors, who had taken up arms to enslave their country and themselves.

49. The next day Sabinus drew up his army on level ground, hoping that his success the previous night would induce the barbarians to risk a battle. But they did not leave their hill forts and the surrounding heights. He therefore blockaded them by a number of redoubts which he had already begun to fortify at strategic points. A ditch and breastwork linked these together into a system four miles in circumference. Little by little he drew his lines tighter, to deprive the enemy of water and fodder. An earthwork was constructed to allow stones, spears, and firebrands to be hurled down on the enemy. But the worst of all their hardships was thirst. A single fountain only was left to supply a huge number of warriors and non-combatants. As is usual with barbarians, the horses and cattle

had been shut up with them, and were now starving for lack of fodder. Beside them lay the corpses of men who had died from wounds or thirst. The whole place was a shambles of blood, stench, and putrefaction.

50. To crown all their miseries came that supreme one—discord. One party wanted to surrender: a second to seek death by killing each other: yet a third wished to sell their lives dearly in a death-charge. This last proposal was opposed, not merely by the common people, but by an aged chief, Dinis, who knew from long experience both the might and the clemency of Rome. He urged that they should lay down their arms, the only course now open in their calamities. With his wife and children he was the first to surrender; his example was followed by the feeble in age or sex, and those who cared more for life than honor.

The young men were split between Tarsa and Turesis. Both were resolved to die free men: but Tarsa, calling for a speedy end making done with hopes and fears, showed the way by plunging his sword into his breast. Others followed him. Turesis and his followers waited for night to fall. The Roman general knew their plans. He strengthened forces in the outposts with reinforcements. A wild, stormy night was fast thickening. On the Thracian side there were savage cries, and then intervals of silence, so that the besiegers grew puzzled. Sabinus went around his men to encourage them, saying they must on no account let uncertain noises, or feigned inactions, give an opportunity for surprise. "Every man stand to his post!" he ordered. "Don't waste missiles on targets you can't see!"

51. Meanwhile, the enemy bunched and charged downhill. They hurled stones, sharpened stakes, and the limbs of trees against our rampart, and filled the ditches with branches, hurdles, and corpses. Some brought planks and scaling ladders, previously made, up to the turrets, grasping them and throwing them down, and getting to close quarters with their defenders.

The Romans pushed them back with spears and shield-bosses; they hurled down heavy spears, and the ammunition of the catapults. They had already won the victory, and would be signally disgraced if they lost now. For the Thracians, it was their last throw; the laments of their wives and mothers standing by spurred them to valor. The Thracians were emboldened by the night. The Romans were terrified: they struck out aimlessly, unable to tell friend from foe, thus inflicting unforeseen wounds on their own men. The echo from the mountain gorges caused some shouts to come from their rear: such was the confusion that the Romans actually abandoned a part

of their defenses as though there had been a break-in. But only
a very few of the enemy actually got inside. The rest, with all
their bravest men killed or wounded, were pushed back shortly
before dawn to their hill fort. Finally they were forced to surrender. The neighboring tribes voluntarily laid down their
arms. The early winter of the Haemus Mountains, in all its
savagery, rescued the others from defeat in battle or siege.

ROME. THE DISTRESS OF AGRIPPINA

52. At Rome, confusion reigned in the imperial house. The
first of the chain of events leading to the downfall of Agrippina
was the prosecution of her cousin Claudia Pulchra. Her accuser
was Domitius Afer. Recently praetor, he had had an undistinguished career, but would stop at nothing for the sake of
advancement. The charges were adultery with Furnius, attempting to poison the Emperor, and the use of witchcraft
against him. Agrippina, hotheaded as usual, rushed to Tiberius.
She found him sacrificing to Augustus, and that gave her her
cue. "It is hardly consistent," she exclaimed, "to sacrifice victims to the deified Augustus, and to persecute his descendants!
His divine spirit has not passed into these dumb statues: I am
its living embodiment: I spring from his divine blood! I wear
this mourning because I know my danger. Pulchra's prosecution is irrelevant. The sole cause of her ruin is that the foolish
woman has befriended Agrippina. She forgot Sosia Galla, and
how that was once her ruin, too!"[37]

This outburst drew from Tiberius' secretive mind one of its
rare pronouncements. Seizing hold of her he quoted in Greek
the line, "It is no injustice that you do not reign."[38] Pulchra
and Furnius were convicted. At once Afer took rank with the
leading orators of the day. He had shown his talents, and they
were supported by a remark of the Emperor's: "He is an orator
by right of nature." In prosecution and for the defense, he
was better known for eloquence than for incorruptibility. In
extreme old age he badly tarnished even his reputation for
eloquence: his mind grew enfeebled, but still he could not bear
to remain silent.

53. Agrippina was unappeased. Once when she was unwell
and Tiberius visited her, she had a long fit of silent weeping.
At last she came out with an embittered *cri de coeur*. "I am so
lonely! Help me to find a husband! I am still young, and marriage is the only solace for a virtuous woman. There are plenty
of men in Rome who would be honored to take into their home

the wife and children of Germanicus." The Emperor saw very clearly the political implications of her request. But he did not wish to seem either displeased or apprehensive, and returned no answer, though she pressed it repeatedly. This incident does not find mention in any of the historians. I came across it in the memoirs of her daughter, Agrippina the Younger (mother of Nero), in which she set down for her descendants the record of her own life and the fortunes of her family.

54. Reckless and distraught, Agrippina received a deadlier blow from Sejanus. In the guise of friendship, his agents warned her of an attempt to poison her; she must avoid the hospitality of her father-in-law. Agrippina never knew how to dissemble. Placed next to the Emperor, she sat speechless and impassive, her food untouched. Tiberius noticed this (or perhaps he was told). To put matters to the test, he praised a dish of fruit as soon as it was brought to the table, and handed some to his daughter-in-law. Agrippina's suspicions were aroused, she said nothing, and passed it to her slaves. Tiberius made no comment to her; but, turning to his mother, he remarked, "Small wonder if I have something unpleasant in mind for a woman who would make me out to be a poisoner!" This gave rise to a rumor that the Emperor did indeed mean to poison her, but did not dare to do so openly, and so was trying to find a secret method.

ROME. THE CONTEST OF THE CITIES OF ASIA

55. To quench this rumor Tiberius was assiduous in attending the Senate. He heard the cities of Asia arguing as to where his new temple should be erected, a case which took up several days. There were eleven contestants, not equally distinguished, but all equally zealous. There was not much to choose between them when they pleaded their own antiquity and their services to the Roman people in the wars with Perseus, Aristonicus, and other kings. Hypaepa, Tralles, Laodicea, and Magnesia were all eliminated as too unimportant. Even the people of Troy, though they claimed to be the mother-city of Rome, could find nothing to cite but their venerable antiquity. The claim of Halicarnassus was not dismissed out of hand: they urged that in twelve hundred years of existence they had never had an earthquake, and could build the temple on the living rock. The people of Pergamum—though in their own eyes this was their strong point—were felt to be sufficiently honored in having a temple of Augustus. Ephesus and Miletus seemed to have

enough on their hands in the cults of Diana and Apollo respectively. The final round was between Sardis and Smyrna. The people of Sardis produced a decree of the Etruscan League to claim kinship with them. For Tyrrhenus and Lydus, sons of King Atys, had divided up the nation as being too populous: Lydus had stayed in his ancestral dominions, Tyrrhenus had been allowed to found a new kingdom. The two peoples had taken their names from their kings, the Lydians in Asia, the Etruscans in Italy.[39] Later, the power of the Lydians had been further increased by the dispatch of colonists to Greece, whence the name of the Peloponnesus, from Pelops.[40] They also produced letters of Roman generals and treaties struck with us during the Macedonian wars. Finally, they spoke of their rich rivers, the temperate climate, and the fertile countryside around them.

56. The delegation from Smyrna spoke of their ancient origin, whether from Tantalus, son of Jupiter, or Theseus (himself of divine origin), or from one of the Amazons. Then they passed to the claims on which they placed chief reliance—their services to the Roman people, the dispatch of naval forces to our help, not merely in foreign wars but even in Italy—and the fact that they were the first to set up a temple to the city of Rome. This was in the consulship of Marcus Porcius Cato.[41] Rome was then a great power, but not supreme, for Carthage still stood, and there were powerful sovereigns in Asia. They were also able to cite the testimony of Lucius Sulla. When his army was in great distress owing to the severity of the winter and their lack of clothing, and when this was announced in the Assembly at Smyrna, all present immediately took off some of their own clothes and gave them to the Roman legions. So, when it came to a vote, the Senate preferred the claim of Smyrna. Vibius Marsus proposed the appointment of a supernumerary legate to Manius Lepidus, governor of the province, to be entrusted with supervision of the temple. The ex-praetor, Valerius Naso, was chosen by lot, since Lepidus modestly refused to make a choice of his own.

THE RETIREMENT OF TIBERIUS

57. It was at this juncture that Tiberius at last carried out his plan, long conceived and often postponed, of retiring to Campania. His pretext was the dedication of temples, to Jupiter at Capua, to Augustus at Nola. But he was firmly resolved to live far from Rome. In attributing his withdrawal to the ruses

of Sejanus I am following the general opinion of historians. But he lived in the same seclusion for six years after Sejanus' death, so that I sometimes wonder whether the cause did not rather lie in Tiberius himself. His deeds made his cruelty and lusts conspicuous; geography might do something to hide them. Then again, some thought that he grew ashamed of his bodily deformities in his old age. For he was very thin, stooped in spite of his height, and was completely bald: moreover, his face was covered with boils and often plastered with ointments. At Rhodes he had grown accustomed to avoiding company, to taking his pleasures in secret. Again, it is said that it was his mother's overbearingness that drove him away, for he was unwilling to make her the associate of his power yet unable to get rid of her, since that power itself had been her gift to him. Augustus had hesitated whether to place Germanicus, his great-nephew and universally beloved, in power at Rome. But he gave way to his wife's entreaties: Germanicus was adopted by Tiberius and Tiberius by Augustus. Livia was always taunting him with her services—and demanding payment.

58. He left Rome with a very scanty retinue. There was one senator of consular rank, Cocceius Nerva (a distinguished lawyer) and (apart from Sejanus) one knight of some standing, Curtius Atticus. The rest were mere scholars—Greeks most of them—whose conversation he found amusing.[42] Astrologers said that Tiberius' departure from Rome coincided with such a conjunction of the planets that he could never return. This caused disaster to many men, who prophesied a speedy end for him and noised it abroad. They failed to foresee the extraordinary issue—that for eleven years he would deliberately absent himself from his country. It was soon apparent how thin is the dividing line between true prediction and falsehood, and how deep the obscurity which veils truth. That he would not return to the city was an authentic prophecy; but of its concomitants they knew nothing. For he was often in the surrounding country, and on the coast, and even approached the very walls of Rome. And he lived to a ripe old age.

ACCIDENT AT SPELUNCA

59. These idle rumors were accentuated by a chance occurrence which brought Tiberius into grave danger, at the same time giving him reason for increased confidence in the loyalty and friendship of Sejanus. He was dining in a natural cave at a villa called Spelunca,[43] between the coast of Amyclae and

the hills of Fundi. Suddenly the rocks at the entrance of the cave collapsed, and several of the attendants were buried. This caused a general panic, and the guests at the dinner rushed out. Sejanus, on hands and knees, covered the Emperor against falling rocks, and was found in that position when soldiers came in to the rescue. This increased his power: though he urged to disastrous courses, his advice carried the weight of one who was personally disinterested.

He now began to assume the role of a judge against the children of Germanicus. *Agents-provocateurs* were found to play the part of accusers. They concentrated on Nero Caesar, next in line to the throne. The young prince bore himself modestly enough, but not always with the circumspection demanded by his situation. For his freedmen and dependents, avid for power, kept on urging him to a display of energy and confidence. "That is what the Roman people want," they exclaimed; "so does the army. Sejanus will never dare to oppose you. He thrives now on the passivity of an old man and the diffidence of a young one!"

60. When he listened to such observations, Nero had no thought of disloyalty. But he did let fall some remarks which were imprudent and tactless. Instantly, the men set to watch him reported them, in an exaggerated form, to Tiberius. Nero got no chance to defend himself. Then he began to find different reasons for anxiety. People would avoid meeting him, or turn away when he had greeted them, or begin a conversation and break it off. Sejanus' partisans stood by and jeered. Tiberius' face wore a scowl—or a false smile. Whether the young man spoke or kept silent, he looked guilty. His very nights were dangerous: every sleepless night, every dream, every sigh, was carried by his wife (Julia) to her mother, Livilla, and by her to Sejanus. The latter even won over Nero's brother, Drusus Caesar, to his side, holding out to him the hope of supreme power if he could get his elder brother out of the way—"and he is already slipping." Drusus was hot-tempered, greedy for power: he had another motive, besides the hatred usual between brothers—jealousy. For their mother, Agrippina, made Nero her favorite. But Sejanus' flattery of Drusus did not exclude plans for his future ruin. He had taken note of his headstrong character, and how it made him all the more vulnerable to evil designs.

61. Two eminent men died at the end of the year. Asinius Agrippa came of a family that was distinguished rather than ancient; his life brought them no disgrace. Quintus Haterius was of a senatorial family, and a famous orator in his day. The surviving specimens of his genius are not highly consid-

ered now. Dash, rather than attention to detail, was his strong point. Other men's painstaking, studious work lasts in the judgment of posterity, but the resounding, copious eloquence of Haterius went with him to the grave.

27 A.D. Consuls Marcus Licinius Crassus Frugi and Lucius Calpurnius Piso

CATASTROPHE AT FIDENAE

62. This year was marked by an unforeseen calamity, in which the loss of life was on the scale of that of a great war. It began, and was over, in an instant of time. A certain Atilius, a freedman by descent, constructed an amphitheater at Fidenae for the holding of gladiatorial shows. He failed to build it on solid ground, and its superstructure was made of wood and insecurely fastened—the kind of negligence to be expected from a man who undertook the work, not as a generous benefactor or a candidate for office, but merely from the sordid motive of profit. Devotees of gladiatorial shows flocked there in immense numbers, deprived as they were of their pleasures under Tiberius. It was at a convenient distance from Rome, and it attracted crowds of both sexes and all ages.[44] This led to worse disaster. For, when the huge structure was filled to capacity, it suddenly burst asunder: part of it collapsed inward, part outward, and it dashed headlong or buried vast numbers of human beings, spectators and bystanders alike. Those who died at the outset of the disaster did at least escape the worst agonies (apart from those of violent death). Much more pitiable was the lot of those whose bodies were mutilated but who did not die immediately. They knew their wives and children were there, too; they saw them by day and heard their groans at night. As the news spread, people rushed to the spot, stricken with grief for a brother, a relative, or a parent. Even those whose friends or relatives had left Rome for some other reason were filled with alarm. Since the identity of the victims of the disaster was not yet known, uncertainty made apprehension yet more widespread.

63. When they began to clear away the debris, there was a

rush to embrace and kiss the bodies of the dead. Quarrels broke out, in cases where features were no longer recognizable but identities had been mistaken because of likeness of age or physique. Fifty thousand people[45] were crushed to death or mutilated in this catastrophe. The Senate passed a decree enjoining that for the future no one should give a gladiatorial show unless possessed of a capital of at least 400,000 sesterces, nor should an amphitheater be built unless on a site of proven solidity. Atilius was condemned to exile. After the disaster, the nobles threw open their houses, and medical attention and first aid were freely provided. Gloomy as the city was through these days, it bore some resemblance to the good old times, when after great battles the wounded were given help and attention.

THE GREAT FIRE AT ROME

64. Scarcely had this calamity faded from mind, when the city was assailed by a fire of exceptional severity, which ravaged the entire Caelian Hill. Men began to say that it was an ill-omened year, and to find reasons for their afflictions—for the mob must have a scapegoat—in the Emperor's decision to leave Rome. But Tiberius, making grants available in proportion to the loss incurred, nullified their complaints. For this he was thanked by the leaders of the Senate, and gained credit with the people, especially since it was all done without the intercession of friends or thought of reward. Indeed, this generosity often extended to complete strangers, responding to the invitation to apply. There was a feeling that the Caelian Hill should henceforward be known as the Hill of the Emperor, since the only thing to escape the conflagration was a statue of Tiberius, which stood in the house of the senator Junius. It was recalled how the same thing had happened to the statue of Claudia Quinta: twice it escaped the fury of the flames, and was then dedicated by our ancestors in the temple of Cybele. Obviously the house of the Claudii was dear to the gods, and a cult should be established in a place where heaven had shown such a mark of respect to the Emperor.

65. It may not be out of place to recall that the ancient name of this hill was the Hill of Oaks, from that tree growing there in great numbers. It received the appellation Caelian from Caeles Vibenna, the Etruscan leader who came as an ally and received a grant of land from Tarquinius Priscus—or from some other king, for accounts differ on this point. But on the rest of the tradition there is no ambiguity—his large

forces settled on the flat ground, so close to the Forum Romanum, and from these immigrants the Vicus Tuscus gets its name.

ROME. THE FLOOD OF PROSECUTIONS UNABATED

66. Thus the zeal of the nobility and the generosity of the Emperor were some comfort in that time of disasters. But the flood of prosecutions continued daily to rise; there was no alteration of that savagery. Varus Quintilius, for all that he was wealthy and the Emperor's kin, was assailed by Domitius Afer, who had secured the condemnation of his mother Claudia Pulchra. No one felt surprise that a man who had long been indigent, and had but recently acquired dishonest gains, should use them badly for a fresh round of crimes. But it was astonishing to find Publius Dolabella abetting him as an informer: he came of noble ancestry, was closely related to Varus, and was a traitor to his own blood and class. But the Senate resisted the attack and resolved that they must wait for the return of the Emperor—that was the only refuge available against the pressing disasters of these years.

TIBERIUS AT CAPRI

67. By now Tiberius had completed the dedication of the temples in Campania. An imperial decree forbade any interruption of his privacy, and soldiers were posted to prevent the local townsfolk gathering in crowds. But he had a profound distaste for the cities and towns of Campania, and indeed for the mainland itself. So he withdrew to Capri, an island situated about three miles from the farthest headland of the Sorrento promontory. It was, I suppose, its privacy that was the chief attraction. There are no harbors on the seas that surround it: even small vessels can scarcely approach; no one can land without the guards being aware. It has a temperate climate. The winters are mild because a range of hills gives protection from the winds: it is delightful in summer, facing the west wind, and with the open sea all round. It looks out on a most beautiful bay—beautiful, that is, before the eruption of Mt. Vesuvius changed the face of the landscape.[46] Report has it that Greeks settled in the district, and that Capri was inhabited by the Teleboi. At this time, however, Tiberius took up residence in twelve great villas, each with a name of its own.[47]

As once he had been zealous for public affairs, so now he focused his energies on his peculiar vices, on that leisure of evil import. He retained, however, his propensity for suspicion and credulity. Sejanus had encouraged these qualities, even in Rome: now he made no secret of the plots he was preparing against Agrippina and Nero Caesar. Soldiers attached to them reported every messenger, audience, or secret plan, as accurately as though writing a history. Some even advised them to flee to the armies in Germany, or else to grasp the image of Augustus in the Forum at the busiest hour of the day, and implore the help of the Senate and people. This advice they rejected; but it was held against them as though they had adopted it.

28 A.D. Consuls Gaius Junius Silanus and Publius Silius Nerva

ROME. THE DEATH OF TITIUS SABINUS

68. The year had an evil beginning, for Titius Sabinus, a distinguished Roman knight, was dragged off to prison because of his friendship for Germanicus. He had, in fact, never failed in his attentions to Germanicus' wife and children: a constant visitor at their house, a faithful attendant in public, he was the only one of all Germanicus' many friends to remain loyal. With the better sort this earned him praise; the wicked hated him. Latinius Latiaris, Porcius Cato, Petilius Rufus, and Marcus Opsius (all ex-praetors) attacked him. They all wanted the consulship: this was to be had only through Sejanus: the price for Sejanus' backing was through crime, and crime alone. So they decided that Latiaris, who had some acquaintance with Sabinus, should concoct a plot against him, and the rest would be witnesses; then the accusation could be launched. Latiaris began with some casual remarks, then began to praise Sabinus' constancy: unlike others, he had stood by a once flourishing house in the hour of its distress. He spoke with respect of Germanicus, with pity of Agrippina. In disaster men's minds soften. Sabinus burst into tears and laments. Latiaris egged him on. He boldly attacked Sejanus for his

cruelty, arrogance, and ambition, and did not refrain from criticism of Tiberius. They had talked of forbidden topics, and this seemed a bond of close friendship. Sabinus sought Latiaris out, came often to visit him, told him all his troubles, as though to a friend he could trust.

69. The four men I have named now began to consult on how to give wider publicity to the affair. The place they met in must seem to be private. If they stood behind closed doors, there was a risk of being seen, or overheard, or of some chance detection. So these three Roman senators squeezed themselves in between the roof and the ceiling—an ignominious hiding place for a detestable trick—and put their ears to chinks and cracks. Meanwhile, Latiaris had met Sabinus in the street. Pretending to have fresh news to impart, he took him home and into the bedroom; there he poured out a flood of past and present grievances—they were in abundant supply—and added some new terrors for good measure. Sabinus joined him, and at greater length; for once these pent-up feelings find expression, there is no holding them. Now the accusation had made headway. The four conspirators wrote to Tiberius, explaining the nature of the trap and exposing their own infamy. Never had Rome been more anxious and panic-stricken. People refused to talk, even to their own kin: all meetings and conversations were avoided: they shunned the ears of friend and stranger alike. Walls and ceilings—dumb things though they are—came under suspicion.

70. In the course of a letter read in the Senate on the first of January, Tiberius, after the formal New Year's greetings, took up the subject of Sabinus. Saying that he had suborned some of the Emperor's freedmen and plotted against his life, he demanded vengeance in no uncertain terms. The Senate were not slow to respond. Sabinus was condemned and dragged away, crying out (as well as he could for the cloak over his head and the noose round his neck)—"This is the New Year sacrifice, and the victims are for Sejanus!"[48] But wherever his eyes were turned or his words directed, there was panic and solitude—streets were emptied, fora deserted. But then others trickled back and displayed themselves, alarmed that they had shown alarm. "Will there ever be a day free of punishments," they whispered, "if noose and chains are present on a day when custom forbids even a profane word? Tiberius has deliberately incurred this odium. It is carefully designed to show beyond any doubt that these new magistrates, when they open the shrines and altars, are also opening the execution cells."

A second letter from the Emperor thanked the Senate for

punishing a public enemy, saying that he had reason to believe that his life was in danger, that certain enemies were plotting against him. No names were mentioned, but it obviously pointed at Nero Caesar and Agrippina.

71. Were it not my plan to relate events under the year in which they happened, I should take great pleasure in anticipating, and recounting the grisly ends to which Latiaris, Opsius, and the rest of these miserable criminals came—both under Gaius Caesar and under Tiberius. For Tiberius always protected the accomplices of his crime against attack from others, but he frequently grew tired of them himself. Then, when new recruits for villainy enrolled themselves, their burdensome predecessors would be liquidated. But there will be a time to recount the punishment of these and other evildoers.

Asinius Gallus—of whose children Agrippina was an aunt—now begged the Emperor to bring his fears to the Senate, and have them removed. Now, among what he was pleased to call his virtues, Tiberius took particular pride in dissimulation. He greatly disliked disclosing what he had suppressed. But Sejanus soothed him down—not, of course, out of any love for Gallus but to give the Emperor's procrastination time to take effect. He knew very well that Tiberius reached decisions slowly: but once flash-point was reached, ominous words were soon followed by terrible deeds.

The younger Julia[49] died at this time. A granddaughter of Augustus, she had been banished for adultery to the island of Trimerum, off the coast of Apulia. There she had endured twenty years of exile, sustained only by the help of the Empress Livia. The Empress had secretly ruined her stepdaughter's family, in their good days: now she was able to make a public display of benevolence toward their ruin.

GERMANY. REVOLT OF THE FRISII

72. In this year rebellion broke out among the Frisii,[50] a people who live east of the Rhine. Roman greed rather than Frisian disloyalty was the cause. Drusus Caesar had imposed on them a moderate tribute—for they were an indigent people—no more than a supply of hides for the commissariat of the army. But no one had prescribed the quality or dimension of these hides, until Olennius, a former first-rank centurion, declared that the hide of the wild ox was the standard required.[51] Other peoples would have found this hard to meet; for Germans it was intolerable. Their forests may be full of

huge wild beasts, but their domesticated cattle are small. So
the Frisii lost first their cattle, then their lands; finally, the persons of their wives and children were taken and sold into
slavery. Infuriated, they sent in complaints: there was no
redress. Now they sought refuge in arms. The soldiers who
came to collect the tribute were seized and hanged on the
gibbet. Olennius escaped the hostile tribesmen by taking refuge
in a fort called Flevum, where a powerful force of Roman and
auxiliary troops guarded the Atlantic coast.

73. As soon as Lucius Apronius, governor of Lower Germany, heard this news, he called for task forces from the
legions in Upper Germany. Strengthening them with picked
auxiliary units, cavalry and infantry, he brought the combined
forces down the Rhine against the Frisii. The fort was no
longer under siege, and the Frisii had gone to protect their own
tribal territory. So causeways and bridges were constructed
over the nearer estuaries, to allow the crossing of heavy units.
Fords were discovered, and a cavalry squadron of the Can-
ninefates, together with German infantry units serving in the
Roman force, was sent to surround the enemy. But the Frisii,
in battle order, routed the auxiliary cavalry and the legionary
cavalry sent to their support. Then three German infantry
units went into action, then two more: after an interval, the
auxiliary cavalry followed. If their assaults had been coordi-
nated, they would have been strong enough for their objective: entered piecemeal, they failed to rally the routed cavalry
and caught the infection themselves.

Then the remnants of the auxiliaries were put under the
command of Cethegus Labeo, commander of the Fifth Legion.
He found his troops in such disorder and the situation so
critical that he hastily sent messengers to ask for substantial
reinforcements from the legions. The men of the Fifth, rushing
ahead of the others, drove off the enemy after a stiff engagement and rescued the auxiliary infantry and cavalry, suffering
from wounds and exhaustion. But the Roman general failed
either to chastise the enemy or bury the dead, although many
senior legionary and auxiliary officers, as well as centurions
of note, were among the fallen. Deserters reported that in
fighting prolonged to the next day, nine hundred Romans were
massacred in the Grove of Baduhenna;[52] another body, four
hundred strong, having occupied the farm of the discharged
soldier Cruptorix, had killed each other because they were
afraid of treachery.

74. The Frisii gained a great name among the Germans by
this action. Tiberius concealed our losses: he was not anxious
to appoint a commander for a campaign. Nor was this a time

when the Senate was greatly concerned over reverses on distant frontiers. They had their troubles nearer home, and sought to remedy them by flattery. Though meeting for other business, they passed a decree to erect an Altar to Mercy and another to Friendship, both flanked by statues of Sejanus and Tiberius. Both men were entreated to allow themselves to be seen. But they came neither to Rome nor to its neighborhood: it seemed good enough to leave Capri and hold audiences on the nearest part of Campania.

There flocked the Senate, knights, and a good part of the common people, all anxious to pay court to Sejanus. He had made himself hard to reach: it could only be done by intrigue and entering into his plans. It is well known that his arrogance throve on this open display of sycophancy. In Rome, crowds are an everyday occurrence, and in so great a city a man's business is not obvious. But in Campania, crowded together in the fields on the shore, men endured by day and night the favor or the insolence of his doorkeepers. Then even this fell under ban, and they returned to Rome, some panic-stricken because he had not deigned either to see or to speak to them, others elated—mistakenly, for a tragic end was in store for their ill-omened friendship.

ROME. MARRIAGE OF AGRIPPINA THE YOUNGER

75. Meanwhile, Tiberius had personally bestowed his grandniece Agrippina, daughter of Germanicus, on Gnaeus Domitius. Now he decreed that the wedding should take place in Rome. Domitius had been chosen for his ancient lineage and for his kinship with the Caesars: Octavia was his grandmother, and through her he could claim Augustus as his great-uncle.

BOOK V (A Fragment)

29 A.D. Consuls Gaius Fufius Geminus and Lucius Rubellius Geminus

ROME. THE DEATH OF THE EMPRESS LIVIA

1. Both the consuls of this year bore the name of Geminus. It saw the death of the Empress Livia, in extreme old age.[1] A Claudian by birth, adopted into the Julian and the Livian houses, she belonged to the highest rank of the aristocracy. Her first marriage (by which she had children) was with Tiberius Nero, who fled from Rome at the time of the Perusian War and returned after the treaty between Sextus Pompeius and the Triumvirs.[2] Then Octavian, inflamed by her beauty, took her away from her husband, whether by her consent or not. So precipitately did he act that he did not wait for the birth of her child, but took her into his own house, pregnant by another man. She bore no more children; the marriage of Germanicus and Agrippina gave her a blood relationship to Augustus, and they had great-grandchildren in common. She preserved the chastity of her home with the strictness of an earlier age, save that the ladies of that day would not have approved of her affability. A demanding mother, she was a compliant wife. In her, her husband's craft and her son's dissimulation met their match. Her funeral was undistinguished, and it was long before the terms of the will were carried out. The funeral laudation was delivered by her great-grandson Gaius Caesar, the future Emperor.

ROME. THE REIGN OF TERROR

2. Tiberius did not attend the last rites for his mother; he did not even interrupt his pleasures on her account. In a letter to the Senate he pleaded the excuse of important business, and, with a show of modesty, deprecated the honors which the Senate had lavishly proposed for her. Of these, a few only were accepted, and any decree of divine honors was expressly forbidden. "This was her wish." In this very letter there was a criticism of "petticoat influences"—an indirect attack, this, on the consul Fufius. He had owed his rise to the friendship of the Empress, and indeed he had those qualities which women find attractive. He was witty, too, and was given to passing cutting remarks at the expense of Tiberius. Such things linger long in the memories of the great.

3. From this time on despotism became incessant and absolute. So long as the Empress lived, there had been some refuge: Tiberius never outgrew a feeling of respect for his mother, and even Sejanus did not dare to oppose her authority. But now—like horses taken off the rein—they were both free for a headlong gallop. A letter was sent attacking Agrippina and Nero Caesar: the popular belief was that it had been held up by the Empress: certainly it was read in the Senate immediately after her death. It was couched in terms of studied harshness. It made no complaints against Nero of conspiracy or revolutionary designs, merely of homosexuality and unnatural practices. Against Agrippina there was nothing so damning—simply a complaint of impertinent language and a froward temper. There was a panic-stricken silence in the Senate. Then—for at a time of public calamity there are always individuals who see a way to win favor for themselves—a few senators (who could do themselves no good by honorable courses) demanded that a motion be put. Cotta Messalinus was primed with a savage proposal. But the other leading members and the magistrates still hesitated: the Emperor had certainly made a harsh attack, but had left his real objects in doubt.

4. There was in the Senate a certain Junius Rusticus, appointed by Tiberius to write up the minutes of the Senate,[3] and therefore credited with insight into his private thoughts. Either through the agency of fate—for he had never previously shown any signs of courage—or by some misguided cunning, which led him to forget the imminent dangers in his dread of un-

certain hazard, this man intruded himself among the doubting senators. He advised the consuls not to put a motion. "A little weight," he repeated, "will tip the balance when great issues are at stake. Sometime the old gentleman might regret the destruction of the house of Germanicus."

Meanwhile the people gathered round the Senate House, bearing in their hands the effigies of Agrippina and Nero. They professed loyalty to Tiberius, but loudly proclaimed that the letter was a forgery, for the Emperor would never plan the destruction of his own house. So no terrible action was taken on that day. Moreover, leaflets under the names of men of consular rank passed from hand to hand, purporting to be resolutions they had drafted against Sejanus. Their numerous authors, being themselves anonymous, were able to give free rein to their imaginations. Sejanus was drawn into a passion, and had ample material for denunciation. "The Senate," he cried, "has made the Emperor's complaint look ridiculous. The people are disloyal, they are hearing revolutionary speeches and reading forged decrees of the Senate; the next step will be a resort to arms. What is to stop them choosing, as leaders and generals, the very persons whose images they have followed like banners to rebellion?"

5. So Tiberius set out again his denunciation of his grandson and his daughter-in-law. An edict rebuked the people. The Senate received a complaint that the action of one of their number had exposed the imperial majesty to public insult. He demanded that the whole issue should be handled *de novo,* by himself. The Senate held no long debates. They could not pass the death sentence (that was in any case forbidden), but they protested that only the hesitation of the Emperor was holding them back from vengeance. . . .

(At this point the manuscript breaks off and the rest of Book V is missing. We lose the account of the death of Sejanus, a climactic episode on which Tacitus must have lavished all his powers—also of Tiberius' discovery of the poisoning of Drusus, and the death of Livilla.)

BOOK VI

(In the manuscripts, the gap at V: 5 is followed by six disconnected fragments below, generally regarded by modern editors as belonging to the [lost] early sections of Book VI. They refer to events following the fall of Sejanus. The numbering of the sections of Book VI here begins with the continuous narrative.)

SPEECH AND DEATH OF AN UNKNOWN SUPPORTER OF SEJANUS

Fr. 1. Forty-four speeches were delivered in the Senate on this theme.[1] In certain cases the motive was fear, in the majority, sycophancy . . .

". . . I thought that I could only bring either shame to myself[2] or obloquy on Sejanus. Fortune has now reversed, and he who once called Sejanus his colleague and 'son-in-law'[3] today forgives himself. All the rest, who once fawned upon Sejanus, now pursue him with criminal accusations. I do not feel capable of deciding whether it is a more miserable condition to accuse a friend or to be accused because of that friendship. I have no wish to test who is merciful, who is vindictive. I am a free man, my conscience is clear, and I shall anticipate my fate. Remember me, gentlemen, with happiness, not with sorrow. Add my name to the list of those who

185

have made a good end to escape from the calamities of our country."

Fr. 2. He spent part of the day with his friends: in talk and conversation if they wished to stay; bidding farewell if they wished to leave. There was still a great throng around him. Attention was riveted on his resolute countenance, and they thought the end was not yet. But suddenly he drew a sword from under his cloak and fell on it. Tiberius never attacked the dead man with charges or slanders, as he did so violently in the case of Blaesus.[4]

THE CASES OF VITELLIUS AND POMPONIUS

Fr. 3. The cases of Publius Vitellius and Pomponius Secundus were taken next. Informers had charged Vitellius with having proffered the keys of the treasury,[5] of which he was the controller, and the use of military funds, for purposes of sedition. Pomponius was accused by the ex-praetor Considius of friendship with Aelius Gallus, who, after the punishment of Sejanus, had taken refuge in his gardens, as the safest hiding place. The only help the two defendants had in their hour of danger was in the loyalty of their brothers, who stood bail for them.[6] Vitellius' case was constantly adjourned, and he found the alternation of fear and hope intolerable. Calling for a penknife (as though he wanted to write) he made a trifling incision of a vein, and died—a victim of his own infirmity of purpose. But Pomponius, a man of refined character and high intellectual powers, endured his adverse fortune patiently, and saw Tiberius into his grave.

THE FATE OF SEJANUS' CHILDREN

Fr. 4. It was next decided to proceed against Sejanus' remaining children,[7] although the anger of the mob was now diminishing, having been glutted by the earlier death sentences. So they were taken to prison. The boy knew very well what fate threatened him. But the little girl[8] was quite unsuspecting, and kept saying, "What have I done? Where are you taking me? I won't do it again! You could give me a smacking, like other children!" Contemporary historians say that, since it was thought unprecedented to carry out the death sentence on a virgin, she was raped by the executioner, with the rope at her side. Their necks broken, the corpses of these children were thrown on the Gemonian Stairs.

THE FALSE DRUSUS

Fr. 5. At this time Asia and Achaea were thrown into alarm by a rumor that was short-lived but explosive. This asserted that Drusus Caesar, son of Germanicus, had been seen, first in the Cyclades, then on the mainland. It was really a young man of the same age, whom certain of the Emperor's freedmen had pretended to recognize.[9] Their feigned support and the name of Drusus attracted others: Greeks are easily allured by anything novel or strange. A story was invented— and instantly believed—that he had escaped from prison, that he was going to his father's armies, that he would invade Egypt or Syria. The youth of the region flocked to join him, public support increased: he was optimistic and puffed up with vain hopes. But then the affair came to the ears of Poppaeus Sabinus, who as governor of Macedonia also had Achaea in his charge. True or false, he thought the matter should be nipped in the bud. Making full speed past the Toronaic and Thermaic gulfs he went by way of the Aegean island of Euboea, Piraeus (on the coast of Attica), then past Corinth and the Isthmus, and finally through the Ionian Sea to the Roman colony of Nicopolis. Here he learned that thorough cross-questioning had elicited from the young man that he was actually the son of Marcus Silanus: many of his adherents had deserted, and he had taken ship as though for Italy. Sabinus reported this to Tiberius, but I have failed to discover anything further about the origins or issue of the affair.

FEUD BETWEEN THE CONSULS

Fr. 6. At the end of the year there was a public display of the ill-feeling that had long been building up between the consuls. Trio, a skilled lawyer and a man apt to provoke enmity, criticized Regulus by hinting that he was sluggish in putting down the adherents of Sejanus. Regulus was not an aggressive man unless he was aroused: now he not merely refuted his colleague's accusation but brought him up for investigation as involved in the conspiracy. Many senators begged them to drop a feud which could only have a disastrous outcome; but they continued to be at loggerheads and breathing out threats until they laid down their office.

(End of Fragments)

32 A.D. Consuls Gnaeus Domitius Ahenobarbus and Lucius Arruntius Camillus Scribonianus

1. As the new consuls entered on their office, Tiberius crossed the strait between Capri and Surrentum, and coasted along the shores of Campania. He was uncertain whether to visit Rome—or, perhaps, having decided against it, wished to make it seem that he would. He made several landings in the vicinity of the city, and got as far as the Garden of Caesar, across the Tiber.[10] But then he sought again the crags of his sea-bound retreat, ashamed of the lusts and crimes which now dominated him as completely as though he were some Oriental despot. By this time, the children of Roman citizens were the object of his debauches: his lusts no longer sought for youth and beauty alone, but found titillation now in childish innocence, now in noble descent. It was then that new names had to be found for perversions hitherto unknown—*sellarii* and *spintriae*, descriptions suited to their obscene postures and pathic complexity. Slaves were appointed his pimps and procurers. They had rewards for prompt compliance, threats for recusancy. If a parent or relative offered resistance, they kidnaped the children and made them the victims of their own lickerishness, as if dealing with helpless captives.

2. In Rome, as though Livilla's misdeeds were newly known and insufficiently punished, savage resolutions were passed against her statues and her very memory. Sejanus' property was transferred from the public treasury to that of the Emperor—for what difference that might make. Men bearing the names of Scipio, Silanus, and Cassius moved these resolutions, in similar or identical terms of sycophancy.

Suddenly, Togonius Gallus[11] inserted his vulgar person into the company of these great names, and provoked general ridicule. He begged the Emperor to nominate senators from whom twenty should be chosen by lot to bear arms and protect his person whenever he entered the Senate House. He was taking literally the letter which requested the help of one of the consuls to permit Tiberius to go in safety from Capri to Rome. But Tiberius, with his usual mixture of the genuine and the absurd, solemnly thanked the Senate. He declared himself obliged to the Senate for their thoughtfulness. "But," he went on, "on what principle shall some senators be chosen, and others left? Shall the same men always serve, or will there be others from time to time? Will they be young men, or those who have reached the end of their careers, private individuals or holders of office? It will be an impressive sight when they gird on their swords at the entrance to the Senate House! Personally, I think life not worth living if I need arms to protect me." To Togonius himself the reply was lenient: it merely asked that the proposal be annulled.

3. But when Junius Gallio proposed that veterans of the Praetorian Guard should have the privilege of seats within the fourteen rows reserved for the knights, he got a very sharp rebuke. As though at a personal interview, the Emperor asked, "What has Gallio to do with soldiers? They receive their orders and get their rewards from the Emperor, and from him alone. Has Gallio discovered some principle which escaped the intelligence of the divine Augustus? Or is this satellite of Sejanus fostering discord and sedition—trying to subvert discipline under the guise of offering privileges?" Such was the reward Gallio gained from his readiness to please. He was expelled, first from the Senate, then from Italy. He chose the famous and delightful island of Lesbos for a retreat: but it was objected that it was far too good for him. So he was brought back to Rome and committed to the custody of the magistrates.

The same letter from Tiberius contained an attack on Sextius Paconianus, the ex-praetor, much to the delight of the Senate. He was a shameless evildoer, with a flair for the investigation of other people's private affairs. Sejanus had selected him for the setting of a trap for Gaius Caesar. When this became known there was a great outburst of hostility, and it was only by turning informer that he escaped death.

4. When he denounced Latinius Latiaris, accuser and accused together provided a heart-warming spectacle. This same Latiaris, as I have said,[12] was the chief agent in the destruction of Titius Sabinus—and he was now the first to pay for it. At this juncture Haterius Agrippa attacked the retired con-

suls. They had assailed each other, he said; why the present silence? Fear and complicity in guilt bound them together—but the Senate was bound to divulge what it had heard. Regulus said that he was awaiting a suitable time for retaliation, and would lay the matter before the Emperor. Trio said jealousy between colleagues and the indiscretions it had promoted were best forgotten. Haterius persisted, but Sanquinius Maximus, a former consul, begged the Senate not to add to the Emperor's cares by stirring up bitterness. The Emperor would see to what needed remedy. So Regulus was saved, and the downfall of Trio postponed. Haterius was a despicable creature. Effete with somnolence, lustful when awake, lethargy like his left no target for the Emperor's cruelty. Between his gluttony and his lusts he had time to plan the ruin of his betters.

5. Next, as soon as opportunity offered, there was an attack on Cotta Messalinus. His hand was to be seen in every savage proposal, and a grudge against him had long been mounting. He was accused of having called Gaius Caesar a homosexual, of having described a priestly banquet, given in honor of the Empress Livia's birthday, as a "funeral feast." Moreover, complaining about the influence of Marcus Lepidus and Lucius Arruntius, with whom he had a dispute over money, he had said, "The Senate will back them: my little man Tiberius will back me." All this was proved against him by leading senators: when they pressed the charge he appealed to the Emperor. Soon after came a letter from Tiberius, phrased as a defense of Cotta. It traced the beginnings of their friendship, recounted his many services, and ended by a request that words deliberately distorted, or let fall in the frankness of the dinner table, should not be manufactured into a charge against him.

6. The opening phrases of Tiberius' letter seemed significant. "What I am to write to you, members of the Senate, or how, or what not to write at this time—if I know that, may the gods destroy me with worse than the death I feel overtaking me every day!" So surely had his crimes and wickedness returned to torment him. Well did the wisest of philosophers[13] proclaim that, if we could look into the minds of tyrants, we should find therein bruises and lacerations, seared into the spirit, like blows on the body, by cruelty, lust, and evil designs. Neither Tiberius' imperial rank nor his secure retreat could prevent him from revealing his tortured heart and the penalties he had brought upon himself.

7. Next came an instruction to the Senate to take cognizance of Caecilianus, the senator who had played the chief

part in attacking Cotta. Against him was decreed the same punishment that had been inflicted on Aruseius and Sanquinius, the prosecutors of Lucius Arruntius. This was the greatest compliment Cotta ever received. Of high rank, but beggared by his excesses, and of evil reputation because of his bad conduct, a parity of vengeance had set him by the side of the impeccable attainments of Arruntius.

After this proceedings were begun against Quintus Servaeus and Minucius Thermus. Servaeus had been praetor, and a friend of Germanicus. Minucius, a Roman knight, had been the intimate of Sejanus but had never abused his position. Both aroused sympathy. But Tiberius attacked them as criminals of the most dangerous kind, requiring Gaius Cestius (the elder) to reveal in the Senate what he had written to the Emperor. Cestius took up the prosecution. Of all the calamities of that age this was the worst—that leading senators were willing to serve as the basest of informers. Some did it openly, more in secret. Suspicion rested equally on relatives and outsiders, on friends and strangers, on recent events and those forgotten by the lapse of time. Remarks let fall on chance subjects, in the Forum or over the dinner table, were brought up as charges. There was a competition to be first in denouncing a victim: in some cases this was in self-defense, but more often it was by a sort of contagion, as in an epidemic. Minucius and Servaeus both turned informer on being condemned. This involved two other men in the same fate—Julius Africanus, from the Santones tribe in Gaul, and a certain Seius Quadratus—whose family origins I have been unable to trace. I am well aware that the great majority of historians omit many of these trials and the verdicts. They find the sheer bulk of them bewildering, as at once too numerous and too affecting, and fear that a like satiety may overcome their readers. My own researches have brought to light many cases which seem worth recounting, though others have deliberately passed them by.

THE CASE OF MARCUS TERENTIUS

8. For example, a certain Marcus Terentius, a Roman knight, found himself accused of friendship with Sejanus. Others had (falsely) shrugged off this charge: he boldly accepted it. His plea to the Senate was in these terms: "In my situation, it might do me less good to accept the indictment than to deny it. But come what may, I shall freely declare that

I was a friend of Sejanus, that I sought to become so, and was delighted when I succeeded. I had seen him, with his father, as commander of the Guard. Later he had high office both in the army and in the city administration. His friends and relations were rewarded with dignities. Intimacy with Sejanus conferred influence with the Emperor: his frown was reason enough for fear and the suppliant's garb. I do not wish to name cases. At my personal risk, I speak for all of us who took no part in his last, criminal designs. In those days we gave our respect not to Sejanus of Vulsinii, but to a member of the Julian and Claudian house to which he was related by marriage—to your 'son-in-law,' Caesar, to your colleague in the consulship, to the man who acted as your adjutant in affairs of state. It is not for us to pass judgment on the man whom you elevated above all others, nor to ask why you did so. Heaven has placed you in charge of the highest issues—our glory is in our obedience. We see only what lies on the surface—who it is to whom you have given wealth and office, and a large license to protect or assail. And no one can deny that man was Sejanus. The motives of the Emperor are secret; research into them is forbidden, dangerous, and not necessarily rewarding. Gentlemen of the Senate, do not think of Sejanus' last day, but of his sixteen years of power. Even a Satrius or a Pomponius won our respect. We thought it a distinction to be recognized by his freedmen and porters. What?—you ask—does this defense hold good in all cases and without distinction? By no means. But let us see that the dividing line falls where it should. Treacherous designs against the state, plans to assassinate the Emperor, must be punished. But if we put an end to friendship and its obligations at the same time as you, Caesar, that should absolve us as well as you."

9. This was a courageous speech; it gave expression to what everyone was thinking, and its effect, together with their own criminal records, was to bring exile or death upon all who accused Terentius.

SEXTIUS VISTILIUS AND OTHERS

Next a letter from Tiberius attacked Sextius Vistilius (an ex-praetor and an intimate friend of his brother Drusus), whom he had promoted to his personal staff. Vistilius—whether rightly or wrongly—was charged with having attacked Gaius Caesar as a profligate. For this he was banished from the Emperor's table. With his senile hand he tried to open his veins: then he bound them up, and sent a note to Tiberius appealing for mercy. The reply was unrelenting, and he opened them again. Then—bracketed together—came a charge of high treason against Annius Pollio, Appius Silanus, Scaurus Mamercus, and Sabinus Calvisius. Vinicianus Pollio was included with his father. All were of high family, and some held offices of state. The Senate shuddered with apprehension—for who could claim to have no connection through friendship or kinship with all these distinguished men? But then, Celsus, who commanded a battalion of the city guard and was one of the informers, rescued Appius and Calvisius from their peril. Tiberius adjourned the other three cases for joint investigation by himself and the Senate. In so doing, he made some ominous comments on Scaurus.

VITIA

10. Even women were in danger. They could hardly be accused of political ambitions, but their tears spoke against them. Thus an old lady called Vitia, mother of Fufius Geminus, was put to death for having wept for the judicial murder of her son. This case was decided by the Senate. The Emperor showed equal cruelty in condemning two of his oldest friends, Vescularius Flaccus and Julius Marinus. Both had followed him to Rhodes and were his inseparable companions at Capri. Vescularius had been the go-between in the plot against Libo Drusus; Marinus had helped Sejanus to ruin Curtius Atticus. That their dirty devices had recoiled on their own heads caused particular pleasure.

A NATURAL DEATH

Yet at the same time, Lucius Piso, Pontifex Maximus, died a natural death—a remarkable occurrence in a man of his eminence. He had never voluntarily associated himself with any cruel measure: when necessity constrained, he had acted with moderation and wisdom. I have mentioned his father's censorship: he lived to be eighty years of age, and won triumphal honors in Thrace. But his chief claim to fame was the high degree of tact he had shown as prefect of the city: that office had only recently been placed on a permanent footing, and was highly unpopular.

THE OFFICE OF CITY PREFECT

11. In earlier times, kings or republican magistrates, before leaving Rome, had appointed someone to administer the laws and to act in an emergency. Thus the city would not be with no one in authority. Tradition says that this office was conferred on Denter Romulius by Romulus, and (later) by Tullus Hostilius on Numa Marcius and by Tarquinius Superbus on Spurius Lucretius. Later the consuls handled the matter: a fossil form of this is the custom whereby someone is appointed to take over the consul's office at the time of the Latin Festival.[14] In the civil wars, Augustus placed a Roman knight, Cilnius Maecenas, in charge of the whole population of Rome and Italy. Later, when he had won power, the numbers of the population and the delay which attended the operation of the law made him choose a man of consular rank to control the slaves and that part of the citizen body who are disposed to restlessness unless there is force to contain them. Messala Corvinus, the first to hold this post, resigned after a few days, not knowing how to discharge it. Then came Statilius Taurus, who fulfilled his duties admirably despite his great age. Next Piso held office for twenty years, amid universal approval. He was honored by a public funeral on the authority of the Senate.

THE ISSUE OF THE SIBYLLINE BOOKS

12. Next Quintilianus, a tribune of the plebs, raised in the Senate the matter of a book of sibylline prophecies,[15] which Caninius Gallus, a member of the College of Fifteen, wished to include as authentic. The matter was carried without a discussion. But Tiberius sent a letter containing a mild rebuke for the tribune, whose youth might excuse his ignorance of ancient custom. Gallus was severely censured: for, well versed as he was in ceremonial and procedure, he had brought up this matter on untrustworthy information and before a thinly attended meeting of the Senate.[16] This, too, without waiting for the opinion of the college, and without the officers of the college having read and pronounced on the poem. He further recalled how Augustus had named a day on which all such poems were to be deposited with the urban praetor, after which none were to remain in private possession. This was

because of the many false verses in circulation under the name of the sibyl. There had been a similar decree in the times of our ancestors, when the Capitol was burned during the Social War.[17] At that time, there was a general search for sibylline verses—whether their authors were one or many—throughout Samos, Ilium, Erythrae, and even Africa and Sicily and the Italian colonies. The pontifices were charged with the task of determining—so far as human power permits—which were true and which were false. With this precedent, the book in question was submitted to the College of Fifteen for their ruling.

DISCONTENT IN THE CITY

13. This same year the exorbitant price of grain all but led to a rebellion. For several days in the theater grievances were voiced in bolder terms than were usually directed toward the Emperor. Tiberius was highly incensed. He criticized the magistrates and the Senate for not using their authority to control the people: he enumerated the provinces from which he had collected grain, pointing out that this had been got in much greater quantity than under Augustus.

So a Senate resolution was drafted in terms of archaic stringency to rebuke the people, and the consuls lost no time in publishing it. That the Emperor kept silence was not, as he had hoped, taken as a sign of restraint, but as a token of arrogance.

MORE PROSECUTIONS

14. At the end of the year, Geminius, Celsus, and Pompeius, all Roman knights, succumbed to a charge of conspiracy. Geminius had been a friend of Sejanus, but that had been purely because of his excessive wealth and luxurious style of living—it had no political results. Julius Celsus, who was a tribune of the plebs, loosened the chain that bound him, put it around his neck, and broke his spine by throwing all his weight against it. Then Ruberius Fabatus was arrested: he seemed to have despaired of things at Rome, and to have fled to the mercy of the Parthians. Arrested in the Strait of Messina, and dragged back to Rome by a centurion, he failed to provide adequate reasons for setting out on his long voyage. Still, he remained alive—forgotten rather than forgiven.

33 A.D. Consuls Servius Sulpicius Galba and Lucius Sulla

ROME. MARRIAGE OF TIBERIUS' GRANDDAUGHTERS

15. Tiberius had long had in mind the choice of husbands for his two granddaughters, Julia and Drusilla, now of marriageable age. His final selections were Lucius Cassius and Marcus Vinicius. Vinicius was of small-town origin; he was born at Cales. His father and grandfather had been consuls, but the rest of the family were of knightly rank. He was a man of kindly character, and with an elaborate oratorical style. Cassius came from a Roman plebeian family, though it was ancient and had held high office. His father had brought him up on old-fashioned lines, though he himself found favor for complaisance rather than energy. Drusilla was bestowed on Cassius, Julia on Vinicius. They were the daughters of Germanicus. Tiberius reported the matter to the Senate, with some perfunctory compliments to the two bridegrooms.

Then he gave some rather casual excuse for his absence, and passed to more serious topics. He had made many enemies in the public service, and he now asked that Macro, commander of the Praetorian Guard,[18] and a few centurions should accompany him whenever he entered the Senate House. The Senate granted this privilege in the widest terms, with no stipulation as to the number or rank of the bodyguard. Even so, Tiberius never again entered Rome, much less a meeting of the Senate. Often he would follow devious routes to circle, and avoid, the city of his birth.

THE PROBLEM OF USURY

16. Meanwhile there was a spate of prosecutions against those who enriched themselves by usury, contrary to the law of the dictator Julius Caesar which controlled loans and land investments in Italy. It had passed into disuse, since private

profit is invariably preferred to the public good. This whole matter of usury was an evil of long standing at Rome, and a most prolific source of uprisings and enmities. Hence, even in an earlier and less corrupt society, attempts had been made to keep it in check. The earliest enactment, in the Twelve Tables, prescribes that no rate of interest should exceed 10 per cent (previously it had been set at the whim of the rich). Then came a bill of the tribunes reducing it to 5 per cent; finally interest was prohibited altogether. Frequent measures were passed in the Assembly of the People against evasions; but however often these were suppressed, marvelous ingenuity was exercised to revive them.

Now, however, the praetor Gracchus, who was in charge of the investigations, could only refer the matter to the Senate, since so many were imperiled. The senators, in dismay (for none of them were blameless), sought the Emperor's indulgence. He prescribed a period of eighteen months, to allow everyone to arrange his finances in accordance with the law.

A FINANCIAL CRISIS

17. The result of all this was a financial crisis. There was a simultaneous calling-in of all debts; moreover, in consequence of the numerous confiscations and forced sales, currency had become concentrated in the public and imperial treasuries. The Senate therefore decreed that all who lent out money should invest two-thirds of their capital in Italian land.[19] But creditors at once called for full payment, and this placed debtors under an obligation to respond. There was an immediate and clamorous demand for loans, then a rush to the praetors' tribunal. The object of the decree enjoining land purchases and sales had been to afford relief; its effect was the exact opposite, for the creditors laid aside all the money they received, waiting for bargains in land. Large-scale selling reduced prices: the more heavily a man was in debt, the greater the difficulty in selling his estate. Many lost their entire fortunes: and with loss of estate went an immediate loss of dignity and rank. Finally Tiberius came to the rescue. He made available through land banks a sum of a hundred million sesterces to provide interest-free mortgages over a period of three years, provided that a borrower could give security for twice the amount advanced. Confidence was thus restored, and little by little private lenders began to appear. But the purchase of lands was not carried out in accordance with the terms of

the Senate's resolution. As so often happens, it made a brisk beginning, but was only slackly applied in the end.

THE REVIVAL OF THE TERROR

18. A recrudescence of the Terror followed. Considius Proculus was accused of high treason; he was celebrating his birthday, wholly at ease, when he was rushed to the Senate House, condemned, and executed almost on the spot. His sister Sancia was deprived of fire and water at the instigation of Quintus Pomponius. This was a man of unstable character, who professed that he acted in this and similar cases to win the Emperor's favor and rescue his brother Pomponius Secundus from danger. Pompeia Macrina was sent into exile: her husband Argolicus and father-in-law Laco, from one of the leading families in Greece, had already been destroyed by Tiberius. Her father, a distinguished Roman knight, and her brother, an ex-praetor, committed suicide when they saw prosecution impending. The charge was that their great-grandfather, Theophanes of Mytilene, had been a friend of Pompey the Great, and that this same Theophanes had received divine honors after his death through the flattery of the Greeks.

19. Their case was followed by the condemnation of the richest man in Spain, Sextus Marius. He was accused of incest with his own daughter, and was flung from the Tarpeian Rock. But it was clear beyond doubt that his great wealth had destroyed him; all his copper and gold mines became public property and were transferred by Tiberius to the imperial treasury. Maddened by bloodshed, Tiberius now ordered the liquidation of all those held in prison on the charge of friendship with Sejanus. There was a huge mound of dead, of both sexes, all ages, noble and plebeian, lying singly or piled in heaps. Relatives were forbidden to stand by or mourn for them, or even to look at them for long. Guards, who noted every expression of grief, surrounded the rotting bodies as they were dragged to the Tiber, to be carried off by the stream or grounded on the bank. None could touch them, none cremate them. The force of fear had cut them off completely from human sympathy. As the Terror mounted, so was pity held at bay.

20. At this time Gaius Caesar, who had accompanied his grandfather to Capri, married Claudia, daughter of Marcus Silanus. Beneath a show of modesty he concealed an abominable character. Not a word escaped him when his mother was

sentenced, when his brothers were done to death. He put on the mood which Tiberius had chosen for the day; he even echoed his very words. Later men were to remember the clever saying of the orator Passienus. "No man was ever a better slave—or a worse master."

TIBERIUS AND ASTROLOGY

I must not fail to recount the prophecy that Tiberius made about the consul, Servius Sulpicius Galba. After summoning him and questioning him on various topics, he said in Greek, "You, too, Galba, shall one day savor the taste of Empire." He was able to forecast the late and brief principate of Galba by his skill in the astrology of the Chaldeans. He had had the leisure to acquire this skill at Rhodes, with Thrasyllus for his tutor, whose learning he put to this purpose.

21. Whenever he wished to consult an astrologer, he made use of a lofty portion of his house, and the services of a single freedman, illiterate but of great physical strength. The house backed onto a cliff, and this freedman would conduct, over a steep and rocky traverse, the consultant whose skill Tiberius had decided to put to the test. On the way back, if there had been any hint of incompetence or deceit, the freedman would hurl him down into the sea, so that no one should live to betray the secret. Thrasyllus was brought there by this same cliff path, and when Tiberius put his questions, aroused his interest by the skill with which he foretold the future, including his accession to the throne. Then Tiberius asked, "Have you cast your own horoscope? If so, what is portended for this particular day of this particular year?" Then Thrasyllus measured out the position and distances of the stars. First he seemed incredulous, then alarmed: the further he followed his investigations, the greater was his astonishment and distress. Finally he said, "I am in great danger, and the issue may be fatal." Then Tiberius embraced him, saying, "I congratulate you on your prophecy of danger. You shall be spared." From then on he treated him as an intimate, and believed his prophecies as though they came from an oracle.

THE PROBLEM OF FATE AND FREE WILL

22. When I hear such stories as these I find my judgment divided as to whether human affairs are ruled by fate and

necessity, or are the product of chance. One finds that the founders of the great philosophical schools of antiquity and their disciples are in disagreement on this issue. Some[20] hold that the gods care neither for our endings nor our beginnings— nor for mankind at all. Hence we so often find that the good suffer, and the wicked prosper. Others[21] again believe that things are indeed ordered by fate, but that this depends, not on the planets, but on the principles and sequences of natural causation. Thus we are left with the choice of a path of life: once you have chosen it, the sequence to follow is determined. Adversity and prosperity, they think, are not as the vulgar believe; for many who seem to be in affliction are truly happy, and many are unhappy in the midst of great wealth—in the former case if they bear their misfortunes with courage, and in the latter if they make ill use of their prosperity. Yet the greater part of mankind does not readily abandon the belief that a man's destiny is determined at the hour of his birth. If some things turn out contrary to prophecy, that is due to the fallacious pronouncements of ignorant seers, which tend to bring into disrepute a science so well attested in both ancient and modern times. This digression must proceed no further; but in its place I shall recount a prophecy made by Thrasyllus' son about the principate of Nero.

DEATH OF ASINIUS GALLUS

23. In this same year the death of Asinius Gallus was announced. Starvation was certainly the cause of death, whether enforced or voluntary. Tiberius was asked for permission to bury him, and did not blush to give it: indeed, he even regretted the chance which had removed a defendant before he could investigate the case. An interval of three years, it seems, was too little to bring to trial a man of consular rank, father of so many consuls!

DEATH OF DRUSUS

Then Drusus met his end. For eight days he had miserably sustained himself by eating the straw of his pallet. Some say that Macro had instructions, should Sejanus proceed to arms, to fetch the young prince from his custody on the Palatine and proclaim him to the people as their leader. Later, as the rumor gained ground of a reconciliation between Tiberius and

Agrippina and Drusus, the Emperor's thoughts turned again to ferocity rather than repentance.

24. Indeed, he accused Drusus after his death of personal depravity, of planning to assassinate his relatives, and of being a traitor to the state. He ordered a public recitation of a record of the prince's daily doings and sayings—the worst feature of the cruelty toward him. It is almost incredible to think that confidential agents should have stood over him for so many years, to set down every change of expression, every sigh, every private utterance, and that his own grandfather should hear and read them, and allow them to be published; but the reports of the centurion Attius and the freedman Didymus even gave the names of the slaves who had threatened or struck Drusus as he came out of his bedchamber. The centurion also recorded his own brutal words, thinking this a merit. He added the dying words spoken by Drusus, who had at first simulated madness, then, as hope of life left him, pronounced the most studied and solemn curses against Tiberius. "As he has murdered his daughter-in-law, nephew, and grandchildren, and steeped his house in blood, so let him pay the penalty he owes to his name, his ancestors, and his posterity!" As though horrified, the senators interrupted the recital. Their real emotions were of fear and surprise—that one so clever and so practiced at hiding his crimes as Tiberius should be so unconcerned that he could, as it were, throw aside the walls of the prison to reveal his own grandson being beaten by a centurion, begging in vain for the last necessities of life, and receiving the blows of slaves.

DEATH OF AGRIPPINA

25. Grief for Drusus had hardly died away when news came of the death of Agrippina. No doubt the murder of Sejanus had caused her to live in hope; but, seeing no abatement in Tiberius' brutality, she committed suicide. It is possible, though, that she was deprived of food, so that her death should look like suicide. She, also, was vilified abominably by Tiberius. There were charges of immorality and of adultery with Asinius Gallus, whose death deprived her of the wish to live. Now Agrippina hated a rival and was avid for power; but she had a man's vices, not a woman's frailties. She died on the same day of the year as Sejanus had done, two years before. Tiberius thought this should be set on record, congratulating himself at the same time that he had not had her

strangled, nor thrown down the Gemonian Stairs. For this, a thanksgiving was decreed in the Senate, and it was enacted that the eighteenth of October, the day of the two murders, should be sacred to Jupiter.

SUICIDE OF COCCEIUS NERVA

26. Not long after this Cocceius Nerva, an intimate friend of the Emperor, an expert in human and divine law, resolved to die, though he was in perfect health and there was no threat to his position. As soon as he heard this, Tiberius hastened to visit him. He asked for his reasons and implored him to desist, protesting that it would rest on his conscience and reflect on his reputation if his closest friend chose to escape from life with no motive for seeking death! Nerva refused to speak to him, or to take food. Those privy to his thoughts asserted that, knowing from the inside the evils of the state, he was so horrified and so indignant that he determined to make an honorable end while still secure and unassailed.

END OF PLANCINA

Oddly enough, the death of Agrippina was also fatal to Plancina. She had been the wife of Piso, and had publicly rejoiced at the death of Germanicus. When Piso himself died, the entreaties of Livia and (no less) the enmity of Agrippina preserved her life. When hatred and influence were both removed, the law could take its course. She was charged with offenses which were notorious, and with her own hand discharged a penalty which was delayed rather than undeserved.

UNSUITABLE MARRIAGE OF JULIA

27. Distracted by so many griefs, the state had further cause for mourning when Drusus' daughter Julia, once wife of Nero Caesar, married into the house of Rubellius Blandus. Men could remember his grandfather, a Roman knight from Tivoli. At the end of the year a public funeral marked the death of Aelius Lamia, who had become city prefect after his release from his fictitious governorship of Syria.[22] He came

of high lineage, and his old age was active: that he was forbidden to proceed to the province redounded to his credit.

The death of his successor, Pomponius Flaccus, drew a letter from Tiberius, complaining that men of distinction, capable of high military command, were refusing to take office, and that he was forced to beg consuls to accept a province. He had forgotten that Arruntius had, by now, been kept out of Spain for nine years.

Manius Lepidus was another who died in this year. I have paid my tribute, in an earlier book, to his moderation and wisdom: his noble ancestry stands in no need of proof. The house of the Aemilii has always been productive of good citizens: even its black sheep have been persons of consequence.

34 A.D. Consuls Paulus Fabius Persicus and Lucius Vitellius

EGYPT. THE YEAR OF THE PHOENIX

28. In this year, at the end of a long cycle of years, the phoenix made its appearance in Egypt.[23] This miraculous phenomenon provided a rich topic for discussion among Egyptian and Greek scholars. It is interesting to set out the points on which they agree, as indeed the (more numerous) problems which are not substantiated, yet not wholly fanciful. All who have depicted this creature agree that it is sacred to the sun and unique, its beak and plumage entirely different from those of all other birds. Accounts differ as to its life span. Five hundred years is the figure generally given; others assert that the cycle is one of 1,461 years and that the bird first appeared in the reign of Sesosis, then in the reign of Amasis, and a third time in that of Ptolemy, the third of the Macedonian dynasty.[24] In each instance the bird flew to Heliopolis, attended by a great crowd of other birds who marveled at its extraordinary aspect. Antiquity veils its earlier appearances: however, between Ptolemy and Tiberius the interval is less than 250 years, and hence some have thought this a false phoenix and not the true Arabian bird. Indeed, it did not perform the functions with which it is credited by tradition.

For when the cycle of years is accomplished, and death at hand, it is supposed to build itself a nest in Arabia. Over this it sheds its genital fluid, and a phoenix chick is born. The first task of the new phoenix, when grown, is to bury its father. This is done in no haphazard way. Taking on its back a load of myrrh, it essays a long trial flight. Then, having tested its capability for weight and distance, it takes its father's body on its back, carries it to the Altar of the Sun, and there cremates it. The details are disputed, and are embellished by myth. What is certain is that this bird does appear in Egypt from time to time.

ROME. CONTINUANCE OF THE TERROR

29. Meanwhile, the Terror went on at Rome. Pomponius Labeo, whom I mentioned as governor of Moesia, opened his veins and bled to death: his wife Paxaea followed his example. Fear of the executioner prompted such deaths as these: moreover, those who were sentenced to death were refused burial, and their estates were confiscated, while those who disposed of themselves were granted interment and their wills were allowed to stand. This put a premium on speed. Tiberius now sent a letter to the Senate, citing the ancient custom whereby friendships were ended by forbidding one's house to a person; this finished the relationship. He had revived this custom in the case of Labeo, but the latter, under suspicion for misgovernment of his province and other charges, had tried to conceal his guilt by arousing odium against the Emperor; he had needlessly terrified his wife, for, though guilty, she was in no danger.

Then there was a second attack on Mamercus Scaurus, an aristocrat and a distinguished lawyer, though a man of dissolute life. It was not the friendship of Sejanus that was his undoing, but the scarcely less potent hostility of Macro, who was beginning to practice the same evil arts in a less obvious way. He denounced the theme of a tragedy which Scaurus had written, quoting lines which could be made to reflect on Tiberius.[25] However, the ostensible charges, brought by Servilius and Cornelius, were adultery with Livia and the use of witchcraft. Scaurus anticipated his sentence by suicide, as befitted a member of the ancient house of the Aemilii. He was encouraged to do so by his wife Sextia, who both urged the deed and followed his example.

30. Even so, whenever opportunity offered, the accusers

were visited with retribution. Servilius and Cornelius had made themselves infamous by the downfall of Scaurus: having taken a bribe to abandon the prosecution of Varius Ligus, they were deprived of fire and water and banished to an island. So too with the former aedile Abudius Ruso: his attack on Lentulus Gaetulicus (under whom he had commanded a legion) for having promised his daughter in marriage to Sejanus, actually resulted in his own conviction and banishment from Rome. At this juncture Gaetulicus was in command of the legion in Upper Germany. He was immensely popular with his troops because of his kindly character and mild discipline: through his father-in-law Lucius Apronius he had influence with the army in Lower Germany. Persistent rumor credits him with the audacity of writing to Tiberius in these terms: "My connection with Sejanus was not voluntary, but on your advice. I can make a mistake no less than you: and the same misjudgment must not be excusable in your case, fatal in that of others. My loyalty is unshaken, and it will endure so long as you practice no trickery against me: the naming of a successor I should regard as a death-warrant. Let us strike a bargain. You rule the rest of the world: I keep my province." This is an extraordinary story, but it gains verisimilitude from the fact that, alone of all the friends of Sejanus, Gaetulicus survived and remained in high favor. Tiberius may have reflected on the hatred felt for him, on his extreme old age, and on the fact that his position rested on prestige rather than power.

35 A.D. Consuls Gaius Cestius Gallus and Marcus Servilius Nonianus

EASTERN AFFAIRS

31. In this year a delegation of Parthian nobles came to Rome without the knowledge of King Artabanus. Fear of Germanicus had kept Artabanus loyal to us and benevolent toward his subjects. Later, relying on the successes he had won in wars with neighboring peoples, he began to develop arrogance to Rome and cruelty to his own people. He despised

Tiberius as senile and unwarlike, and coveted Armenia, where he had imposed his oldest son Arsaces as king on the death of Artaxias. A mark of insult had been the dispatch of agents to demand the return of the treasure Vonones had left in Syria and Cilicia.[26] In a mixture of boastfulness and menace Artabanus talked about reconquering the old empires of the Persians and Macedonians, and invading the lands once held by Cyrus and Alexander.[27]

The man chiefly responsible for the Parthian secret mission was Sinnaces, a person of noble family and great wealth. He was seconded by the eunuch Abdus, for barbarians do not consider this condition degrading; indeed, with them it frequently leads to high influence. They summoned together other notables, and since there was no other prince of the Arsacid line whom they could place on the throne (for most of them had been murdered by Artabanus, or else were minors), they sought the return from Rome of Phraates, son of the king of that name. "All we need," they argued, "is the royal name, and the backing of Tiberius: then let the scion of the house of Arsaces show himself on the bank of the Euphrates!"

32. This was exactly what Tiberius wanted. He gave Phraates the insignia of royalty, and the means to recover his father's throne—holding fast to his maxim of employing guile and diplomacy in the conduct of foreign affairs, without recourse to arms. Meanwhile Artabanus had discovered the treachery being plotted against him. His first reaction was a paralysis of panic, then a passionate desire for revenge. To Orientals, delay is servile, and instant action becomes a king. None the less Artabanus heeded expediency to the extent of inviting Abdus to a feast under the guise of friendship and putting him out of action with a slow poison. Against Sinnaces he used dissimulation, providing both amusements and business to hold him in check. Phraates, on reaching Syria, dropped the Roman style of living he had been used to for years and took up a Parthian mode of life: but his people's customs proved too much for him, and he fell ill and died. Even so, Tiberius did not abandon his designs. As a rival for Artabanus he chose Tiridates, a member of the same family; and for the recovery of Armenia his candidate was Mithridates, a prince of Iberia, whom he reconciled to his brother Pharasmenes, the ruler of that country. Moreover, he placed Lucius Vitellius in general charge of Eastern affairs. I am well aware that Vitellius' reputation in Rome was a bad one, and much that is scandalous is recorded about him. But as a provincial administrator he showed the virtues of an earlier age. On his return from the

East, fear of Gaius Caesar and intimacy with Claudius converted him to sycophancy of the basest kind; indeed, a later
generation saw him as the archetype of all flatterers. So his
earlier achievements were overlaid by his later ignominy, and
a virtuous youth annulled by an infamous old age.

33. The first of the petty kings to take action was Mithridates. By treachery and force he compelled Pharasmenes to
help him in his plans: between them, they bribed Arsaces'
attendants (for a high price) to do away with him. At the
same time, a powerful Iberian force invaded Armenia and
captured Artaxata. Immediately he learned of this, Artabanus
dispatched a force of Parthians under his son Orodes to take
revenge, and sent out envoys to enlist mercenaries. Pharasmenes countered by enlisting the Albani and invoking the help
of the Sarmatians. Their chieftains took bribes from both parties—a national custom—and enlisted on opposite sides. But
advantage of ground lay with the Iberians: they rushed their
force of Sarmatians over the Caucasus Pass[28] and invaded
Armenia. Those Sarmatians who rallied to the Parthian cause
were easily kept at bay: all the passes were closed to them by
the enemy, and the one remaining road was that between the
eastern end of the Albanian mountains and the Caspian Sea.[29]
But this route is impracticable in summer, when the annual
gales flood all the coastline.[30] (In winter, the southerly winds
drive back the floods and the coastal shallows are drained.)

34. When his reinforcements had come in, Pharasmenes
challenged Orodes to fight. The latter, devoid of allies, refused.
But the Iberians harassed him, riding up to his camp and
depriving him of fodder—indeed, even surrounding him with
pickets as though in a regular siege. The Parthians were not
accustomed to insults: they gathered around their king and
begged for battle. They were strong only in cavalry; Pharasmenes also had a useful force of infantry. For the Albani and
the Iberians are mountaineers, well accustomed to hardship
and adversity. They claim Thessalian descent, from the time
when Jason again sought out Medea and her children and
occupied the empty palace of Aeëtes and the kingless land of
Colchis. They retain many legends about Jason, and support
an oracular shrine of Phrixus. The ram sacrifice is prohibited
there because Phrixus was carried on a ram (whether the
actual animal or on a ship with a ram for figurehead).

When both sides had been drawn up in battle array, Orodes
addressed his troops. He spoke of the Parthian empire, and
the glories of the house of Arsaces, in contrast to the base-
born Iberians and their mercenary soldiers. Pharasmenes told
his men that they had never been the subjects of Parthia: the

greater their hopes, the greater the honor in victory, or the danger and disgrace in defeat. Pointing to his own savage troops, and the glittering array of the Parthians in their golden robes, he exclaimed, "Here are the men: there's the booty!"

35. His voice was not the only one to be heard among the Sarmatians. They all shouted: "Don't let's have an archers' battle: let's make a charge, and then get to grips!" A confused action followed. The Parthian cavalry, trained to pursuit and withdrawal, opened the ranks to allow room to shoot. The Sarmatians abandoned their bows, which have a shorter range, and charged in with pikes and swords. At one period there would be the charges and retreats of a regular cavalry engagement: at another, the lines would interlock in a stand-up battle, every man pushing, and being pushed by the full weight of arms and bodies. Then there would be a rush of Albanians and Iberians to seize the riders and drag them off their horses. The enemy forces were thus trapped in two ways—harassed by cavalry, and assailed by infantry at close quarters. Pharasmenes and Orodes were both conspicuous, supporting the active fighters and rallying the laggards. They recognized each other, shouted, and charged. Pharasmenes showed the greater dash; he pierced Orodes through the helmet and wounded him in the head. But the speed of his horse carried him beyond the range of a second blow, and Orodes' guards covered the wounded man. But a false report of Orodes' death caused much alarm among the Parthians, who admitted defeat.

36. It was not long before Artabanus sought revenge with all the forces of his empire. The Iberians, through their knowledge of the terrain, had the better of the fighting, but Artabanus would not have withdrawn if Vitellius had not mustered the legions and spread a rumor of an invasion of Mesopotamia. Fear of a war with Rome made the Parthian king desist. So Armenia was abandoned, and the cause of Artabanus began to decline. The bribes of Vitellius induced the Parthians to abandon a king who was cruel in time of peace and suffered disasters in war. So his enemy Sinnaces induced his father Abdagaeses and others privy to the plot to revolt, attracting further support from those disillusioned by the continuous succession of defeats. Little by little they gained the adherence of men who had followed Artabanus from fear rather than loyalty, and had plucked up their courage now that leaders had appeared. All that Artabanus now had was his foreign bodyguard, exiles from their own country, men who cared nothing for right or wrong, but were the paid agents of crime. Taking these with him, he fled to Scythia (which, though distant, marches with Parthia), where he had hopes of sup-

port through his connections in Hyrcania and Carmania. Meanwhile, too, the Parthians, who liked their kings when in exile and were fickle to those on the throne, might change their minds about him.

37. Now that Artabanus had fled and the Parthian people were expecting a new king, Vitellius urged Tiridates to seize his opportunity. He took the main force of the legions and allies to the bank of the Euphrates. While sacrifices were being offered—by the Romans, the bull, ram, and boar to Mars; by Tiridates, a horse to appease the river—natives brought in a report that the Euphrates was rising, though not swollen by rain, to an unusual height, and its white foam formed eddies, like crowns, to prophesy a successful crossing. A more sophisticated interpretation ran thus: "The affair will begin well, but it will not last. The more reliable portents are those seen in the earth or the heavens: water is the unstable element; its omens are no sooner shown than they are washed away."

Then a bridge of boats was constructed, and the crossing of the river took place. The first to join them was Ornospades, who brought with him several thousand cavalry. Once an exile, he had done good service under Tiberius in the Dalmatian war,[31] and been rewarded with Roman citizenship. Then, restored to high favor with the Parthian king, he had been made governor of the plain which is called Mesopotamia,[32] situated as it is between the famous rivers Euphrates and Tigris. Soon afterwards, Sinnaces came in, accompanied by the real pillar of his cause, Abdagaeses, who brought with him the royal treasure and insignia. Vitellius thought that this display of Roman force had achieved its purpose. He exhorted Tiridates to remember the good qualities of his grandfather Phraates IV and foster-father Augustus, while urging his nobles to remain loyal to their sovereign, respectful to Rome, and true to their own honor and good faith. Then he led the legions back to Syria.

ROME. THE TERROR CONTINUED

38. My reason for making a continuous narrative out of the events of two summers is to afford some relief from the disasters at Rome. It was three years since the death of Sejanus. On other men such influences as time, prayers, satiety, have a pacifying effect; not so on Tiberius. He continued to punish doubtful or forgotten offenses as savagely as though they were heinous and recent. For this reason Fulcinius Trio could not bear to wait as the prosecutors mustered their charges against

him: in his will he gave expression to violent denunciations of Macro and of the chief freedmen of Tiberius. The Emperor himself he described as a man in his dotage, whom continued absence had made almost an exile. His heirs suppressed this passage, but Tiberius ordered it to be recited—thus making a display of his tolerance of freedom of speech in others, or his contempt for his own reputation. Perhaps, too, having been ignorant for so long of the crimes of Sejanus, he thought that what was being said about him should be published by every means available. Flattery obscures the truth; he would learn it from insults. At this period the senator Granius Marcianus, accused of treason by Gaius Gracchus, laid violent hands on himself: the ex-praetor Tarius Gratianus was condemned and executed on the same day.

39. A like fate overtook Trebellenus Rufus and Sextius Paconianus. Trebellenus was the suicide; Paconianus was strangled in prison for the libelous poems he had there composed against the Emperor. All these executions Tiberius learned of not, as once, across the strait or by messages from a distance: he was close to the city, he could write to the consuls on the same day, or overnight: he had a clear view, as it were, of the tides of blood, swollen by suicides or the executioner's hands.

Poppaeus Sabinus died at the end of the year. Of an undistinguished family, it was his friendship with Emperors which brought him his consulship, triumphal honors, and the governorships of important provinces over no less than twenty-four years. No outstanding qualities secured him these posts; his merit lay in being competent, and no more.

36 A.D. Consuls Quintus Plautius and Sextus Papinius

40. That Lucius Aruseius (and others) were executed in this year attracted little notice, since men's minds were now hardened to evil. But a sensation was produced when the Roman knight, Vibulenus Agrippa, on the conclusion of the

case for the prosecution, took out a phial of poison from his clothing in the Senate House itself, collapsed, and was carried out, dying, by the lictors. They took him to prison, where he was strangled, though already dead.[33] Tigranes, formerly king of Armenia, and then on trial, found the royal rank no protection against the penalty inflicted on Roman citizens. The former consul, Gaius Galba, and the two Blaesi committed suicide. Galba had received threatening letters from Tiberius, forbidding him to take part in the draw for the provinces. In the case of the Blaesi, priesthoods destined for their family in the days of prosperity were now, in its ruin, treated as vacant and given to others. They saw this as a death sentence, and took their cue.

Aemilia Lepida (whose marriage with Drusus I have mentioned)[34] continued to accuse her husband. Detestable as this was, she acted with impunity so long as her father Lepidus was alive. After his death, informers denounced her for adultery with a slave. There was no doubt about her guilt; she committed suicide without putting up a defense.

REBELLION IN CAPPADOCIA

41. At this time the tribes of the Cietae, subjects of King Archelaus of Cappadocia, were compelled to undergo a census and be assessed for taxation as though they were Roman provincials. They withdrew to the recesses of the Taurus Mountains, where they were able to use their knowledge of the ground to defend themselves against the unwarlike forces of the king. But at length the legionary commander Marcus Trebellius, dispatched by Vitellius, governor of Syria, with a force of four thousand legionaries and a picked body of allies, besieged the two hills which these barbarians had occupied, and which were called Cadra and Davara. Those who tried to break out were killed: thirst forced the others to surrender.

EVENTS IN PARTHIA

Meanwhile Tiridates, with Parthian consent, had occupied several cities—Nicephorium, Anthemusias, and other Macedonian foundations which bore Greek names, and also the Parthian cities of Halus and Artemita. This gave satisfaction to those who hated Artabanus for the cruelty he had learned among the Scythians, and hoped to find in Tiridates a mild disposition, the product of Roman civilization.

42. The inhabitants of Seleucia outdid the rest in flattery. With its great fortifications theirs is a powerful city: it has never been barbarized, and it keeps green the memory of its founder Seleucus. It has a senate of three hundred, chosen for wealth or sagacity; the people, too, have a political function. Whenever they act in unison, their city can defy the Parthian king. But when they fall out, and each side calls him for support against its rival, then the Parthian, though summoned against one side, dominates them both. That had happened when Artabanus was king; he had delivered the people into the power of the aristocracy, to suit his own purpose. For the rule of the people makes for freedom, while an oligarchy is better suited to a despot's whims. When Tiridates reached Seleucia he was loaded with all the honors given to the ancient Persian kings, and indeed with the most lavish innovations of recent times. Insults were directed at Artabanus, an Arsacid only on his mother's side, and of low descent on the other. Tiridates gave control of Seleucia to the democratic party. As he was considering the choice of a day for the solemn ceremony of coronation, he received letters from Phraates and Hiero, governors of the most powerful provinces, requesting a brief delay. It seemed wise to await the arrival of these powerful figures. In the meantime Tiridates went to Ctesiphon, capital of the Empire. But the delay dragged on from day to day. Finally, amid rejoicing crowds, the Surena[35] crowned him with the diadem, according to Parthian custom.

43. Had Tiridates gone at once to the central provinces to win over the other peoples of the Empire, the waverers would have overcome their doubts and all would have directed their loyalty to him, and to him alone. But by besieging the fortress to which Artabanus had sent the royal treasures and the harem, he provided a chance for the breaking of engagements. Phraates, Hiero, and others who had not come to the coronation on the appointed day (some through fear, others through jealousy of the power of Abdagaeses, who was supreme at court and had the new king firmly in his control) now began to look toward Artabanus. He was discovered to be in Hyrcania, squalid and neglected, and living by what he could shoot. At first he was apprehensive of treachery; then when they swore that they had come to secure his restoration, his spirits rose, and he asked to know the reasons behind the change. Then Hiero began to abuse Tiridates as a mere lad, saying that power was no longer in the hands of an Arsacid,

but there was a shadow monarchy only, attaching to an unwarlike prince who had been corrupted by foreign luxury—
that the real power lay with the house of Abdagaeses.

44. Artabanus' long experience of rule had taught him that
while the loves of his subjects might be false, their hates were
genuine. Staying only long enough to summon reinforcements
from Scythia, he took the field at once, forestalling his enemies'
intrigues or a change of heart by his friends. To win the favor
of the mob, he retained his squalid appearance. He used fraud,
entreaties, and every other device that might serve to seduce
waverers and to encourage loyalty. Soon he was approaching
Seleucia with a large force.

Tiridates was greatly alarmed by the news, and later by
the presence of Artabanus. He could not decide whether to
meet him face to face, or engage in a war of attrition. Those
who favored a battle and a quick issue pointed out that
Artabanus' troops were scattered and weary after their long
march. Even in their minds there was no steady loyalty toward
him: only lately they had turned traitor and opposed him, and
then they had changed to take up his cause once more. But
Abdagaeses counseled a retreat into Mesopotamia. Then, with
the river between them, and strengthened by reinforcements
from Armenia and the Elymaei—besides what the Roman
commander might send—Tiridates could put his fortune to
the test. This advice prevailed, for Abdagaeses wielded the
greatest authority, and Tiridates had little stomach for a fight.
But the withdrawal looked uncommonly like a rout. First the
Arabs, then the other tribal contingents, went home or deserted to the camp of Artabanus. Finally Tiridates withdrew
with a small bodyguard to Syria, thus excusing the general
abandonment of his cause.

ROME. THE FIRE ON THE AVENTINE

45. That year there was a great fire in Rome. It burned to
the ground that part of the Circus Maximus which adjoins the
Aventine, and the Aventine Hill itself. Tiberius shouldered
the cost of restoring the houses and tenements destroyed, and
won much prestige by so doing. He contributed a hundred
million sesterces for this purpose; and popular gratitude was
the more marked because he had spent so little on private
building. Indeed, only two public buildings were constructed
under him—the temple of Augustus and the stage buildings
for the Theater of Pompeius.[36] Even when these were com-

pleted, he did not dedicate them, either because he scorned to make a display, or because he was too old. For assessing the damage caused by the fire he appointed the husbands of his four granddaughters—Gnaeus Domitius, Cassius Longinus, Marcus Vinicius, and Rubellius Blandus—and (on the nomination of the consuls) Publius Petronius. Members of the Senate competed with each other in devising and approving compliments to the Emperor. Which he accepted or rejected is uncertain because of his approaching end.

37 A.D. Consuls Gnaeus Acerronius Proculus and Gaius Petronius Pontius

For soon the last consuls of Tiberius' reign, Gnaeus Acerronius Proculus and Gaius Petronius Pontius, entered their office. By now the power of Macro had become excessive. He had always paid court to Gaius Caesar; now he did so more keenly with every day that passed. After the death of Claudia (whose marriage to Gaius I have recorded), Macro made his own wife Ennia affect a guilty passion for the prince and seduce him under promise of marriage. Gaius was nothing loth; anything to gain power. Indeed, though naturally brusque of temper, he had acquired a perfect mastery of dissimulation at his grandfather's knee.

THE PROBLEM OF THE SUCCESSION

46. Tiberius became aware of this, and it caused him to hesitate in his plans for the succession. As between his grandsons, Drusus' son (Tiberius Gemellus) was of his own blood and closer to his affections, but as yet no more than a child; Gaius, son of Germanicus, was in his young manhood, and the favorite of the people—and so his grandfather hated him. He even considered Claudius, who had in his favor years of discretion and a taste for literary culture, but he was disquali-

fied as weak-minded. If they had to look beyond the imperial house for a successor, there was a fear that the memory of Augustus and the name of the Caesars would be the object of ridicule and insult. Tiberius' mind looked not so much to current popularity as to the approbation of posterity. Infirm of mind and irresolute of body, he found the choice beyond him, and left it to fate.

But many remarks betrayed his insight into the future. It was a riddle easily read when he reproached Macro for turning from the setting to the rising sun. When Gaius Caesar happened to sneer at Lucius Sulla in casual conversation, Tiberius said. "You will have all Sulla's vices, and none of his virtues." And again, when with many tears he was embracing his grandson, Tiberius Gemellus, and Gaius was looking on with a scowl, he said, "You will kill this child, and someone else will kill you!" As his health failed he kept up all his depravities. He was at pains to put on a show of health: he had always derided the medical arts, and made fun of anyone who, having reached the age of thirty, needed someone else to tell him what was good or harmful for his body.

ROME. LAST PHASE OF THE TERROR

47. Meanwhile, in Rome, the seeds were being sown of murders to come after the death of Tiberius. Laelius Balbus prosecuted Acutia, formerly the wife of Publius Vitellius, on a charge of treason. When she was condemned, and a reward voted to her prosecutor, the tribune Junius Otho interposed his veto. This caused enmity between them and, later, the downfall of Otho. Then Albucilla, notorious for her many lovers (wife of that Satrius Secundus who had denounced the conspiracy of Sejanus), was accused of disloyalty to the Emperor. Among the paramours denounced with her were Gnaeus Domitius, Vibius Marsus, and Lucius Arruntius. I have spoken of the high lineage of Domitius: Marsus too was of an old family, and a man of literary distinction. Documents submitted to the Senate showed that Macro had supervised the interrogation of the witnesses and the torture of the slaves. But no letters of denunciation came from the Emperor, and the suspicion was aroused that most of this evidence was false, collected by Macro—in the Emperor's illness and perhaps even without his knowledge—to gratify his notorious enmity toward Lucius Arruntius.

48. So Domitius and Marsus prolonged their lives: Do-

mitius preparing his defense, Marsus ostensibly on a hunger strike. Arruntius' friends counseled procrastination and delay, but he replied, "Different people make different choices. I have lived long enough. My only regret is that my old age has been so beset by insults and dangers. I have always had the enmity of the powerful: for so long, of Sejanus, and now of Macro. My only fault is intolerance of crime. I could survive the few days to see this Emperor into his grave: but a stripling is to follow; how can I outlast him? If Tiberius, with all his experience, has succumbed so completely to the corruption of absolute power, what of Gaius? He is barely out of his childhood, he knows nothing, he has been brought up on the worst of examples. Will he change for the better under Macro's tutelage? Macro was chosen as the greater villain, to suppress Sejanus: he has committed more crimes and done even more harm to the state. I foresee a yet more grievous slavery ahead: I am resolved to liberate myself from the horrors of the past and the horrors yet to come." These words he uttered with all the fervor of an oracle. Then he opened his veins. The sequel was to show that Arruntius had been wise to die. Albucilla vainly tried to kill herself, and was conveyed to prison on the instruction of the Senate. Of those who had ministered to her lusts, the ex-praetor Carsidius Sacerdos was banished to an island, and Pontius Fregellanus expelled from the Senate. So was Laelius Balbus, but this caused the Senate much pleasure; his was an aggressive eloquence, ever ready for employment against the innocent.

THE CASE OF SEXTUS PAPINIUS

49. At this time Sextus Papinius, a man of consular family, chose to meet a sudden and shocking death—by defenestration. His mother was at fault. Long repelled, her complaisance and attentions had finally involved the young man in a situation from which the only escape was death.[37] Summoned before the Senate, she fell on her knees, pleading the grief which everyone, and above all a poor weak woman, must feel in a pitiable strait like hers. Much more to this effect, all couched in the same melting strain. Nonetheless, the Senate banished her from Rome for ten years, until her younger son should be past the slippery years of youth.

The Grand Cameo of France (Cabinet des Medailles, Paris)
Giraudon

*Center: Tiberius and Livia, seated on throne. Left,
Germanicus, Agrippina, and the young Gaius.*

*Above: Winged horse bears Germanicus (?) to greet Augustus
and Aeneas (?).*

Below: German and Parthian prisoners.

Augustus. Prima Porta Statue (Vatican Museum, Rome)
Alinari

Messalina and her children
(Cabinet des Medailles, Paris)

Giraudon

Top right: the busts of Britannicus and Octavia, on either side
of the portrait of Messalina.

Head of Caligula (National Museum, Rome)
The Bettman Archive

Bust of Claudius
(Vatican Museum,
Rome)
Alinari

Bust of Nero
(Uffizi Gallery,
Florence)
Alinari

Dp. *Tiberius:* Divus Augustus pater/S C, *Temple c. 22–23 A.D. Radiate; head of Augustus; reverse, Temple of Vesta on the Palatine. (The continuity of the Augustan Tradition).*

Sest. Civitatibus Asiae restitutis, *Tiberius seated c. 22–23 A.D. cf. Annals, II. 47.*

Dp. *Tiberius:* Iustitia *c. 22–23 A.D. Tiberius' interest in judicial equity. cf. Annals, I. 75.*

Sest. *Tiberius:* Divo Augusto s p q r, ob cives ser, *shield, wreath, capricorns c. 36–37 A.D. Recalls the beneficence of Augustus, and Tiberius' public generosity in 33 A.D.—the fiftieth year of the new saeculum begun by Augustus in 17 B.C. cf. Annals, VI. 17.*

Sest. *Gaius:* Agrippina M f mat C Caesaris Augusti/
S p q r memoriae Agrippinae, *carpentum*

*37–41 (?) A.D. Gaius recalls the memory of
Agrippina the Elder.*

Dp. *Gaius:* Germanicus Caesar, *Germanicus in quad-
riga*/Signis recept devictis Germ, S C, *Germanicus as
imperator*

*37–41 (?) Gaius recalls the German campaigns,
the recovery of the standard of Varus,
and the defeat of Arminius.*

Aur. *Claudius:*
Paci Augustae,
Pax

*49–50 A.D.
Peace as the
keynote of
Claudian policy.*

Aur. *Claudius:* De
Britann, *statue on
arch*

*46–47 A.D.
Claudius com-
memorates the
conquest of
Britain in
43 A.D.*

Aur. *Claudius:*
Agrippinae
Augustae

*52–54 A.D.
The influence of
Agrippina the
Younger stressed
by her appearance
on the coins.*

Aur. *Claudius:* Nero Claud Caes Drusus Germ princ iuvent

52–54 A.D.
The growing influence of the young Nero.
cf. *Annals XII. 41.*

Aur. *Nero:* Agripp Aug divi Claud Neronis Caes mater/Neroni Claud divi f Caes Aug Germ imp tr p, ex s c *in wreath*

54 A.D. Agrippina still powerful.
cf. *Annals XIII 5.*

Aur. *Nero:* Nero Caesar Augustus/Augustus Augusta, *Nero and Empress*
64–68 A.D. The Empress is Poppaea.

Sest. *Nero:* S C August, port Ost, *ships in Ostia harbor*
64–66 A.D. The Imperial musician is compared with Apollo.

As. *Nero:* Pontif max tr pot imp p p S C, *Nero "citharoedus"*
64–66 A.D. The competition at the Claudian harbor at Ostia.

Sest. *Nero:* Pace p r terra mariq parta Ianum clusit, S C, *closed temple of Janus*
64–66 A.D. The Temple of Janus was closed in 166 A.D., after Corbulo's eastern victories. The coins were perhaps struck in anticipation.

THE DEATH OF TIBERIUS

50. Health and strength were now leaving Tiberius. Dissimulation remained. There were the same iron will, the same vigor of speech and expression. But now there was an occasional parade of geniality, to hide a failing that was all too obvious. He changed his quarters restlessly, but finally settled in a villa on the promontory of Misenum that had once belonged to Lucius Lucullus. That his end was at hand was discovered in the following manner. There was a famous physician called Charicles, not the Emperor's regular medical attendant, but called in from time to time as a consultant. On taking his leave to attend to private affairs, Charicles grasped the Emperor's hand[38]—as though out of respect—and felt his pulse. Tiberius noted this. Annoyed, possibly, and for that reason concealing his annoyance, he ordered new courses to be brought and sat longer than usual at table, as though in honor of his departing guest. But Charicles assured Macro that vitality was ebbing: Tiberius could not last more than another two days.

Arrangements were therefore put in hand[39] by conferences among those present, and by the sending of dispatches to the provincial governors and the armies. On the sixteenth of March the Emperor's breathing stopped: it was thought that he had reached the end of his mortal span. Gaius Caesar issued forth for the official beginning of his reign, surrounded by a huge crowd of well-wishers. But suddenly came the news that Tiberius had recovered his voice and sight: he was asking for food to strengthen himself after a fainting fit![40] Panic and general confusion ensued. The crowd dispersed, each man assuming a look of sadness—or of ignorance. Gaius Caesar stood in a silent catalepsy: his high hopes in ruins, and the worst to fear. But Macro kept his nerve. He ordered them to smother the old man in a pile of bedclothes, and to leave the room. So Tiberius came to his end, being then in his seventy-eighth year.

CHARACTER OF TIBERIUS[41]

51. His father was Tiberius Claudius Nero, and he belonged to the Claudian house on both sides, though his mother

Livia passed by adoption first into the Livian, then the Julian house. From his earliest infancy he knew hazard and danger. He followed his father into exile: as a stepson in the house of Augustus he suffered many rivals, so long as Marcellus and Agrippa, then Lucius and Gaius Caesar, were alive. Even his own brother Drusus was dearer to the hearts of the people. But his greatest peril derived from his marriage to Julia (daughter of Augustus), when he had either to tolerate or escape her immoralities. When he returned from Rhodes he was, for twelve years, unchallenged heir in Augustus' house: he ruled supreme in the Roman world for three-and-twenty years. His character, too, went through a wide range of phases. As a private citizen, or holding military command under Augustus, his conduct and reputation were excellent. While Drusus and Germanicus lived, craft and equivocation provided a screen of virtues. While his mother was alive, Tiberius still showed good and bad qualities: while he had Sejanus to love (or to fear), his cruelty was appalling but his perversions remained hidden. In his last phase, there was a great eruption of crime and vice; set free from shame and fear, he stood out at long last in no other character but his own. . . .

(At this point the manuscript breaks off, to resume with Book XI. We are deprived of four books, and the opening chapters of Book XI, in which was contained the narrative of the years 37–47 A.D. The chief events were: the accession of Gaius and his principate: his murder in 41; the accession of Claudius; the campaigns in Mauretania and the establishment of two provinces, 41–42; the invasion of Britain, 43; the triumph of Claudius, 44; the campaigns of Aulus Plautius, 43–47.)

BOOK XI

47 A.D.

1. . . . For Messalina believed that Valerius Asiaticus, who had twice held the consulship, had been a lover of Poppaea Sabina's. Moreover, she was consumed with envy of his gardens, which Lucullus had created and which he had embellished with great lavishness.¹ So Suillius was launched in attack against them both. He was assisted by Sosibius, the tutor of Britannicus, who was ordered, under the guise of benevolence, to warn Claudius of power and wealth ill disposed to the imperial house. Asiaticus, he said, had been the leading spirit in the murder of Gaius: he had not hesitated to admit this at an assembly of the Roman people, and even to glory in it. This had made him famous in Rome; moreover, the provinces were full of rumors of a projected visit to Germany. Born at Vienne, his numerous and influential connections would make it very easy for him to stir up trouble among the tribes of his native province. Claudius lost no time in investigation. The prefect of the Guards, Crispinus, was sent with a force of soldiers large enough to put down a rising: he found Asiaticus at Baiae and brought him in chains to Rome.

2. Asiaticus was denied access to the Senate, and the case was heard in the Emperor's bedchamber. Messalina was present. Suillius accused him of corrupting the troops, by bribery and sexual license, to all sorts of outrages. His adultery with Poppaea was next brought up; the last charge was one of ef-

feminacy. At this point Asiaticus broke his silence. "Ask your sons, Suillius!" he said. "They will confess that I am a man!" When he began his defense, Claudius was powerfully affected. Even Messalina was in tears. Slipping from the room to dry her eyes, she whispered to Vitellius, "Don't let the defendant get away!" Then she hurried off to complete the ruin of Poppaea Sabina, sending agents to menace her with prison and thus drive her to suicide. So successfully was this kept from Claudius that, when Publius Cornelius Scipio, Poppaea's husband, was dining with him a few days later, he was asked why he had not brought his wife. The reply was that she had died.

3. Consulted as to the acquittal of Asiaticus, Vitellius shed tears, recalling their old friendship and devotion to the Emperor's mother, Antonia. Then he recounted the offices Asiaticus had held, touched on his recent military service in Britain, and other matters that might seem to urge clemency. Finally he said that Asiaticus ought to be allowed to choose his own manner of death. Claudius at once pronounced a similar formula of mercy. Some of Asiaticus' friends urged him to seek an easy death by abstaining from food; his reply was to decline the favor. After his usual exercises in the gymnasium, he took a bath, and dined cheerfully. Then, with the remark that it would have been more honorable to die from Tiberius' plotting or Gaius' brutality than from a woman's treachery and Vitellius' filthy tongue, he opened his veins. Before this, he had inspected his own funeral pyre, and ordered it to be moved to another part of the gardens, lest the flames should damage the leaves of the trees. Such was his composure in the last hours of his life.

FURTHER PROSECUTIONS BY SUILLIUS

4. Then the Senate was summoned, and Suillius proceeded to indict two Roman knights called Petra. The reason for their violent end was that they had lent their house for the meetings of Poppaea and the dancer Mnester. But the published charge against one of the two was that he had had a dream in which Claudius appeared, wearing a garland of grain with the ears turned down, and had interpreted this as a prophecy of a failure of the grain supply. Another account was that the wreath was of shriveling vine leaves, and the interpretation that the Emperor would die in the autumn. What is certain is that a dream—whatever its nature—was fatal to Petra and his brother. Crispinus received 1,500,000 sesterces as a reward

and an honorary praetorship. Vitellius proposed a million sesterces for Sosibius, for instructing Britannicus and advising Claudius. When Scipio was asked for his opinion, he replied, "Since I share the general view about Poppaea's misdeeds, you must assume that I say the same as everyone else"—a neat compromise between his love as a husband and his duty as a senator.

5. Suillius now showed a savage and unbroken energy in prosecution, and his ruthlessness found many imitators. By concentrating all the functions of the law and the executive in his own person, the Emperor had opened up an easy road to plunder. In the open market, the treachery of an advocate was the readiest commodity. Things reached such a point that Samius, a distinguished Roman knight, paid Suillius a fee of four hundred thousand sesterces and then found that he was on the other side. He fell on his sword at Suillius' house. At this the Senate, led by the consul-designate Gaius Silius—whose power and fall I shall later recount—rose and demanded that the Cincian Law,[2] enacted by our ancestors against the acceptance of money or gifts for legal services, be effectively enforced.

LEGAL FEES

6. There was a violent protest from those likely to be injured by the measure. Silius hated Suillius, and spoke in bitter terms. "Remember," he said, "the great orators of old, who looked to present and future fame as the reward of their eloquence. What would else be the noblest of talents is debased by this sordid money-making: where the object is profit, even honor cannot be secure. If there were no legal fees, there would be fewer actions at law; the present system incites to enmities, charges, hatred, and malevolence. Just as the prevalence of disease is profitable to doctors, so a diseased legal system puts money in the pockets of lawyers. Think of Asinius Pollio, Messala, or, more recently, Arruntius and Aserninus: these great men reached the top of the tree by immaculate probity and eloquence!" This speech of the consul-designate met with support, and a motion was drafted to include offenders under the law against extortion. Suillius, Cossutianus, and the rest, however, who saw that this meant, not a trial—for they were clearly guilty—but punishment, crowded round Claudius and begged him not to make it retroactive.

7. He assented, and they proceeded to put their case.

"Who," they said, "is so self-confident as to assure himself of eternal fame? A lawyer simply tries to meet a need arising from the business of life, so that no man shall be at the mercy of powerful enemies through lack of anyone to plead his case. Eloquence is not acquired without cost: to attend to another man's affairs a lawyer must neglect his own. Many senators earn a living by military service, some by farming. No profession attracts recruits unless they can count on a reward. It is easy enough for Asinius and Messala, who made their fortunes out of the wars between Augustus and Antony, or for the heirs of wealthy families, such as Aserninus and Arruntius, to show themselves high-minded! We on our side could easily quote the huge fees which Publius Clodius and Gaius Curio had demanded. We are simply senators, of modest means, seeking in times of peace no more than a peacetime income. Think how many men of lowly origin have risen to fame at the bar: take away incentives and a profession perishes." This was a less idealistic argument, but Claudius saw the force of it. He therefore decided to set a maximum fee of ten thousand sesterces, with prosecution for extortion when it was exceeded.

EVENTS IN THE EAST

8. At this time Mithridates—whom I have mentioned as the king of Armenia, and prisoner of Gaius—returned to his kingdom at the suggestion of Claudius, relying on the support of Pharasmenes. This man was king of Iberia, and the brother of Mithridates. He reported civil war in Parthia; since the dispute was over the throne itself, all lesser matters were being neglected. For Gotarzes, among many other cruel deeds, had planned the murder of his brother Artabanus, his wife, and his son. Alarmed at this, the other Parthian princes had called in Vardanes.[3] Always ready for great enterprises, Vardanes had covered 350 miles in two days, found Gotarzes unprepared, thrown him into a panic, and finally driven him out. Without delay, he had seized the neighboring provinces, and only the citizens of Seleucia were refusing to recognize his rule.

Not so much for any immediate gain as for his anger against them for having deserted his father, Vardanes laid siege to this powerful city, well protected by fortifications, its river, and its wall, and well provisioned. Meanwhile Gotarzes, reinforced by the armies of the Dahae and Hyrcani, renewed the struggle. Vardanes was forced to raise the siege of Seleucia and to move his forces to the plains of Bactria.

9. The whole forces of the East were thus engaged in a contest of doubtful issue, and Mithridates had an opportunity of seizing Armenia. Roman troops eliminated the fortresses in the mountains, Iberian cavalry scoured the plains. The Armenians made no resistance, once the Satrap Demonax had ventured on a battle and had been defeated. A little delay was caused by Cotys, king of Lesser Armenia, to whom some of the nobles turned. But letters from Claudius brought him to heel, and everything swung Mithridates' way, though his conduct was harsher than was politic at the beginning of a reign. While the Parthian princes were making ready for battle, Gotarzes revealed to his brother a conspiracy among their people, and there was a sudden armistice. They met together, hesitant at first; later they clasped hands and swore on the altars of the gods to avenge their enemies' treachery and to come to terms with each other. Vardanes seemed to have the better claims to the throne, and Gotarzes withdrew to furthest Hyrcania, to avoid any semblance of rivalry. On the return of Vardanes, Seleucia surrendered. It was the seventh year of the siege, and the long resistance of a single city was something of a disgrace to the Parthians.

10. Vardanes then visited the most important provinces, and was eager for the recovery of Armenia, but a threat of a war from Vibius Marsus, governor of Syria, deterred him. Meanwhile Gotarzes began to regret having surrendered the kingdom, and to assemble forces at the instance of the nobility, who found their slavery insupportable in times of peace. Vardanes advanced against him to the river Erindes. In a stiff encounter for the river crossing, victory went to Vardanes, then in a series of successful battles he overran the peoples as far as the Sindes, the river which is the boundary between the Dahae and the Arii. There his successes came to an end, for the Parthians, even when victorious, dislike distant campaigning. So he set up monuments to proclaim his power, and to assert that no previous Arsacid king had ever exacted tribute from these remote tribes. He returned with much glory, which made his rule harsher and more intolerable to his subjects than before. A plot was got up against him: suspecting nothing, he was murdered when out hunting. Vardanes was in his early manhood, yet few among the long-lived kings would have rivaled his glory if he had shown as much zeal to win his people's love as to strike fear into his enemies. His murder was followed by great confusion among the Parthians about the successor to the throne. Many favored Gotarzes, but there was also support for Meherdates, the son of Phraates, who had been a hostage in Rome. Finally Gotarzes prevailed, but the cruelty and ex-

travagance that marked his rule prompted the Parthians to send a secret missive to the Roman Emperor, begging him to set Meherdates free to assume his ancestral crown.

ROME. THE SECULAR GAMES

11. In the same year, it being the eight hundredth anniversary of the foundation of Rome, there was a celebration of the secular games, only sixty-four years after those given by Augustus![4] I pass over the calculations made by these Emperors, having given an adequate account of them in my narrative of the reign of Domitian. For he also gave secular games, and I was closely concerned in them, both as a member of the College of Fofteen and as a praetor of the year.[5] I note this not in any spirit of boastfulness, but because the College of Fifteen is traditionally associated with these rites, and those of them who hold magistracies have especial charge of the ceremonies. Claudius took his seat in the Circus, where the young men performed the Game of Troy.[6] Among them were his son Britannicus and the young Domitius, soon to be adopted into the imperial succession under the name of Nero. Domitius won the greater applause from the people, and this was taken as a sign of coming worth. A story was spread that snakes had watched over his infancy, but this was an invention, modeled on foreign myths.[7] Nero, hardly the man to detract from his own glory, merely said that one snake had been seen in his bedroom.

MESSALINA AND GAIUS SILIUS

12. However, the favor of the people was a survival from the popularity of Germanicus, of whom he was the sole living male heir. Moreover, there was growing sympathy for his mother Agrippina, who suffered much cruelty at the hands of Messalina. The Empress had always hated her, and was only distracted from launching accusers to the attack by a new and almost lunatic love affair. For Gaius Silius, the handsomest young man in Rome, so inflamed her mind that she caused him to divorce his wife Junia Silana, a lady of noble family, so that her own adulterer might be free of marriage. Gaius Silius was well aware of the danger and the scandal. But death was certain if he refused; there was some hope of avoiding detection, and the rewards were very great. So he pushed aside future

dangers to enjoy the delights of the present. The Empress would visit his house, not secretly but with a large retinue; she would keep close to him in public; she showered him with wealth and office. At last, as though there had been a change of fortune, the slaves, freedmen, and treasures of the Emperor began to be seen at the house of the adulterer.

13. Claudius, ignorant of his own marital affairs, was busy exercising his powers as censor. He put down disturbances in the theater with a firm hand: for insults had been hurled at the ex-consul Publius Pomponius, the playwright,[8] and several noble ladies. He also passed a law to check the harshness of creditors, forbidding the issue of loans to a minor for payment after the father's death. He brought into the city water collected from the springs among the Simbruine Hills.[9] He introduced and popularized new letters of the alphabet, having established that even the Greek alphabet was not perfected in a single instant.

ORIGINS OF THE ALPHABET[10]

14. The Egyptians, with their animal pictures, were the first to represent thoughts by means of symbols. Theirs are the most ancient records of humanity still to survive, engraved on stone. They claim, too, to have invented the alphabet, and to have taught it to the Phoenicians, who being supreme at sea, introduced it to the Greeks, and gained the glory of having invented what they actually borrowed. For the story is that Cadmus, who came with a Phoenician fleet, was the first to teach this art among the still illiterate Greeks. Some say that Cecrops of Athens, or Linus of Thebes, and Palamedes of Argos at the time of the Trojan War, invented an alphabet of sixteen letters, and that the remaining letters were added by others, notably Simonides. In Italy, the Etruscans took their alphabet from Demaratus of Corinth, the Aborigines from Evander of Arcadia; the Latin characters were like those of early Greece. But our alphabet too had only a few letters at first, with later additions. With this precedent, Claudius added three letters which were used in his reign and then forgotten. They are still to be seen in public inscriptions in the Forum and on Temples.

15. Next he brought before the Senate proposals for a guild of haruspices, to prevent this most ancient of Italian arts from dying out through disuse. Often at times of public danger the haruspices had been summoned, and on their advice religious ceremonies had been revived and conducted thenceforth in

better form. Etruscan nobles, whether on their own initiative
or at the bidding of the Roman Senate, had kept up the art and
passed it on to their sons. Now it had fallen out of fashion,
through public indifference to noble arts and the prevalence
of foreign superstitions. All was well for the present, but gratitude must be shown for the divine favors, lest the rites which
had been maintained through times of peril should lapse in
prosperity. The Senate responded by asking the pontifices to
see what was required for the upkeep and support of the
haruspices.

EVENTS IN GERMANY

16. The same year the Cherusci sought a king from Rome.
Their nobility had been depleted by civil wars, and only one
member of the royal house was left. He lived at Rome, and his
name was Italicus. On his father's side he was the son of Flavus,
brother of Arminius; his mother was a daughter of Actumerus,
a prince of the Chatti. He was a handsome man, skilled in riding and the use of arms in both the Roman and the German
fashion. Claudius made him a grant of money, provided an
escort, and bade him take up his ancestral honors with a good
heart: for he was the first man born at Rome as a citizen—
no mere hostage—to win a foreign crown. His coming was, at
first, welcome to the Germans. Free from party feelings, he
treated everyone with equal favor: he won renown and respect,
at times by amiability and moderation, qualities universally admired, but even more often by heavy drinking and lustfulness,
which barbarians find congenial. At first his popularity was
local, soon it spread farther afield. But men who found profit
in civil strife began to rouse the neighboring peoples with the
cry that German liberty was in danger, and Roman power on
the increase. Was there no man of native birth who could fill
the office of king? Was the offspring of Flavus—a Roman military scout—to outrank them all? No use to cite Arminius: even
if his son had returned from the enemy's country to rule, his
foreign upbringing, servility, dress, and all his non-German
habits would give grounds for fear. And, if Italicus was like
his father, no one had borne arms more remorselessly against
his country and its native gods than Flavus!

17. There was much support for these views, but Italicus'
followers were still in the majority. He was able to claim that
he had not come against their will, but had been invited because he was of more noble descent than the other claimants:

if they tested his courage, he would show himself worthy of his uncle Arminius, and his grandfather Actumerus. He had no need to blush for his father, who had never wavered in a loyalty to Rome which the Germans had freely assumed. "Liberty" was being falsely bandied about as a catchword by men of no morals, politically dangerous, whose only hope lay in civil war. The people applauded this speech. In a great battle—by German standards—Italicus was the victor. But his good fortune incited him to arrogance; he was expelled, and restored again by the help of the Langobardi. In prosperity and adversity alike he brought trouble to the Cherusci.

CORBULO IN LOWER GERMANY

18. At this time the Chauci, free from internal troubles, took advantage of the death of Sanquinius to raid his province of Lower Germany, before Corbulo could take up his duties. Their leader was a certain Gannascus, who had served in an auxiliary regiment and had then deserted with his small ships. He directed his raids especially on the coasts of Gaul, knowing them to be both rich and unwarlike. But when Corbulo reached the province he showed much energy, and soon acquired that reputation which dates from this great campaign. He brought up his warships by the main stream of the Rhine, and other vessels through estuaries and canals, as the situation warranted. With these he sank the German boats and drove out Gannascus. When the trouble was settled, he turned his attention to his own legions. They had little taste for duties and fatigues, though they were enthusiastic looters, and he was determined to reimpose the old discipline, to prevent falling out on the march or unauthorized combat. Arms were worn for picket and sentry duties, and for all the duties of day or night. A man is said to have been put to death for working at an entrenchment without side arms, and another for carrying only his dagger. These stories may be exaggerated, even invented, but they derive from the general strictness. One can suppose that a man credited with such harshness to light offenses would be severe, even inexorable, to serious charges.

19. Certainly this ruthlessness had opposite effects on the Roman soldiers and on the enemy. Our men gained in courage; the German savagery wilted. The Frisii, who had been unfriendly or unreliable since the death of Lucius Apronius, gave hostages and settled in lands assigned to them by Corbulo. Indeed, he gave them a senate, magistrates, and a legal code.

But he also stationed a garrison among them, to see that they did not violate his orders. Then he sent agents to induce the Greater Chauci to surrender, and laid a trap for Gannascus. It was successful, and being employed against a deserter and a breaker of oaths, it was not shameful. But his murder disturbed the Chauci, and Corbulo had sown the seeds of rebellion. Most Romans approved his action, but from others it drew criticism. "Why provoke the enemy?" they asked. "A reverse will be bad for the country. If he succeeds, so distinguished a general will be suspect under an inactive Emperor, and a danger to peace." So Claudius forbade all further advance in Germany, even ordering the withdrawal of garrisons from across the Rhine.

20. These dispatches reached Corbulo as he was building bases in enemy territory. It was an unexpected blow, and his mind was filled with a confusion of thought—fear of the Emperor, the contempt of the barbarians, the mockery of our allies. Yet his only remark was, "Happy were Roman commanders of old!" Then he ordered the retreat. But, to prevent idleness among the troops, he made them dig a canal, twenty-three miles long, between the Maas and the Rhine, so avoiding the dangers of the ocean. At least Claudius granted him the ornaments of a triumph, though he had forbidden him to campaign.

21. These same honors were won a little later by Curtius Rufus. He had opened a mine in the territory of the Mattiaci in search of veins of silver. It was only worked for a short time and its yield was poor. But the troops suffered severely from the work, digging channels, and laboring underground at tasks which would have been exhausting in the open air. The men were worn out, and since this work was going on in several provinces, a secret letter was sent in the name of all the armies to appeal to the Emperor. The honors of a triumph, they suggested, could well be awarded to generals before they took command of their troops.

Some accounts say that this same Curtius Rufus was a gladiator's son. I do not wish to make up a false report about him, but I shrink from telling the true facts.[11] At any rate, when he grew up, he was a clerk of the quaestor in the province of Africa. Strolling in the noonday heat in a deserted colonnade at Hadrumerum, he saw a vision of a woman of supernatural size, who said, "Rufus, you will one day be governor of this province." His hopes were raised by this omen. Returning to Rome, he used his friends' money and his own energies to become quaestor; then he defeated aristocratic competitors to become praetor. Tiberius backed him, covering Rufus' shameful birth with the words "Curtius Rufus can be his own ancestors." After this he reached a ripe old age. Toward his superiors he was obedient but surly, his inferiors he bullied; with his peers he was difficult. He gained the consulship, triumphal honors, and the province of Africa; then, having fulfilled the omen, he died.

ROME. THE OFFICE OF QUAESTOR

22. Meanwhile, at Rome, and for no reasons obvious at the time or later, a Roman knight called Gaius Nonius was discovered wearing a sword in the throng of callers at an imperial reception. When he was put to the torture, he did not deny his guilt but said nothing to incriminate others. Whether he had accomplices is not known.

In the same year Publius Dolabella carried a proposal that the expense of an annual gladiatorial show should be defrayed by the candidates for the quaestorship. In our ancestors' time that office had been the reward of good character, and all citizens of honorable standing were allowed to seek office. Indeed, no age limits debarred those in their early manhood from holding even the consulship or dictatorship. As early as the kingly period quaestors were appointed, as is shown by Lucius Brutus' restatement of the law passed by the Comitia. But the power of choosing them rested with the consuls, until the people took over selection to that office along with others. Valerius Potitus and Aemilius Mamercus were the first so chosen—sixty-three years after the expulsion of the Tarquins —to supervise expenditure for war. As business increased, two more quaestors were appointed to work in Rome. Then the number was doubled again, with taxes coming in from Italy and the addition of provincial tribute. An enactment of Sulla created twenty, to enlarge the Senate, which now had charge of judicial business. Though the knights recovered this function, the quaestorship still depended on the merits of the candidates, or their popularity with the electors—until Dolabella's proposal put it up for sale.

43 A.D. Consuls Aulus Vitellius and Lucius Vipstanus Publicola

23. In the consulship of Aulus Vitellius and Lucius Vipstanus there were discussions about enlarging the Senate. The great chiefs of Gallia Comata,[12] who already had treaties of alliance and Roman citizenship, put forward demands to hold magistracies in Rome. This caused much discussion and disagreement. The rival views were brought forward in the Emperor's presence. "Italy," said one party, "is not so weak that she cannot supply a Senate for her own capital. Once native-born Romans satisfied the kindred Italian peoples: there is little reason to be ashamed of the old form of government. Even today, the old Roman character is quoted for instances of valor and true glory. Is it not enough that the Veneti and Insubrian Gauls have forced their way into the Senate House?[13] Are we to have a mob of foreigners like prisoners of war? What office will be left to the remnants of our own nobility, or to the impoverished senators of Latium? These wealthy Gauls will fill every office. Their fathers and grandfathers, commanding their tribal armies, defeated the armies of Rome, and besieged Caesar at Alesia.[14] These are recent injuries, but does no memory remain of those who died beneath the Capitol, the very citadel of Rome, at the hands of the ancestors of these Gauls? Let them bear the name of citizen; but do not let them debase the insignia of the senators and the glorious office of Roman magistrate."[15]

24. Such a line of argument did not carry weight with Claudius. He refuted it on the spot, and at a meeting of the Senate spoke as follows.[16] "My own ancestors, going back to Clausus, who, though of Sabine origin, was made a Roman citizen and a patrician at one and the same time, induce me to follow the same policy in public affairs—to import excellence, from whatever source. I recall that the Julii came from Alba, the Coruncanii from Cameria, the Porcii from Tusculum. Leaving aside these venerable parallels, Etruria, Lucania, and

the whole of Italy have sent men to the Senate. Indeed, Italy herself has been extended to the Alps, so that not merely individuals, but whole districts and peoples, have been brought together under the name of Rome. There was solidly based peace at home, and a sound policy abroad, when we brought the nations beyond the Po into our citizenship, when we strengthened our overstrained Empire by adding the best of the provincials to the legionary settlements we spread throughout the world. Do we regret that the Balbi came from Spain, or other men of no less distinction from Gallia Narbonensis? Their descendants are still here, and they vie with us in love of Rome. What else caused the downfall of Sparta and Athens, at the height of their military glory, but the exclusiveness with which they treated conquered peoples as aliens and kept them at arm's length? But our founder Romulus had the wisdom to treat several peoples as first enemies, then in the same day, as Roman citizens. We have had foreign kings. That the sons of freedmen should be elected to office is not, as is often alleged, an innovation; it happened often in early times. 'But,' we are told, 'we fought against the Senones!' Did the Vulsci, then, and the Aequi never face us in arms? 'But we were conquered by the Gauls!' Yes, and we gave hostages to the Etruscans, and we passed under the yoke before the Samnites.[17] Look back over all the wars we have fought, and mark how the Gallic wars took the shortest time to finish. They were straightway followed by a peace that has endured. They are linked to us in customs, culture, and marriage; let them bring their gold and wealth, rather than keep it separate. Members of the Senate, everything that now seems ancient was once a novelty. Plebeians held magistracies after the nobility, Latins after plebeians, the other peoples of Italy after the Latins. This, too, will grow customary with time; what today we justify by precedent, will be a precedent in its turn."

25. The Emperor's speech was followed by a resolution of the Senate, by which the Aedui were the first to obtain the right of becoming Roman senators. This privilege was given them because of the antiquity of their treaty with Rome and because, alone of the Gauls, they claimed the title of "Brothers of the Roman People."[18]

At the same time, Claudius made patrician all senators of long standing, or of distinguished ancestry. Few families indeed remained from what Romulus had termed the greater, or Lucius Brutus, the lesser, nobility. Even the families which the dictator Caesar had elevated under the Cassian, and Augustus under the Saenian law, were now extinct. There was a warm welcome for these measures, and the censor who carried them was very gratified. But he was also worried about how to expel notorious characters from the Senate. The plan he followed was derived from a tolerant modern procedure rather than the severity of the old method. For he advised persons so involved to consider for themselves the wisdom of applying to resign from the order. Permission would be readily granted. Next, expulsions and resignations were published in a single list, so that the mingling of censorial verdicts with the modesty of voluntary withdrawals would lessen the humiliation. For this, the consul Lucius Vipstanus proposed conferring on Claudius the title of "Father of the Senate." The title "Father of His Country" had been lavishly granted; now services to the state deserved recognition by new honorary titles. Claudius checked the proposal as too flattering. Then he held the census at the ritually determined time: the number of citizens registered was 5,984,072.[19]

THE FALL OF MESSALINA

26. This too, was the end of his ignorance of his own affairs. Soon he was compelled to take note of and to punish his wife's scandalous immoralities, though as a result he would himself conceive a desire for an incestuous marriage. By now the mere ease of her adulteries had begun to bore Messalina; she was veering toward vices as yet untasted. At this very moment Silius urged that they should abandon concealment; either a fatal lunacy had seized him, or he thought desperate perils called for desperate measures. "We have not reached the point of waiting for the Emperor to die!" he exclaimed. "Innocent plans suit innocent people; when guilt is obvious, audacity is called to the rescue. We have accomplices who share our fears. I am unmarried, childless, and ready to marry you and adopt Britannicus. If we can only circumvent Claudius, your power, Messalina, will be the same, and you will have security as well. He is slow to detect treachery, but quickly roused to fury!" There was an unenthusiastic response. Not that Messalina loved her husband, but she feared that once Silius won the throne he might turn against his mistress, and then this crime, born of emergency, would stand out in its true light. But she lusted for the name of wife for the sheer enormity of the scandal—depravity's most lasting thrill. Waiting no longer than for Claudius to go to Ostia to perform a sacrifice, she performed all the solemnities of marriage with Silius.

27. Here, I am well aware, we seem to be entering the

realm of fantasy. Could any human beings have such a degree of carelessness in a city where everything was known, and everything talked about? More than that, here is the consul-designate, marrying the wife of the Emperor, on a duly appointed day, in the presence of witnesses, "for the procreation of children": here is the Empress, hearing the auspices, taking the bridal veil, sacrificing to the gods. Together they take their place at the wedding feast among their guests; there is an exchange of kisses and embraces, the night is passed in the delights of honorable marriage. But I invent nothing. I recount, and shall recount, what an older generation heard and wrote.

28. Panic possessed the imperial household, especially those in positions of power, who had most to fear from a revolution. From secret discussions, they passed to open indignation. "It was a disgrace," they said, "when a male ballet dancer insulted the bedroom of the Emperor: yet disaster was still far away. But here is a young aristocrat, handsome and intelligent, due for the consulship, but with higher ambitions still! The sequel to such a wedding can hardly be in doubt!" They then thought —doubtless with alarm—of the sluggishness of Claudius, his subjection to his wife, and the many murders that had been carried out on Messalina's orders. Yet his very pliability offered the hope that, if the enormity of the outrage could be brought home to him, she might be ruined and undone before she could stand trial. The whole issue turned on whether he would give her a hearing, and how they could shut his ears against her, even if she confessed.

29. First, then, Callistus (whom I have already mentioned in connection with the murder of Gaius), next, Narcissus, architect of the murder of Gaius Appius, and the reigning favorite Pallas, discussed the chances of employing secret threats simply to turn Messalina from her affair with Silius, concealing their knowledge of everything else. But this course they abandoned for fear of disaster. With Pallas this was cowardice, but Callistus had learned from an earlier court that power is better safeguarded by caution than by dramatic expedients. But Narcissus continued to persevere with the plan, making only one change—that Messalina should be given no previous inkling of the accuser or the charge. He waited for his opportunity. The Emperor stayed long at Ostia, and by promises and bribes—and by pointing out that once the wife had been removed their influence would be strengthened— he was able to persuade two of the Emperor's favorite concubines to act as his informers.

30. So, at a private interview, Calpurnia (that was the girl's name) flung herself at Claudius' feet and cried out that

Messalina had married Silius. She turned for confirmation to the other girl, Cleopatra, who stood waiting for her cue, and when she nodded, asked that Narcissus should be sent for. Apologizing for having withheld what he knew of Messalina's affairs with Vettius and Plautius, Narcissus protested that even now he would pass over acts of adultery, nor was there to be any thought of demanding back the palace, the slaves, the other fortunes she had heaped on Silius. Let him enjoy them; but he must return his wife and cancel the contract of marriage. "Do you know," he exclaimed, "that you are divorced? The Roman people, the Senate, the army, have all witnessed the marriage of Silius; act quickly, or this new husband will seize Rome."

MESSALINA'S PARTY

31. Claudius summoned his most loyal friends, notably Turranius, prefect of the grain supply, then Lusius Geta, commander of the Guard. When he questioned them, they said the story was true. The rest of his entourage crowded around, exclaiming that he must go to the barracks of the Guard and win their loyalty: safety must come before revenge. It is well known that Claudius was so panic-stricken that he kept asking, "Am I still Emperor? Is Silius a private citizen?" On Messalina's side there was all the carelessness of unbridled excess. It was autumn; she was holding a mock wine harvest on her estate. The presses were at work, the vats brimming; women clad in skins capered like frenzied bacchantes at a sacrifice. The Empress, hair unbound, brandished the thyrsus; Silius, ivy-wreathed, wearing the buskins, stood by her, rolling his head. Around them yelled a dissolute crew. Vettius Valens is said to have climbed a huge tree as a joke, and when asked, "What do you see?" answered, "Dirty weather coming up from Ostia!" The sky may indeed have betokened it, but perhaps this casual remark was taken as a prophecy.

APPEAL OF MESSALINA

32. But by now it was no mere rumor. Messengers kept pouring in, saying Claudius knew everything, and was on his way to exact vengeance. So they separated. Messalina went to the Gardens of Lucullus, Silius, hiding his fears, to business in the Forum. The others were melting away, but they were

arrested by centurions and thrown into chains, as they were
seized in public or in private hiding places. The disaster had
deprived Messalina of the ability to plan. But she had often
profited from meeting her husband and being seen by him,
and she resolved to try once more. Britannicus and Octavia
were ordered to seek their father's arms: Vibidia, senior vestal
virgin, was exhorted to speak to the Emperor, as Pontifex
Maximus, and beg for mercy. Meanwhile, with no more than
three attendants—her retinue had already shrunk to that—she
walked on foot the entire length of Rome. Then, in a cart used
for removing refuse from gardens, she set off along the road
to Ostia. No man pitied her; all were overwhelmed by her fearful crimes.

33. On Claudius' side, also, there was panic. They could
not trust Geta, the Praetorian prefect, whose fickleness could
turn to either good or bad. So Narcissus—and others who
shared his fears—warned Claudius that the only hope of safety
lay in command of the soldiers being entrusted to one of the
freedmen, though only for one day. He offered himself for the
post. He also asked for, and was granted, a seat in the Emperor's carriage, lest on the journey to Rome Lucius Vitellius
and Largus Caecina might have an opportunity of persuading
him to change his mind.

34. There are many reports of the Emperor's contradictory
remarks, as he passed from reproaching his wife's scandalous
conduct to recollections of their marriage and the infancy of
their children. Vitellius said nothing but "How scandalous!—
how disgraceful!" Narcissus kept pressing him to be less ambiguous, and to declare his real sentiments, but could not ex-
tract from him anything but hesitant remarks which could
lead to any conclusion. Largus Caecina followed his example.

By now Messalina was in sight. She called out that a hearing must be given to the mother of Octavia and Britannicus.
Her accuser shouted her down, bringing up Silius and the marriage; then he handed over a detailed inventory of her vices,
so as to attract the gaze of Claudius. Soon after, they entered
the city. Here, the two children they shared were brought forward. Narcissus ordered them to be taken away. Vibidia he
was unable to remove before, with many reproaches, she had
demanded that Claudius should not condemn his wife unheard.
Narcissus replied that the Emperor would give her a hearing
and an opportunity to clear herself; meanwhile, the vestal
virgin should take herself off and attend to her sacred duties.

35. All this time, Claudius was preternaturally silent.
Vitellius looked unconscious of what was happening. All
obeyed the freedman's orders. He ordered the house of the

adulterer to be opened up, and the Emperor conducted thither. In the vestibule he was able to point out a statue of Silius' father, which the Senate had ordered to be destroyed; then all the heirlooms of the Neros and the Drusi which had come to him as the wages of sin. This angered Claudius, who broke out into threats. Narcissus conducted him to the barracks of the Guards, where it had been arranged that he should address the troops. Narcissus spoke first, then Claudius uttered a few words: just though his anger was, shame held him back. The troops then clamored to know the names of the accused and the punishments of the guilty. Silius was pushed forward: he did not attempt to defend himself or to play for time; indeed, he begged for a speedy death. Several noble Roman knights showed the same fortitude. Titius Proculus, who had been appointed "guardian" to Messalina by Silius and who now turned informer; Vettius Valens, who confessed his guilt; Pompeius Urbicus and Saufeius Trogus, privy to the plot—all were condemned to death. The same sentence was pronounced against Decrius Calpurnianus, commander of the watch, Sulpicius Rufus, master of a training school for gladiators, and Iuncus Vergilianus, a senator.

36. Only in the case of Mnester was there delay. Tearing open his clothes, he showed the marks of lashes, and bade Claudius remember the words by which he had placed him under Messalina's orders. Ambition or money had driven the others to sin: necessity was his compulsion. He would have been the first to die, had Silius come to power. This swayed Claudius, always prone to indulgence. But the freedmen urged him not to spare a ballet dancer, after the deaths of so many men of rank; in a crime of this magnitude, the question whether participation was enforced or voluntary was unimportant. Nor did the defense of Traulus Montanus, a Roman knight, find acceptance. A modest young man, but physically handsome, he had been summoned to Messalina's bed and ejected from it in a single night, for she passed with equal caprice from lust to disdain. Suillius Caesoninus and Plautius Lateranus escaped the death sentence—the latter, because of his uncle's distinguished services; the former, thanks to his own vices, for in that rabble of perverts he had played the woman's role.

THE FATE OF MESSALINA

37. Meanwhile, in the Gardens of Lucullus, Messalina fought for life. She composed an appeal, hopeful in some

passages, indignant in others, for she preserved her arrogance
to the last. Indeed, had not Narcissus hastened her end,
calamity would have fallen on her accuser. For Claudius went
home, dined early and, mellowed by wine, ordered a message
to be sent to the "poor woman" (his actual words) to say
that she should attend the next day to plead her case. His
anger was abating, his love returning; any further delay, and
the coming night might renew the memories of conjugal delights. So Narcissus rushed out and ordered the centurions and
the officer, who were standing by, to carry out the murder:
these were the Emperor's instructions. One of the freedmen,
Euodus, was sent to make sure that the deed was done. Bursting into the gardens, they found her lying on the ground, her
mother, Domitia Lepida, sitting beside her. When Messalina
had been in her glory they had quarreled; now, moved to pity,
Domitia had come to be with her daughter in her last hours.
She urged her not to await the assassin's blow: "Your life is
over, all you can now hope for is an honorable death." But
honor found no place in that lust-besotted heart. There were
tears and useless complaints, until the doors gave under the
weight of assailants. Then there was the officer, looking down
on her in silence, and the freedman, hurling his slave's abuse.

38. Then at last she looked her situation in the face, and
took the steel. Next she moved it, in useless panic, from her
throat to her breast: a blow from the officer ran her through.
The corpse was turned over to her mother. Claudius was still
at dinner when he received the news that Messalina was dead,
though it was uncertain whether by her own hand or another's.
He did not bother to inquire. Asking for wine, he went on
with the feast. And, in the days that followed, he gave no sign
of hatred or pleasure, of anger or sadness, nor of any other
human emotion—not even when he saw the rejoicings of the
accusers, or his children in mourning. The Senate helped him
to forget by ordering Messalina's name and statues to be removed from all public and private places.

Narcissus was given an honorary quaestorship, though that
was the least of his reasons for arrogance, since his power
now far exceeded that of Pallas and Callistus.

This action against Messalina was just, but it was to lead
to fearful consequences.

BOOK XII

1. The death of Messalina threw the imperial household into confusion. Competition arose among the freedmen as to who should choose a wife for Claudius, since the Emperor had no taste for a bachelor's life and was used to being under the control of his wives. Fierce rivalry raged between the ladies themselves, each urging the beauty, birth, and wealth that qualified her for so exalted a marriage. The chief contest was between Lollia Paulina, daughter of Marcus Lollius the ex-consul, and Germanicus' daughter Julia Agrippina, backed respectively by Callistus and Pallas; Aelia Paetina, daughter of the noble house of the Tuberones, enjoyed the support of Narcissus. The Emperor's own inclinations kept changing now this way and now that, according to the last person he spoke to; in the end he called the rival backers to a meeting[1] and asked for their advice, supported by reasoned argument.

2. Narcissus took the line that he had been married before to Paetina (who had borne him a daughter, Antonia), that remarriage would bring no unpleasant innovations into his domestic arrangements, and that Paetina would not feel a stepmother's hatred for Britannicus and Octavia—indeed, she would treat them almost as her own children. Against this Callistus insisted that he had divorced her long ago; that this was a disqualification and remarriage would make her arrogant. By far the better course would be to marry Lollia; being childless, she would not be jealous, and would be a mother

to her stepchildren. Pallas, however, insisted that the great merit of Agrippina was that she brought with her the grandson of Germanicus, a boy eminently worthy of imperial rank. It would be wise for Claudius to unite to himself a noble race, the posterity of the Julian and Claudian lines, and not to allow a lady of proved fertility, and still in the flower of youth, to take to another house the illustrious name of the Caesars.

3. These arguments prevailed, not unassisted by the seductions of Agrippina herself; for, using her family connections as an excuse to pay frequent visits to her uncle, she enticed him into giving her the preference, and, indeed, exercised the powers of a wife in advance. Once she had made sure of her marriage, she began to extend her ambitions, and to work for the union of Domitius, her son by Gnaeus Ahenobarbus, with Claudius' daughter Octavia. This called for criminal methods, seeing that Claudius had already betrothed Octavia to Lucius Silanus, and had already won popular favor for the young man (who had other claims to distinction) by granting him the ornaments of a triumph and giving extravagant gladiatorial shows in his name. Still, anything was possible with an Emperor whose likes and dislikes went according to what was suggested or dictated to him.

4. So Lucius Vitellius, who had a sure instinct for future despots, used his post as censor to carry on a servile intrigue. In order to win Agrippina's favor, he took a hand in her plans, and prosecuted Silanus, whose pretty but forward sister, Junia Calvina, had previously been married to Vitellius' son. This provided the pretext for the accusation, for Vitellius put the worst construction on the affection of the brother and sister, which had been unguarded but not incestuous. To this the Emperor lent a ready ear, his affection for his daughter predisposing him to suspicion against his future son-in-law. Silanus knew nothing of the trap. He was praetor for the year; but, although the list of senators was complete and the censor's ceremonies had been performed, he was suddenly expelled from the senatorial order by a decree of Vitellius. At the same time, Claudius revoked his engagement to Octavia; he was forced to resign his office, and was superseded by Eprius Marcellus for the one day of his term still to go.

49 A.D. Consuls Gaius Pompeius Longinus and Quintus Veranius

5. The next year, both rumor and their illicit relationship argued strongly for the impending marriage of Claudius and Agrippina. But to celebrate it openly was something they did not, as yet, dare to do. There was no precedent for the marriage of uncle and niece; indeed, the thing was incestuous, and it was feared that disregard of such a prohibition might bring disaster on the state. Hesitation persisted until Vitellius took it upon himself to arrange things by his own methods. Would the Emperor, he asked, be willing to bow to the demands of the people, to the authority of the Senate? Claudius answered that he was no more than an individual citizen, powerless to resist unanimity. Very well, said Vitellius, let him stay at home. Then he himself entered the Senate House and asked permission to speak first on a matter of the utmost public importance. "The laborious duties of the Emperor," he said,[2] "are worldwide in their scope; they call for support which will enable him to provide for the public good without private worries. What prop and comfort would be more suitable for the Emperor—a very censor in disposition—than marriage with a wife, who would be his companion in good times and in bad, to whom he could entrust his innermost thoughts, and his little children? From his earliest youth he has obeyed the laws; he has never accustomed himself to idleness or dissipation."

6. Applause followed this promising beginning, and the senators seemed disposed to agree. "We are all resolved," proceeded Vitellius, "that the Emperor ought to marry. Now the lady must be of noble birth, proved fertility, unblemished chastity. Agrippina's preeminence in birth is easily established: she has demonstrated her fertility; her virtue is all that can be desired. How admirable—indeed, I see in it the work of heaven—that she should come to the Emperor as a widow, for he knows no wives but his own! You will have heard from fathers, you may have experience yourselves, of wives being

torn away to serve an Emperor's desires. Nothing of the kind is involved in this virtuous arrangement. Let us set up an example, let the Emperor be presented with a wife by the country! Do I hear the objection that marriage between uncle and niece is not customary with us? With other peoples it is usual, and quite legal; here, too, marriage between second cousins has become frequent with the passage of time. Customs change with the times, and this innovation will soon come to be taken for granted."

7. At this, several senators rushed out of the Senate House, protesting that they would force the Emperor, if he delayed any longer. A crowd collected, spontaneously proclaiming that this was the will of the Roman people. Claudius immediately paraded himself in the Forum to receive congratulations, then entered the Senate House and asked for a decree legalizing, from that time forward, marriage with a brother's daughter. Only one person could actually be found anxious to avail himself of this concession—a certain Alledius Severus, of knightly rank, commonly supposed to be seeking to ingratiate himself with Agrippina.

From that time Roman society was transformed. Everything was done to a woman's dictates—and that woman no Messalina, who made public affairs serve only her appetites. Agrippina's was almost a masculine despotism: in public she was austere, even haughty: her private life was free from immorality, unless it served to gain her power. She had an unbounded desire for money, but only as a support of authority.

8. On the very day of the marriage, Silanus committed suicide; whether because that day put an end to his hopes, or because he had made a deliberate choice of it to increase resentment. His sister Calvina was expelled from Italy. Claudius decreed ritual sacrifices, as approved by King Tullus Hostilius, and carried out by the pontifices in the grove of Diana. General ridicule was aroused by the revival of penalties and expiations for incest at this precise juncture. Agrippina, however, lest she become known solely for ill-doing, sought to win favor by securing the recall of Annaeus Seneca,[3] and advancing him to the praetorship. This, she thought, would be well received by the public, owing to the fame of his literary works; besides, she was anxious to have him as a tutor for her son Domitius, and as a consultant in her own plans for power. For Seneca was believed to be faithful to her for benefits received, and hostile to Claudius through resentment of his injury.

BETROTHAL OF NERO AND OCTAVIA

9. They now decided to act without further delay. The ex-consul Mammius Pollio received lavish inducements to urge Claudius to betroth Octavia to Domitius.* Their age made it not unreasonable, and it opened up wider designs, and Pollio's arguments ran along the same lines as those recently used by Vitellius. So Octavia was betrothed; as for Domitius, he was now, in addition to his earlier ties, the Emperor's son-in-law and the rival of Britannicus. This position he had reached through his mother's support, and through the intrigues of those who had attacked Messalina and now feared the vengeance of her son.

EASTERN AFFAIRS

10. I have previously mentioned the dispatch of a Parthian delegation to Rome to ask for Meherdates, then a hostage at Rome. Received in the Senate, they disclosed their instructions as follows. "We are well aware of the treaty between our countries, and we are not disloyal to the ruling house of Parthia, the Arsacids. What we do ask is that the son of Vonones, the grandson of Phraates, should come to deliver us from the tyranny of Gotarzes, which has become intolerable to the nobles and to the people. He has already exterminated his brothers, his kinsmen, and even more distant relations, and is now turning his attention to pregnant women and little children. Idle at home, unlucky in war, he is covering lethargy with the cloak of terrorism. We have an old, publicly sanctioned pact of friendship with you. Now you must come to the help of allies who are your equals in power, but who accord you deference out of respect. It is for precisely this reason that kings' sons are sent to Rome as hostages, so that if we get tired of our rulers at home we can apply to the Emperor and Senate, and obtain a better one, with the advantages of a Roman education."

11. Replying to this, and other similar statements, Claudius launched into a speech about Roman preeminence and Parthian subservience. He compared himself to the deified Augustus, who had sent a king to Parthia (Tiberius had sent kings too,

* The future Nero.

but nothing was said about that). From this, he turned to giving precepts to Meherdates (who was present) and advising him to think in terms of mentor and citizens, not of despot and slaves. Mercy and justice, he said, were qualities which orientals would accept all the more gladly because they were unknown. Then he turned to the deputation and extolled Rome's fosterling, who had given proof of his good character. Still, they must take kings as they were, frequent changes were unprofitable. Rome had now reached a pinnacle of glory, and desired peace for foreign countries. He then entrusted the governor of Syria, Gaius Cassius, with the task of escorting the young prince to the bank of the Euphrates.

12. At this period Gaius Cassius stood high as a jurist—military qualities being unremarked in times of peace, when good and bad generals appear the same. Still, so far as was possible without actual hostilities, Cassius did his best to revive the old Roman discipline, to train the legions in the field, and to show as much planning and forethought as though an attack were imminent. This, he thought, was a debt he owed to his family, that of the Cassii, who had a considerable reputation even in those parts. He therefore summoned the nobles who had asked for Meherdates as king, and pitched camp at Zeugma, the most convenient crossing on the river. There he was joined by some high Parthian nobles, as also by Acbarus, king of the Arabs. Since delay cools the enthusiasm of barbarians, or turns it to treachery, he advised Meherdates to press forward with his plans. The treachery of Acbarus nullified this advice; the young prince identified the royal power with indulgence of appetite and allowed himself to be detained for several days in the city of Edessa. Carenes, governor of Mesopotamia, invited him to come, stressing that everything was ready if he would move quickly. But instead of going at once to Mesopotamia he made a long detour via Armenia, a district quite unfavorable at that time of the year, when winter was approaching.

13. Finally, exhausted by travel through snowbound, mountainous country, they reached the plains and were reinforced by the troops of Carenes. Crossing the Tigris, he went on through Adiabene, whose king, Izates, publicly allied himself with Meherdates, but secretly remained loyal to Gotarzes. Still, they captured the city of Nineveh, the ancient seat of Assyrian power, and the fortress where the power of Persia finally collapsed in the battle between Darius and Alexander. Meanwhile Gotarzes was at Sanbulos,[4] offering prayers to the divinity of the mountain. (This is the seat of that cult of Hercules who, at regular intervals, warns the priests in visions

to station horses ready for hunting by the temple. The horses are loaded with quivers full of arrows, and range loose through the forest, returning only at night, exhausted and with their quivers empty. Then, in a second vision, the god reveals his track through the forests, and the corpses of wild beasts are found all along it.)

14. Gotarzes' army had yet to be reinforced, so he took up a position protected by the river Corma. Although challenging his rival to battle by message and insults, he played for delay, moving from place to place, and sending secret agents to bribe the enemy force to change sides. First Izates with the forces of Adiabene, then Acbarus with his Arabs, went over to him. Treachery comes by nature to these peoples, and experience has shown that they would rather invite their kings from Rome than keep them.

Meherdates, stripped of these powerful allies, and fearing betrayal from the others, saw that his only hope was to risk everything in a battle. Gotarzes was full of confidence, now that his enemy's power was diminished, and a long and bloody battle was fought. The issue was in doubt until Carenes, pursuing his defeated opponents too far, was surrounded and cut off by a fresh enemy force. Now Meherdates had no hope left. Listening to the promises of a dependant of his father's, Parraces, he was bound and surrendered to the victorious Gotarzes. The latter sneered at him as no kinsman of his, no scion of the Arsacids, but an alien and a Roman. He allowed him to live—with his ears cut off—as a proof of his clemency and as a disgrace to Rome. Later, Gotarzes died of an illness, to be succeeded by Vonones, ruler of Media. He won no successes and suffered no losses worthy of mention. After a brief and undistinguished reign he died and was succeeded by his son Vologeses.

WAR IN THE CRIMEA

15. Mithridates, king of the Crimean Bosporus, who had been deposed and was wandering at large, learned that the Roman general Aulus Didius Gallus and his main force had been withdrawn, and that the new kingdom was held by Cotys, an inexperienced youth, and a few cohorts under the Roman knight Julius Aquila. Disdainful of both, he began to rouse the tribes and attract deserters. Finally he got an army together, drove out the king of the Dandaridae, and gained possession of his kingdom. When this became known, and he

seemed on the point of invading Bosporus, Aquila and Cotys became aware of the weakness of their own forces—the more so, since Zorsines, king of the Siraci, had taken up arms again. They too began to look for outside help, and sent a deputation to Eunones, king of the Aorsi. It was easy enough to arrange an alliance by pointing out that the power of Rome was now brought to bear against Mithridates. The agreement was that Eunones should fight the cavalry battles, while the Romans undertook to besiege cities.

16. Then they advanced with a mixed force, the Aorsi in the front and rear, the middle position taken up by auxiliary cohorts and Bosporan troops armed in Roman fashion. This force routed the enemy and reached Soza, a town of the Dandaridae. Mithridates had evacuated it, but the loyalty of its people was uncertain, so it was decided to post a garrison there. Then they proceeded against the Siraci, crossed the river Panda, and surrounded the city of Uspe, which was placed on high ground and fortified by walls and a ditch. However, these walls were not stone-built but made of wickerwork frames with earth in between, poor defense against an assault. Lofty siege towers were built to harass the defenders with burning brands and showers of missiles; indeed, had not nightfall put an end to the fighting, the city would have been beset and captured in a single day.

17. The next day the inhabitants sent envoys to beg for pardon for the whole free population, and offering ten thousand slaves. The victorious army rejected these terms, since it seemed barbarous to massacre the surrendered, but a hard task to guard so many prisoners: better that they should be killed in open warfare. So the soldiers who had got inside by means of ladders were given the order to kill. The people of Uspe were exterminated, and their neighbors terrified. There seemed no safety anywhere: weapons, fortifications, strongly held or lofty positions, ruins, cities themselves, had all been swept aside. Zorsines debated long whether to help Mithridates in his extremity, or to save his own kingdom. Finally, tribal loyalty won the day; he surrendered hostages and prostrated himself before the effigy of the Emperor. This was a great distinction for the Roman army, which had won a bloodless victory and reached a point only three days' journey from the river Don. But its return journey was less fortunate; for some ships went ashore on the voyage back and were surrounded by the barbarians, with the loss of the commander of a cohort and large numbers of auxiliary troops.

18. Meanwhile Mithridates, seeing no hope in arms, was considering to whom he should turn for mercy. He was afraid

of his brother Cotys, who had once betrayed him and was now his enemy. None of the Roman commanders seemed of high enough rank to enable their promises to carry weight. So he turned to Eunones, who bore him no personal grudge and who was strengthened by his recent alliance with Rome. With dress and mien appropriate to his fortunes he entered the royal palace, fell at Eunones' feet, and exclaimed, "Here I am, Mithridates, whom the Romans have sought by land and sea for so many years. Use as you will this descendant of the Persian royal line: my ancestry is all my foes have left me."

19. Eunones was moved by the king's distinction, by the change in his fortunes, and by his dignified entreaty. He raised the suppliant and praised him for turning for refuge to the people of the Aorsi, and to himself personally. At the same time he sent envoys to bear dispatches to the Emperor couched in these terms: Friendship between Roman emperors and the kings of great peoples came from their comparable dignity: he and Claudius were also allied in victory. The noblest ending for war is forgiveness; thus Zorsines had been conquered, but not despoiled. Mithridates merited heavier punishment; so he was not asking for power nor the return of his kingdom, only that he should be spared appearing in a triumph, and death.

20. Claudius was, as a rule, lenient to foreign princes, but he hesitated for some time as to whether he should receive Mithridates as a captive, under a promise of safety, or recapture him in arms. The latter course would gratify resentment of his hostile actions, and the desire for revenge: on the other hand it could be argued that it would involve a war in a trackless country, devoid of harbors, against savage kings, nomad tribes, and on an infertile soil. Delay would be tedious, haste dangerous; victory would bring only moderate renown, and failure much disgrace. Better, then, to seize the opportunity and to keep Mithridates alive as an exile, in destitution, for whom the longer life lasted, the greater his punishment would be. Moved by these considerations, he wrote to Eunones to the effect that Mithridates had indeed deserved the harshest of punishments, which he had the means to enforce. However, the Roman tradition was to be resolute against enemies but merciful to suppliants; as for triumphs, they were earned against whole peoples and nations, not against individuals.

21. So Mithridates was surrendered, and conveyed to Rome by Junius Cilo, imperial finance officer in Pontus. It is said that his demeanor in Claudius' presence was not in keeping with his situation, and one remark of his gained wide currency: "I was not sent back to you: I returned. If you

doubt this, set me free, and see if you catch me again!" He preserved an impassive countenance when he was surrounded by armed guards and displayed to the Roman people beside the Rostra. The insignia of a consul were given to Junius Cilo, and those of a praetor to Aquila.

EVENTS IN ROME

22. In the same year Agrippina's hatred and enmity toward Lollia, her rival for the imperial marriage, led her to fabricate accusations and an accuser against her. The charge was that she had consulted astrologers and magicians, and had inquired of the oracle of Apollo at Claros about Claudius' wedding. Without giving Lollia a hearing, Claudius spoke in the Senate about her noble birth: her mother was the sister of Lucius Volusius, Cotta Messalinus was a great-uncle, and she had once been married to Memmius Regulus. Deliberately, he said nothing of her marriage to the Emperor Gaius. But, he said, she had entertained criminal designs against the safety of the state and she must be deprived of the means of doing wrong: her sentence must be confiscation of her property and exile from Italy. So, of all her immense wealth, she retained no more than five million sesterces.[5] Calpurnia, another lady of rank, came to grief because the Emperor made a comment about her beauty. However, it was merely a passing remark, without amorous intent, so Agrippina's anger did not go to extremes. But as for Lollia, a tribune was sent to order her to commit suicide.

Cadius Rufus was prosecuted for extortion by the people of Bithynia, and condemned.

23. Gallia Narbonensis received a privilege for the respect it had always shown to the Roman Senate. Senators from that province were allowed to visit their property without receiving imperial permission; the same regulation already applied to senators from Sicily.[6]

When Sohaemus and Agrippa, the client-kings of Ituraea and Judaea, died, their kingdoms were added to the province of Syria. It was decided to review and place on a permanent footing the "Solemn Augury for the Welfare of the Roman People," which had not been performed for seventy-five years.

Claudius also extended the pomerium of the city of Rome, according to the archaic custom which permits those who extended the boundaries of the Empire to advance those of the city as well.[7] Yet of all Roman generals who had subdued great nations, only Lucius Sulla and the deified Augustus had ever availed themselves of this privilege.

24. Various reports are given of the vanity or glory of the kings in this respect, but I do not think it will be out of place to give some account of the first foundation ceremony, and of the pomerium traced by Romulus. Beginning, then, from the Cattle Market (where now stands the bronze statue of a bull, the animal used in plowing), the pomerium furrow was drawn, for the purpose of marking out the city, so as to include the great altar of Hercules. Thence its course, marked by stones at set intervals, ran along the lower slopes of the Palatine Hill to the altar of Consus, then to the Old Curia, then to the chapel of the Lares, and from there to the Forum Romanum.

It is supposed that the Forum Romanum and the Capitol were added to the city by Titius Tatius and not by Romulus. Later, the pomerium was enlarged as Rome's fortunes advanced; the limits then laid down by Claudius are easily seen on the ground, and are entered in the state archives.[8]

50 A.D. Consuls Gaius Antistius and Marcus Suillius

EVENTS IN ROME

25. In the consulship of Gaius Antistius and Marcus Suillius the adoption of Domitius was hurried forward on the advice of Pallas, who was a partisan of Agrippina's both as the supporter in her marriage plans and, now, as her lover. Urging Claudius to think of the public interest, as well as to protect the young Britannicus, he pointed out that Augustus had advanced his stepsons, although surrounded by grandchildren, and that Tiberius had adopted Germanicus, although having children of his own. Claudius would do well to link to himself a young man who could take over a part of his burdens. The Emperor was won over by these arguments, and adopted Domitius to a position above his own son, though he was only three years older. In the Senate he made a speech in words which the freedman had composed for him. Antiquarians

noted that this was the first instance of adoption in the patrician branch of the gens Claudia, which had come down without a break from the time of Attus Clausus.[9]

26. Thanks were offered to the Emperor, and flattery to Domitius. A law was passed to grant his adoption into the family of the Claudii, with the name of Nero; and the title of "Augusta" was conferred on Agrippina. When all this had been done, there was no one who did not feel a sympathy for the hard lot of Britannicus. Little by little even the servants ceased paying him any attention, and he himself mocked the attentions of his stepmother, seeing them for the falsehoods they were. Indeed, he is reported to have had a lively intelligence; whether this is really true, or whether the dangers he was in brought him a reputation, was never put to test.

27. Agrippina now wished to make her powers known even to allied nations, and procured the foundation of a colony of veterans at the town of the Ubii, where she had been born. The name was taken from hers,* for it so happened that her grandfather had received the submission of that people when they crossed the Rhine.

THE NORTHERN FRONTIERS

At this period, alarm was caused in Upper Germany by a plundering expedition of the Chatti. The governor, Publius Pomponius, sent levies of soldiers from the Vangiones and Nemetae against them, augmented by some squadrons of auxiliary cavalry. Their orders were to block the raiders' lines of retreat, or, if they dispersed, to surround them unexpectedly. The soldiers carried out these instructions energetically; dividing into two, the left-hand column took by surprise an enemy force which had just returned, and was sleeping off an orgy over its spoils. What was particularly satisfactory was that they were able to redeem from slavery certain survivors of the disaster of Varus, forty years after the event.

28. The right-hand column, which had taken a more direct route, inflicted even heavier losses on the enemy, and returned to its base in the Taunus mountains heavily laden with booty and glory. Here Pomponius was waiting for them with the legions, to see whether the Chatti would be anxious for revenge, and would risk a battle. But they were afraid of being caught between the Roman forces and their inveterate enemies

* It was called Colonia Claudia Agrippinensis—the modern Cologne.

the Cherusci. They therefore sent a delegation to Rome, and gave hostages. Pomponius was awarded triumphal honors: though that plays a small part in the fame accorded him by posterity, which has set a higher value on his poetry.[10]

29. This was also the time at which Vannius was expelled from his kingdom of the Suebi which Drusus Caesar had conferred upon him. That prince had won fame and the loyalty of his people at the outset of his reign, but a long reign turned him into a tyrant, and internal discords and the hatred of his neighbors led to his overthrow. This was brought about by Vibilius, king of the Hermunduri, and by his own sister's sons Vangio and Sido. Claudius was repeatedly asked to intervene, but refused to interfere in the contest of barbarians, though he did promise Vannius safe refuge if he should be driven from his kingdom. To Palpellius Hister, governor of Pannonia, he sent instructions to line the banks of the Danube with a legion and local auxiliaries, to act as support for the losers and to overawe the victors, lest elation at their success might cause them to break their peace with Rome. For immense numbers of the Lugii and other tribes were approaching, drawn by the wealth of the kingdom, which Vannius had further increased by forty years of plunder and exactions. Vannius' own force of infantry, and his cavalry of Sarmatian Jazyges, were unequal in strength to the enemy, so he decided to operate from his forts and to prolong the war.

30. The Jazyges, however, had no use for siege, and scoured the surrounding plains, thus precipitating a battle, since the Lugii and Hermunduri were drawing near. So Vannius left his forts, and met with defeat in open battle. However, he gained credit in adversity for taking a personal part in the combat, and being wounded in front. Then he took refuge with the Roman fleet patrolling the Danube;[11] his dependents followed and were settled on lands granted to them in Pannonia. Vangio and Sido divided his kingdom. To us they showed a steadfast loyalty; by their own people they were much loved while they were winning power and even more strongly hated after they had obtained it—whether this was due to their own character or is inherent in the nature of despotism.

EVENTS IN BRITAIN: THE WAR WITH CARATACUS

31. In Britain the governor, Publius Ostorius, was confronted with a disturbed situation. The enemy had raided the territory of our allies, acting all the more boldly because they

did not think that a new governor, his army untried and with winter drawing on, would take the field against them. Ostorius knew that it is the first results that engender either fear or confidence; he therefore led his light cohorts on forced marches, killed all who made a stand, and followed up the scattered enemy forces. Then—to prevent their rallying again —and to avoid that false armed peace that allows no rest either to a general or to his army—he made preparations for the disarming of all the rebellious tribes, and for the building of forts to control the entire territory on this side of the Trent and Severn.[12] The Iceni were the first to react against this measure. They were a powerful tribe, whose forces were not yet crushed in battle, since they had voluntarily sought our alliance. Neighboring tribes followed their lead, and a place[13] was chosen for battle protected by a crude embankment, and having a narrow approach to prevent the access of cavalry. The Roman general immediately prepared to force this position, though he had only auxiliary forces, without legionary support. Posting his cohorts, and bringing up squadrons of dismounted cavalrymen, he gave the signal to engage, burst through the embankment, and entangled the enemy in their own defenses. Knowing that they had been disloyal, and cut off from any chance of escape, the Britons fought valiantly. It was in this battle that the governor's son, Marcus Ostorius, won the distinction awarded for saving the life of a Roman citizen.

32. The defeat of the Iceni quieted those tribes that were wavering between peace and war, and an expedition was mounted against the Decangi.[14] their territory was laid waste and a good deal of booty taken away; for the enemy never ventured on an open battle, while any attempt to harass our columns was duly punished. Ostorius had nearly reached the sea which looks toward Ireland when an outbreak of civil war amongst the Brigantes forced him to turn back—for he was fixed in his purpose and averse to beginning new projects unless earlier ones were completed. The Brigantes settled down when the few rebels had been killed and the others were granted pardon. But against the Silures neither clemency nor severity was of any avail. Nothing stopped them from waging war, and it became necessary to keep them in check by setting up a legionary base. To promote this end, a powerful colony of veterans was settled on captured lands at Camulodunum; it would serve as a support against rebellion, and imbue our allies with a sense of the duties enjoined by law.

33. Then Ostorius advanced into the territory of the Silures. Besides their own warlike qualities, that people had been

strengthened by their confidence in the prowess of Caratacus,[15] who had won himself a preeminent place among British leaders by a series of victorious or drawn battles. Inferior to us in numbers, he excelled by cunning and a better knowledge of the country. Transferring the fighting to the country of the Ordovices, he was joined by all who feared the *pax Romana*. Finally he decided to stake everything on a battle. He had chosen a site[16] where the approach routes, lines of retreat, and all other factors were to his advantage and our disadvantage. On the one side were steep hills, and where they did offer an easier line of ascent, he had piled boulders to form a rampart. A river flowed in front of the position, and its fords had not been tested, while bands of warriors lined the defenses.

34. The British chieftains went around their tribal levies, making light of their fears, encouraging their hopes, and offering other incentives to arms. Caratacus hastened from one point to the next, proclaiming that this was the day and this the battle which would either win back their freedom, or mark the beginning of eternal slavery. He called on the names of their ancestors, who had put to flight the dictator Julius Caesar; it was through their valor that they lived free from the lictor's ax and the tax collector's demands, and that the bodies of their wives and children were undefiled. These words were greeted with applause, and every man bound himself, with the oath of his people, never to yield to weapons or wounds.

35. Their spirit dismayed the Roman commander, as did the river between the armies, the overhanging ridges, and the fierce warriors who crowded every point. All made up a black picture. But the soldiers demanded battle, saying that valor could carry any position: their officers spoke in the same way and encouraged them still further. Then Ostorius made a reconnaissance to determine which points would yield and which would not, and led forward his eager troops. The river crossing offered no obstacle. When they reached the embankment, there was a sharp exchange of missiles, with the greater number of wounds, and many deaths, on the Roman side. But when they locked shields and made a "tortoise,"[17] hurled down the rudely built rampart, and brought about a hand-to-hand battle on equal terms, the barbarians made a retreat to the hilltop. Here too our men followed them, the light-armed soldiers making use of their spears, the legionaries in close order. The British ranks were thrown into confusion, for they had no protection from breastplate or helmets: if they made a stand against the auxiliaries, they were mown down by the swords and spears of the legionaries; if they turned against the latter, they met

the long swords and pikes of the auxiliaries. It was a glorious victory: the wife and daughter of Caratacus were captured, and his brothers surrendered.

36. Caratacus himself fled to Cartimandua, queen of the Brigantes. But there is no refuge in adversity, and he was bound in chains and handed over to us. This was the ninth year of the war in Britain.[18]

The fame of Caratacus was not confined to the British islands; it had spread through the neighboring provinces and over to Italy. Men were eager to see the chieftain who had withstood our power for so long. Even in Rome, the name of Caratacus was not without its glory, and the Emperor, seeking to extol himself, added to the reputation of the Briton in defeat. The people of Rome were invited as though for a great spectacle; the Praetorian Guard stood to, fully armed, on the parade ground before their barracks. Then there passed in long array the dependents of Caratacus, with the decorations and torques and spoils that he had won in war with foreign tribes. Next his wife, brothers, and daughters were displayed— and finally Caratacus himself. The others disgraced themselves by pleading for mercy, but Caratacus neither lowered his gaze nor made any plea for pity. When he reached the platform he spoke thus:

37. "Had my high birth and rank been accompanied by moderation in the hour of success, I should have entered this city as a friend and not a prisoner. You would not have hesitated to accept as an ally a man of splendid ancestry, and bearing rule over many tribes. My present position is degrading to me, but glorious to you. I had horses, warriors, and gold: if I was unwilling to lose them, what wonder in that? Does it follow that, because you desire universal empire, all must accept universal slavery? Were I now dragged here as one who had surrendered without fighting, no fame would have attached to my fall nor to your victory. If you punish me, they will both be forgotten. Spare me, and I shall be an eternal example of your mercy!" These words won from the Emperor pardon for himself, his wife, and his brothers. Released from their chains, they paid the same thanks and gratitude to Agrippina, who was seated not far off on another raised platform. It was a new thing, quite alien to the custom of our ancestors, that a woman should thus sit before Roman standards, but she was displaying herself as a full partner in the Empire her ancestors had won.

38. After this there was a session of the Senate, and a good deal of inflated rhetoric about the capture of Caratacus. This was hailed as an achievement equal to the capture of Syphax

by Publius Scipio, of Perseus by Lucius Aemilius Paulus, or, indeed to that of any of the other generals who had displayed captured kings to the Roman people.[19] The ornaments of a triumph were voted to Ostorius. Thus far, he had enjoyed success, but soon things took a turn for the worse, possibly because our troops were less eager, assuming that the removal of Caratacus meant the end of war, or also pity for so great a king fanned to a blaze the enemy's desire for revenge. A camp commander and legionary cohorts, left behind to build forts in Silurian territory, were surrounded; had not the news brought up reinforcements to the besieged from the nearest Roman forts, they would have been cut to pieces. Even so, the commander, eight centurions, and all the pick of the men were killed. Immediately afterward, the enemy routed some Roman cavalry squadrons sent in support as they were foraging for supplies.

39. Then Ostorius put in his light infantry battalions, but even this failed to check the rout. Finally legionary troops entered the fighting, and their arrival made the struggle an even one. Eventually the balance swung our way, but the enemy drew off with only very light casualties, since dusk was coming on. There were frequent battles, and much guerrilla fighting in the woods and marshes, as opportunity or individual courage prompted. Some were planned, some were spontaneous; some were fought for plunder, others for revenge; some the enemy generals had ordered, others they knew nothing of. Nothing excited the obstinacy of the Silures so much as a remark of the general's, which had gained wide currency, to the effect that the very name of the Silures should be wiped out, as once the Sugambri had been exterminated or moved across the Rhine into Gaul.[20] Two auxiliary cohorts, tempted by their commanders into rash plundering raids, were cut off: prisoners and spoils were distributed among other British tribes to tempt them to rebellion. At this point Ostorius died, worn out with his anxieties, much to the delight of the enemy, who felt that if they had not destroyed this redoubtable general in battle, they had at least eliminated him in war.

40. Claudius did not want to leave the province without a master, and sent Aulus Didius to take his place. Though he crossed over rapidly to Britain, he found the situation had worsened, for the legion commanded by Manlius Valens had been beaten in battle.[21] This reverse was exaggerated—by the enemy, to alarm the new governor; and by the governor, who in turn magnified the reports he heard in order to improve his credit if he won, or to supply a good excuse if the war dragged on. The Silures, again, had been responsible for that disaster;

indeed they ravaged far and wide, until met and turned back by Didius.

After the capture of Caratacus, the British leader most distinguished for military ability was Venutius of the Brigantes. Earlier, I have mentioned how he was loyal,[22] and supported by Roman arms, so long as his marriage to the queen, Cartimandua, remained intact. But then there was a divorce, and he took up hostilities even against us. The first phases of the fighting were among themselves, and Cartimandua's trickery had trapped Venutius' brother and some of his kinsfolk. Her enemies, infuriated by this action, and by the humiliating prospect of a woman's rule, invaded his kingdom with a powerful force of picked young warriors. We had foreseen this move: cohorts sent to her support were involved in fierce fighting. The issue at first was doubtful, but later we gained the upper hand. Success also attended a legionary battle fought by the troops under the command of Caesius Nasica. Didius was well on in years and already loaded with honors, and so preferred to act through subordinates, and remain on the defensive. These events were conducted by two governors of Britain over a period of years,[23] but I have thought it best to narrate them in a single piece, for if split up they might fail to make due impact. I now return to chronological sequence.

51 A.D. Consuls, the Emperor Tiberius Claudius (for the fifth time), and Servius Cornelius Orfitus

AFFAIRS AT ROME

41. In this year Nero's assumption of the *toga virilis*[24] was brought forward before the usual age, to let it appear that he was now fit for public office. The Emperor readily agreed to the flattering suggestion of the Senate that Nero should hold the consulship in his twentieth year and in the meantime, as consul-designate, he should have proconsular authority outside Rome, and receive the title "Prince of Youth." The troops got a grant of money in his name, as did the public; at the games held in the Circus to win for him the popular favor, he appeared in triumphal dress, Britannicus in the usual dress of

a boy. It was intended that the imperial attire of the one, and the childish dress of the other, should give the Roman people a forecast of their future. All the tribunes and centurions sympathetic to Britannicus were posted elsewhere, some on trumped-up charges, others as a show of promotion. Even those freedmen who remained loyal were got rid of on some such pretext as the following: Nero and Britannicus met; Nero called Britannicus by his proper name, and was addressed by Britannicus as Domitius. Loud complaints to the Emperor from Agrippina: here was the start of a quarrel. Nero's adoption was being nullified: a decree of the Senate and the will of the people was disregarded inside the imperial house. Unless the wickedness of certain ill-disposed people could be turned aside, the result would be a public disaster. Hints and charges such as these persuaded the Emperor to banish or put to death all his son's best tutors; the boy was placed in the care of persons hand-picked by his stepmother.

42. Still, Agrippina did not venture to prepare the last stages of her plan before Lusius Geta and Rufrius Crispinus had been removed from the command of the cohorts of the Praetorian Guard. These men remembered Messalina, and she believed them loyal to Messalina's children. On Agrippina's assertion that the brigade was being divided by rivalry between the commanding officers, and that discipline would be tightened under a unified command, there was a transfer of appointment to Burrus Afranius.[25] He bore a distinguished military reputation—but he knew very well to whose wishes he owed his promotion. Then Agrippina began to exalt her own position to an even higher pinnacle. She drove to the Capitol in a carriage, a privilege previously reserved for priests and objects of worship.[26] All this increased the reverence felt for a lady who, as daughter of a great general and a sister, wife, and mother of Emperors, held a position which remains unrivaled to this day. Yet at this time her great supporter Vitellius, for all his venerable age and influence—so precarious is high position—was involved in a criminal charge brought by the senator Junius Lupus. The charge was high treason and aiming at imperial power, and Claudius was inclined to listen to it. But the threats—rather than the entreaties—of Agrippina caused him to change his mind, and it was the prosecutor who was outlawed. That was all Vitellius had demanded.

43. It was a year of prodigies. Ill-omened birds descended on the Capitol. Frequent earthquakes destroyed houses: panic spread, and in the confusion of the mob the weak were trampled to death. The failure of the harvest and the subsequent dearth were regarded as a portent. Not all the com-

plaints were under cover, for when Claudius was sitting in judgment, a disorderly crowd surrounded him, and began driving him to the other end of the Forum. It needed a company of soldiers to break up the riot. It was calculated that there was fifteen days' food supply for the city, no more: only a mild winter and the favor of heaven saved a desperate situation. And yet did not Italy once export provisions for armies in far distant provinces! The trouble is not infertile soil: we prefer to cultivate Africa and Egypt, and to entrust to the hazards of seafaring the very life of the Roman people.

EASTERN AFFAIRS

44. In this year war broke out between the kingdoms of Armenia and Iberia, which also provoked serious conflict between Rome and Parthia. The Parthian king was Vologeses, son of a Greek concubine, who had won the throne by consent of his brothers. Pharasmenes had long ruled Iberia: his brother Mithridates was king of Armenia with our support. There was a son of Pharasmenes, Radamistus, a handsome and tall young prince, well skilled in all the arts of his countrymen, well thought of by the neighboring peoples. He was loud and frequent in his complaints that his father's longevity was keeping him off the throne of Iberia—as yet—and he made no secret of his ambitions. Pharasmenes noted that his son was eager for power and enjoyed popular support, and he was conscious of his own advancing years. He thought it best to encourage him in other hopes, and so pointed out the situation in Armenia, saying that he had driven out the Parthians and given it to Mithridates. However, he said, better not use force in the first instance: guile was the answer, so as to take Mithridates unawares. So Radamistus simulated a quarrel with his father, and as though unequal to confronting his stepmother's hatred, took himself off to his uncle. Here he found a kind reception and was treated as a son, and so was able to incite the leading Armenians to rebellion, Mithridates the while quite ignorant, and even loading him with honors.

45. Then there was a show of reconciliation, and Radamistus returned to his father to proclaim that guile had produced all the results it could, that force must be employed for the rest. Meanwhile Pharasmenes was thinking up causes for war. When he had been engaged in a struggle against the Albani, and had asked for Roman support, his brother had stood in his way; this insult must now be repaid by his brother's de-

struction. He immediately gave his son a large body of troops. With these Radamistus made a sudden attack on Mithridates, who took panic and shut himself up in the fortress of Gorneae, a naturally secure refuge, and one where he had the protection of Roman soldiers, commanded by Caelius Pollio, and with Casperius as their centurion. The barbarians are quite ignorant of the technical equipment and skill required for siege warfare, a branch of military science which we have thoroughly mastered.[27] Radamistus' attempts at a siege or an assault were either useless or costly; when his military strength went for nothing, he had tried to bribe the acquisitive Caelius Pollio. Casperius protested strongly at the ruin, by criminal corruption, of a loyal ally, and of the kingdom of Armenia which had been given to him by the Roman people. But Pollio was able to plead the enemy's superior numbers, Radamistus his father's orders. Casperius therefore arranged a truce and left, intending either to deter Pharasmenes from war or to make the position in Armenia clear to Ummidius Quadratus, governor of Syria.

46. Once the centurion had gone, Pollio felt that he was no longer under supervision, and began to urge Mithridates to conclude an agreement. There was the tie of brotherhood, and Pharasmenes was the older. There were other family connections as well—for he had married Pharasmenes' daughter, and Radamistus had married the daughter of Mithridates. The Iberi were disposed for peace, though at present their strength was greater. "Don't trust the Armenians," he said; "you know their treachery. Your only protection is a badly provisioned fort. Don't risk the hazards of war rather than conclude a bloodless peace." Mithridates hesitated over this, disliking the advice of Pollio, who had seduced one of the royal mistresses, and was a man who had his price for any form of wickedness. Meanwhile Casperius had reached Pharasmenes, and demanded that the Iberi should abandon the siege. In public, the king's answers were cryptic, though tending to be favorable. In private, he sent messages to Radamistus to urge him to hasten the siege by all possible means. The price of treachery then increased, and Pollio induced the Roman troops also to come forward with a demand for peace, and threaten to abandon their arms. Mithridates had no option but to agree to a date and a place for a treaty, and left the fort.

47. At first Radamistus hurled himself into his embrace, feigned obedience, and saluted him as parent and father-in-law. He next took an oath not to slay him by sword nor poison; then he drew him aside into a nearby grove, saying that everything was ready for a sacrifice there, so that the gods might be witnesses of the peace agreed. Now these Eastern kings have

the custom, when they are going to make an alliance, of joining their right hands together, with their thumbs tied together
and squeezed tight by a knot. Then when the blood has flowed
into the extremities they make a slight incision and let it out,
and each in turn licks it. A mystic sanction is thought to be
conferred by this exchange of blood.[28] On this occasion, the
man who was to fasten the cords pretended to slip, caught
Mithridates around the knees, and brought him to the ground.
Several others at once fell on him, and he was bound in chains.
Then he was dragged away by his fetters—which barbarians
consider particularly degrading—and soon the people who had
suffered from his harsh rule were loading him with blows and
insults. Some, however, took pity on so dramatic a reversal of
fortune, especially as his wife and little children followed him,
all weeping loudly. But they too, were hustled away in covered
carriages to await Pharasmenes' instructions. But Pharasmenes
heart was one in which the lust for power counted for more
than a brother or a daughter, and his will was primed for
atrocity. However, he spared his gaze the spectacle of their
murder, which was carried out secretly. As for Radamistus, he
strictly observed his oath not to use sword or poison against his
sister and his uncle. He had them flung to the ground, covered
with layers of heavy clothing, and thus smothered to death.
The children of Mithridates were killed for having shed tears
at their parents' murder.

48. When Ummidius Quadratus, governor of Syria, learned
of the betrayal of Mithridates and the seizure of the kingdom
by his murderers, he summoned a meeting of his council. He
put before them what had happened, and asked whether they
thought punitive measures were called for. A few members
showed some concern for Roman honor: most played for
safety. They urged that all criminal acts among foreigners
should be positively welcomed, and that discord should actually be fostered. How often had Roman Emperors bestowed
this same Armenia, outwardly as a token of generosity, but
really to unsettle the minds of the barbarians! So, let Radamistus keep his ill-gotten gains, so long as he was hated and in
bad odor; expediency was much better served in that way than
if he had gained his kingdom honorably.[29] This was the opinion
that prevailed. But to avoid the risk of seeming to condone the
crime—or of receiving imperial instructions to reverse their
policy—messages were sent to Pharasmenes ordering him to
withdraw from Armenia and recall his son.

49. The imperial agent in Cappadocia was a certain Julius
Paelignus, a man as contemptible for the meanness of his mind
as for the absurdity of his person. Nonetheless, he was an inti-

mate of the Emperor, who had employed the idle hours before his accession in the company of such buffoons. This individual had begun to collect auxiliary forces as though for the recovery of Armenia, but he caused a good deal more damage to the provincials than to the enemy. Finally, his troops deserted him, the barbarians began to make inroads, and quite devoid of help he fled to Radamistus. The latter loaded him with presents: the delighted Paelignus urged him to assume the royal insignia: indeed, at the ceremony he stood as his satellite and sponsor. When this shocking news spread abroad, Ummidius Quadratus felt it necessary to show that all Romans were not on the model of Paelignus. He therefore sent a legion under Helvidius Priscus to clear up the disturbed situation as seemed best on the ground. Helvidius quickly crossed the Taurus Mountains and settled things by tact rather than force. Later, he was recalled to Syria lest he should provoke Parthia to war.

50. For Vologeses, king of Parthia, saw in this an excellent opportunity of invading Armenia, once a possession of his ancestors, and now seized by a foreign king under disgraceful circumstances. He mustered his forces, and prepared to establish his brother Tiridates on the throne, on the principle that every prince of the royal house should have a kingdom of his own. At the approach of the Parthians the Iberi withdrew without a battle, and the Armenian towns of Artaxata and Tigranocerta submitted to their yoke. But a fearful winter followed; this, and the feeble supply system of the Parthians, led to an epidemic which caused Vologeses to withdraw. Armenia was vacant once more and Radamistus invaded it yet again, more truculent than ever, treating every one as a traitor who would all some day rebel again. The Armenians were well used to slavery, but now their patience was at an end, and they surrounded the palace in arms.

51. All that saved Radamistus, and his wife, was that he had some swift horses. But the poor lady was pregnant. At first she endured the journey as best she could because she feared the enemy and loved her husband. But with the continuous galloping her womb and her very entrails were so shaken that she begged for death, to rescue her from the shame of captivity. Radamistus at first embraced her and tried to cheer and encourage her: he was divided between admiration for her courage, and a desperate fear that another man would have her if he left her there. But he was frenzied with love, and not unpracticed in deeds of violence: drawing his scimitar he ran her through and dragged her, wounded, to the banks of the Araxes, then threw her in, so that even her body should be carried away. He made off at a headlong gallop to his own king-

dom of Iberia. Meanwhile Zenobia (that was the lady's name) was found by shepherds on a quiet backwater, still breathing and showing signs of life. They could tell from her beauty and dignity that she was some noble person, so they bound up her wound, used some rustic remedies, and, when they heard her name and story, took her to Artaxata. From there she was sent at public expense to Tiridates, who received her kindly and treated her with royal honors.

52 A.D. Consuls Faustus Cornelius Sulla and Salvius Otho

EVENTS IN ROME

52. In this year Furius Scribonianus was sentenced to exile on a charge of consulting astrologers about the death of the Emperor. His mother Vibia was also named in the charge, as always complaining of a previous sentence of banishment. The father, Camillus, had placed himself at the head of an armed rebellion in Dalmatia; Claudius counted it to his clemency that he had twice spared this disloyal family. Scribonianus did not long survive his exile: whether his death was due to natural causes or poison was a matter on which everyone had his own opinion. The Senate had passed a decree to banish astrologers from Italy, as severe as it was unenforceable. Then the Emperor made a speech in praise of those who voluntarily resigned from the Senate through lack of means; those who hung on were expelled, as adding impudence to poverty.

53. Next he referred to the Senate a proposal for penalties against free-born women who became the concubines of slaves. The decision was that any woman guilty of such misconduct should, if the slave owner was unaware, become his slave; if he had agreed, she was to be treated as a freedwoman. The Emperor gave it out that Pallas had drafted this proposal, and the consul-designate, Barea Soranus, recommended that he should be granted an honorary praetorship and fifteen million sesterces. Seconding this, Publius Cornelius Scipio proposed a public vote of thanks to Pallas, who, though descended from ancient Arcadian kings, had rather thought of the public good

than of his noble lineage, and allowed himself to be numbered among the Emperor's servants. Claudius protested that Pallas was content with that distinction, and wished to live within the limits of his humble means. The senatorial decree was set up in letters of bronze—and thus an ex-slave worth 300,000,000 sesterces was heaped with praise for showing old-world frugality.

EVENTS IN JUDAEA AND CILICIA

54. A similar parsimony was not to be seen in the conduct of his brother Felix, governor of Judaea, who looked on his powerful backing as a license for all classes of criminal behavior. The Jews had shown unrest earlier, when the Emperor Gaius had ordered his own effigy to be set up in the Temple. On the news of his assassination this had not been enforced, but the fear remained that another Emperor would renew the demand. Ill-timed penal measures by Felix accentuated the discontent; and his misdeeds were emulated by the governor, Ventidius Cumanus—for Judaea was so divided that Galilee was administered by Ventidius, and Samaria by Felix. Their inhabitants had always been at loggerheads, and their contempt for their governors led them to give their hatred full rein. They started to raid each other's territory, formed bands of brigands, laid ambushes, and sometimes fought regular pitched battles; spoil and booty were banked with the Roman governors. This suited the two very well at first, but then the trouble got out of hand and they had to intervene with armed forces. Some Roman soldiers were killed, and the whole province would have been ablaze with war but for the intervention of Ummidius Quadratus from Syria. There was no hesitation about putting to death Jews who had killed Roman soldiers; but the cases of Cumanus and Felix presented some embarrassment, since Claudius, after learning the causes of the rebellion, had entrusted to Quadratus the task of dealing with these officials himself. Quadratus displayed Felix on the judge's bench, to damp down the zeal of his accusers. Cumanus was sentenced for the misdeeds of both. Peace was now restored to the province of Judaea.

55. Shortly afterward the wild tribes of Cilicia, the Clitae, under their chief Troxoboris, who had often been up in arms, fortified an inaccessible mountain and began to make raids on the cities and the coast. They made audacious attacks on countrymen and townsmen, and often on traders and shippers. They

laid siege to the city of Anemurium, and when a relief force of
cavalry was sent from Syria under Curtius Severus they threw
it into confusion: for the rough ground favored the infantry-
men and was unsuitable for cavalry engagements. Finally,
Antiochus (of Commagene), ruler of the coastal districts, split
the barbarian forces by cajoling the soldiers and tricking their
leader. Troxoboris and a few ringleaders were put to death, and
the rest settled down under amnesty.

EVENTS IN ROME AND ITALY: CONTRETEMPS AT THE FUCINE LAKE

56. At this time the tunnel between the Fucine Lake and
the river Liris had been completed.[30] To make a public display
of this superb piece of engineering a naval battle was staged on
the lake itself. Augustus had once displayed a similar spectacle
on an artificial lagoon adjoining the Tiber, but that was with
lighter ships and on a smaller scale. Claudius produced triremes, quadriremes, and nineteen thousand armed combatants.
The area of the fighting was surrounded by a floating barrier
of rafts, to prevent escape, but there was plenty of room for
vigorous rowing, skillful steering, ramming of ships, and the
usual incidents of naval battles. Squadrons of cavalry and
troops of the Praetorian Guard were posted on the rafts, which
were equipped with ramparts from which the fire of catapults
and ballistae could be brought to bear. The rest of the lake was
patrolled by marines in decked ships. An enormous throng
crowded the banks of the lake, and all good viewpoints on the
hills and mountains, as though in a theater. They came from
the nearby cities, and even from Rome itself, avid for sightseeing or anxious to do honor to the Emperor. Claudius himself, in a splendid military cloak, and Agrippina next to him
wearing a mantle of cloth of gold, presided at the spectacle.
The combatants were all condemned criminals, but they fought
like brave men; after much letting of blood their lives were
spared.

57. After the end of the spectacle the waterway was formally opened. At once the shoddiness of the engineering became apparent: the tunnel had not been sunk to the lowest,
or even the medium, depth of the lake. So the channel was
excavated further, and in due course, another crowd was assembled, this time to witness an infantry battle fought by gladiators on pontoons. A banquet was served close to the lake's
outlet, but all the guests were driven to panic by a sudden rush

of water which swept off everything in the vicinity. Even those some distance away were terrified and shocked by the roar and crash. The Emperor's alarm was used by Agrippina to accuse Narcissus, who had supervised the project, of graft and corruption. To this he had his answer, speaking pointedly of feminine arrogance and unbridled ambition.

53 A.D. Consuls Decimus Junius Silanus and Quintus Haterius Antoninus

A GENERAL REVIEW

58. In this year Nero, then aged sixteen, married the Emperor's daughter Octavia. To display his learning and skill in oratory, he took up the cause of the people of New Troy, setting out at some length the origins of the Roman people in Troy, Aeneas the founder of the Julian house, and various other ancient tales not far removed from myth.[31] The result was the complete exemption of the people of Ilium from public burdens. His advocacy also won for the people of Bononia a grant of ten million sesterces after their city had suffered a disastrous fire. The Rhodians were given their liberty once again (so often forfeited for domestic strife, or conferred in times of war). A five-year remission of taxes was granted to the people of Apamea, which had suffered from an earthquake.

59. But Claudius was now constantly goaded into acts of savagery by the wiles of Agrippina. She brought down Statilius Taurus, famous for his wealth, whose gardens she coveted. Tarquitius Priscus was her tool in this: he had been legate under Taurus when the latter was governor of Africa. When they were back in Rome, he made some accusation of extortion against him, though the real charge was that of practicing magic rites. Statilius could not endure a lying accuser and the humiliation of being prosecuted, and committed suicide before the Senate had pronounced judgment. Indeed, so indignant were the senators at the prosecution that they expelled Tarquitius from the order, in spite of the influence of Agrippina.

60. During this year the Emperor was often heard to declare that the decisions of his agents ought to have the same validity

as if he had pronounced them. Lest this should be regarded as
a casual remark, a decree of the Senate established the point
in ampler terms and with greater emphasis than before. It was,
after all, the late Emperor Augustus who had granted the imperial agents in Egypt powers of jurisdiction, and who had laid
down that their decisions should have the same force as those
of a Roman magistrate. Later in the other provinces and in
Rome, imperial agents handled business formerly dealt with
by praetors. Claudius granted to them all those judicial powers
which had once been the cause of armed conflicts—when the
Lex Sempronia handed them over to the equestrian order,
when the Lex Servilia restored them to the Senate, and when
they provoked, more than anything else, the wars between
Marius and Sulla. But then the contests were between different
classes of the commonwealth, and the results benefited the
whole order. Caesar's agents, Gaius Oppius and Cornelius
Balbus, were the first who handled issues of peace and war.
Names of later powerful knights, such as Matius and Vedius,
are scarcely worth mentioning, since Claudius gave to the freedmen who administered his own estates powers equal to those
of the Emperor and of the law.

61. He next proposed the exemption of Cos from taxation.
He had a great deal to say about the antiquities of that island.[32]
Its first inhabitants had been Argives, or perhaps Coeus, father
of Latona. Then Aesculapius had brought the art of healing, in
which his descendants had achieved so great a fame. Their
names were recited, together with the appropriate dates. His
own family physician, Xenophon, was of their number, and as
a result of his petition the people of Cos ought to be exempted
from all future taxation, holding their island as a sacred place,
ministering to the service of the god. They had, in fact, rendered many services to the Roman people, and been our allies
in many a victory, but this he did not mention. No external
arguments were used to dress up what he granted, with his
usual compliance, as a favor to a single individual.

62. But when the Byzantines complained about the size of
their tax assessment, they gave a full review of all their services
to Rome. They began with the treaty struck with them at the
time of our war with the king of Macedon, known from his
doubtful origins as pseudo-Philip. Next they instanced their
services against Antiochus, Perseus, and Aristonicus, then the
help they had given Antonius in the war against the pirates,
also to Sulla, Lucullus, and Pompey, and, more recently, to the
Emperors. All this arose from their situation, convenient for
the passage of generals and armies by land or sea, and for the
procurement of supplies.

63. The Greeks had founded Byzantium at the far extremity of Europe, where it approaches most closely to Asia. When they had asked Apollo at Delphi where they should found a city, he had replied, "Opposite the country of the blind." This saying referred to the people of Chalcedon, who were the first to survey the advantages of the site, but had then proceeded to choose a worse one. For Byzantium has a fertile soil and a teeming sea: great shoals of fish come out from the Black Sea, and are scared by underwater shoals into the harbors on the European shore, avoiding the inlets of the Asiatic side. This had once been the source of wealth and prosperity for the inhabitants, but now their financial burdens were such that they asked for concessions. The Emperor backed their plea, arguing that their exhaustion in the Thracian and Bosporan wars made them a deserving case. Their taxes were remitted for a period of five years.

54 A.D. Consuls Marcus Asinius Marcellus and Manius Acilius Aviola

THE MURDER OF CLAUDIUS

64. In this year numerous portents gave warning of a change for the worse in public affairs. Fire from heaven struck the standards and huts of the army; a swarm of bees settled on the pediment of the Capitoline temple; there were monstrous births, half human and half animal; a sow produced a piglet with claws like a hawk. Among these manifestations was noted the death of Roman magistrates of every rank: within a few months there died a quaestor, an aedile, a tribune, a praetor, and a consul. Agrippina was especially panic-stricken, alarmed by a remark made by Claudius in his cups. "My destiny," he said, "is to endure the wickedness of my wives; but I punish it in the end." She decided to act—and to act quickly. Feminine jealousy caused her to begin with Domitia Lepida, a lady who looked on herself as Agrippina's equal, since she was the daughter of the younger Antonia,[33] the grandniece of Augustus, Agrippina's first cousin, once removed, and the sister of Agrippina's first husband, Domitius. There was indeed little

between them in beauty, age, and wealth; they were both dissolute, notorious, and violent; they vied with each other in
vices as well as in the gifts of fortune. But the real issue between them was whether the mother or the aunt should have
the greater influence with Nero. Lepida was in the process of
cozening his adolescent mind with gifts and flattery. Threats
and violence were Agrippina's methods; she wanted to bring
her son to power but could not bear that he should use it.

65. The charges brought against Lepida were, first, that she
had sought the death of the Emperor's wife by witchcraft, and
second, that her uncontrolled gangs of slaves[34] in Calabria
were a menace to the peace of Italy. Death was the sentence
pronounced. Narcissus urged every objection to this, for he
grew ever more suspicious of Agrippina, and is said to have
spoken thus to his intimates: "Whether Nero or Britannicus
gains power, I am doomed for certain. But I owe so much to
Claudius that I will gladly risk my life in his service. They
condemned Messalina and Silius: there will be another occasion for such a charge, if Nero is going to be Emperor. If
Britannicus is the heir, Claudius has nothing to fear. But now
a stepmother's hatred poisons the atmosphere of the imperial
household: it is worse than if I had kept silent about the immorality of his first wife. Immorality, indeed, there is now,
with Pallas as her lover, so that none can doubt that she holds
everything—beauty, honor, her own body—as cheap compared
with power." With such words as these he would embrace
Britannicus, begging him to grow up fast; stretching out his
hands now to the gods, now to the boy, he would pray that he
would reach a man's years, scatter his father's enemies, and
take vengeance on the murderers of his mother.

66. With all this load of care Narcissus was struck down
by illness, and took himself off to Sinuessa to recuperate in its
mild climate and healing waters. Agrippina had long been
resolved on the deed; she was ready to seize her opportunity,
and had no lack of ministers. She now sought advice on the
choice of the poison to be employed. One that acted too suddenly and precipitately would betray the crime: if she chose
a slow and wasting drug, Claudius might detect the plot in his
last extremities, and revive his feelings for Britannicus. Something of a very refined nature was to be desired, something
that would derange his mind yet postpone the end. A specialist
in such matters was chosen, a certain Locusta, recently condemned on a charge of poisoning, and long employed as an
accessory of despotism. By her ingenuity the poison was concocted; it was administered by one of the eunuchs, Halotus,
who used to serve the Emperor at table, and acted as his taster.

67. Later, the whole episode became known, and contemporary authors say that the poison was inserted into a choice mushroom.[35] The full effect of the drug was not at first apparent, either through Claudius' constitutional sluggishness or through his drunkenness; and a movement of the bowels was thought to have saved him. Agrippina was desperate: but since the worst was to be feared, she brushed aside short-term disrepute and called in the Emperor's physician, Xenophon, whose complicity she had already won. He is reported to have pushed a feather lined with quick-acting poison down the Emperor's throat, while pretending to help him to vomit. Xenophon had grasped the truth that major crimes are dangerous in their earlier stages, but are attended by great rewards in the end.

68. Meanwhile, the Senate was summoned. Public prayers were offered by the consuls and the priests for the recovery of the Emperor, whose dead body was wrapped in blankets and poultices, while the necessary preparations were made for securing the transfer of power to Nero. Agrippina had a leading role in this. As though broken with grief, and looking for comfort, she took Britannicus in her arms, calling him the living image of his father, and employing every device to prevent him from leaving his room. She also detained his sisters Antonia and Octavia, and secured every doorway with guards. Frequent bulletins were issued to the effect that the Emperor's condition was improving—the object being to preserve morale in the army, and to await the moment that the astrologers had pronounced to be propitious.

ACCESSION OF NERO

69. At last, precisely at noon on October 13, the gates of the palace were thrown open, and in company with the Praetorian prefect, Nero came out to the company of the Guard which, according to regulations, was on duty. At their officer's command, the troops acclaimed him, and placed him in a litter. It is said that some of the men hesitated, looking around and asking where Britannicus was. But no countersuggestion was made to them, so they took the choice to hand. Nero was carried to the barracks and spoke appropriately to the occasion, promised a donative on the same scale as that of Claudius, and was duly saluted as Emperor. The army had decided; now a decree of the Senate showed solidarity; the provincial armies did not waver.

Divine honors were decreed for Claudius, and a state funeral on a scale as grand as that for Augustus. This was because Agrippina wanted to emulate the magnificence of her great-grandmother Livia. But there was no reading of the will. The public might have sensed a certain unfairness and injustice in the open preference of a stepson to a son.

BOOK XIII

The Reign of Nero

1. The first death of the new reign was plotted by Agrippina, unknown to Nero. It was that of Junius Silanus, proconsul of Asia, and was in no way due to any violent element in his character.[1] Indeed, earlier Emperors had despised him, and Gaius Caesar found a name for him—"the Golden Sheep." But Agrippina had contrived the death of his brother Lucius, and was afraid he might take revenge for that. Besides, there was popular talk to the effect that it might be better to have for Emperor a man of mature age, blameless life, noble blood, and a descendant of the Caesars—a factor then taken into account —rather than Nero, a mere boy, who had won his position by a crime. For Silanus too was a great-great-grandson of Augustus—and this was the direct cause of his murder. The agent was a certain Publius Celer, a knight, and a freedman, Helius —both administrators of the imperial estates in Asia. These two gave the proconsul poison at a banquet, but too openly to escape detection.

Narcissus also, whose conflicts with Agrippina I have already described, was hurried off to death. Harsh treatment in prison and the threat of execution led him to put an end to his life. Nero did not approve of his death, for Narcissus' qualities of greed and prodigality were nicely attuned to the young Emperor's unformed vices.

2. A reign of terror would have set in had not Afranius

Burrus and Annaeus Seneca prevented it. They were Nero's governors, and by mutual sympathy uncommon in those who share power, they established by different means an equal hold over him. Burrus did this by soldierly qualities and an austere character; Seneca by his lessons in oratory and his dignified courtesy. They helped each other to control the young prince's dangerous years of adolescence, laboring to see that if he were going to spurn virtue, he should at least be guided toward permissible indulgence. They united to oppose the savagery of Agrippina, who, inflamed with all the wicked passions of despotism, had the help of Pallas, on whose advice Claudius had destroyed himself by promoting his incestuous marriage, and the disastrous adoption of Nero. But to be ruled by slaves was not to Nero's tastes, and the haughtiness of Pallas, so inappropriate to his station, moved him to disgust. But publicly Agrippina was paid every honor. When the duty officer of the Guard, according to custom, asked the Emperor for the password, the one he gave was "The Best of Mothers."[2] The Senate granted her two lictors, and made her a priestess of Claudius; Claudius was voted a public funeral, and later received divine honors.

FUNERAL OF CLAUDIUS

3. On the day of the funeral Nero pronounced the eulogy. During his recital of the antiquity of Claudius' family, the consulships and triumphs that his ancestors had gained, he and his audience were in a serious mood. Reference to his literary distinction, and to the fact that no external disasters had afflicted the state in his time, found ready acceptance. But when he touched on Claudius' foresight and wisdom, laughter was unrestrained. Yet the oration had been prepared by Seneca, in a highly polished style, well adapted to the taste of the times. An older generation, who occupied their leisure in comparing the past and the present, noted that Nero was the first Roman Emperor who had needed to borrow another man's eloquence. The dictator Julius Caesar could hold his own with the greatest orators, and Augustus had a ready and flowing style, well suited to an Emperor. Tiberius was a past master at weighing his words: he could put a point forcefully, or be purposely ambiguous. Even Gaius' powers of oratory had not been weakened by his mental instability. Claudius could be graceful enough, providing he kept to a prepared text. But from boyhood Nero

had directed his lively mind to other things—carving, painting, singing, and riding. He even composed poems himself—a token of at least the elements of an education.[3]

NERO'S POLICY

4. His exercises in counterfeit sorrow duly performed, Nero attended the Senate and paid tribute to their support and the agreement of the army. Then he spoke of his admirable advisers, and the example of a good Emperor which had been placed before him. His youth, he declared, had not been steeped in civil wars nor in palace quarrels: he brought with him no hatreds, no sense of injustice, no vendetta. Then he outlined his future policy, stressing especially the renunciation of all that had brought unpopularity in the previous reign. He was not going to take all judicial business himself, thus increasing the power of a few individuals by shutting up defendants and prosecutors in the same building. In his house, there would be no room for bribery or favoritism: there would be a strict division between private and public business. The Senate should exercise its ancient functions, and people from Italy and the provinces would have access to its tribunals, while he looked after the armies entrusted to him.

5. These promises were kept. The Senate decided many affairs: forbidding counsel to receive gifts or fees, excusing quaestors-elect from holding public games. Agrippina regarded the latter as a reversal of the policy of Claudius and objected to it, but the Senate persisted, although the meeting had been called at the palace for her convenience, and she was standing behind a curtain at a door specially built to enable her to hear without being seen. When, on another occasion, a deputation from Armenia was pleading its case before the Emperor, she actually prepared to mount the dais and take a seat beside him. Everyone was horrified and alarmed, but Seneca signed to Nero to rise and greet his mother. Thus a scandal was avoided by a display of filial piety.

EASTERN AFFAIRS

6. At the close of the year, there were rumors of disturbances in the East. The Parthians had again broken loose and were ravaging Armenia, and had driven out Radamistus, who

had so often occupied that kingdom, and equally often evacuated it. Now he had once more given up the contest. Rome was
always avid for gossip, and the current speculation was as to
how an Emperor barely seventeen years of age could cope with
a danger so formidable, still less repel it. Nero was a boy, and
under a woman's government; what good could he be? Could
battles and sieges and the other operations of war be conducted
by tutors? Against this there were those who argued that the
prospect was better than if the summons to battle had come under an old dotard like Claudius, under the influence of slaves.
At least Burrus and Seneca were well tried in the conduct of
affairs, and Nero was not far from manhood. At the age of
eighteen Gnaeus Pompeius had shown himself able to cope
with civil war, as had Augustus at nineteen. Guidance and
counsel, not arms and physical strength, were what counted at
the top. The Emperor would soon show whether he followed
good or bad advice, according to whether he ignored jealousies
and appointed a distinguished general, or chose a rich favorite
backed by influence.

7. Such was the public talk. Meanwhile Nero ordered that
the recruits drafted from the nearby provinces to bring the
Eastern legions up to full strength were to be moved up and
the legions themselves stationed near the Armenian borders.
The two veteran client-kings, Agrippa and Antiochus, were
asked to assemble an expeditionary force to invade Parthia, and
bridges were flung across the river Euphrates. Lesser Armenia
and Sophene were entrusted, with the royal insignia, to Kings
Aristobulus and Sohaemus. Acceptably enough, a rival arose
against the Parthian king, Vologeses, in the person of his son
Vardanes: as a result the Parthians withdrew as though abandoning the war.

8. But in the Senate these advantages were much exaggerated. Votes were passed of public thanksgiving, and of days
on which the Emperor should enter the city in triumph, wearing
a triumphal robe. His statue was to be set up in the temple
of Mars the Avenger, equal in size to that of the god himself.
There was in this partly the now customary element of flattery, but also a feeling of relief that the appointment of Domitius Corbulo to the Armenian command did seem to indicate
that a career was open to ability. The distribution of forces in
the East was as follows: to Ummidius Quadratus, governor
of Syria, half the auxiliaries and two legions; to Corbulo, an
equal number of Roman and auxiliary troops, plus the infantry
and cavalry in winter quarters in Cappadocia. The allied kings
were instructed to serve wherever they were needed, but their
inclination would have been to serve under Corbulo. Corbulo,

eager to reap advantage from his reputation, and knowing how much that counts in all new enterprises, advanced rapidly to the city of Aegeae, in Cilicia. There Quadratus went to meet him, lest all eyes should be turned on Corbulo if he entered Syria to take up his command. For he was a tall man, speaking in high-flown language, and besides genuine wisdom and experience, he had all those superficial qualities which command attention.

9. Both generals now sent messages to the Parthian king, urging him to opt for peace and not war, and to show the same reverence toward Rome as his predecessor by offering hostages. Vologeses duly handed over the most eminent members of the royal house. He may have wanted to prepare for war at a more convenient opportunity: he may equally have wished to eliminate dangerous rivals. The hostages were received by the centurion Insteius, sent by Ummidius for that purpose. As soon as Corbulo heard this, he detailed a company commander, Arrius Varus, to take them over. This led to scenes between the centurion and the commander. To eliminate this unedifying spectacle before the eyes of foreigners, the decision was left to the hostages and the envoys who were escorting them. They all chose Corbulo, because of his recent successes, and also because he was popular even among our enemies. This led to a quarrel between the two generals. Ummidius maintained that he had conducted the negotiations, but had been robbed of the fruits of them. Corbulo said that the offer of hostages by the Parthians was subsequent to his own appointment, and that this was what had converted the Parthian hopes into fears. Nero settled the quarrel by decreeing that the fasces should be wreathed with laurel "because of the victories of Quadratus and Corbulo." These events actually ran over into the next year, but I have narrated them consecutively.

10. This year the Emperor asked the Senate to approve a statue of his father Gnaeus Ahenobarbus and consular insignia for his tutor Asconius Labeo. He declined an offer to erect statues of himself in silver or gold. And though the Senate had decreed that years should in future begin with the month of December, in which Nero was born, he adhered to the custom, hallowed in the old calendars, of beginning the year in January. He blocked the prosecution of a senator, Carrinas Celer, on the denunciation of a slave, and also of the knight Julius Densus, accused of supporting Britannicus.

55 A.D. Consuls Claudius Caesar Nero Augustus and Lucius Antistius Vetus

11. When the magistrates were taking their annual oath of office, Nero prohibited his colleague Antistius from swearing to obey his acts. The Senate approved this in extravagant terms, in the hope that if Nero's youthful mind were fired with the credit for minor good actions, he might pass on to something more substantial. Leniency was shown to Plautius Lateranus, who had been removed from the Senate for adultery with Messalina, and who was now restored. Nero bound himself to clemency in a number of speeches which had been put into his mouth by Seneca, who wished to publish to the world through the mouth of the Emperor what excellent advice he gave—or what a good orator he was.

THE INTRIGUE WITH ACTE

12. By now, Agrippina was gradually losing her influence over Nero through his passion for a freedwoman named Acte, who had once been a slave. Two young men of rank were in his confidence in this affair, Marcus Otho, a man of consular family, and Claudius Senecio, whose father was one of the Emperor's freedmen. At first, Nero's mother knew nothing about it; later her opposition was ineffectual. Nero became obsessed with the intrigue, in all its debauchery and secretiveness. His older friends offered no opposition; indeed they were pleased to find all his ardors satisfied by a woman of low rank, with no harm done to anyone. Nero detested his wife, the noble and virtuous Octavia, either through the workings of fate, or because stolen joys are sweeter; and they were afraid that if they thwarted his passion in this affair, it would only burst out in attacks on the virtue of ladies of the aristocracy.

13. But not Agrippina. She raged in a woman's fashion at

having a freedwoman for her rival, a servant girl for her daughter-in-law. She refused to wait until her son began to regret his fancy—or to be bored with it—and the more violently she reproached him the more eager he became. In the end he threw off all obedience to his mother and turned to Seneca, one of whose intimates, Annaeus Serenus, had acted as go-between. This man pretended also to a violent passion for Acte, so that the first stages of Nero's intrigue could be carried on under a cloak of secrecy, and he could openly offer her the presents which really came from Nero. Agrippina then followed a new line. She exerted all her blandishments on Nero, offering him the use of the privacy of her own rooms for an affair which, after all, his youth and his high position fully excused. She had, she confessed, been too hard with him, and she proffered the use of her own resources, which were scarcely less than those of the Emperor. Once she had shown excess in trying to curb him; now she was going to the other extreme in indulgence. But this changed attitude did not deceive Nero, while his friends begged and implored him to beware the treachery of this woman—always terrible, and now playing the hypocrite as well.

It happened that during this period Nero inspected the magnificent gowns and jewelry that had been worn by the ladies of the imperial house. He selected a dress and some jewels and sent them—generously and spontaneously—as a present to his mother. There was nothing niggardly about this gift, for he gave her the finest and most desirable of all. But Agrippina complained that he was not adding these to her wardrobe, but keeping her out of the rest; he was giving her a small dole only, though he owed everything to her.

THE BREACH WITH AGRIPPINA

14. Some read a more sinister meaning into these remarks. As for Nero, he had turned violently against the supporters of this domineering woman, and dismissed Pallas from the post of treasurer to which Claudius had promoted him, and from which he had virtually ruled the Empire. As he left the Palatine Hill with his huge train of attendants Nero is said to have remarked, wittily enough, "There goes Pallas to swear that his hands are clean!"[4] And indeed Pallas had stipulated that there should be no going back into any of his past actions, and that his accounts with the state should be taken as balanced.

By now Agrippina was alarmed, and resorted to threats and

menaces. She took good care to let Nero hear her say that Britannicus was grown up, that he was the true heir, and worthy of his father's position—which was held by an adopted supplanter through the iniquities of his mother. She laid bare every secret of the ill-fated imperial house, not least her own marriage and the poisoning of her husband. The one prudent measure that could be credited to her—and the gods—was that her stepson was alive. She would take him to the barracks of the Praetorian Guard; that would be the place for a hearing between Germanicus' daughter on the one side, and on the other, the cripple Burrus with his deformed hand, and the refugee Seneca, with his professor's voice, who claimed to rule the world! Gesticulating, screaming abuse, she would call to witness the deified Claudius, the ghosts of the Silani, and all the other crimes she had committed in vain.

15. Nero was gravely alarmed at this. Britannicus' fourteenth birthday was rapidly approaching; and Nero pondered on his mother's violent nature, and also on the character of Britannicus, which had recently become known through a minor incident that won him wide popularity. It was the feast of the Saturnalia,[5] and among their other youthful amusements they were playing the game of dicing for a king of the feast. The lot fell on Nero. On all the others he laid trifling and innocuous commands, but he bade Britannicus to get up, come out into the center, and give them a song. He hoped the boy would make a fool of himself, being unused as yet even to sober dinner parties, much less to drunken orgies. But Britannicus rose and, with great steadiness of nerve, recited a poem which told how he had been pushed out from his father's house, and from the throne itself. Much sympathy was thus aroused, and at that late hour and in the atmosphere of a party there was no attempt to hide it. Nero saw that he had incurred odium, and turned all his hatred on Britannicus. Agrippina's threats prompted him to action. But there was no charge he could bring, and he could not openly order his brother's murder. He decided to act secretly, and gave orders for poison to be prepared. It was to be administered by an officer of the Guard, Pollio Julius, in whose custody had been placed the notorious Locusta, now convicted on a charge of poisoning. The precaution had long been taken of surrounding Britannicus with persons who cared nothing for loyalty and right. The young prince received the first dose of poison at the hands of his tutors, but a motion of the bowels rendered it ineffective, or perhaps it had been watered down to prevent immediate action. But Nero became impatient with murder by inches. He began to threaten the officer, and ordered the poisoner to be executed, saying

they were endangering his safety while they were considering public opinion and preparing their own defense. They promised the preparation of a poison that would act as swiftly as a sword stroke. Their laboratory was next to the Emperor's bedroom: the poisons in the mixture had been tested for potency and quick action.[6]

DEATH OF BRITANNICUS

16. Now it was the custom for the young princes of the imperial house to dine with others of their age at a separate table, where the fare was simpler and they were under the eyes of their relations. There sat Britannicus, but he had a special attendant who tasted his food and drink. A trick was therefore invented which would allow the custom to be observed, without betraying the crime by the death of two persons. A cup of mulled wine, previously tasted, and so far without poison, was handed to Britannicus. But it was too hot to drink, and he refused it. The poison was then put in with some cold water. Its action was so immediate on his whole system that he at once lost the power to speak or breathe. The other guests were appalled. Some were foolish enough to rush out of the room, but the more intelligent waited, their eyes fixed on Nero. He lolled at ease, pretending to know nothing. Then he remarked that Britannicus had had fits of epilepsy since childhood, but his vision and senses would soon return. Agrippina tried to compose her features, but her fear and agony of mind showed quite clearly that she knew as little of the deed as did Britannicus' sister Octavia. She saw her last support gone, and, before her eyes, the example of a kinsman's murder. As for Octavia, young as she was, she too had learned to hide sorrow, affection, or emotion of any kind. So there was a brief pause—and then the merriment of the feast was resumed.

17. The same night saw the murder and the cremation of Britannicus. Preparations for the funeral had been thoughtfully provided. Its scale was modest. But such furious storms attended the burial of his ashes in the Campus Martius that the people believed the gods were showing their anger at the crime. Most men, however, found an excuse for it, saying that brothers ever hated brothers, and that a kingdom could never be shared. Some contemporary authors[7] assert that, for several days before the murder, Nero had taken advantage of the boy's innocence to commit homosexual acts on his person. Thus his death cannot be considered atrocious or untimely—even though

it did occur at the sacred board, with no time to embrace his sisters, and under the very eyes of his foe. Such was the death of the last prince of the Claudian line, violated first by lust, then by poison!

The Emperor published an edict to excuse the brief funeral obsequies. Ancestral custom, he said, bade them conceal from the eyes of the public the funeral of the young, avoiding alike lavish display and funeral speeches. He had lost a brother's help, and now all his hopes were placed in the state. All the more readily should Senate and people rally to the support of an Emperor who was the last survivor of a house born for imperial power.

18. Nero then lavished presents on his principal friends. There were those who were critical of men who professed Stoic austerity, yet were now dividing up among themselves town and country houses as though they were so much booty. Others thought they had no option: the Emperor was conscious of his guilt, and hoped to buy forgiveness by bribing the most powerful.

INTRIGUES OF AGRIPPINA

But no munificence could assuage Agrippina's anger. She embraced Octavia's interests, held secret conferences with her friends, collected money from all sources for her cause, even beyond the limits of her natural greed. She gave a gracious reception to tribunes and centurions, and herself courted such noblemen of birth and ability as still existed. She was looking around for a party, and for a leader to put at its head.

Nero discovered this, and withdrew the personal guard, which she had received as the wife, and retained as the mother, of the Emperor, and also those German guardsmen who had recently been added to it as a mark of respect. He gave her a separate house—the one formerly owned by Antonia—to prevent her from giving great receptions. Whenever he paid a visit there, it was with numerous guards in attendance, and after a perfunctory embrace he would take his leave.

19. Nothing in human affairs is so transitory and precarious as the reputation for power without the means to support it. Agrippina's threshold was at once deserted: no one comforted her, no one came to call, except a few women, who could have done so from hatred as much as from love.[8] Now one of these ladies was Junia Silana, whose divorce from her husband by the doing of Messalina I have recounted above. She was dis-

tinguished by high birth, beauty, and lasciviousness. Agrippina had once loved her dearly, but later enmity had grown up between them because Agrippina had dissuaded the youthful Sextus Africanus from marrying Silana, whom she described as immoral and aging. She did not want Africanus for herself, but she had no mind to see a husband for Silana, who was both rich and childless. Here was Silana's chance of revenge. She suborned two of her clients, Iturius and Calvisius, to bring accusations against Agrippina, not the old and threadbare charges of mourning for the death of Britannicus or publishing Octavia's wrongs, but of preparing a plot to bring forward Rubellius Plautus, who was descended from Augustus, on his mother's side, in the same degree as Nero. She herself was to become his wife and control the Empire once more. This story the two told to Atimetus, freedman of the Emperor's aunt Domitia. Atimetus rejoiced in his opportunity—for there was implacable enmity between Agrippina and Domitia—and he persuaded the actor Paris, another freedman of Domitia's, to go at once and present the charge in the most forceful terms.

20. It was night, and Nero was far in his cups. To him entered Paris, who usually appeared at that hour to give a fillip to the Emperor's dissipations, but now wore an expression of gravity. Point by point he related the accusation. Nero became so terrified that he thought not only of killing Agrippina and Plautus, but also of removing Burrus from the command of the Guards, on the ground that he was under obligation to Agrippina for the promotion she had won for him and was now paying his debt. Fabius Rusticus asserts that the brevet was drafted to Caecina Tuscus, appointing him to the command, and that it was at Seneca's instance that Burrus was retained. Pliny and Cluvius do not suggest that there was any doubt of Burrus' loyalty: admittedly Fabius is partial to Seneca, to whose friendship he owed his success. (I intend to follow the authorities when they agree, and to mention them by name only when they differ.)[9] Nero was so terrified and anxious for the execution of his mother that the only thing which could restrain him was a promise from Burrus that she should certainly suffer if guilty. But everyone, said Burrus, especially a parent, must be given an opportunity for defense. No prosecutors had presented themselves; they were going on the word of a single man, from an unfriendly household. They must also have regard to the late hour, the night spent in merrymaking, and all the other factors which made for a hasty and unfounded judgment.

21. Thus the Emperor's fury was appeased. At dawn, Burrus went to Agrippina to inform her of the charge, so that

she could either clear herself or pay the penalty. This instruction he discharged in the presence of Seneca: there were also some freedmen to take note of what was said. Burrus took a threatening attitude, setting out the charges and the accusers. Agrippina had lost none of her spirit. "I am not surprised," she said, "that Silana, who has never borne a child, is totally ignorant of a mother's feelings. Parents do not change their children as easily as adulteresses change lovers. If Iturius and Calvisius have devoured all their fortunes, and are now doing the old woman the last favor of bringing an accusation against me, is that a reason for my attempting my son's murder, or the Emperor burdening his conscience with matricide? As for Domitia, I should be grateful for her enmity if she were vying with me to benefit Nero; but she is only using her lover Atimetus and the actor Paris to trump up lying melodramas. She was looking after her fishponds at Baiae when I was procuring Nero's adoption, the granting of proconsular power, and the rank of consul-designate—everything, in short, that was the prologue to the imperial theme. If I have intrigued with the cohorts of the Guard, tampered with the loyalty of the provinces, or corrupted slaves or freedmen, let witnesses be produced. If Britannicus had been in power, should I be alive? If Plautus or anyone else does win the Empire and sit in judgment over me, will there be any lack of accusers then? No, and they will charge me, not with a few hasty words spoken from a mother's love, but with real crimes of which only my son can absolve me." Those who were present were moved by these words, and sought to calm her temper. But she demanded to see her son. To him she spoke not a word of her innocence, as if it were in doubt, nor of her service to him, as if in reproach. What she did seek—and win—was vengeance on her enemies and rewards for her friends.

OTHER EVENTS OF THE YEAR

22. Faenius Rufus was placed in charge of the grain supply. Arruntius Stella undertook the preparation of the games to be given by the Emperor. Tiberius Balbillus became prefect of Egypt. Publius Anteius was nominated governor of Syria, but various excuses were found to put him off, and in the end he was detained in Rome. Silana received a sentence of exile: Calvisius and Iturius of relegation to an island. Atimetus was executed. Paris was too useful in the Emperor's debauches to

suffer any penalty. For the time being, no action was taken against Rubellius Plautus.

23. Then Pallas and Burrus were accused of plotting to win the Empire for Cornelius Sulla, of noble family and linked to Claudius by marriage with his daughter Antonia. A certain Paetus brought this charge, a man of bad reputation through his trafficking in old treasury debts. The charge he brought was obviously false. But the pleasure caused by Pallas' innocence was more than offset by the repugnance felt for his arrogance. When certain of his freedmen were named as his accomplices, he had answered, "I give all the orders in my house by a nod or a gesture: if anything more explicit is needed, I put it in writing, to avoid being on speaking terms with them." Burrus, although accused, gave his vote as one of the judges. Paetus was sentenced to exile, and his account books, containing notes of long-overlooked debts to the treasury, were burned.

24. At the close of the year the company of soldiers usually posted at the public spectacles was withdrawn. The purposes were to give an appearance of greater freedom, to avoid corruption of the troops by the license customary in the theater, and to show whether the crowd could control itself in the absence of guards. On the advice of the haruspices, the Emperor carried out a purification of the city, since the temples of Jupiter and Minerva had been struck by lightning.[10]

56 A.D. Consuls Quintus Volusius Saturninus and Publius Cornelius Scipio

EVENTS IN ROME

25. This was a year of peace abroad, but of shameful excesses at home. Nero in slave's disguise would roam the streets and brothels and taverns of the city with a group of wild companions, who would snatch away goods displayed for sale and assault anyone they met. So little were they detected, that the Emperor himself received blows and bore the marks on his face. When it became known that this brigand was Nero, there were more cases of assault on men and women of high rank. Indulgence once granted, there were others who formed gangs

of their own and performed the same outrages unpunished. Rome at night became like a captured city. Finally one Julius Montanus, of senatorial rank though he had never held office, met the Emperor in the streets after dark, and resisted very stoutly on being attacked. However, he recognized his attacker and begged his pardon: this apology was taken to imply reproach, and he was forced to commit suicide. After this Nero took fewer risks. He provided himself with an escort of soldiers and gladiators, with the instructions that private quarrels were to be allowed to go on if they were not serious, but if there was serious resistance from the assaulted, they should intervene with weapons.

He also converted the brawls in the theater, caused by the supporters of rival actors, into something like pitched battles, with prizes and immunity from prosecution. He would watch them himself, sometimes openly, sometimes incognito, until at last the public disorder and the fear of things getting really out of hand left him no remedy except to expel the actors from Italy and once more set an armed guard over the theater.

DEBATES IN THE SENATE

26. At this time there was a discussion in the Senate about the behavior of freedmen, and a strong demand that the patron should have the right of revoking the gift of freedom in cases where it had been abused. This view found support. But the consuls did not like to take a vote without consulting the Emperor, to whom they wrote putting the views of the Senate. He consulted a few advisers and found opinions divided. Some said that the impudence engendered by freedmen had now reached such a pitch that freedmen actually asked their patrons whether they should go to law about their rights, or assert them by force. They even threatened violence, or were impertinent enough to prescribe their own punishment. For what punishment could the injured patron inflict, other than that of banishing a freedman beyond the hundredth milestone —to the seaside in Campania? All other kinds of lawsuits were open on the same terms to both parties: what was needed here was the provision of some weapon that could not be defied. It would do the freedmen no harm to have to retain their liberty by the same sense of obedience by which they had won it. Notorious offenders, on the other hand, deserved to be returned to slavery: they needed to be restrained by fear, if they were insensitive to kindness.

27. The arguments on the other side were: admittedly it was equitable that the guilty minority should be punished, but the order as a whole should not suffer in its rights. It was very numerous, supplying as it did the majority of the voters, servants of public offices, attendants to magistrates and priests, and soldiers even in the city cohorts. Many of the knights, even of the senatorial order, had no other origin; if the freedmen were to be segregated, the freeborn would be shown to be very thin on the ground.[11] When our ancestors designated degrees of rank, they had very properly made freedom the common property of all. Again, two methods of liberation had been established, to leave room either for a change of heart, or for a second grant of favor. Those whose patron had not "liberated by the wand"* were left in a semiservile condition. Patrons ought to consider each case carefully on its merits, and be slow to grant what could not later be revoked. This argument prevailed, and Nero wrote back to the Senate saying that individual charges brought by patrons against freedmen should be carefully investigated, but that no action should be taken against the order as a whole. Not long after this Nero's aunt Domitia lost her freedman Paris, ostensibly by process of law: since Nero issued the decree of freeborn status, he earned not a little discredit.

28. Still, for all this, there was still some semblance left of a free country. When there was a dispute between the praetor Vibullius and the tribune Antistius, who ordered the release of two disorderly supporters of actors who had been arrested by the praetor, the Senate ratified the arrest, and censured Antistius for his impudence. They took the occasion to prevent the tribunes from assuming the powers of consuls and praetors, or from summoning litigants from Italy to appear in Rome. The consul-elect, Lucius Piso, added the clause that they must not exercise jurisdiction in their own homes, and that the quaestors must not enter up any fines levied by them in the public account books for a period of four months, within which time appeals could be lodged, to be decided by the consuls. The aediles suffered some loss of power, since the amounts by which the curule magistrates and the aediles of the people could levy fines or distrain was defined by statute. Helvidius Priscus, tribune of the people, had a quarrel with a treasury official, whom he accused of excessive harshness over the compulsory sales of the property of persons in distressed circumstances. This led the Emperor to transfer custody of the

* The text in this whole passage is very corrupt.

public accounts from the finance officers to a body of special commissioners.

29. This was a matter that had undergone frequent and various changes. Augustus allowed the Senate to select commissioners for the treasury: then there arose a suspicion of canvassing for votes, and they were chosen by lot from the praetors available. That did not last long, for the lot produced some very unsuitable persons. Claudius reverted to the system of finance officers, promising them accelerated promotion to make sure that they would not hesitate to take action through fear of giving offense. However, these young men did not carry the weight for so important a first post, so Nero established the appointment of ex-praetors of proved capacity.

30. In this year Vipsanius Laenas was convicted of rapacity in his governorship of Sardinia. The prosecution by the Cretans of Cestius Proculus, on a charge of extortion, was unsuccessful. Clodius Quirinalis, prefect of the fleet at Ravenna, who by his extravagance and cruelty treated Italy as though it were the most contemptible of nations, took poison before sentence could be pronounced. Caninius Rebilus, among the foremost in wealth as well as in legal sagacity, escaped the sufferings of old age and sickness by opening his veins. A man of notorious effeminacy, he was not generally credited with the resolution to commit suicide. Lucius Volusius left a great name when he died. Rich and virtuous, he had reached the age of ninety-three, and provoked to malevolence none of all these Emperors!

57 A.D. Consuls Nero Caesar (for the second time) and Lucius Piso

31. Very little worthy of record occurred during this year, except for those historians who choose to pad out their pages with praises of the timbers and foundations of the enormous amphitheater built by Nero in the Campus Martius. The dignity of the Roman people requires only notable names for its annals: such topics as the above are the proper concern of the

daily journals.[12] The colonies of Capua and Nuceria were now strengthened by veterans; a bounty of four hundred sesterces per head was distributed to the Roman plebs; a deposit of forty million sesterces was added to the treasury to buttress public credit. The 4 percent sales tax on the sale of slaves was remitted, though this was in appearance rather than in fact, for the tax was now collected from the seller and, naturally, was passed on to the purchaser. The Emperor forbade any magistrate or procurator to hold any show of gladiators or wild beasts, or any other spectacle, within his province; for in the past this sort of generosity had oppressed the provincials as sorely as the greed of the officials—who protected themselves with pageantry against retribution for the wrongs they had committed through wantonness.

32. A measure of the Senate served the interests of vengeance and security alike. It provided that where a man was murdered by his slaves, any of them set free by the will, but still remaining in the house, should suffer the same fate as the rest. Lurius Varus, an ex-consul, was restored to the Senate, having been expelled on charges of extortion. A noble lady called Pomponia Graecina, wife of that Aulus Plautius whose ovation for a British victory I have recorded,[13] being accused of adherence to a foreign superstition, was handed over for judgment to her husband. He followed the ancient custom, sat in judgment on his wife in the presence of her relatives, and pronounced her not guilty. This same lady lived a long life of unbroken sorrow. For forty years, from the day Julia, daughter of Drusus, was murdered through the treachery of Messalina, she never put off her mourning, and never abated her grief. This earned her no punishment while Claudius lived; later, it brought her glory.

33. It was a year of prosecutions. The province of Asia prosecuted Publius Celer: Nero could not decently acquit him, but let proceedings drag on till he died of old age. This was the Celer who, as I have related, murdered the proconsul Junius Silanus: gratitude for this great crime threw a screen over his other misdeeds. The people of Cilicia accused Cossutianus Capito. A man of base reputation and profligate life, he had had the impertinence to suppose that he might behave in a province with the same license as in Rome. But his accusers persisted and brought him to bay: in the end he abandoned any defense, and was condemned under the law of extortion. The Lycians, also, claimed reparation from Eprius Marcellus. But so much influence was brought to bear on his behalf that some of his accusers were sentenced to exile for having endangered an innocent man.

58 A.D. Consuls Nero Caesar and Valerius Messala Corvinus

EVENTS IN ROME

34. In his third consulship, Nero's colleague was Valerius Messala. Some of the oldest senators recalled that his great-grandfather, the orator Corvinus, had held that office with Augustus, the great-great-grandfather of Nero. As a mark of honor for that noble house, Messala received an annual grant of 500,000 sesterces, to enable him to support his blameless poverty. Aurelius Cotta and Haterius Antoninus also received annual grants from the imperial treasury, though in their case the family fortunes had been dissipated by extravagance.

EVENTS IN THE EAST—THE CAMPAIGNS OF CORBULO

The beginning of the year saw a vigorous resumption of the Roman-Parthian war over Armenia, which had been feebly begun and intermittently pursued. The Parthian king, Vologeses, had no mind to allow his brother Tiridates to give up the kingdom he had conferred on him, nor yet to hold it as a gift from a foreign power. Corbulo thought that the dignity of the Roman people demanded the recovery of the lands once conquered by Pompey and Lucullus.[14] The Armenians wavered in their loyalty, and invited in the armies of both sides. Geography, the customs of the country, and frequent intermarriage made them more akin to the Parthians; they had no conception of freedom, but they preferred a Parthian to a Roman master.

35. But Corbulo had more trouble from the slackness in his own army than from the treachery of the enemy. His legions had been brought up from Syria, where they had long grown idle in peacetime service. They could not tolerate the duties of a camp. Veterans there certainly were who had never manned an outpost nor stood a watch, who had never seen

a ditch or a rampart, who had no issues of helmet or breast-plate! Sleek and prosperous, they had done their military service in towns. Those unfit for service by age or health were discharged, and their places filled by troops levied in Galatia[15] and Cappadocia, with the addition of a legion from Germany and auxiliary cavalry and infantry units. The whole army was kept under canvas,[16] although the winter was so severe that the frozen ground had to be dug out to allow tents to be pitched. There were many cases of limbs lost by frostbite; men died on guard. One man was seen carrying a load of wood: his hands were so frostbitten that they stuck to the load and dropped off, leaving him with only the stumps. The general himself went about the camp lightly clad, bareheaded; he was present on marches and fatigues, with a word of praise for the energetic, of cheer for the sick, an example to the whole army. But the harsh climate and rough conditions led to many desertions and derelictions, and he had to adopt a policy of toughness. In other Roman armies first or even second offenders are forgiven: with Corbulo death followed immediately for desertion of the colors. This was shown by experience to be salutary, and better than a more sympathetic policy. Corbulo had fewer desertions than in armies where pardons were given.

36. Corbulo meanwhile kept his legions in camp until the spring was well advanced. His auxiliary infantry were posted at various selected points, under orders not to provoke an engagement. These posts were under the command of an officer called Paccius Orfitus, who had been first centurion in his legion. Paccius reported that the barbarians were taking no precautions, and there was a good chance of gaining a success, but he was ordered to keep within his defenses and wait for reinforcements. This command he disobeyed. A few cavalry squadrons came in from neighboring posts, clamoring for battle: he led them against the enemy, and was defeated. Moreover, those units that should have come to his rescue took fright at the defeat, and retreated to their own camps. Corbulo was furious. He reprimanded Paccius severely, and ordered him and his men to pitch their tents outside the camp. In that humiliating position they were kept until the entreaties of the entire army secured their release.

37. Tiridates by now had reinforcements from his brother Vologeses as well as his own levies, and began openly, rather than stealthily, to harry Armenia. He ravaged those peoples whom he suspected of being pro-Roman, moving rapidly around to avoid forces sent against him, and caused panic by his reputation rather than by any military deeds. Corbulo's repeated attempts to force a battle came to nothing. Imitating

the methods of the enemy, he enlarged the theater of the war, and disposed his forces so that legionary commanders and officers in charge of auxiliary units could make simultaneous attacks on various objectives. King Antiochus of Commagene was ordered to invade the territories closest to his kingdom. King Pharasmenes of Iberia had put his son Radamistus to death as a traitor, and was very ready to demonstrate his pro-Roman sympathies by reviving his old feud with the Armenians. The tribe of the Moschi were also won over for the first time, and ravaged remote parts of Armenia. They have shown themselves very faithful friends of Rome.

These measures nullified Tiridates' policy. He therefore sent a delegation to register a protest in his own name and that of the Parthians. How was it, they asked, that after giving hostages and resuming his friendship with Rome—and incidentally opening up new possibilities of favor from Rome—he now found himself being pushed out of his old kingdom of Armenia? Vologeses so far had made no move only because they would rather rely on their rights than on force; but if the war did go on, the house of the Arsacids would again show the courage and good fortune that had produced so many Roman disasters.[17] Corbulo knew well that Vologeses was occupied with a rebellion in Hyrcania. He therefore advised Tiridates to apply to the Emperor—that way lay the possibility of securing the throne without bloodshed: it would be well to prune vague ambitions for the future and grasp the better choice within his reach.

38. Since these exchanges did nothing to promote peace, it was resolved to fix the time and place for a top-level conference. Tiridates announced that he would come with a guard of a thousand cavalry: no limit was set for Corbulo, and he could bring troops of any kind he liked, providing they discarded helmets and breastplates as a token of their peaceful intentions. Now anyone at all—especially a wily and experienced old general—could hardly fail to detect the barbarian's treachery. The limited numbers on his side, and the carte blanche to Corbulo, were of course a trap; if men without armor were exposed to cavalrymen skilled at using the bow, numbers would be useless. But Corbulo did not let it appear that he saw through the trick. His answer was that matters of public concern were best discussed in the presence of both their armies, and he selected a place for the conference where gentle hills on one side were suitable for infantry, and an open plain on the other for cavalry maneuvers. Corbulo came first on the appointed day. He placed the auxiliary units, and the levies from the client-kings, on the wings. The center was held

by the Sixth Legion, which had been strengthened by about three thousand men from the Third, brought up from another camp under cover of night. They all stood to under one eagle, as though belonging to only a single legion. Toward evening, Tiridates established himself at a distance from which he could be seen rather than heard. They did not meet together, and the Roman general ordered his men to return to their own camp.

39. At once the king drew off, either because he suspected guile from the sight of Roman troops moving in several directions, or because he wanted to intercept Roman supply columns coming by way of the Black Sea and Trapezus. But our troops held the mountain passes, and he was unable to attack the convoys. Corbulo, to prevent the war from dragging on, and to force the Armenians onto the defensive, prepared to storm the forts. For himself he chose the strongest place in the district, Volandum:[18] less important points were assigned to the legionary commander Cornelius Flaccus and the camp commandant Insteius Capito. He inspected the defenses, and assembled everything necessary for a siege. Then he called on the troops to expel from his lair a slippery enemy, ready neither for peace nor for war, who by his flight had confessed his cowardice and treachery, and to fight for both booty and glory. Then he divided his force into four parts. One, in tortoise formation, was to undermine the rampart; a second brought scaling ladders against the walls; others were to discharge spears and incendiary missiles from artillery. Places were marked for slingers to use their bolts, and to send a hail of bullets from a distance to prevent help coming at any point to an enemy unit hard pressed. The attack was pressed so hard that within a few hours the defenders had been driven off the walls, the barricades in the gateways demolished, the ramparts scaled, and all men of military age put to the sword, with not a man lost on our side, and very few wounded. Noncombatants were sold into slavery, everything else was treated as booty. The legionary commander and the camp commandant were equally successful. In a single day three forts were stormed, and the others surrendered in panic—or sometimes willingly. Thus encouraged, Corbulo planned to attack Artaxata. But he did not march the legions there directly: had he crossed the Araxes by a bridge close to the walls, he would have come under fire. The river crossing was therefore made by broader fords some way off.

40. In the mind of Tiridates fear contended with shame. If he allowed the siege to go on, he showed himself powerless; to attempt to raise it could only entangle himself and his cavalry in difficult country. He decided to make a show of

military force and, when opportunity offered, to engage in
open battle or make a feigned retreat which might lead to
an ambush. He suddenly surrounded the Roman army, but
Corbulo, realizing his purpose, had prepared his army both
for marching and for battle. The Third Legion was on the
right flank, the Sixth on the left, picked troops from the Tenth
were stationed in the center. All the baggage was within the
lines. A thousand cavalry protected the rear: they were to
resist an attack, but had orders on no account to pursue an
enemy withdrawal.[19] The wings were occupied by the foot
archers and the rest of the cavalry. The left wing was prolonged along the base of the hills so that an enemy penetration
of our lines could be met both from the front and from the
flank. Tiridates feinted a frontal assault, but never came
within range; now he threatened attack, now he pretended to
panic, in the hope of drawing out our units and cutting them
to pieces. But our men made no such move, except for one
foolish cavalry officer who moved out and was instantly
riddled with arrows. This example suggested to the others that
it was wise to obey orders. With fall of darkness Tiridates
retired.

41. Corbulo constructed a camp on the ground he held.
Thinking that Tiridates had gone to Artaxata, he debated
whether to make a forced march with the legions and besiege
the city. But his scouts reported that the king had set off for
a long march, either to Media or Albania, so he waited for
daylight. Then he sent on the lighter forces to surround the
walls and invest the city at a distance. The inhabitants, however, threw open the gates and surrendered themselves and
their possessions to us. Well for them that they did, for their
lives were spared. But Artaxata was fired, destroyed, and
leveled to the ground: the circuit of its walls made it impossible to hold without a powerful garrison, and our numbers
were too low to divide between a garrison force and a field
army; again, had it been spared and left ungarrisoned, its
capture would have been neither useful nor honorable. Then
occurred what seemed a divine portent. The sun was shining
brilliantly right up to the city walls, but a sudden darkness,
with flashes of lightning, enveloped the whole space within
them. It looked as though hostile gods were giving up the city
to destruction.

These victories brought Nero repeated salutations as "Imperator"; by senatorial decree statues, triumphal arches, and
successive consulships were conferred on him, thanksgivings
were held, and the day on which the victory had been won,
that on which it had been announced, and that on which they

had passed these motions, were made festive days. There were other proposals of the kind, in so extravagant a vein that Gaius Cassius was moved to declare that he agreed with the honors proposed, but if the gods were to be thanked for all their bounties, the year would not be long enough. It would be better to distinguish clearly between holy days and days of business on which men could carry on divine worship without neglecting human affairs.

EVENTS IN ROME

42. Publius Suillius was then accused. He had known many changes of fortune and made himself many enemies, yet his condemnation brought much discredit on Seneca. In Claudius' reign Suillius had been both cruel and corrupt; now the change in affairs had not brought him so low as his enemies would have liked, and he himself would rather appear as a criminal than a suppliant. It was to crush him that the Senate proposed to renew the decree against those who pleaded for pay, and to attach the penalties provided by the Lex Cincia.[20] Complaints and recriminations followed from Suillius, who had a violent temper and the outspokenness of old age. He censured Seneca for his hostility to the friends of Claudius, under whom, he said, Seneca had very properly been sentenced to exile. "Seneca is used to profitless learning and the company of unformed youths: he has a grudge against those who can use their oratory with courage and effect for the good of their fellows. I was Germanicus' quaestor; Seneca was an adulterer in that house.[21] Which is better, to receive money for honorable work from grateful clients, or to violate the bedchamber of young princesses? What learning, what school of philosophy, has taught Seneca to accumulate three hundred million sesterces in the four years he has been the Emperor's favorite? In Rome he collects wills and legacies as though with a hunter's net: Italy and the provinces are bled white with loans at an exorbitant rate.[22] As for me, I have earned my modest fortune—I will face an accusation, a conviction, anything rather than allow my long-standing and self-made position to give place to this sudden prosperity of an upstart."

43. There were those who reported these words, or an exaggerated version, to Seneca. Accusers were found to charge Suillius of plundering provincials, when governor of Asia, and of embezzlement of public funds. A delay of twelve months was granted for the investigation, so it seemed better to begin

with charges for offenses committed in Rome, where witnesses could easily be collected. He was accused of having forced Quintus Pomponius to the extremity of civil war by the harshness of his persecution, of having caused the deaths of Julia, daughter of Drusus, and Poppaea Sabina, of having ruined Valerius Asiaticus, Lusius Saturninus, Cornelius Rufus, and countless Roman knights; indeed, all the cruelties of Claudius were charged to Suillius. His defense was that none of this was his doing, that he had only obeyed the Emperor's command. Nero put an end to this line by saying that he had ascertained, from his father's private journals, that he had never enforced prosecution against anyone. Then Suillius pleaded the orders of Messalina, but this too broke down. Why was it, it was asked, that no one else was ever selected to be the mouthpiece of that violent and shameless woman? The agents of atrocities must be punished, especially when they enjoyed the rewards of their crimes and imputed the blame to others. So Suillius was banished to the Balearic Islands, and half his fortune confiscated. (The rest was granted to his son and granddaughter, together with their whole legacy from their mother and grandmother.) Neither his danger nor his sentence broke his spirit; a well-supplied and easy life made his seclusion bearable. The accusers followed up the hatred of the father by charging his son Nerullianus with extortion, but the Emperor felt that vengeance had been served and used his veto.

OCTAVIUS SAGITTA

44. The case of Octavius Sagitta, tribune of the people, occurred at this time. He fell passionately in love with a married woman, Pontia, won her with expensive gifts to become his mistress, then induced her to promise to leave her husband and marry him. But when the lady was free, delays began: her father disapproved of the marriage, and so on; then she abandoned her promises altogether on finding the chance of a wealthier husband. Octavius tried threats and complaints: his honor was ruined, his money gone, all he had was his life, and that he put in her hands. All was in vain. Finally, he asked for a single night, as a consolation, after which he would control himself. The night was agreed upon: Pontia told one of her maids and asked her to watch the bedroom. Octavius came, with a single freedman, and hiding a knife under his cloak. There followed a scene of lovers' quarrels. Tears, reproaches, accusations, apologies, and inter-

vals of love-making took up most of the night. Pontia suspected nothing: but Octavius, as though in a frenzy of love, stabbed her with his knife, wounded the maid when she ran to help, and rushed out of the bedroom. The murder was discovered the next day, nor could there be any doubt of the murderer, for they had obviously passed the night together. But the freedman insisted on confessing to the deed, saying that it was done in vengeance for his master. Such devotion shook the belief of many, but then the maid recovered and told the full facts. The woman's father laid an accusation of murder before the consuls, and when Octavius vacated his office as tribune,[23] he was condemned under the Lex Cornelia by the Senate.

POPPAEA SABINA

45. There was another notorious example of lust in that year, and one which marked the beginning of much evil for the state. There was in Rome a lady called Poppaea Sabina.[24] She was a daughter of Titus Ollius, but she had taken the name of her maternal grandfather, the famous Poppaeus Sabinus, distinguished by his consulship and triumphal decorations; for Ollius had fallen a victim to his friendship for Sejanus before he could begin a public career. This woman had every gift— except virtue. Her mother had been the greatest beauty of her day, and she inherited her looks and her distinction; her wealth was equal to her birth. Her conversation was charming, her mind lively; her outward behavior was discreet—her life depraved. She seldom appeared in public, and then with part of her face veiled. She meant her beauty to have a scarcity value—and found the fashion becoming to her. She cared nothing for her reputation, and made no distinction between husbands and lovers. Her own affections, and those of others, counted for nothing with her: her passions were adjustable, as expediency called. Rufrius Crispinus, a Roman knight, had married her, and she had borne him a son: but Otho seduced her by his youth and extravagance, and also because he was thought to be Nero's most intimate friend. Their liaison soon turned into marriage.

46. Otho was always praising her beauty and graces to Nero. It may have been a lover's indiscretion, or it may have been a wish to arouse his interest, so that sharing the same woman would be a bond to increase Otho's power. He was often heard to rise from table at the palace with the words,

"I am going to Poppaea. She has brought me beauty and nobility: all men pray for such gifts; a fortunate few attain them." Under such promptings there was no long delay. When she was admitted to the palace, Poppaea made her way with a practiced flirtatiousness: she found Nero's looks as irresistible as her own passions. But as the Emperor's passion grew, she became haughtier. If she were kept for one or two nights in the palace, she would insist that she was a married woman, and had no desire to lose her marriage. "I am devoted to Otho," she would say. "No one else lives in such style: wealth and culture are united in him, he is equal to any fortune. Nero has a slave girl for a mistress: he is tied down by Acte's company; an intrigue with a servant is a mean and squalid affair!" Otho lost his intimacy with the Emperor; then he was expelled from court and from his suite. Finally, lest he should stay in Rome as a rival, he was sent to govern Lusitania. This post he held up to the civil wars, and discharged it honorably and well, quite out of keeping with his earlier habits. A playboy in his private life, he showed self-discipline in his public office.[25]

47. So far, Nero had tried to throw a screen over his crimes and excesses. He had become very suspicious of Cornelius Sulla, whose lethargic nature he misinterpreted as one of cunning and dissimulation. These fears were played upon by an elderly freedman called Graptus, who had been versed in palace intrigue since the days of Tiberius. In those days the Milvian Bridge was crowded with night resorts, and it was a favorite haunt of Nero, who could indulge himself with less restraint outside the city. Now it was known that he usually returned by way of the Via Flaminia; and Graptus invented the story that on a certain night an ambush had been laid for him, which he had escaped only by the chance that he went by the Gardens of Sallust instead. Sulla was denounced as the author of this plot, the whole story being based on the fact that a few revelers had created a groundless panic among Nero's attendants on their way home—a common enough piece of youthful folly. No slave or freedman of Sulla was ever identified, and his timid and contemptible nature would have been quite unequal to such a deed. Nonetheless, as if he had been convicted, he was forced to quit Rome and live within the walls of Massilia.[26]

48. The same year saw two separate deputations sent by the senate and people of Puteoli. The former complained of the violence of the populace, the latter of the greed of the magistrates and the leading citizens. The disorders had already reached the point of stone-throwing and threats of arson; to

prevent armed bloodshed Gaius Cassius was chosen to find a solution. But the inhabitants found his rule too harsh, and at his own request the mission was transferred to the brothers Scribonius. A Praetorian cohort was summoned, there were a few executions, and the citizens were restored to their former harmony.

49. My only reason for mentioning an unimportant decree of the Senate affecting the citizens of Syracuse (it allowed them to exceed the quota set for the number of gladiatorial shows), is that it was opposed by Paetus Thrasea,[27] who thus gave a handle to his critics. "Why," they demanded, "if Thrasea thinks the state needed a free Senate, does he waste time on such trifles? Why not speak on peace or war, on tariffs or laws—the really decisive issues? All senators have the right to raise any topic whenever they speak, and to demand a motion on it. Is the abundance of shows in Syracuse the only thing needing reform? Is everything, everywhere, in every part of the Empire, as well arranged as if Paetus, and not Nero, were in charge? If matters of great moment are to pass without debate, how much more important to ignore trivialities!" His friends asked for an explanation, and Thrasea's reply was that it was not through ignorance of the present state of affairs that he offered criticism in such matters, but that he paid the Senate the compliment of assuming it would be clear to them that those who concerned themselves with minor matters were not likely to hide their interests in what was more important.

50. There was a great protest this year against the extravagant demands of the tax collectors. Nero even thought of abolishing all indirect taxes, a veritable boon to humanity. But members of the Senate[28] dissuaded him from this generous impulse (after praising the grandeur of the conception). The Empire, they said, would perish if the revenues which supported the state were diminished. If indirect taxes were abolished, there would be a demand for the abolition of tributes. Most of the tax-collecting companies had been founded by consuls and tribunes of the people in the full freedom of the Republic; since that time every care had been taken to balance revenue and expenditure. Some check was admittedly needed on the cupidity of tax gatherers, lest taxes paid for years without complaint should engender ill-will through new exactions.

51. The Emperor therefore ordered that the regulations for each tax, hitherto confidential, should be publicly displayed. Arrears were not to be recoverable after twelve months: lawsuits against the tax collectors should be given priority, in Rome by the praetor, in the provinces by the propraetor or proconsul. Soldiers were to enjoy tax exemption, except for articles

that they sold; and there were other excellent provisions, which were observed for a time, and then lapsed. However, the 2½ and 2 percent duties were abolished, together with other inventions of the tax collectors, and this has remained in force to our own times. Overseas provinces found easier terms for the shipment of grain, and merchant ships were exempted from assessment and payment of property tax.

52. Two former governors of Africa, Sulpicius Camerinus and Pompeius Silvanus, were tried and acquitted by the Emperor. Camerinus, accused by a few private individuals, had been charged, not with extortion, but with cruelty. Silvanus was attacked by numerous prosecutors, who asked for time to produce witnesses. But Silvanus asked to be heard immediately. He was rich, old, and childless, and this combination served him so well that he outlived those whose expectations had brought about his acquittal.

EVENTS ON THE GERMAN FRONTIER

53. Up to that time things had been quiet in Germany. This was the choice of the Roman generals, for triumphal honors had been awarded with such prodigality that they felt they would earn greater merit by keeping the peace. Paulinus Pompeius and Lucius Antistius Vetus then held command.[29] To prevent the troops from being idle, Paulinus completed the levee, begun sixty-three years earlier by Drusus, to control the flood waters of the Rhine. Vetus prepared plans for a canal to connect the Moselle and Saône, so that sea-borne freight could be sent through the Mediterranean, then up the Rhone and Saône, through the canal to the Moselle, and thence by the Rhine to the ocean. By removing the difficulties of overland transport this would make a shipping link between the western Mediterranean and the northern shores of Europe. This project aroused the jealousy of Aelius Gracilis, governor of Gallia Belgica,[30] who had no wish to see Vetus bringing his legions into another man's province and winning the favor of the Gauls. He therefore hinted to Vetus that the Emperor would be alarmed at the undertaking—an argument which has been fatal to so many admirable schemes.

54. But the continued inactivity of the Roman armies gave rise to a rumor that the governors had been forbidden to attack the enemy. On the strength of this the Frisii led their young warriors through the swamps and forests, moved the noncombatants across the lagoons, reached the banks of the

Rhine, and settled on unoccupied lands reserved for the use of the Roman army.[31] This was under the leadership of Verritus and Malorix, kings of that people—if Germans may be said to have kings. They had built houses, sown crops, and were working the land as though it were their ancestral domain when Dubius Avitus (Paulinus' successor in Lower Germany) ordered them out. By threatening that Roman force would be used against them unless they returned to their old lands, or petitioned the Emperor for new territory, he forced Verritus and Malorix to make the appeal. They reached Rome to find Nero occupied with other business. On the round of sightseeing usually prescribed for barbarians, they were taken to the Theater of Pompey, to see the huge audience. Idling away the time (for they were too ignorant to get any pleasure from the show), they began asking about the seating arrangements in the auditorium and especially the reserved seats for the different orders—where were the knights, the senators, and so on—and then they saw a number of persons in foreign dress sitting in the senatorial rows.[32] They asked who these people were, and were told that this honor was granted to ambassadors from foreign nations notable for valor and for their friendship to Rome. "No people on earth," they exclaimed, "are more valiant and loyal than the Germans!" And with that they moved down the gangway and sat down among the senators. The spectators were delighted with this old-fashioned impulsiveness and honorable pride in themselves. Nero gave them both Roman citizenship, but ordered the Frisii to leave their new lands. This order they opposed, but the unexpected sending of a cavalry squadron brought them to heel, after a few of the more obstinate tribesmen had been killed.

55. The same lands were next occupied by the Ampsivarii,[33] a more powerful tribe both in themselves and in the sympathy they enjoyed from their neighbors because they had been expelled from their lands by the Chatti, and were then homeless refugees looking for somewhere secure to settle. Their case was put by one Boiocalus, of high repute in these parts, and of proven loyalty to us. "I was imprisoned by Arminius," he said, "in the revolt of the Cherusci; I served under Tiberius and Germanicus; after fifty years of loyalty I am now bringing my people within your Empire. How little of all this land will ever be needed for the occasional pasturing of army flocks and herds! Reserve lands for cattle—though men are starving—but do not choose an empty wilderness in preference to friendly peoples. The Chamavi once held these lands, then the Tubantes, and finally the Usipi. Heaven has been given to the gods, the earth to men: empty lands are free for all." Then he raised his

eyes to the sun and, invoking it and all heavenly bodies, he
demanded, as if face to face with them: "Do you want to look
down on empty lands? Rather bring the sea to flood out those
who rob others of their soil!"

56. This plea had an effect on Avitus. But his answer was
that men must obey their betters: the very gods they invoked
had given the Romans power to give and take away as they
chose: and the Romans would admit no other judges than
themselves. This was his official reply to the Ampsivarii. To
Boiocalus he gave the private promise of a grant of land as
a recompense for his long loyalty. Boiocalus indignantly rejected this as the wages of treachery, adding the words: "We
have not land to live on, but we shall not lack land in which
to die!" They parted as enemies, and the Ampsivarii asked the
Bructeri, Tencteri, and even more distant tribes to join them
in war. Avitus wrote to Curtilius Mancia, commander of the
forces in Upper Germany, asking him to cross the Rhine and
make a show of force in the rear. Then he led his own legion
into the territory of the Tencteri, threatening to wipe them
out unless they abandoned the Ampsivarii. They withdrew
from the alliance; the same threats alarmed the Bructeri, and
the remaining tribes also declined to fight other people's battles. So the Ampsivarii were left alone. They fell back from
the Rhine into the lands of the Usipi and Tubantes: expelled
from there, to the Chatti, and finally to the Cherusci. In their
long wanderings in alien lands they were treated first as guests,
then as beggars, finally as foes. In the end all their fighting men
were killed, and the noncombatants shared out as booty.[34]

57. The same summer saw a great battle between the
Hermunduri and the Chatti. The dispute was over a salt-
producing river which divided their lands. Besides the Germanic passion for settling everything by force of arms, they
had a religious motive, for they believed that those lands were
especially close to heaven, so that nowhere did the gods respond more readily to human prayers. Indeed, they thought
that it was by a dispensation of providence that salt was produced in this river and these forests, for the method was not
the usual one of evaporation from pools of salt water. Instead,
they poured the water onto a burning mass of logs and timber,
and the salt was produced from the fusion of two opposite elements, fire and water.[35] The Hermunduri won the battle; disaster fell on the Chatti. For both sides, if victorious, had vowed
the enemy army to Mars and Mercury, a vow which involves
the complete destruction of men, horses, everything. So their
boastful threats recoiled on themselves.

An allied people, the Ubii, suffered an unforeseen calamity.

Fires started in the ground[36] and burned farms, crops, and villages, reached right up to the walls of the newly founded colony.[37] They could not be put out by rain nor river water nor any other liquid. But in the end, the country people, desperate for a remedy and infuriated at their losses, began hurling rocks at them from a distance and then, when the flames were halted, coming to closer quarters with them and beating them with cudgels and other instruments as though they were driving wild animals away. Finally they snatched the very clothes off their backs and hurled them on—the older and dirtier the clothes, the more effective as a fire extinguisher.

58. This same year the fig tree by the Comitium known as the Ruminalis—the tree which 830 years earlier had sheltered the infants Romulus and Remus,[38] showed some dead branches and began to wither in its trunk. This was taken as a prodigy, but it revived and sent out new shoots.

BOOK XIV

59 A.D. Consuls Gaius Vipstanius and Gaius Fonteio

THE MURDER OF AGRIPPINA

1. Nero put off no longer the crime he had planned for so long. Length of rule had made him bolder than ever, while his passion for Poppaea grew more ardent every day. She knew very well that there would be no marriage for her, nor divorce for Octavia, so long as Agrippina lived. She kept reproaching the Emperor, or mocking him as no more than a ward, devoid not only of power but even of his own freedom, and under the control of others. Why did he postpone their marriage? Did he mistrust her beauty, or dislike the glory of her ancestors? Did he doubt that she could give him children, or that she loved him truly? No: he feared that if she spoke as a wife, she would make it clear how the Senate was humiliated and the people annoyed by his mother's arrogance and greed. If Agrippina's idea of a daughter-in-law was someone who hated her son, she herself would go back to her marriage with Otho—indeed, she would go anywhere, and would rather hear than see the Emperor's degradation, and be involved in the dangers that went with it! These pleas, accompanied by all a mistress's tears and tricks, had their way with Nero, and none opposed them. All were longing to see his mother's power broken: none could believe that the son's hatred would extend to murder.

2. Cluvius says that Agrippina was so bent on clinging to power that several times at midday, when food and wine had inflamed Nero,[1] she displayed herself to him, primed and ready

for incest. Intimates marked their sensual kisses, the embraces that were the prelude to the crime. Seneca thought a woman the best counter to another woman's seductions, and sent in to him the freedwoman Acte, who was alarmed both for Nero's reputation and for her own safety. She it was who warned him that his incest was public property, and that Agrippina was boasting of it: also that the soldiers would never endure the rule of a sacrilegious Emperor. Fabius Rusticus says that the incest was by Nero's desire, not Agrippina's, and that it was the same freedwoman who broke it up. But other authors give the same account as Cluvius, and tradition supports them. Perhaps Agrippina really did intend this abomination; or perhaps it was simply that such novel sexual indulgence seemed quite credible in a woman who, in her early youth, had committed adultery with Lepidus for the sake of power, who had for the same objective lowered herself to become the mistress of Pallas, and whose marriage with her own uncle had perfected her in every kind of debauchery.

3. So Nero avoided meeting her in private. When she withdrew to her gardens, or to her country houses at Tusculum or Antium, he would commend her for planning to rest. At last he decided that, wherever she was, she was intolerable. His only remaining doubt was whether to kill her by poison, by the sword, or by some other means. Poison was his first choice: but if she were poisoned at the Emperor's table, it would scarcely be ascribed to chance in the light of the death of Britannicus; and to bribe her servants would be difficult in view of the precautions she now took against plots. In any case, she had strengthened her physical resistance by a course of antidotes. No one could think of how to stab her and avoid detection: and there was also the possibility that the selected agent might recoil from his frightful mission. But a plan was submitted by the freedman Anicetus, now commander of the fleet at Misenum,[2] but once Nero's tutor, and linked to Agrippina by mutual hatred of long standing. He demonstrated that it was possible to build a ship with a part that could be detached at sea, and drop her overboard unawares. Accidents could happen at sea, if anywhere: if she were the victim of shipwreck, who would be so cynical as to suspect human agency in what was clearly the work of winds and waves? A further installment of the plan would be the provision, by the Emperor, of a temple and altars for the dear departed, together with other public marks of filial affection.

4. It was an ingenious plan, and it was accepted. Moreover, it came at a good time of the year, for Nero usually spent the festival of Minerva[3] at Baiae. There he lured his

mother, saying that one should bear a parent's hasty temper and show a conciliatory spirit. All this gave a general impression of reconciliation, and was so interpreted by Agrippina, who had all her sex's credulity toward good news. She landed from Antium, and Nero met her on the shore. Stretching out his arms, he embraced her, and escorted her to Bauli, a mansion on the bay between Cape Misenum and the waters of Baiae. Several ships were moored there: one, finer than the others, was obviously a mark of honor for his mother, who was used to traveling in a warship manned by marines. Then she was invited to dinner, so that the crime could take place under cover of night. It is well known that the plot was betrayed by an informer, but Agrippina was uncertain whether to believe it. At all events, she traveled to Baiae in a sedan chair. Here her fears were dispelled by her kind reception: Nero was most affable, and seated her next to himself. They had a long conversation: Nero was friendly and boyish, or else grave, as he made her his confidante on serious themes. It was a lengthy visit, and he saw her off at her departure, clinging to her and looking into her eyes. This may have been the final touch of hypocrisy; or perhaps this last sight of his mother as she went to her death touched even Nero's cruel heart.

5. It was a bright, starry night, and the sea was calm—as though heaven were determined to reveal the crime. The ship had not gone far, and Agrippina was attended by two of her friends. Crepereius Gallus was standing by the tiller, while Acerronia leaned over her recumbent mistress's feet and chatted gaily about the repentance of Nero and the restoration of his mother's influence. Then the signal was given: the cabin roof, weighted with lead, at once fell in. Crepereius was crushed and killed instantly; Agrippina and Acerronia were saved by the projecting framework above the couch, which, by chance, was too strong to be crushed. The ship did not fall to pieces, for in the general confusion the majority who knew nothing of the plot got in the way of those who did. Some of the crew thought of hurling themselves to one side to upset the boat, but it took them too long to carry out this improvised plan, and the others bore in the opposite direction, providing a gentler fall into the water. Acerronia foolishly called out, "I am Agrippina! Help the Emperor's mother!" She was at once dispatched by blows from oars, poles, or whatever other fittings lay to hand. Agrippina kept quiet, and was unrecognized. She had a wound in her shoulder, but she was able to swim until picked up by men in small boats. They brought her to the Lucrine lake, and then she was carried to her villa.

6. There she was able to think things over. She realized how treacherous were the letters which had brought her invitation, and the mark of special honor. No wind had driven the ship, the shore was hard by, and it did not strike a rock. It had begun to collapse at the top, like a piece of stage apparatus used on land.⁴ Then there was Acerronia's death, and her own wound: the only way to escape the plot was to feign ignorance. She therefore sent her freedman Agerinus to inform Nero that, thanks to divine mercy and his own good fortune, she had escaped a terrible accident. He was to stress that, however alarmed Nero might be at his mother's danger, he should not give himself the trouble of calling on her as yet; rest was what she needed now. She made a pretense of unconcern, while applying restoratives for her wound and her general condition. She gave instructions to search for Acerronia's will and seal up her goods; no pretense was needed here.

7. Nero was waiting impatiently for news that the deed was done. Instead, he was told that she had escaped, with only a slight wound, but after undergoing dangers such that she knew very well who was responsible for them. He was beside himself with terror, and kept calling out, "She will soon be here! She'll come for vengeance! What if she arms the slaves, or rouses the soldiers? She may bring in the Senate and people, and blame me for the shipwreck, her wounds, and her friends' murder! How can I save myself? Can Burrus and Seneca suggest anything?" They were awakened and sent for: whether they had been in the plot earlier is uncertain. There was a long silence. Neither wished to try to dissuade him, and be rejected; or they may indeed have felt that matters had gone so far that Nero would be murdered if Agrippina were not forestalled. At last Seneca summoned up his courage to the extent of looking at Burrus and asking whether a soldier might not be ordered to carry out the murder. The answer was that the Guards were devoted to the whole imperial family, and to the memory of Germanicus; on no account would they do violence to one of his descendants. Let Anicetus, said Burrus, fulfill his engagements. As for Anicetus, he made no delay in asking to be put in charge of the crime. When Nero heard him, he exclaimed that this day had given him an Empire—and that the giver of this splendid gift was a freedman! "Go at once," he ordered. "Take with you men who know how to obey instructions!" Meanwhile Agrippina's messenger Agerinus had arrived. Nero at once set the scene for an accusation, throwing a sword at the man's feet as he was delivering his message and ordering him to be arrested, as if caught red-handed. Now Nero could say

that his mother had plotted the Emperor's murder and, when the plot had failed, had herself committed suicide.

8. By now everyone knew of Agrippina's perilous experience, which was, however, believed to be an accident. As soon as they heard the news, they rushed to the shore, some climbing on the breakwaters, others getting into skiffs. Some even waded out to sea, so far as they were able, stretching out their hands. The whole shore reechoed with shouts and prayers, the noise of many inquiries, and the ignorant answers. A great crowd assembled, carrying lights. When it became known that she was safe, they made ready to celebrate; but the appearance of a menacing column of armed men dispersed them. Anicetus surrounded the villa, broke down the doors, arrested any servant who crossed his path, and forced his way to the door of her bedroom. A few servants were still on guard; the rest had been frightened away by the invasion. The room was dimly lit; a single maid was in attendance. Agrippina became more and more alarmed: no one had come from her son, not even Agerinus; if things were going well, everything would be very different: now the silence followed by a sudden uproar could only be taken for the worst. Her maid slipped away. "You are leaving me, too?" she called; and, turning, she saw behind her Anicetus, and with him a captain of a trireme, Herculeius, and the centurion of marines, Obaritus. "If you have come to pay me a visit," she exclaimed, "you can say that I am better: but if you are planning a crime, I don't believe my son has a part in it—he never gave orders for his mother's murder!" The murderers closed around her bed. The first blow was struck by the captain, who hit her on the head with a club. As the centurion drew his sword for the death blow she thrust out her stomach and cried, "Strike my womb!";[5] then she died of many wounds.

9. This much is generally agreed. Some assert, others deny, that Nero inspected his mother's corpse and praised her figure. She was cremated that very night, with minimum rites, and on a couch taken from a dining room. So long as Nero lived, her grave was not covered with a mound, nor enclosed in a stone tomb. Later, her household staff saw to it that she had a modest tomb; it stood by the road to Misenum, where Julius Caesar's villa looks out over the bay. At the cremation, one of her freedmen, called Mnester, committed suicide; he may have loved his mistress, or he may have feared his own murder. So Agrippina met the death she had expected, undaunted, for so many years. When she had asked the astrologers to cast Nero's horoscope, they had told her that he would be Emperor, but would

kill his mother. "Let him kill me, so long as he reigns!" was her reply.

10. As for Nero, it was only when the crime was done that he realized its full horror. The rest of that night he spent in a state of fear and paralysis. Sometimes he would start to his feet; beside himself with terror, he waited for the dawn of what he thought would be his last day. At Burrus' suggestion, centurions and tribunes of the Guard came to flatter him, clasping his hand, congratulating him on having escaped the unforeseen dangers of his mother's evil deed. This was the first thing that caused him to hope. Then his friends crowded to the temples; the hint was taken by the towns of Campania, which demonstrated their joy by offering sacrifices and sending deputations. Nero's hypocrisy took the opposite line. He simulated sorrow, as though upset at his own escape, and grieving for his mother's death. But the face of nature is not so easily changed as the face of man: here before his gaze was the grim spectacle of that sea and shore, now reechoing (as some thought) with trumpet blasts from the high hills, and with keenings from his mother's grave. So Nero left for Neapolis. To the Senate a dispatch was sent, to the effect that the freedman Agerinus, a confidential agent of Agrippina's, had been caught with a sword in his hand, and that Agrippina had committed suicide, conscious of her guilt in having planned the murder.

11. To this were added charges dredged up from the distant past. Agrippina had wanted to share the imperial power; she had intended the Guard to take the oath of loyalty to herself —a woman!—and had expected that the Senate and people would undergo the same humiliation. When this had been denied her, she conceived a hatred for the army, the Senate, and the people. She had opposed donations to soldiers and gratuities to the people, and had contrived the ruin of eminent men. It had been all Nero could do to stop her from entering the Senate House, from giving answers to foreign embassies. There followed indirect attacks on the reign of Claudius, whose scandals were ascribed to Agrippina. Her death was a piece of public good fortune, as was shown by the shipwreck. But the vainest fool could hardly regard that as accidental; nor suppose that a single shipwrecked woman could dispatch an assassin through the imperial guards and fleet. It was therefore no longer Nero—whose monstrous cruelty towered above reproach—but rather Seneca who took the blame, since he had composed the dispatch which was a confession of guilt.

12. There followed a remarkable competition for favor among the eminent. Thanksgivings were voted at every shrine —the feast of Minerva (when the plot had been discovered)

was to be commemorated by annual games, a golden statue of Minerva was set up in the Senate House, next to the statue of the Emperor: Agrippina's birthday became a black day in the calendar. Thrasea Paetus, who used to pass over earlier flatteries with silence or a curt word of assent, now walked out of the Senate House. This endangered his own life, but did nothing to advance the cause of public freedom.

There were numerous prodigies, all quite purposeless. A woman gave birth to a snake: another was struck by lightning in her husband's embrace: the sun was eclipsed: every one of the fourteen districts of Rome was struck by lightning. These were not, in any sense, the work of divine providence; there were still many years ahead for Nero's reign and Nero's crimes. Still, to aggravate dislike for his mother, and to show his own clemency now that she was gone, he summoned back two noble ladies, Junia and Calpurnia, and restored to their estates two ex-praetors, Valerius Capito and Licinius Gabolus, all of whom she had exiled. He even gave permission for the ashes of Lollia Paulina to be brought home, and for a tomb to be erected. An amnesty was granted to Iturius and Calvisius, whom he had banished himself. Silana had already died, after having returned to Tarentum from her distant exile when Agrippina, whose enmity had caused her downfall, became less vindictive—or less influential.

13. Even so, Nero lingered on in Campania. How he should enter Rome, what kind of reception the Senate would give him, how he stood with the people—all these questions gave him cause for alarm. Meanwhile, all men of evil purpose—and no palace ever grew a more fertile crop of them—urged on Nero that Agrippina's very name was loathed, and that he had gained in popular favor by her death. Let him enter the city boldly, and see how he was beloved. They asked to be allowed to precede him, and found an even greater show of enthusiasm than they had promised. The tribes went to meet him, the Senate was in formal dress, wives and children were suitably disposed, according to sex and age. Along his route there rose tiers of seats as though for a triumph. An arrogant Emperor, triumphant over the slavery of Rome, Nero went to the Capitol and discharged his vows. Then he gave full rein to every form of wickedness, which some lingering respect for his mother had perhaps delayed, though it could not halt.

14. Nero had long desired to compete in chariot races; equally degrading was his ambition to sing to the lyre, as a professional.[6] He was fond of recalling that chariot racing had been the sport of kings and of generals in the good old days; it had won the praise of poets, and formed a part of the worship

of the gods. Apollo was, after all, the god of singing: statues of that powerful and prescient divinity, dressed as a lyre player, were to be found in Greek cities, and also in Roman temples. To stop him was out of the question, but Seneca and Burrus hoped to forestall both vices by conceding one of them. So an enclosure was built in the Vatican valley for him to practice chariot racing.[7] At first this took place in private, but before long there was an open invitation to the people of Rome. They praised Nero to the skies, having all a crowd's passion for pleasure, and delight if the Emperor should share it. But the scandal and publicity did not damp Nero's ardor; they merely provoked it further. With the idea that there would be less disgrace if more were corrupted, the descendants of noble families who had fallen on hard times were bribed to appear on the stage. They are dead, and I shall not name them; I think their ancestors deserve that much consideration.[8] For blame attaches also to the man who paid them to offend, rather than not to do so. Some Roman knights, too, were induced to offer their services in the arena by means of what might be called huge gifts, were it not that a certain imperative attaches to the gifts of the man who can command.

15. As yet, however, Nero was unready to debase himself by appearing in the public theater. Instead, the Festival of Youth was founded and attracted many volunteers. Nobility, age, and office alike failed to deter men from the practice of the Greek or Latin actor's art, not stopping short of effeminate performances. Noble ladies took indecent parts. In the groves where Augustus had built the Naval Lake, houses of assignation and taverns were constructed, and every inducement to debauchery displayed for sale. Largesses were granted which the virtuous spent under compulsion, the licentious for vanity. Immorality and degradation flourished; even though morals had long been debased, this filthy scum fostered debauchery as never before. Even in a moral society, public decency is hard to uphold; here, in this competition of vice, no room was left for modesty or chastity or any scrap of moral feeling. Finally, the Emperor himself made his debut; there was much scrupulous tuning of the lyre, and rehearsing of preliminary notes. The audience was swollen by a troop of soldiers, complete with the officers. Burrus grieved—and applauded. Then was first enrolled the company of Roman knights known as Augustiani—powerful young men, endowed with impudence by nature or ambition. They kept the applause going day and night and bestowed on Nero's beauty of person and voice epithets reserved for the gods. They won respect and honor as though they had performed some deed of real merit.

16. The display of the Emperor's talents was not confined to the stage. He affected a taste for poetry, and issued invitations to dinner to men with a talent for versifying who had not yet made their mark. They would sit on over dinner, stringing together verses they had brought with them or produced extempore, or amplifying the Emperor's compositions—such as they were. Nero's poems bear witness to this method of writing; they lack vigor and feeling, and are in a medley of styles. After dinner, he would devote some time to professors of philosophy. Amusement was to be had from their quarrelsome assertions of flatly opposed arguments, and there was no lack of men ready to contribute sour remarks and gloomy expressions[9] for the entertainment of the court.

OTHER EVENTS OF THE YEAR

17. At this time, a bloody contest broke out between the citizens of the colonies of Nuceria and Pompeii. It arose from a trifling cause at a gladiatorial show given by one Livineius Regulus, whose expulsion from the Senate I have already mentioned. With the license usual in these country towns, they passed from the exchange of insults to the throwing of stones, and finally to the sword. The people of Pompeii were the more numerous, since the show was in their amphitheater. Many wounded Nucerians were brought to Rome as evidence, and very many had to mourn the loss of parents or children. The Emperor referred the matter to the Senate, and they, in turn, to the consuls. When it came back to the Senate, the people of Pompeii were prohibited from such assemblies for a period of ten years, and the illegal guilds which had grown up among them were dissolved. Licinius and others who had fostered the disorder were sent into exile.

18. Pedius Blaesus was expelled from the Senate, having been charged by the people of Cyrene of robbing the temple of Aesculapius, and of having used bribery and favoritism in the conduct of the levy for the army. The same people of Cyrene prosecuted Acilius Strabo. He had been sent with a praetor's powers by Claudius to inquire into the problem of the royal estates of King Ptolemy Apion,[10] which had been left to the Roman people together with the whole kingdom. These had been invaded by neighboring landowners, who now cited their long-standing usurpation as fair title to possession. When Acilius pronounced against them, he became exceedingly unpopular; the Senate decided that it did not know what instructions had

been given by Claudius, and referred the matter to Nero. Nero upheld the decision of Acilius, but, to help Roman allies, wrote to legalize their title to the lands on which they had squatted.

19. Two notable deaths followed these events—those of Domitius Afer and Marcus Servilius. Both were famous orators, both won high office. Domitius had been an advocate; Servilius, after many years at the bar, won fame as a Roman historian. A man of refined tastes, this set him above his rival, whose talents were no less brilliant.

60 A.D. Consuls, The Emperor Nero (for the fourth time) and Cornelius Cossus

20. A five-yearly stage festival was instituted at Rome, on the Greek model. As is usual with innovations, it had a mixed reception. Some recalled the earlier criticism of Pompey when he built a permanent theater.[11] (Previously, performances had been given with improvised seating and on a temporary stage; or, to go back further still, the audience had had to stand, for fear that if they were allowed to sit down, they might waste days together in idleness.) They thought it best to preserve the old-fashioned custom for theatrical displays under the patronage of the praetors, which did not oblige any Roman citizen to compete. They argued that traditional morals, already in decay, had been wholly corrupted by this imported luxury. Everything debased and tending to corruption was now to be seen in Rome, the youth demoralized by foreign influences into a pack of athletes, shirkers, and homosexuals! It was all the fault of the Emperor and the Senate: not only had they granted a license to vice, but they were taking active measures to force the Roman upper classes to degrade themselves by declaiming or singing on the stage. The end could only be that they would strip themselves for fist-fighting, and regard pugilism as a substitute for service in the army. Would public justice be better served, would the panels of Roman knights give sounder verdicts, if they had an expert ear for effeminate music and sweet voices? The nights were now given over to lust, and no place

was left for virtue. Every debauchee, in these promiscuous crowds, could practice by night the lusts he had conceived in fantasy by day.

21. The majority found this license to their taste, though they disguised it under honorable names, declaring that our ancestors had not shrunk from the pleasures of public spectacles, so far as the resources of the times had allowed. Actors had been imported from the Etruscans, horse races from Thurii; dominion over Greece and Asia had led to ever more elaborate standards of display. Yet in the two hundred years since Lucius Mummius at his triumph had first exhibited these performances in Rome, no single Roman of good birth had ever degraded himself by professional acting. A permanent stage building was an actual economy, since it would save the large expense of construction and demolition every year. Nor would the magistrates have to be so lavish with their private funds as formerly, and the people would not be so prone to demand Greek spectacles if the cost of the shows were met from public funds. The proposed prizes for poetry and rhetoric would encourage talent; as for the judges, it would in no way degrade them to lend their ears to honorable pursuits and pleasures. Gaiety, not lust, was the object to which these nights were devoted—a few out of a span of five years—and in the blaze of light nothing forbidden could be concealed. At all events, the spectacle passed off without open scandal: there were no instances of public disorder, even on a small scale, for although the ballet dancers were allowed to return to the stage, they were debarred from the sacred performances. The prize for eloquence was not awarded, but the Emperor was proclaimed the winner. Greek costume, which many had worn throughout the festival, suddenly fell out of favor.

RUBELLIUS PLAUTUS

22. At this time a comet blazed in the heavens, which popular opinion regards as betokening a change of kings. There was speculation as to who would succeed Nero, as if he were actually dethroned. Rubellius Plautus was the name on everyone's lips: his nobility lay in his mother's connection with the Julian house. He followed the principles of his ancestors and was a man of serious bearing, impeccable morals, and retired life. This retirement, due to fear, only added to his fame. The rumors set on foot by the comet were further inflamed by an equally idle interpretation of a flash of lightning. For when

Nero was dining in his villa, known as Sublaqueum, by the Simbruine lakes, lightning struck the banquet and shattered the very table. Since this happened in the territory of Tivoli, the ancestral home of Plautus' father's family, it was taken to mean that he had been singled out by the will of heaven. He was much courted by those whom a greedy and misguided ambition drove on to a premature display of partisan zeal. Nero, alarmed by this, wrote privately to Plautus, asking him, in the interests of public order, to withdraw himself from the company of those who were spreading malicious gossip: he had ancestral estates in Asia ideally suited to the safe passing of his youthful years. Thither Plautus withdrew, with his wife Antistia and a few friends.

This was a time when excessive indulgence of his whims brought scandal and even danger upon Nero. He ventured to swim in the waters of the Aqua Marcia (which supplies the city); the immersion of his body in the sacred waters was regarded as a defilement of the sanctity of the place. A serious illness confirmed the anger of the gods.

EVENTS IN THE EAST

23. After the destruction of Artaxata,[12] Corbulo thought that the fear thus engendered should be used to secure the occupation of Tigranocerta. Its destruction would cause the enemy to panic: equally, by sparing it, he could win a reputation for clemency. To that city, then, he proceeded. The army took no hostile action, so as not to deprive the Armenians of hope of pardon; but there was no relaxation of watchfulness, for he knew how fickle that people could be, sluggish in the face of danger, but very quick to seize an opportunity for treachery. As each was prompted by his nature, the natives gave themselves up, or else left their villages and took refuge in the wilderness. Some hid themselves and their families in caves. The Roman general followed a flexible policy: merciful to the surrendered, he was swift in the pursuit of fugitives. Merciless to those in hiding, he burned them out by blocking the entrances of their caves with brushwood and fagots. As he traversed their territory, he was attacked by the Mardi, old hands at brigandage, who relied on the protection of their mountains. But Corbulo launched the Iberi against them, thus securing the ravaging of their territory and the repulse of their attack without the loss of Roman blood.

24. General and army were becoming worn out with fa-

tigue, though they had had no losses in battle. Meat was all
they had to hold starvation at bay;[13] water was scarce, the summer blazing hot. On the long marches their general's stamina
was their only asset; he endured all the exertions of the common soldier, and more. At last they reached cultivation, and
were able to harvest the crops. The Armenians had taken refuge
in two forts, one of which was taken by storm. The other withstood the first assault, to be captured by siege. Next he passed
into the district of Tauraunitis, where he escaped an unexpected
danger: a barbarian of high rank was arrested with a weapon
close to Corbulo's tent; under torture, he revealed a plot of
assassination, and gave the names of his associates. Those who
plotted the murder under the guise of friendship were brought
to trial and punished. Soon afterward a deputation from Tigranocerta announced that the city gates were open, and the
people waiting to receive his orders. They offered him a gold
crown as a welcome. This he accepted politely, and refrained
from making any demands on the city so as to win their loyalty
unimpaired.

25. A brave band of warriors had manned the fortress of
Legerda, which did not surrender without a struggle. They were
confident enough to engage in a battle in the open, then, driven
within the walls, it was only after a siege-mound had been built
and an entrance forced that they finally surrendered. Our successes came more easily because the Parthians were hampered
by a war against the Hyrcani. These people sent to the Emperor to treat for an alliance, citing as a guarantee of their
friendship that they were tying down Vologeses. As the embassy was on its way back, in order to prevent them from
being trapped by the Parthians at the crossing of the Euphrates,
Corbulo gave them an escort as far as the shore of the Caspian
Sea. Thus they were able to reach their own country without
entering Parthian territory.

26. Finally, however, Tiridates entered Armenia on the east
from Media. Corbulo sent auxiliaries ahead under the command of Verulanus, then made a rapid advance at the head of
the legions, so forcing him to retire and abandon any hope of
fighting. Districts known to be unfriendly to us were burned
and laid waste, and Corbulo held on to Armenia until the arrival of Tigranes, grandson of Archelaus, king of Cappadocia
and Nero's candidate for the throne. His long period as a hostage in Rome had left him with a slave's docility. This, and the
fact that the Arsacid pretender still had supporters, meant that
his reception was anything but unanimous. But most Armenians
detested Parthian arrogance, and preferred a king supplied by
Rome. A garrison was supplied of one thousand legionaries,

three allied infantry battalions, and two of cavalry. For the better protection of the new reign, the frontiers of Armenia were assigned to neighboring friendly rulers, Pharasmenes, Polemo, Aristobulus, and Antiochus.* Corbulo now withdrew to Syria, a province which the death of its governor Ummidius had left to its own devices.

OTHER EVENTS OF THE YEAR

27. This same year Laodicea, one of the famous cities of Asia, was destroyed by an earthquake. It was rebuilt from its own resources, without any subsidy from us. In Italy, the ancient town of Puteoli was given the status of a colony and acquired a title from Nero. Veterans were assigned to the towns of Tarentum and Antium; but this did nothing to remedy the depopulation of these districts, for they soon slipped away to the provinces in which they had done their military service: unaccustomed to taking wives and bringing up families, they left their old homes without a younger generation. In former times, these colonies had been drawn from entire legions, complete with centurions, tribunes, and soldiers of every rank; they had formed a community based on affection and mutual ties. But now, strangers to each other, drawn from different units, with no acknowledged leader, without common loyalties, they were an aggregate of human beings rather than a Roman colony.[14]

28. At the election of praetors, normally conducted by the Senate, the intervention of the Emperor was necessary. Feeling ran high, but the three candidates in excess of vacancies were provided with the command of a legion. The Emperor also increased the standing of the Senate by requiring that appeals from civil tribunals to the Senate should put up the same deposit as those to the Emperor; such appeals had previously been free and not subject to penalty. At the end of the year Vibius Secundus, a Roman knight, was convicted of extortion on the prosecution of Mauretania. He was expelled from Italy, and only the influence of his brother, Vibius Crispus, saved him from a severer sentence.

* Of Iberia, Pontus, Lesser Armenia, and Commagene, respectively.

61 A.D. Consuls Caesennius Paetus and Petronius Turpilianus

DISASTER IN BRITAIN

29. In the consulship of Caesennius Paetus and Petronius Turpilianus a terrible disaster was suffered in Britain.[15] I have already narrated how, in that province, the governor Aulus Didius had done no more than maintain the *status quo:* his successor Veranius made a number of raids against the Silures, but died before he could extend the war further. In his life his reputation was one of self-restraint, but the last words of his will convicted him of vanity, for after gross flattery of Nero he added that he would have presented him with the whole province, subjugated, had he lived two years longer. But by now Suetonius Paulinus[16] was in charge of Britain. He was Corbulo's rival in military skill, as in popular gossip, which leaves no one without a rival, and he was eager to achieve military victories to match the glory of the reconquest of Armenia. He therefore planned an expedition against the island of Mona, which was itself thickly populated and had offered sanctuary to many who fled from Roman power. Flat-bottomed boats, built to cope with the shifting shallows, transported the infantry; the cavalry got across by finding the fords, or, in deeper waters, swimming beside their horses.

30. The shore was lined with the enemy in battle array, a dense mass of armed warriors, with women rushing to and fro among their ranks, dressed in black like furies, their hair disheveled, brandishing torches; and all around were Druids with their arms raised to heaven and calling down terrible curses.[17] The soldiers, paralyzed by this strange spectacle, stood still and offered themselves as a target for wounds. But at last the promptings of the general, and their own rallying of each other, urged them not to be frightened of a mob of women and fanatics. They advanced the standards, cut down all who met them, and swallowed them up in their own fires. After this, a garrison was placed over the conquered islanders, and the groves sacred to savage rites were cut down; for their religion

315

enjoined them to drench their altars with the blood of prisoners, and find out the will of the gods by consulting the entrails of human beings. While Suetonius was thus engaged, he was informed of a sudden rising in the province.

31. Prasutagus, king of the Iceni, distinguished by the prosperity he had long enjoyed, had died, and left the Emperor as heir, together with his two daughters. His hope had been that with such subservience the kingdom and his own property would remain inviolate, but it fell out far otherwise. Both were plundered as though they were the spoils of war, the kingdom by centurions, the royal household by the procurator's slaves. The first outrage was the flogging of his wife Boudicca and the rape of his daughters: then the Icenian nobles were deprived of their ancestral estates as though the Romans had been presented with the whole country, and the king's relatives were treated as though they were household slaves. These outrages and the fear of worse now that they had been reduced to the status of a province, moved the Iceni to arms. They were joined by the Trinobantes and other tribes who were unsubdued by slavery, and who had secretly conspired together to regain their freedom. The veterans were the special object of their hatred. These men, recently settled at Camulodunum, had been turning them out of their homes, taking away their lands, and calling them captives and slaves. The soldiers did nothing to check the insolence of the veterans, for they were men of the same stamp and hoped for similar license when their own time came. To add to this, the temple of Claudius[18] seemed to have been established as the very citadel of enduring slavery, and its chosen priests, under the guise of a religious cult, were squandering the wealth of the whole country. To attack a position undefended by fortifications seemed no arduous undertaking; indeed, the Roman governors had scandalously neglected to take precautions, putting amenities before the needs of defense.

32. At this point, and for no apparent cause, the statue of Victory at Camulodunum fell down, its back turned as though yielding to an enemy. Frenzied women prophesied destruction, saying that barbarian yells had been heard in the Senate House, the theater had echoed with shrieks, and a vision of the colony had been seen in the Thames estuary, sacked and destroyed: the very ocean was blood-red, and the ebbing tide had left on the shore what appeared to be human corpses. All this induced hope in the Britons and fear in the veterans. But the governor was away, and they sent for help to the procurator, Catus Decianus. He sent them hardly two hundred men, without proper equipment; there was a small garrison on the spot: and they relied on the temple as a strong point. Hampered by undercover

adherents of the rebellion, who threw their plans into confusion, they took no steps to construct a rampart or ditch, nor to evacuate women and old people and defend the place with men of military age. Devoid of precautions as though in time of peace, they let themselves be surrounded by huge numbers of barbarians. Everything else was overrun in the attack, or went up in flames, but the soldiers concentrated in the temple and held out for two days. Then it was overwhelmed. The victorious Britons routed Petilius Cerialis, the commander of the Ninth Legion, as he was marching to the rescue.[19] His infantry was cut to pieces: he himself escaped to the legionary camp with his cavalry and took shelter behind its walls. The procurator Catus Decianus, whose greed had driven the province into war, was so horrified by this disaster and by the hatred against him that he fled to Gaul.

33. But Suetonius, with remarkable steadfastness, pressed on through the midst of the enemy to Londinium,[20] a place not dignified by the name of a colony, but crowded with merchants and provisions. He was uncertain whether to make it a military center, but after discovering its lack of troops, and well aware of the price paid by Cerialis for his rashness, he decided to save the whole situation by the sacrifice of this single town. No tears, no laments for those who begged his help could prevent him from giving the signal for departure. Those who could keep up with him were given a place in the column: but all who, because of their sex or age, or love for the place, chose to stay, were butchered by the enemy. The same fate overtook the *municipium* of Verulamium.[21] For the barbarians paid no attention to forts or garrisons, but made for the richest booty under the feeblest protection, for they loved plunder and shrank from toils. It has been established that some seventy thousand persons, Roman citizens and allies, were massacred in the three places I have mentioned. The Britons had no thought of taking prisoners or selling them as slaves, nor of any of the usual commerce of war, but only of slaughter, the gibbet, fire, and the cross. They knew they would have to pay the penalty, and meanwhile they hurried on to avenge their wrongs while they could.

34. By now Suetonius had with him the Fourteenth Legion, and a detachment of the Twentieth, together with auxiliary troops from the nearest fort, a total of some ten thousand men, and he decided to make an end of delay and to seek engagement in battle. He chose a position in a narrow defile, protected from behind by a forest.[22] Here he could be sure that there would be no enemy except in front, where an open plain gave no cover for ambushes. He therefore drew up the legionaries

in close order, with the light-armed auxiliaries on either flank, and massed the cavalry on the wings. The British forces, on the other hand, ranged over a wide area in bands of infantry and cavalry. Never had they massed in such great numbers, and they were so confident of victory that they had brought their wives and children with them to witness it, and placed them in wagons at the edge of the battlefield.

35. Boudicca drove around in a chariot, her daughters with her. As they reached each tribal contingent, she proclaimed that the Britons were well used to the leadership of women in battle. But she did not come among them now as a descendant of mighty ancestors, eager to avenge her lost wealth and kingdom. Rather was she an ordinary woman, fighting for her lost freedom, her bruised body, and the outraged virginity of her daughters. Roman greed no longer spared their bodies; old people were killed, virgins raped. But the gods would grant a just vengeance: the legion which had dared to fight had perished: the others were skulking in their camps and looking for means of escape. They would never face the roar and din of the British thousands, much less their charges and their hand-to-hand fighting. Let them consider how many they had under arms, and why! Then they would know that on that day it was victory or death. That was her resolve, as a woman; the men could live, if they liked, and be slaves.

36. Suetonius, too, did not keep silent at this moment of crisis. Confident as he was of his men's courage, he thought it best to add encouragement and appeals: "Don't pay attention to the noises of these savages," he said, "nor to their empty threats: there are more women than soldiers in their ranks. They are unwarlike and ill-armed; when they see the weapons and valor of troops who have beaten them so often, they're going to crack. Even in a force with many legions, it is only a few who give the decisive impulse to a battle: what glory awaits you, a small band that is going to win the renown of a whole army! Keep together: throw your javelins: then continue the slaughter with your swords and the points of your shields. Don't give a thought to booty: once you've won the victory, it will all be yours." His words were received with enthusiasm; the battle-hardened soldiers were itching to throw their javelins. Suetonius knew he could count on victory, and gave the signal for battle.

37. At first the legion stood motionless, using the defile for protection. When the enemy approached more closely up the slope, they discharged their javelins with unerring aim. Then they burst forward in wedge formation, as did the auxiliary forces, and the cavalry, lances at the ready, broke down all serious resistance. The rest of the Britons turned to flight, but

this was made difficult by the ring of wagons. The Romans did not spare the women, and the bodies of pack animals, pierced with spears, were added to the piles of corpses. It was a glorious victory, equal to those of the good old days: some estimate as many as eighty thousand British dead: there were only four hundred Romans killed, and scarcely more wounded. Boudicca ended her life with poison. As for Poenius Postumus, camp commandant of the Second Legion,[23] he fell on his sword when he heard of the honors won by the Fourteenth and the Twentieth—for he had cheated his own men of a like distinction and disobeyed his commander's orders, in defiance of army regulations.

38. Then the whole army was concentrated and kept under canvas to finish the war. The Emperor increased their strength by sending as reinforcements from Germany two thousand legionary soldiers, eight auxiliary infantry battalions, and a thousand cavalry. These were enough to bring the Ninth Legion up to strength: the infantry and cavalry were stationed in new winter quarters: the territory of all tribes that had been hostile or neutral was laid waste with fire and sword. But famine was the worst of their hardships: they had omitted to sow the crops and brought every man into the army, regardless of age, expecting that they could secure our supplies for themselves. But the British tribes were obstinate and little inclined for peace— especially as the procurator, Julius Classicianus,[24] who had replaced Catus and did not get on with Suetonius, allowed his private dislikes to interfere with the public interest. Indeed, he kept urging them to wait for a new governor who would be lenient to the conquered, without the bitterness of an enemy and the arrogance of the victor. He reported to Rome that there would be no end to campaigning unless Suetonius was superseded; and he attributed his failures to his base qualities, his victories to luck.

39. So Polyclitus, one of the imperial freedmen, was sent out to investigate affairs in Britain. It was Nero's hope that his authority would be sufficient to reconcile the governor and the procurator, and to pacify the warlike and rebellious Britons. Polyclitus played his part, burdened Italy and Gaul with a huge retinue, and after crossing the ocean, struck terror even into a Roman army. The barbarians only thought him ridiculous: liberty still prevailed with them, and they had as yet no acquaintance with the power of a freedman. They could not understand how an army and general who could complete so great a war should obey the commands of slaves. However, everything was toned down in the report to the Emperor. Suetonius' term of office was prolonged, but when, shortly afterward, he

lost a few ships and their crews on the shore, he was superseded, as though protracting the war, by Petronius Turpilianus,[25] who had just laid down his consulship. The latter
neither provoked the enemy nor suffered loss at their hands,
conferring the honorable name of peace on what was really
sluggish inaction.

EVENTS IN ROME

40. The same year witnessed two noteworthy crimes in
Rome, one the work of a senator, the other of a presumptuous
slave. Domitius Balbus was an ex-praetor, but extreme old age,
childlessness, and great wealth made him vulnerable to trickery.
His relative Valerius Fabianus—a man destined for a public
career—forged a will in his name, with the assistance of two
Roman knights, Vinicius Rufinus and Terentius Lentinus, who
in their turn brought in Antonius Primus and Asinius Marcellus. Of these two, Antonius Primus was the more daring;
Marcellus was distinguished by the fact that he was a great-
grandson of Asinius Pollio, and his own character was respectable—save for the fact that he regarded poverty as the worst of
evils. With these accomplices, and others of less note, Fabianus
sealed the will. All were convicted in the Senate, and Fabianus
and Antonius, together with Rufinus and Terentius, were condemned under the Lex Cornelia.* Marcellus, by the memory of
his ancestors and the prayers of the Emperor, escaped punishment—but not infamy.

41. The same day's work involved Pompeius Aelianus, a
young ex-quaestor, as being privy to the crimes of Fabianus.
He was banned from Italy and from Spain (the country of his
birth). Valerius Ponticus was similarly disgraced for having
brought the case before the praetor, to prevent it going to the
city prefect. There was a show of legality in this, though its
real objective was to avoid sentence by collusion. The senatorial decree therefore contained a clause to the effect that
anyone who bought or sold means of collusion in such a case
should be liable to the same penalties as if convicted of false
accusation in a criminal suit.

42. Shortly afterward, the city prefect, Pedanius Secundus,
was murdered by one of his own slaves. The cause may have
been that he had been refused his freedom, after a price had
been agreed upon, or that the slave could not tolerate his
master's rivalry in a homosexual love affair. At any rate, when

---

* A law of Lulla against falsification of wills, enacted in 81 B.C.

the ancient custom of condemning to death the entire slave household lodged under that roof was brought forward, there was a great gathering of the people anxious to protect the numerous innocent victims. It came very close to a riot, and the Senate House was besieged. Even there, some opinions were opposed to undue severity, though the majority opposed any change. Gaius Cassius, who belonged to the latter group, spoke as follows[26] when his turn came:

43. "Gentlemen, I have often been present in this House when proposals have been brought forward for departure from the laws and customs of our ancestors. I have not opposed them, although I am fully convinced that for every purpose the existing provisions are better and wiser, and that every change could only be for the worse. However, I did not wish by too great zeal to seem to be exalting my own profession, the law; nor did I wish to destroy any authority I might have with you through being perpetually in opposition. Better, I thought, to preserve it unimpaired for a time when the state should really need it. That occasion has come today. A former consul has been murdered, by his own slave and in his own household. Nobody stopped him, nobody denounced him; though we have not yet repealed the decree that threatened the entire household in such a case! Exempt them from punishment, and who will be protected by his rank, if the city prefect was not protected? Who will be protected by the number of his slaves, when the four hundred of Pedanius Secundus availed him nothing? Who can rely on his household for help, if even their own danger does not alert them to our perils? Some are so unprincipled as to suggest that the slave was avenging his own wrongs. We shall be told next that he had been arranging his family fortunes, or had lost his ancestral estates! Why not bring in a verdict of justifiable homicide on the person of the master!

44. "Would you wish to question the grounds of a decision already reached by those who are wiser than we? But even supposing we were making the decision for the first time, can you really believe that a slave could conceive a plan for killing his master, and not breathe a word of it nor utter some threat? Assuming that he kept his design hidden, that no one knew he had prepared a weapon, how could he possibly pass through the guards, open the doors of the bedroom, bring in a light, and commit the murder—all without a single witness? There are many advance warnings of a crime. If slaves will betray them, we can live in safety, though one among many, because they fear for themselves: or, if we are to die, we shall not do so unavenged. Our ancestors had a distrust of the characters of slaves, though in those days they were born in the same estates

or houses, and knew their master's affection from birth. But now we have aliens in our households; they have foreign rites and beliefs—or none at all. Fear is the only thing to check this rabble. We are told that some innocent people will die. Well, if any army is beaten and decimation is applied, the good soldiers have to draw lots just like the rest. Every large-scale case of exemplary punishment involves some injustice; but the wrong to the individual is offset by the advantage of the community."

45. No single person ventured to oppose Cassius, but voices of protest were raised against the idea of involving so many people, of all ages and both sexes, and most of them undoubtedly innocent. But the party in favor of the full rigor of the law prevailed. However, a crowd gathered, armed with stones and torches, and the sentence could not be carried out. Then Nero published a dispatch censuring the people, and lined the whole route along which the prisoners had to pass to execution with a military guard. Cingonius Varro proposed that the freedmen from this household should be deported from Italy. This proposal was vetoed by Nero, lest an ancient custom which had not been tempered by mercy should be aggravated by brutality.

46. The same year saw the condemnation of Tarquitius Priscus on a charge of extortion, at the instance of the Bithynians. The Senate found this highly gratifying, remembering how he had once prosecuted his own governor, Statilius Taurus. In the Gallic provinces a census was conducted by Quintus Volusius, Sextius Africanus, and Trebellius Maximus. Volusius and Africanus were rivals in nobility, and both despised Trebellius; as a result, he rose above both.

47. In this year died Memmius Regulus. He had won to fame—so far as anyone could under the towering preeminence of the Emperor—by influence, determination, and good name. Once when Nero was gravely ill, and the flatterers around him were saying that it would be the end of the Empire if anything were to happen to him, he replied that the state yet had support in reserve. When they asked whom he meant by this, he replied, "Memmius Regulus." Yet Memmius lived on, even after this: his quiet life, recent elevation in rank, and moderate fortune were his safeguards.

This year Nero dedicated a gymnasium and, with Greek lavishness, furnished free oil even to senators and knights.

62 A.D. Consuls Publius Marius and Lucius Afinius

48. In this year the praetor Antistius, whose highhanded conduct as a tribune has already been mentioned, composed libelous poems against Nero, and recited them at a well-attended dinner party in the house of Ostorius Scapula. He was at once charged with treason by Cossutianus Capito, recently restored to senatorial rank at the entreaty of Gaius Tigellinus, his father-in-law. This was the first occasion on which the law of treason was revived. The object was generally thought to be, not so much to encompass the death of Antistius, as to glorify the Emperor, who could use his tribunicial power to nullify a death sentence passed by the Senate. The host, Ostorius Scapula, testified that he had heard nothing, but the hostile witnesses were believed. The consul-designate, Junius Marullus, proposed that Antistius should be deprived of his praetorship and put to death in the ancient manner. The rest of the Senate were for accepting the proposal. But Thrasea Paetus, after complimenting the Emperor in warm terms, and rebuking Antistius, took the line that the condemned man need not suffer the extreme penalty, since under so excellent an Emperor the Senate was under no compulsion. The executioner and the rope were by now obsolete: penalties had now been established by law which absolved the judges from harshness and the times from infamy. Antistius should have his property confiscated and be banished to an island: the longer he lived the more miserable he would be, but he would be a shining example of official mercy.

49. Thrasea's boldness caused the others to shed their servility. When the consul put the matter to the vote his proposal was carried, with only a few to oppose it. Aulus Vitellius was one of the grossest sycophants; like all cowards, he was very ready to insult any decent person, but collapsed when they hit back. The consuls did not dare to carry out the Senate's decree, but wrote to the Emperor to inform him of the feeling

323

of the Senate. Anger and conscience caused him to hesitate: finally he wrote back to remind the Senate that Antistius, quite unprovoked, had grossly insulted the Emperor. The Senate had been asked to punish him, and should have imposed a penalty in keeping with the enormity of the crime. But he would have opposed undue severity, and he would not forbid their leniency. They could decide as they chose: they were quite free to acquit him, if they so wished. This and similar comments were read aloud, and it was obvious that Nero was much annoyed. But the consuls adhered to the motion, Thrasea did not withdraw his proposal, and the others stuck to their decision. Some wanted to avoid putting the Emperor in the wrong; others saw safety in numbers. Thrasea showed his usual resolution of mind—and did not wish to miss his hour of glory.

50. A similar charge struck down Fabricius Veiento, who had uttered a string of insults against senators and members of the priestly colleges in a work which he entitled "My Will."* His prosecutor, Tullius Geminus, added the charge that he had accepted bribery and sold official commissions. Nero took up the case in person; Veiento was convicted; he was expelled from Italy, and his writings were burned. There was a great run on them, and they were widely read, so long as it was dangerous to do so; when the ban was lifted, they were soon forgotten.

DEATH OF BURRUS AND FALL OF SENECA

51. Public affairs deteriorated from day to day, and the forces to support them were progressively enfeebled. Burrus died: whether through natural causes or by poison is uncertain. Natural causes might be deduced from the gradual growth of a tumor in the throat, which finally blocked his windpipe and made it impossible for him to breathe. Majority opinion, however, insisted that Nero, under the show of prescribing a cure, had ordered that his throat should be painted with poison.[27] Burrus, it was said, was perfectly aware of the crime, and when the Emperor came to visit him and asked how he was, he merely turned his face to the wall and said, "*I* am doing well enough." His death caused general sorrow. Men remembered his virtues, and noted his successors, one harmless but idle, the other a hardened criminal. For Nero made a dual

* Freedom of expression was traditionally allowed in wills, and had been upheld by Augustus. Many opponents of the imperial regime availed themselves of this, their last means of satisfaction.

appointment to the post of prefect of the Praetorian Guard, namely, Faenius Rufus, because of his popularity (he had managed the grain supply without lining his own pockets), and Sofonius Tigellinus, whose long record of debauchery and evil reputation the Emperor found attractive. They lived as their characters would suggest. Tigellinus had more influence with the Emperor, and shared his private debauches: Faenius Rufus was popular with the Guard and the people, and therefore disliked by Nero.

52. Burrus' death brought the influence of Seneca to an end. Honest counsels carried less weight now that one of their champions was gone, and Nero was lending his ear to worse advisers. They brought a multiplicity of charges against Seneca. His wealth was excessive, quite inadvisable for any subject, and still increasing. He made bids for the favor of Roman citizens; his wonderful gardens and superbly appointed mansions surpassed anything the Emperor had. They accused him of monopolizing all distinction in oratory, and of writing poetry with excessive zeal, once Nero had shown his taste for it. He publicly criticized the Emperor's accomplishments, disparaging his ability as a charioteer and ridiculing his singing. How long was nothing to carry distinction in Rome except by license of Seneca? Nero was a child no longer; he had reached man's estate. It was time to discharge his tutor: his ancestors would provide all the instruction required.

53. Seneca knew of this criticism, for those who still had some care for decency kept him informed. Since Nero increasingly avoided his company, he sought an audience, and spoke as follows:[28] "Fourteen years have passed, Caesar, since I was called on to guide your youthful hopes; eight, since you have been Emperor. In all this time you have so loaded me with office and with honors that all that is lacking to my happiness is that it should know some bounds. Let me put some notable precedents before you, selected from your station in life, not mine. Your great-great-grandfather, Augustus, allowed Marcus Agrippa to retire to Mytilene, and permitted Gaius Maecenas almost a stranger's leisure in Rome itself. The former had been his partner in war, the latter had borne many burdens at Rome; greatly had they labored, and great was their reward. I have no claim on your generosity except for my academic learning, acquired in peaceful seclusion; the renown it has won—solely because it aided your early education—is ample reward. But you have given me boundless influence, wealth beyond counting—I often ask myself, Am I, the provincial, from a mere equestrian family, counted among the leaders of the state? Does my *parvenu* standing display itself

among those great families, with their long array of famous names? Where is my old spirit, once contented with little? Laying out these splendid gardens, stalking through its great estates, counting its broad acres, its immense revenues? And the only answer I can find is that it would have been wrong to resist your generosity.

54. "But now we have reached the limits: you, of what a prince should give his friend: I, of what a friend should accept from his sovereign. Anything more can only lead to envy. You will not notice it; such things lie beneath your greatness. But I do, and I ask for some relief. As in warfare, or as on a journey I might be tired and ask for a stick, so now, on this journey of life, I ask for support. I am an old man, unfit even for the lightest task, and I can no longer sustain my own wealth. Take it, let it be administered by your agents, and be incorporated with your property. I am not plunging myself into poverty, but I am dazzled with all you have given me. The time I shall save from looking after mansions and gardens I mean to devote to the care of the mind. You have strength to spare; for years you have known what it is to dwell on the pinnacle of power. We, your older friends, can ask for repose. It will be to your honor that you elevated to power men who would have been happy in a more modest station."

55. The gist of Nero's answer was, "The first debt I owe you is that I know how to answer, impromptu, your carefully prepared speech. You have taught me how to deliver prepared and unprepared orations. It is true that my great-great-grandfather Augustus permitted Agrippa and Maecenas to claim retirement after their labors. But he had reached years when his authority could be cast over any arrangement he made, whatever its nature. And Augustus did not deprive them of the rewards he had given them. They had been won in battle, among dangers: for thus was the youth of Augustus employed. You would have supported me in the field, if I had gone to war; as it was, you supported my childhood and my youth with reason, with advice, with philosophy, as circumstances required. The gifts you have given me will be with me as long as life lasts; what I have given you—gardens, wealth, mansions—are at the mercy of fortune. They may seem ample: but others less worthy have been given more. I shall not, for very shame, mention those freedmen who are obviously wealthier, but I blush to think that you, my dearest friend, are still by no means the richest of men.

56. "But come, you are still in good health, fit for active life and all its glittering prizes. My reign is only in its early stages.

Do you rank yourself below Lucius Vitellius who has held three consulships, or do you think I am less open-handed than Claudius? Shall my generosity do less for you than his lifelong savings did for Volusius? If I stumble on the slippery paths of youth, be at hand to guide me; you shaped my manhood's strength; show still greater devotion in guiding it. If you give back your wealth, if you desert your Emperor, they will not praise your moderation. No, they will all speak of *my* greed, of your fear of *my* cruelty. And whatever praise your self-denial wins, no true philosopher can gain credit from a course of action that brings his friend into contempt." With these words, he clasped Seneca to his embrace. Nature had endowed him, and practice had perfected him, in the art of concealing his hatred under deceitful endearments. Seneca returned thanks—the invariable end of all conversations with tyrants. But he changed his way of living from that of his days of power. Lavish receptions were abandoned, his train of attendants shunned. He was seldom seen in Rome, giving out that ill-health, or his researches into philosophy, kept him at home.

57. When Seneca was removed, it was an easy matter to bring down Faenius Rufus on a charge of friendship with Agrippina. Tigellinus' influence grew stronger every day. His evil talents were his only assets, and he thought these would be more acceptable if he could bind the Emperor to him by making him a partner in crime. He cast around to discover the source of the Emperor's fears, and established that the two men he dreaded most were Sulla, who had recently been banished to Narbonese Gaul, and Rubellius Plautus, who had been sent to Asia. He called attention to their noble descent, and the fact that one of them was close to the army of the East, the other to that of Germany. "I myself," he said, "unlike Burrus, have no dual allegiance: your safety is my one concern. In Rome, at least, it can be guarded from attack, but who can suppress sedition from afar? Sulla's name, with its echoes of the dictator, excites all the provinces of Gaul: the peoples of Asia are no less affected by the renown of Plautus' great ancestor, Drusus. Sulla is poor—a great stimulant to daring—and under a show of idleness is merely waiting the opportunity for a bold stroke. Plautus, with his great wealth, does not even pretend a longing for retirement. He affects to imitate the old Roman austerity; in reality he is a true follower of the Stoics, that arrogant sect of provokers of sedition and meddlers in politics." There was no delay. Six days later, Sulla's murderers reached Massilia, before any rumors or

alarms could reach him. He was murdered as he was sitting down to dinner. It is said that when his head was shown to Nero the Emperor jeered at its disfigurement by premature gray hairs.

58. Similar secrecy could not be observed for the murder of Plautus. For one thing, more people cared for his safety: for another, the great length of the journey by land and sea, and the time it took, caused rumor to spread. The common belief was that he had taken refuge with Corbulo, who was then in command of large armies and high on the danger list if there was to be a massacre of the great and innocent. Also, that Asia had taken up arms in Plautus' favor, that the soldiers who had been sent to kill him, being few in number and lacking in zeal for their task, had joined the rising when they had failed to accomplish their mission. Like all rumors, this became exaggerated through lack of critical examination. But a freedman of Plautus, with the help of favorable winds, was able to outstrip the centurions and carry a message from his father-in-law, Lucius Antistius, to this effect: "Escape a passive death, so long as help is possible! You will find good men to pity a great name, brave ones to help it. Don't disdain any means of support for the present. Repulse these sixty soldiers (all that have been sent) and while the messenger goes back to Nero, while another task force is prepared, there could be developments—even to the extent of war. Finally, either you will save yourself by this policy, or you will meet no worse fate by boldness than by timidity."

59. But Plautus made no response to this appeal. Unarmed as he was, he may have had no resources to use, or perhaps he could no longer support doubt and suspense. Again, his motive might have been his love for his wife and children, and the thought that Nero would be more lenient to them if he was not disturbed by any alarm. Some accounts say there was a second message from Antistius, denying that any danger was imminent. Others say that his philosophic advisers, the Greek Coeranus and the Etruscan Musonius Rufus,[29] advised him to meet death with constancy rather than face a life of uncertainty and fear. What is certain is that the assassins reached him at noon, as he was stripped for exercise. A centurion dispatched him, just as he was, under the supervision of a eunuch, Pelago. Nero had placed this creature over a Roman officer and his men, like some oriental despot's slave over his retinue. The murdered man's head was sent back; on seeing it Nero (and here I shall quote his very words) exclaimed, "To think I was ever afraid of that long-nosed

fellow!"[30] Laying aside his fears, he pushed forward with plans for the marriage to Poppaea, which they had caused to be postponed, and for removing Octavia, for though her conduct was modest, he hated her for her father's name and her popularity with the people. Meanwhile, letters were sent to the Senate, which said nothing about the murders of Sulla and Plautus, but proclaimed them both to be of a rebellious nature, and stressed Nero's solicitude for the safety of the state. Public thanksgivings were decreed, and Sulla and Plautus removed from the Senate. This farcical procedure caused even greater offense than the crimes themselves.

THE FATE OF OCTAVIA

60. When he learned of this decree, Nero felt that all his sins would be accounted virtues. He divorced Octavia on a charge of barrenness and married Poppaea. She had long been his mistress: she had ruled Nero when he was her lover, and she ruled him as his wife. She now induced one of Octavia's household to accuse Octavia of adultery with a slave. The man designated was Eucaerus, a skilled flute player from Alexandria. Octavia's handmaidens were questioned; under torture a few made admissions that were untrue, but most of them stubbornly asserted their mistress' innocence. One even said to Tigellinus, as he stood over her, "Her privy parts are cleaner than your face!" Nonetheless, she was divorced by the common procedure. She received the house of Burrus and the estate of Plautus—ominous gifts. Before long, she was sent to Campania and a guard posted over her. The common people complained of this loudly and often: they lack worldly wisdom, and their humble station renders them less exposed to danger. At their insistence,[31] Nero seemed to repent of his wrong-doing, and recalled Octavia to be his wife.

61. Joyfully the Roman people climbed the Capitol, at long last able to thank heaven. Poppaea's statues were thrown down, those of Octavia borne aloft, flowers were cast on them, and they were set up in the Forum and the temples. They even began to worship the Emperor again.[32] A gratified, noisy crowd swarmed into the palace; but bands of soldiers dispersed the rioters with blows and drawn swords. The statues displaced in the riot were replaced, and those of Poppaea restored to their original positions. She had always hated Octavia; now she was driven to desperation by panic, lest the people should

turn to mob violence, or their obvious partisanship have its effect on Nero. Clasping his knees, she exclaimed, "Things have come to such a pass that I am not now struggling for my marriage, though that means more to me than life itself! But my life is gravely threatened by Octavia's servants and dependents. They pose as the Roman people, they have dared in peace what could hardly be achieved in war! These arms are leveled at the Emperor: all they lack is a leader, and that will easily be found when sedition gets under way, when she leaves Campania and comes to Rome! A nod from her, even from a distance, and disorders begin. And what have *I* ever done? Whom have I injured? Is it because I am going to give a true-born heir to the house of the Caesars? Would the Roman people prefer to see an Alexandrian musician's offspring thrust into the imperial dignity? Well, if you think it best, take her back and be her slave: but don't be coerced into it; do it of your own free will. Otherwise, think of your own safety. The first tumult was duly punished and did not end in violence; but if they abandon hope of seeing Octavia as Nero's wife, they will find another husband for her!"

62. She suited her arguments to his fears and his anger, and Nero was both alarmed and enraged. But the charges against Octavia's slave were not enough to go on, and the questioning of her maids had brought them to nothing. It was decided to find someone to whose confession of adultery a charge of revolution could be added. Anicetus, murderer of Agrippina, seemed a good candidate. He was (as I have said) prefect of the fleet at Misenum; immediately after the crime he had been not ill-regarded, but later Nero grew to hate him, since the sight of one's tools in a terrible deed is a standing reproach. He was summoned to the presence, and reminded of his former services. He alone had come to the Emperor's rescue when his mother was plotting his murder. Now he could earn equal gratitude by ridding him of a hated wife. No need, now, of violence or weapons: all that was needed was to confess to adultery with Octavia. He was promised rich rewards—unspecified, for the present—and safe retirement. If he refused, death. So warped was his nature, so easily did he take crime in his stride from his earlier deeds, that he invented and confessed, before a special session of Nero's privy council, even more than had been ordered. He was expelled to Sardinia, where his exile was not penurious, and his death was due to natural causes.

63. But now Nero could issue an edict proclaiming as ascertained facts that Octavia had seduced the prefect of the

fleet, as a step to revolution, and then—the recent charge of sterility being conveniently forgotten—conscious of her immorality, had procured an abortion. Octavia was then imprisoned in the island of Pandateria. No other exiled lady ever won such sympathy from those who saw her. Some still remembered how Agrippina the elder had been banished by Tiberius, and they recalled the more recent exile of Julia by Claudius. But these were ladies of mature age; they had known what happiness is and in their present misfortunes could console themselves with their memories of better days. But for Octavia, the very day of her marriage had been the beginning of her death. She had come to a house where she had known nothing but sorrow: her father had been poisoned, to be soon followed by her brother; her maid had been preferred to herself; then Poppaea could achieve marriage only by ruining the legitimate wife. And now this accusation, the worst calamity of all.

64. So this young wife, in her twenties, passed into exile among centurions and soldiers. Presentiments of disaster told her she no longer belonged to the world of the living, but she did not yet know the peace of the grave. But after a few days, there came the order for her death. She said she was a wife no longer, and no more than a sister to Nero, but she called on their common tie with the two Germanici*—and, as a last resort, even on the name of Agrippina, during whose lifetime her marriage had been unhappy enough, but at least not fatal. She was bound in chains, and arteries opened in every limb, but she was so terrified that the blood only flowed slowly. The steam from a very hot bath put an end to her. Then—a refinement of cruelty—her head was cut off, taken to Rome, and shown to Poppaea.

What point would be served in recounting the thank offerings that now poured into the temples? All readers of the history of those terrible times, in my pages or another's, may fairly assume that the gods were thanked for each instance of banishment or murder ordered by the Emperor. Indeed, such occasions, once the sign of public rejoicing, now marked only public disaster. But I shall still record senatorial decrees that plumbed new depths of sycophancy, or established new records of servility.

65. The same year, Nero is thought to have poisoned two of his chief freedmen—Doryphorus, for opposing the marriage

---

* These complicated relationships are explained by the facts that (a) Nero was, by adoption, Octavia's brother, and (b) the title of "Germanicus" had come into Octavia's family through her grandfather, the elder Drusus. Nero also acquired it through adoption.

to Poppaea, and Pallas, for keeping his immense riches to himself by living so long. A certain Romanus denounced Seneca secretly on a charge of conspiring with Gaius Piso, but Seneca turned the tables on his accuser. This served to alarm Piso, and was the beginning of a complex, ill-fated conspiracy against Nero.

BOOK XV

1. Vologeses, king of Parthia, had by now[1] learned of Corbulo's doings. The alien, Tigranes, had been imposed as king of Armenia, and his own brother Tiridates driven out. He was eager to avenge the insult to the dignity of the Parthian royal house, but Roman power and his respect for a long-standing agreement pointed the other way. Hesitant by nature, he was further impeded by the rebellion of the powerful nation of the Hyrcani and the many campaigns resulting from it. But while he was trying to make up his mind, he was jolted into action by the news of a fresh humiliation. Tigranes had sallied forth from Armenia and invaded the territory of the neighboring kingdom of Adiabene, and this on a scale much too large and too destructive to be treated as a mere raid. The Parthian nobles were outraged; had they really, they asked, sunk so low in esteem that they were not even attacked by a Roman general but by a venturesome hostage who had for years been regarded as a slave? Monobazus, king of Adiabene, further aroused their resentment when he asked what support he could expect and where he was to go for it. Armenia was lost, the borderlands were going: if no help came from Parthia, he would get better terms of subjection by surrendering to Rome rather than by being defeated. Tiridates, now exiled from his kingdom, was the more effective because his reproaches were restrained, or even suppressed. "Great empires," he said, "are not held together by inertia. Arms and men must

333

be put to the test. At the highest levels, might is right: a private household can win praise by keeping what it owns, a king only by fighting for the possessions of others."

2. These words moved Vologeses, and he summoned his council. Placing Tiridates next to him, he spoke as follows: "This man, born of the same father as myself, yielded the position of king of kings to me by right of age. I granted him possession of Armenia, the kingdom which ranks third in honor, since Pacorus was already ruling Media. I thought I had acted in contradistinction to the traditional feuds and rivalries between the princes of our house, and reached a just settlement. But the Romans forbid this, and although they have never prospered after breaking peace with us, have broken it again. It will lead them to disaster! I will not conceal from you that I should have preferred to rely on justice rather than on bloodshed, on right rather than weapons, to preserve our patrimony. But if my hesitation has been at fault, my valor shall redeem it. Your courage and glory have suffered no diminution; it has been enhanced by the fame of moderation. That, no man is too lofty to scorn, and it is dear to heaven." He then placed the diadem on the head of Tiridates. Then he gave command of the royal Horse Guards, who were ready for action, to a nobleman named Monaeses, together with some auxiliary units from Adiabene. He gave instructions for Tigranes to be expelled from Armenia, while he broke off operations against the Hyrcani, mobilized the reserve, and took over the main burden of an offensive against the Roman provinces.

3. As soon as Corbulo got reliable intelligence of these moves, he sent two legions to the support of Tigranes, commanded by Verulanus Severus and Vettius Bolanus. Their secret orders were to act with circumspection rather than haste; Corbulo preferred to have a state of war rather than actual campaigning. To the Emperor he wrote that the defense of Armenia called for a separate command: the threat of invasion by Vologeses was chiefly directed at Syria. The remaining legions he posted on the bank of the Euphrates, hastily levied a force of provincials, and blocked the routes of entry with garrisons. Water supplies are scarce in that area, so certain springs were protected by building forts, others put out of use by filling them with sand.

4. Such were Corbulo's preparations for the defense of Syria. Meanwhile Monaeses was pressing on at full speed, hoping to catch Tigranes before his movements were detected. But he failed to find him unready or unprepared, for he had occupied Tigranocerta, a powerful position both from the size

of the garrison and the strength of the fortifications. Furthermore, the river Nicephorius—a fairly broad one—protects part of the wall, and a huge moat had been built when the river was inadequate. A garrison of Roman troops was in position, duly furnished with supplies. It is true that a few rash foragers who went too far had been surprised and ambushed, but these served to enrage rather than alarm their fellows. The Parthians had no stomach for the hand-to-hand fighting required by a siege; their feeble discharges of arrows failed to alarm the defenders, and did nothing for their cause. When the soldiers from Adiabene brought up scaling ladders and siege engines they were easily repulsed; then, when our men made a sally, they were cut to pieces.

5. Although Corbulo's affairs were going well, he thought it prudent to be moderate in the hour of success. He therefore sent to Vologeses to complain of the attack on the province, of the blockade of an allied king, and the siege of Roman troops. The siege must be lifted, or he too would encamp in enemy territory. Casperius, the centurion chosen to take the letter, found the king at Nisibis, thirty-seven miles from Tigranocerta, and delivered his message in unmistakable terms. Vologeses had a settled and well-established policy of avoiding war with Rome; moreover, things were not going well with his plans. The siege was bogged down: Tigranes was well garrisoned and well supplied; the assault party had been turned to flight; Roman legions had been dispatched to Armenia, and others were on the Syrian frontier, poised for an invasion. His own cavalry were enfeebled by a shortage of fodder, for a plague of locusts had devoured every leaf and blade of grass. So—hiding his fears—Vologeses answered in mild terms, saying he would send a delegation to Rome to discuss the Armenian claim and to establish peace. Then he ordered Monaeses to raise the siege of Tigranocerta, and withdrew his own forces to Parthia.

AFFAIRS IN THE EAST. DISASTER UNDER CAESENNIUS PAETUS

6. These achievements were generally acclaimed as redounding to the credit of Rome, and springing from the king's fears and Corbulo's threats. But there was another view. This deduced a secret agreement; a cessation of hostilities on both sides, and Tigranes to leave Armenia, as Vologeses withdrew from Syria. Otherwise, why had the Roman army evacuated Tigranocerta? Why leave in peace what had been defended in

war? What advantage had there been in passing the winter on the eastern frontier of Cappadocia—in improvised hutments—rather than in the capital of the kingdom which had recently been protected from attack? The war had been postponed, in effect, to allow Vologeses to contest it with someone other than Corbulo; Corbulo had no mind to endanger further the laurels he had won in so many years of warfare. Indeed, as I said earlier, Corbulo had suggested that a general should be sent for the specific task of protecting Armenia, and now it was reported that Caesennius Paetus was on his way. When he arrived the forces were divided. The Fourth and Twelfth legions, together with the Fifth, which had just been posted from Moesia, and all the auxiliaries from Pontus, Galatia, and Cappadocia, were under Paetus' command. The Third, Sixth, and Tenth legions, and the forces originally in Syria, remained under Corbulo. The remaining troops formed a pool, to be drawn upon as circumstances required. But Corbulo had little use for a rival. As for Paetus, he might well have been content with second place, but he expressed disdain for Corbulo's solid achievements: there had been no battles or bloodshed, he said; the token occupation of cities had been represented as capture by siege. He was going to impose tribute, law, and Roman administration instead of a shadowy client-king.

THE DESIGNS OF PAETUS

7. At this time the ambassadors of Vologeses—whose dispatch to Rome I have recorded—came back without an agreement, and the Parthians openly took up hostilities. Paetus accepted the challenge. With two legions, the Fourth (at that time) under Funisulanus Vettonianus, and the Twelfth under Calavius Sabinus, he entered Armenia. The omens were bad. Crossing the Euphrates (by bridge), the horse which carried the consular insignia took fright for no obvious reason and turned back: the sacrificial victim which was being kept for the building of winter quarters broke out when the work was only half completed, and escaped beyond the ramparts; the soldiers' spears caught fire—an omen of special significance, because the Parthian foe fought with missiles.

8. But Paetus disregarded the omens. Without completing the winter quarters, without any provision of a grain supply, he set off on a crossing of the Taurus range. The object was given out as the recapture of Tigranocerta and the devastation of the territories which Corbulo had left undamaged. Some

fortresses were captured, and both booty and glory were won on a scale that would have been satisfactory if the glory had been claimed with moderation or any care taken to protect the booty. But in his far-ranging marches he had overrun more territory than he could hold, the grain he had taken was spoiled, and winter was drawing on. He returned to base, and drafted a dispatch to the Emperor as though the war were over—grandiose in wording, but empty of content.

MOVES OF CORBULO

9. Corbulo had never neglected the Euphrates defenses, but now he still further strengthened the river line. To prevent bridge-building being disturbed by the enemy's cavalry squadrons (and they were maneuvering with great show on the plains by the river) he moved across the stream some very large ships, connected by planks and equipped with towers. Then, with catapults and ballistae he broke up the enemy, for the stones and spears from our artillery far outranged the arrows which the Parthians used in reply. Then work was resumed on the bridge, and the hills on the opposite bank occupied by auxiliary units, and finally by the camps of the legions themselves. This speedy and massive display of strength was such that the Parthians abandoned all preparation for the invasion of Syria and concentrated their hopes on Armenia. Paetus, wholly unaware of the threat, had sent the Fifth Legion off to Pontus, and had weakened his remaining forces by the indiscriminate granting of leave to the troops. At this point news reached him that Vologeses was at hand in great strength and hostile array.

DISASTER TO PAETUS

10. The Twelfth Legion was now hastily summoned. Paetus had hoped to give the impression of having reinforced his army; actually, he laid bare his weakness. Even so, he could have held his base, or frustrated the Parthians by protracting the war, if he had shown any consistency of policy, whether his own or another's. But when the advice of men of experience had braced him to face the imminent dangers, he suddenly turned to opposite and inferior courses, to show that he had a mind of his own. Then he left winter quarters and led

out the legion as though for battle, proclaiming that arms and men, not ramparts and a ditch, were his weapons against the foe. But when a single centurion and a few men who had been sent forward to observe enemy movements were lost, he returned in panic. But Vologeses did not follow up this success; Paetus regained his nerve and posted a picked force of three thousand legionaries on the nearest ridge of the Taurus to bar the Parthian advance, stationed the best of his cavalry—the Pannonian units—on a part of the plain, and hid his wife and son in the small fort of Arsamosata with an infantry unit to protect them. He had thus dispersed a force which, if concentrated, might readily have withstood the enemy's sporadic attacks. Report says that it was only with difficulty that he was persuaded to inform Corbulo of his danger. Corbulo did not hurry. The more acute the danger that threatened Paetus, the greater the credit to the rescuer. Still, he ordered one thousand infantry from each of the other three legions, eight hundred cavalry, and an equal number of auxiliary infantry[2] to stand by for action.

11. Vologeses was aware that the infantry and cavalry of Paetus barred his way. But he did not change his plans at all; by action, or the threat of it, he threw the cavalry into a panic and crushed the legionaries. Only one centurion, Tarquitius Crescens, ventured to defend the tower he was occupying. He made numerous sallies, and killed all the barbarians who came within range, but finally he was overwhelmed by a shower of firebrands. Any of the infantry who survived fled into the distant wilderness. The wounded regained camp, to spread alarmist reports of the king's valor, and the fierceness of his people. These were readily believed by men who shared the same fears. Paetus showed no courage in adversity. Abandoning all military duties, he sent another message to Corbulo, begging him to come to the rescue of the eagles, the standards, and what was left of the prestige of his unlucky army, and assuring him that they would hold out loyally so long as life remained.

12. Corbulo remained calm. Leaving part of his forces in Syria to hold the Euphrates defenses, he made for Armenia by the shortest route that offered provisions. This lay through part of Commagene, then Cappadocia. Besides the usual preparations of an expeditionary force, he had with him a large number of camels, loaded with grain; for he had to cope with famine as well as the enemy. The first of the beaten army he met with was one Paccius, a senior centurion; then there followed many soldiers. They put forward a great diversity of excuses for their desertion, but he told them to rejoin their

regiments and seek mercy from Paetus—he himself had a hard
heart, except for men who had won a battle. Then he spoke
to his own legions, encouraging them with reminders of past
victories, and the prospect of fresh ones. The objectives now
were not Armenian towns and villages, but Roman camps and
the two legions they contained—an ample reward for toil.
Individual soldiers could win from the Emperor's own hand
the supreme distinction of the civic crown for saving a Roman
life; what a distinction if a whole army could be decorated for
rescuing a force as large as itself! These and similar arguments kindled their enthusiasm (and some had the further
inducement of the danger of brothers or kinsmen) and a
forced march was maintained night and day.

13. Vologeses therefore pressed on with the siege. Now
threatening the legionary camp, now the small fort where the
noncombatants were guarded, he approached closer to the
ramparts than is usual with the Parthians, to see whether this
display would lure the enemy out to fight. But the Roman
forces scarcely left their quarters, save to man the ramparts.
With some this was because of the general's orders, but in
other cases it was cowardice, under the guise of waiting for
Corbulo. As the enemy attack intensified, their minds turned
to the disasters of the Caudine Forks and of Numantia. The
Samnites, after all, a single Italian people, could hardly be
compared with the Parthians, Rome's rivals for world empire.
Even the brave and highly praised ancients had thought of
their own safety when fortune turned unkind. The general
despair induced Paetus to write to Vologeses. He did not ask
for terms at first, but affected to complain of the Parthian
action in support of Armenia, which had always been under
the rule of Rome, or of a king chosen by the Roman Emperor.
Both sides stood to gain from peace. He should try to look
beyond the present circumstances: the king was attacking two
Roman legions with all the forces of his kingdom, but Rome
could muster the forces of the entire world for the rest of the
war.

14. Vologeses evaded the issue, and said he must wait for
his brothers, Pacorus and Tiridates. Now was the place and
time appointed for deciding the destiny of Armenia: heaven
had appointed a further task worthy of the royal house of
Parthia—to decide the fate of the two Roman legions. Paetus
then sent messengers to ask for an interview with the king,
who replied by sending Vasaces, commander of the cavalry.
On his arrival, Paetus gave him an account of Lucullus and
Pompeius and all the Roman Emperors who had succeeded
in conquering or disposing of Armenia. Vasaces retorted that

the appearance of keeping or giving the crown had been ours, but the real power had always belonged to Parthia. They had a long discussion, but the next day Monobazus, king of Adiabene, was brought in to witness the agreement which had been reached. This was to raise the siege of the legions, to withdraw the whole of the Roman forces from Armenia, and to hand the forts and their supplies over to the Parthians. When this had been done, Vologeses was to have the opportunity of sending an embassy to Nero.

15. Meanwhile, Paetus built a bridge across the river Arsania, which flowed past the camp. He pretended that this was for a retreat, but in fact the Parthians had required it to be built as a proof of their own victory. And, indeed, they used it; our forces retreated by a different route.

Rumor added that the legions passed under the yoke, and suffered other humiliations.[3] The behavior of the Armenians would seem to support this, for they entered the fortifications before the Roman army had left them; lining the roads, they would recognize some captured slave or draught animal and seize it; clothing was seized and weapons torn from the terrified soldiers, who did not dare to resist for fear of starting a battle. Vologeses piled together the bodies and weapons of the fallen to testify to the Roman defeat. He did not, however, witness the withdrawal of the retreating legions; he had satisfied his pride, and now he sought to win a name for moderation. He forded the river on elephant back, while his staff crossed on their horses, for it was reported that the bridge had been treacherously designed so as to collapse under a weight; but those who ventured on it found it secure and trustworthy.

A SHAMEFUL RETREAT

16. However, it is certain that the besieged were so well supplied with grain that they fired the granaries, while Corbulo has revealed[4] that the Parthians were so short of provisions and fodder that they were on the point of raising the siege, and that he himself was no more than three days' march away. He also asserts that Paetus had sworn an oath, before the standards and the witnesses sent by the king, that no Roman would set foot in Armenia until Nero's dispatches had shown whether he would agree to peace. Granted that these reports may be fabrications to increase Paetus' disgrace, there are other facts which are not in doubt. Paetus marched forty miles in a single day, abandoning all the wounded, and the panic on his retreat

was as disgraceful as cowardice in battle. Corbulo and his army met him on the Euphrates. There was no display of decorations and weapons, such as might seem to point the contrast between the fate of the two armies. Corbulo's men were downcast, and so dismayed at the plight of their fellow soldiers that they could not restrain their tears: the lamentations were such that they could barely carry out the ceremony of saluting the standards. Gone were the old rivalry in valor, the desire for glory. Such emotions belong to success; now there was room only for pity, and especially among the lower ranks.

17. The generals held a brief conference. Corbulo complained that his work was undone, for the Parthians could have been put to flight and the war ended. Paetus' reply was that nothing had been lost. "Let us join forces," he urged, "and reoccupy Armenia, which Vologeses' withdrawal has left undefended." Corbulo answered that he had no such instructions from the Emperor. Only his anxiety for the safety of Roman legions had induced him to leave his province; Parthian plans being unpredictable, he would now return to Syria. The best that could be hoped for was that his infantry, tired from their long marches, would yet be able to intercept the Parthian cavalry, who could move so easily over open ground.

Paetus then went into winter quarters in Cappadocia. Vologeses sent an embassy to Corbulo to demand the destruction of the Roman forts across the Euphrates, and the reestablishment of the frontier along that river. Corbulo countered with the demand that all foreign garrisons should be withdrawn from Armenia. At last the king gave way: Corbulo leveled the fortifications he had built across the river; Armenia was left without an overlord.

EVENTS IN ROME

18. At Rome, trophies won from the Parthians and a triumphal arch had been set up in the middle of the Capitoline Hill.[5] They had been voted by the Senate before the disaster to Paetus, and the order was not abandoned. Regard for appearances triumphed over knowledge of the facts. To distract attention from the serious crisis in foreign affairs, Nero threw into the Tiber a large quantity of grain which had been intended for public consumption, but had gone moldy. This was intended to produce confidence in the grain market.[6] No advance in price was allowed, although almost two hundred

grain ships were destroyed at Ostia in a violent gale, and another hundred accidentally lost by fire after they had been brought up the river to Rome. He then appointed a commission of three—Lucius Piso, Ducenius Geminus, and Pompeius Paulinus—to supervise public revenues. He criticized earlier Emperors whose expenditure had regularly exceeded their revenues, pointing out that he himself was paying an annual subsidy to the state of no less than sixty million sesterces.[7]

19. At this time there was a widespread use of a pernicious practice whereby, when an election or a ballot for a provincial governorship was due to be held, childless candidates would acquire sons through fictitious adoptions. Later, when they had won their praetorship or governorship by lot, they would emancipate the persons adopted. The real parents protested loudly to the Senate. Theirs were the natural claims, they protested, for they had had the cares of bringing up the children; and their claims were very different from the fraudulent and transient nature of these adoptions. The childless already had their compensations in the ease and facility with which, free of cares and financial burdens, they could acquire influence and win office. Their own privileges, for which they had waited so long, were no more than a laughingstock when some "parent" (so-called), whose childless condition was not due to bereavement, could acquire without effort an office which natural parents had sought for years. A senatorial decree therefore provided that adoption should carry no weight in the matter of public office, nor indeed in the claiming of bequests.

20. There followed the prosecution of the Cretan, Claudius Timarchus. The charges against him were, in general, those commonly brought against influential provincials whom great wealth has enabled to tyrannize over their inferiors. But one remark of his went so far as to insult the Senate, for he had asserted more than once, "It depends on me whether Roman governors of Crete get an address of thanks or not!" However, Paetus Thrasea was able to turn this to the public advantage. Proposing the defendant's expulsion from Crete, he added, "Experience has shown us, gentlemen, how good laws and proper penalties among honorable men result from the misdeeds of others. I quote the Lex Cincia on the abuse of advocates, the Lex Julia on corruption among candidates for office, the Lex Calpurnia against avarice on the part of magistrates. Punishment follows the crime, correction comes after abuse. This latest example of provincial arrogance must be corrected as befits the honor and dignity of Rome. We need a measure which, without diminishing the protection due to provincials, makes it quite clear that the reputation of a Roman is de-

pendent on absolutely nothing but the verdict of his fellow citizens.

21. "We once sent out private individuals—not simply consuls and praetors—to inspect the provinces and report back on the loyalty of individuals. Nations trembled at their verdict. But now we flatter and pander to foreigners; at the nod of a single man they thank—or more often prosecute—the Roman governor. By all means let provincials retain this method of displaying their power; but let us restrain false thanks, exacted by entreaties, as being as undesirable as malice or cruelty. More sins are committed by being obliging than by being unjust. Certain virtues are bound to be unpopular—I instance unbending strictness, and a mind steeled against corruption. That is why Roman magistrates do so much bettter at the beginning of their term than at the end, when they have to go around drumming up support like election candidates. If we can stop this, provincial administration will be fairer and more consistent. Fear of prosecution has restrained avarice; the banning of votes of thanks would put an end to the search for popularity."[8]

22. His opinion was warmly received, but no senatorial decree resulted, for the consuls refused to treat it as business before the Senate. However, the Emperor took the initiative in enacting that no vote of thanks to governors of either imperial or senatorial provinces should be presented to the Senate, and that no provincial should take part in any embassy for such a purpose.

In the same year the gymnasium was destroyed by lightning, and a statue of Nero which it contained reduced to a shapeless mass. A large part of the populous Campanian town of Pompeii was destroyed by an earthquake.[9] The vestal virgin Laelia died, her place being taken by Cornelia of the Cossian house.

63 A.D. Consuls Memmius Regulus and Verginius Rufus

23. In this year Poppaea bore Nero a daughter. His joy at the event knew no bounds: the child was given the title of Augusta, and Poppaea received the same distinction. The birth took place at the colony of Antium, where Nero himself had been born. The Senate had earlier asked for divine protection for Poppaea's pregnancy, and had offered vows. These were now discharged and with interest. There were public thanksgivings, a temple to fertility, a competition on the lines of the festival of victory after Actium.[10] Golden statues of the Two Fortunes of Antium were to be placed on the throne of Jupiter Capitolinus, and circus games were to be held at Antium for the Claudian and Domitian houses—like those at Bovillae for the Julian house. But all this was transitory; within four months the baby was dead. A fresh outburst of flattery followed—the infant was declared a goddess, received a priest and a temple, and a place at the banquet of the gods.[11] As for Nero, his grief was as immoderate as his earlier joy. When the Senate streamed out to Antium to congratulate on the birth of a child, it was noted that Thrasea was expressly forbidden to attend. This insult—a warning of his approaching death—he met with unflinching courage. Subsequently, Nero is said to have boasted to Seneca that he was reconciled to Thrasea, and Seneca congratulated him. This brought new glory—and fresh dangers— to those eminent men.

AFFAIRS IN THE EAST

24. At the beginning of spring in this year the Parthian embassy arrived, bringing messages from Vologeses and letters to the same effect. He said that his earlier claim to Armenia, so often repeated, would now be passed over in silence. "The

344

gods," he went on, "are the judges of the affairs of even the mightiest nations, and they have conferred possession on the Parthians, not without some disgrace to Rome. I besieged Tigranes: I could have destroyed Paetus and his two legions, but I let them go in safety. I have given sufficient proof of my power; I have also shown a proof of my clemency. Tiridates would not refuse to come to Rome to claim the crown of Armenia, were there no religious scruples to forbid him.[12] He will certainly be prepared to go before the Roman standards and the statues of the Emperor, to inaugurate his reign in the presence of the Roman legions."

25. Such were the letters of Vologeses. Paetus' dispatches told a very different story, suggesting that the war had yet to reach an issue. A centurion who had accompanied the embassy was therefore questioned as to the true state of affairs in Armenia; his reply was that all Romans had withdrawn. The mockery of the Parthian request was now revealed: they were asking for what they had already seized. Nero asked his council which to choose—dishonorable peace or a hazardous war. Unhesitatingly, they voted for war. Sole command was given to Corbulo, with his long experience of the troops and of the enemy. They did not want a new disaster through the incompetence of another general, and they were disgusted with Paetus. The envoys were dismissed with their mission not completed. But presents were given them to suggest the hope that if Tiridates made the same request, submissively and in person, it would not be refused. Syria was entrusted to Gaius Cestius, and the army to Corbulo. Added to this was the Fifteenth Legion, transferred from Pannonia under the command of Marius Celsus. All tetrarchs and client-kings, all governors of neighboring provinces, of whatever rank, received instructions that they were to obey Corbulo. Indeed, his powers were now virtually as great as those which the Roman people had granted to Pompey on the eve of the War against the Pirates.[13] Meanwhile, Paetus had returned, fearing the worst. But the Emperor was content to let him off with a sarcastic rebuke, to wit, "I am going to grant you an immediate pardon: for a man as timid as you might fall ill under the strain of a long period of uncertainty!"

26. Corbulo sent the Fourth and Twelfth legions back to Syria. They had lost all their best men, the rest were shaken, and they no longer seemed battleworthy. In their place he sent for the Sixth and Third legions, which were up to strength and toughened by many successful campaigns, and led them to Armenia. They were joined by the Fifth, whose service in Pontus had caused it to escape the disaster, by the Fifteenth,

newly arrived, by picked detachments from Illyricum and Egypt, and by all the auxiliary units, infantry and cavalry, together with contingents from the client-kingdoms. All these forces were concentrated at Melitene, the point chosen for the crossing of the Euphrates. There was a ritual purification[14] of the army, followed by an address from the commander-in-chief. There were some fine phrases about the Emperor's auspices and his own achievements; reverses were ascribed to Paetus' incompetence. All this in the confident tones which soldiers use as a substitute for eloquence.

27. He then advanced along the route opened up by Lucius Lucullus, after clearing away the obstacles which had accumulated in the course of time.[15] When ambassadors came from Vologeses and Tiridates to negotiate for peace, he did not rebuff them. Indeed, he sent centurions with them whose instructions were in mild terms. Things had not, he said, reached the point where a fight to a finish was the only course. The Romans had gained many victories, the Parthians had known some successes—a warning against overconfidence. Much better for Tiridates to receive as a gift a kingdom undevastated by war; much better for Vologeses, and to the interest of the Parthians, to make an alliance with Rome rather than proceed to the infliction of mutual injury. He knew very well the internal stresses of the Parthian kingdom and the ungovernable ferocity of its peoples. By contrast, his own sovereign ruled over a realm at peace—and had only one war on his hands.

At the same time he added intimidation to advice. Those Armenian chieftains who had first defected from Rome were driven from their homes, and their forts demolished. Mountain and valley, strong and weak, were smitten with alarm.

28. But Corbulo's name was not regarded by the barbarians with bitterness, nor with the hatred usually felt for an enemy, and so his advice was felt to be trustworthy. Vologeses therefore was not for going to extremes on the main issue, and sought an armistice for certain provinces; Tiridates asked for a conference at an appointed day and place. An early date was agreed upon: the Parthians asked for the place to be that where Paetus' legions had recently been besieged, because of its association with success. Corbulo made no objection: the contrast in fortune could only redound to his glory. How little he was stirred by Paetus' disgrace he made very obvious by ordering the latter's son, then a military tribune, to take his men and bury the dead of that shameful battle. On the appointed day, the Roman knight Tiberius Alexander, who was attached to the campaign as a commissary, and Annius

Vinicianus, Corbulo's son-in-law, and acting commander of the Fifth Legion, entered the camp of Tiridates. This was a mark of distinction to him, and a pledge against treachery. Then each took a guard of twenty cavalrymen. On sighting Corbulo, Tiridates at once dismounted. Corbulo followed, and on foot they clasped hands as a solemn pledge of friendship.

29. Corbulo immediately complimented the young prince on his good sense in following wise counsels and avoiding rash action. Tiridates began with a long disquisition on the nobility of his family, but the rest of his speech was in moderate terms. He said he would go to Rome, and bring to Nero a new distinction—the homage of a Parthian royal prince, although Parthia had suffered no reverse. It was then agreed that Tiridates should lay his crown before the statue of Nero, and should only take it up again from his hands. The interview ended with an embrace. At the meeting which followed a few days later there was a splendid display by both armies.

On the Parthian side the cavalry were drawn up regiment by regiment, each with their national ensigns. On the Roman side the legions stood in line, their eagles and standards glittering brightly, and with the images of the gods displayed as in a temple. A chair of state stood in the middle of the tribunal, and on it was placed a statue of the Emperor. Tiridates advanced towards it. After the usual sacrifices had been made, he took the crown from his head and placed it before the statue. On all sides this produced a deep impression. The spectacle of the siege and massacre of a Roman army was fresh before men's eyes; but now it seemed that the tables were turned. If Tiridates was going to make a display of himself before the nations, was he not virtually a prisoner?

30. The courtesy and hospitality displayed by Corbulo added further to his glory. The king wanted an explanation for every novelty he saw—the centurions announcement of the changing of the guard, the bugle call at the end of mess, the altar and the torch to light it before the general's tent. All this, explained in colorful terms, aroused his admiration for ancient Roman customs. Next day, he asked for permission to visit his mother and brothers before starting on his long journey. Meanwhile, he gave his daughter as a hostage, and sent submissive letters to Nero.

31. He found Pacorus in Media, and Vologeses at Ecbatana, much concerned for his brother's interests. Indeed, he sent messengers to Corbulo to request that his brother should not be required to show any outward mark of subjection—he should be allowed to keep his scimitar, be entitled to salute provincial governors with an embrace, and not be kept wait-

ing at their doors. In Rome, he was to have the honors of a consul. Used to oriental ostentation, he did not understand the Roman attachment to the realities of power, and its disdain for the trappings.

ROME. OTHER EVENTS OF THE YEAR

32. This same year the Emperor granted Latin rights to the peoples of the Maritime Alps. Roman knights were allotted seats in the Circus in front of those of the people. Previously, they had had no reserved places because the Lex Roscia had only prescribed fourteen rows for the Senate. The gladiatorial games of that year were held with the same magnificence as before; the number of senators and ladies of high rank who disgraced themselves by appearing in the arena exceeded all records.

64 A.D. Consuls Gaius Laecanius and Marcus Licinius

ROME. NERO ON THE STAGE

33. Nero showed daily an ever-increasing passion for making a public appearance on the stage. Previously, his performances had been in private, or at the Festival of Youth held in his gardens, but these he dismissed as too thinly attended, and unworthy of a voice of such quality. But he did not venture on a debut at Rome. Naples was selected as being a Greek city: this would be the first stage of a progress which would take him to Greece, to the award of those great prizes long known to fame, and to a reputation which would win the favor of the citizens of Rome. The theater at Naples was filled with a crowd from all the Greek cities, and from the neighboring Roman colonies and municipalities, whom this event had attracted. There were, too, those whose office or employment caused them to wait on the Emperor, and even certain units of troops.

34. At Naples took place what most people regarded as an evil omen, though Nero thought it favorable, and a sign of heaven's protection. For the theater collapsed, but the crowd had left it and there were no casualties. Nero composed an elaborate poem recounting the incident and recording his thanks to the gods. Then, on his way to a crossing of the Adriatic, he made a stop at Beneventum, where a well-attended gladiatorial show was given by Vatinius. This same Vatinius was one of the filthiest creatures of his court. The son of a cobbler, deformed in body, and with an abusive wit, he had been taken up as a butt. Before long, his attacks on every person of decency had so exalted him that he was preeminent, even among scoundrels, for his influence, wealth, and power to do harm.

35. His were the games that the Emperor attended. But he did not allow his pleasure to interrupt his crimes. These were the days when Torquatus Silanus was driven to his death because, in addition to the fame of the Junian house, he boasted Augustus as his great-great-grandfather. The accusers were primed to bring against him a charge of extravagance on a scale that left revolution his only hope. Moreover, they declared, he had freedmen to whom he gave the titles of secretary for correspondence, secretary for petitions, and finance officer: these were the titles of the imperial bureaucracy; Torquatus must be preparing for the day. His intimate servants were removed in chains; seeing that conviction was impending, Torquatus opened his veins. As usual, Nero proclaimed that, although Torquatus was guilty and merited his death, he would have been allowed to live had he thrown himself on the mercy of his judge.

36. Soon after this, for some unknown reason, Nero gave up the plan for a visit to Greece. He returned to Rome, but private fantasies now dwelt on the Eastern provinces, and especially on Egypt. He issued an edict to declare that his visit would be a short one, and that the government would continue to function with undisturbed efficiency. Then he made offerings to the Capitoline temple for his journey. After worshiping its divinities, he also entered the temple of Vesta; there he was seized with a sudden fit of shivering in all his limbs. It might have been fear of the goddess, or it is possible that the thought of his crimes kept him in a perpetual state of panic. At any rate, he abandoned this journey also, asserting that for him patriotism overruled everything. He had seen the sad faces of the people of Rome, heard their private complaints about his coming travels so far afield. Even his short absences abroad they found hard to bear, accustomed as they were to

solace themselves for the hardships of life by the sight of the Emperor. In private life, one's nearest and dearest must come first; for him, this meant the people of Rome, and he must obey their appeal to stay at home. Such pronouncements always tickled the fancy of the lower classes, who were fond of their amusements; besides, they had a particular anxiety that the price of grain would go up if the Emperor were absent. To the Senate and the aristocracy, it was a moot point whether Nero was more abominable present or absent. Later, as happens in all frightful experiences, they came to believe that the worst was what had actually taken place.

37. Nero now tried to pretend that Rome was really his favorite place. There were feasts in the public squares as though the whole city were his private house. The most notorious, as it was the most elaborate, of those banquets was the one given by Tigellinus. I shall quote it as a model of its kind, having no taste for the repeated description of orgies.[16] A raft was built on the lake of Agrippa,[17] and here the banquet was served while the raft was towed about by other vessels. These were fitted out in gold and ivory; their rowers were selected perverts, divided according to their age and the vices which were their specialties. Rare birds, wild animals, even marine monsters from the ocean, had been procured. On the quays of the lake were brothels, filled with women of rank, and opposite them naked prostitutes, with lewd posturings and obscene gestures. At nightfall, the nearby woods and houses reechoed with songs, and were ablaze with lights. Nero tried every pleasure, licensed and unlicensed. It seemed that there were no further depths of degradation for him to plumb. But then, after a few days, he entered on an actual parody of marriage with one of the filthy crowd of homosexuals, called Pythagoras. The Emperor wore the bridal veil; witnesses were present, there was a dowry, wedding torches, and a nuptial couch. Everything was in public, even down to those items which are usually performed in darkness when the bride is a woman.

THE GREAT FIRE OF ROME

38. Disaster followed, in the form of the most terrible and destructive fire Rome has ever known. Whether this was accidental, or elaborately contrived by the Emperor, is uncertain; historians give both versions. It began in the part of the Circus Maximus which is close to the Palatine and Caelian hills, and

among shops whose wares included inflammable goods. The fire took hold at once, and the wind very quickly spread it the length of the Circus, where there were no palaces or temples with outer walls, nor indeed anything else to check it. First it swept through all the level ground, then climbed the hills, then returned again to destroy the lower districts. The speed with which it spread, and the all too inflammable nature of the old city, with its narrow winding streets and irregular buildings, nullified all attempts to contain it. All movement was blocked by the terrified, shrieking women, by helpless old people or children, by those who sought their own safety or tried to help others—some carrying invalids, others waiting for them to catch up, some rushing headlong, others rooted to the spot. When they looked back, outbreaks of fire threatened them from the front or the flanks. When they reached a neighboring quarter, that too was alight: even what they had supposed to be remote districts were found to be affected. Finally, utterly at a loss as to what to avoid or where to go, they filled the streets, or collapsed in the fields. Some who had lost everything they had—even their food for the day—and others who had lost their loved ones in the flames, preferred death, though they could have escaped. No one dared to fight the flames. Menacing gangs threatened anyone who dared to try to put out the fire; indeed, some men openly cast on torches, and said they had their instructions. They may have been acting under orders, or they may simply have wanted a freer hand to loot.

39. Nero was then at Antium. He did not return to Rome until the flames were threatening the house he had built to link the Palatine with the Gardens of Maecenas. But the fire could not be checked before it had destroyed the Palatine itself, the house, and everything in the vicinity. As a refuge for the terrified, homeless people he threw open the Campus Martius and the buildings of Agrippa.[18] He also opened his own gardens, and constructed emergency huts to house the thousands of helpless refugees. Supplies were brought in from Ostia and the neighboring towns, and the price of grain was reduced to three sesterces a peck. These were meant to be popular measures, but they earned no gratitude, for a widespread report had it that as the city was burning Nero entered his private theater and sang of the fall of Troy, comparing the modern with the ancient calamity.

40. The fire was brought to a halt on the sixth day at the foot of the Esquiline, where houses had been demolished over an enormous tract, so that its unbroken violence was faced with an open horizon and bare ground. But before terror was allayed, or hope could revive in the people, there was a fresh

outbreak in the more open parts of the city. Here actual loss of life was less, but the destruction of temples and amenities such as colonnades was even more widespread. This second fire was the more suspicious because it started on the estates of Tigellinus in the Aemilian district.[19] Nero, it seemed, longed for the glory of founding a new city, and giving it his own name. For indeed, of the fourteen regions into which Rome was divided, only four remained intact, and three were destroyed to ground level; in the other seven a few houses survived, but half burned and severely damaged.

41. It would be a long task to enumerate all the palaces, blocks of apartments, and temples that were destroyed. Among famous and ancient shrines, there perished Servius Tullius' temple of Luna, the great altar and shrine which Evander dedicated to Hercules, the temple of Jupiter Stator vowed by Romulus, the Regia, and the shrine of Vesta with the penates of the Roman people.[20] There perished too the spoils of so many victories, the masterpieces of Greek art, and the ancient and authentic manuscripts of so many of the great writers of Roman literature.[21] For all the beauty of the rebuilt city, there are many of an older generation who remember these losses as unique and irreplaceable. It was noted in some quarters that the fire began on July 19, the very day on which the Senonian Gauls burned the city. Others went so far as to calculate that between the two fires there elapsed the same number of years, plus months, plus days.[22]

42. Nero made good use of this disaster to his country. He built himself a palace[23] remarkable not so much for its gold and jewels—these are the ordinary trappings of luxury and have become commonplace—as for its meadows, its lakes, its artificial wilderness, now of woods and now of open spaces, and its vistas. Severus and Celer were the architects and engineers: their skill and daring essayed what nature had denied, and went far beyond the resources even of the Emperor. For they had undertaken to build a ship canal the whole way from Lake Avernus to the mouth of the Tiber, despite its rocky coastline and the impeding mountains. The only available supply of water was from the Pontine marshes, for everything else was either precipitous or waterless: if a channel could have been dug, the labor would have been intolerable and the expense unjustifiable. However, Nero ever longed for the impossible, and so he tried to cut through the hills by Lake Avernus. A few remains today attest the failure of his hopes.

43. In the part of the city not reserved for the palace, the rebuilding was not at random or uncontrolled, as after the

Gallic fire. Regulations prescribed the alignment of roads, the width of streets, and the height of houses. They stood in spacious building plots, and colonnades were added to the blocks of apartments so as to protect their street frontage. Nero undertook to construct these colonnades at his own expense, and clear up all building sites before restoring them to their owners. Rewards were announced, in proportion to the standing and resources of individual citizens, for the completion of private houses or blocks of apartments by a given date.

The marshes by Ostia were designated for the dumping of rubble, and instructions were given that the ships employed to bring grain up the river should make the return trip loaded with rubble.

A portion of all buildings had to be made without timber and of stone from Gabinum or Albano, which is fireproof. Water inspectors were appointed to insure a better and more efficient service from the public supply, which had suffered from the tapping of unauthorized individuals. Each householder had to keep fire-fighting apparatus ready to hand. Party walls were forbidden; buildings must be surrounded by walls of their own. Necessity caused these measures to be accepted, and they certainly added to the city's amenities. Some, however, thought the old city had been a healthier place to live in, arguing that the narrow streets and tall buildings offered protection against the intense heat of the sun, while now the open spaces, devoid of shade, blaze with oppressive heat.

PUNISHMENT OF A SECT CALLED CHRISTIANS

44. Such were the remedies of human forethought. Later, means of appeasing the gods were sought, and the Sibylline books were consulted. These advised the offering of prayers to Vulcan, Ceres, and Proserpine, and the propitiation of Juno by the matrons of Rome. This took place first on the Capitol, then on the nearest point of the coast, whence water was drawn to sprinkle the temples and statues of the gods. Women whose husbands were living performed night-long rituals, and there were solemn banquets. But no human aid, no largesse from the Emperor, no supplications to heaven, did anything to ease the impression that the fire had been deliberately started. Nero looked around for a scapegoat, and inflicted the most fiendish tortures on a group of persons already hated by the people for their crimes. This was the sect known as Christians.[24] Their founder, one Christus, had been put to death

by the procurator Pontius Pilate in the reign of Tiberius. This checked the abominable[25] superstition for a while, but it broke out again and spread, not merely through Judaea, where it originated, but even to Rome itself, the great reservoir and collecting ground for every kind of depravity and filth.[26] Those who confessed to being Christians were at once arrested, but on their testimony a great crowd of people were convicted, not so much on the charge of arson, but of hatred of the entire human race. They were put to death amid every kind of mockery. Dressed in the skins of wild beasts, they were torn to pieces by dogs, or were crucified, or burned to death: when night came, they served as human torches to provide lights. Nero threw open his gardens for this entertainment, and provided games in the Circus, mingling with the crowd in a charioteer's dress, or else standing in the car. These Christians were guilty, and well deserved their fate, but a sort of compassion for them arose, because they were being destroyed to glut the cruelty of a single man and for no public end.

A DRIVE FOR FUNDS

45. Meanwhile, the whole of Italy was ransacked to provide money, and the provinces, the allies, and the so-called free cities brought to disaster. Even the gods fell in that drive for booty. The temples in Rome were despoiled, robbed of all their treasures which every generation of the Roman people had vowed to them in the hours of triumph or of fear. In Asia and Greece not only the temple treasures but the very images of the gods were plundered by Nero's two commissioners, Acratus and Secundus Carrinas. The first was a freedman, ready to undertake any crime, the latter a self-proclaimed admirer of Greek culture, though it had done nothing to improve his character.

Seneca is said to have asked permission to retire to a distant country seat, to avoid being involved in the infamy of sacrilege. When it was not granted, he kept to his bedroom on the excuse of an attack of rheumatism. Some say that, on Nero's orders, poison was administered to him by the freedman Cleonicus. But Seneca escaped, either because the man betrayed his mission, or because of his own suspicions, which enabled him to prolong his life by a very simple diet of fresh fruit and water direct from the fountain.

46. At this time there was a rising of gladiators from the imperial training school at Praeneste. It was suppressed by

soldiers of the guard, but already there was talk of Spartacus[27] and other ancient disasters among the people, who find revolution fascinating and alarming. Soon afterward came a severe loss at sea. Not, indeed, in battle—for never had peace reigned more widely—but because Nero had ordered the fleet to return to its Campanian bases on a given date, making no allowance for the hazards of the sea. The steersmen therefore set out from Formiae, although a storm was raging; and as they tried to round Cape Misenum, a violent southwester drove them ashore and wrecked many triremes and smaller vessels.

OTHER EVENTS OF THE YEAR

47. At the end of the year, there was much talk of prodigies announcing impending catastrophes. Never had lightning struck more frequently, and there was a comet, atoned for by Nero, as usual, by the shedding of noble blood. Two-headed offspring, animal and human, were thrown into the streets, or discovered in those sacrifices which demand pregnant victims. In the district of Placentia,[28] a calf was born by the public road, with its head adhering to one of its legs. Soothsayers interpreted this as a sign that there was coming into being a new head of the world; yet this would be neither strong nor kept secret, either because the beast had been deformed in the womb or because it had been given birth at the roadside.

65 A.D. Consuls A. Licinius Nerva Silanus and M. Julius Atticus Vestinus

ROME. THE CONSPIRACY OF PISO

48. At the very beginning of the year a great conspiracy formed and made headway. Senators and knights, even women, vied with each other to join it, their motives being hatred for Nero and love of Gaius Piso. A member of the Calpurnian house, he was connected on his father's side with many illustrious Roman families, while he was popular with the Roman people for his virtues, or what passed for virtues. He used his eloquence for the defense of his fellow citizens; he was gen-

erous to his friends, affable and accessible to strangers. Besides all this, he had the accidental advantages of being tall and handsome. But he had no soundness of character, and could not control his pleasures: he was fickle, ostentatious, and prone to debauchery. These very characteristics made him popular to most men, who find vice highly seductive and do not care for austerity and puritanism on the throne.

49. But it was not the ambitions of Silanus that launched the conspiracy. Indeed, it is hard to say who it was, or who gave the first impulse to a movement which was joined by so many. That leading roles were played by Subrius Flavus, an officer of the Praetorian Guard, and by the centurion Sulpicius Asper is attested by the courage with which they met their deaths. Lucan and Plautius Lateranus contributed embittered hatred to the cause. Lucan had personal reasons for this, for Nero's jealousy and vain opinion of himself had injured his poetic reputation and prohibited his public display. Lateranus, who was consul-designate and could have had no wrongs to avenge, made one of them out of regard for the good of the state. Flavius Scaevinus and Afranius Quintianus, both of senatorial rank, belied their reputations in becoming leaders of so great an enterprise. For Scaevinus had ruined his brain in debauchery, and led a lethargic life: Quintianus was a notorious pervert whom Nero had attacked in a libelous poem, and who now sought to avenge the insult.

50. These men talked among themselves, and in the houses of their friends, about the Emperor's crimes, the impending termination of his rule, and the need to choose someone who would come to the country's aid in its hour of need. They were joined by Claudius Senecio, Cervarius Proculus, Vulcacius Araricus, Julius Augurinus, Munatius Gratus, Antonius Natalis, and Marcius Festus, all Roman knights. Of these Senecio was on intimate terms with Nero, and since this friendship was ostensibly unbroken he was in a very dangerous position; Natalis shared in all Piso's secrets; the rest stood to gain personally from revolution. Military men in the conspiracy—besides Subrius and Sulpicius, whom I have already mentioned—were Gavius Silvanus and Statius Proxumus, officers of the Praetorian Guard, and the centurions Maximus Scaurus and Venetus Paulus. Their great strength lay in Faenius Rufus, prefect of the Guard. His honorable life and good reputation were inferior in the Emperor's mind to the cruelty and wickedness of Tigellinus. He was the constant target of accusations by Tigellinus, and was endangered by the charge of having committed adultery with Agrippina, and being driven to seek revenge through love of her. So, when

the Praetorian prefect joined the conspirators and repeatedly protested his loyalty, they began to talk in most urgent tones about a date and place for the murder. Subrius Flavus was said to have taken a sudden impulse to attack Nero when he was performing on the stage, or when he was wandering unguarded at night when the palace blazed. The latter occasion seemed to offer solitude, the former the advantage of a crowd of witnesses to so brave a deed. But the wish for survival had held him back, a factor always adverse to high enterprise.

51. So they hesitated between fear and hope. Meanwhile a woman called Epicharis, who had wormed out their secret—how is uncertain, for she had never shown any previous interest in virtuous actions—began to encourage and reproach the conspirators. Finally, she grew disgusted at the delay, and being in Campania, began to tamper with the loyalty of the naval officers at Misenum and involve them in the conspiracy. A ship's captain in that fleet, Volusius Proculus, had taken part in the murder of Nero's mother, and considered that he had never been advanced in proportion to the merits of his crimes. He became friendly with Epicharis—whether then or earlier—and told her of his services to Nero and how ill rewarded they had been, how aggrieved he felt, and how he would seize an opportunity for revenge if it ever occurred. This raised the hope that he could be stirred into action and might bring in others; moreover, the fleet would be useful in providing opportunities, since Nero enjoyed sailing in the neighborhood of Misenum and Puteoli. So Epicharis took a further step: she denounced the Emperor's crimes, one by one, adding that the Senate was now impotent. But plans had been laid to avenge Rome's ruin: all that was now needed was for Volusius to act with energy and win over the best men in his command; he could expect a worthy reward. The names of the conspirators she did not reveal. Although Proculus told all he had heard to Nero, his denunciation could not be made to stand. For when Epicharis was arrested and confronted with him, he had no witnesses to support him, and she refuted him quite easily. However, she was kept in custody, for Nero suspected that the information might not be false, though it could not be proved to be true.

52. By now, the conspirators dreaded exposure. They planned to murder Nero in Piso's villa at Baiae, whose amenities drew him as a frequent visitor for baths or feasts, unguarded and with no imperial retinue. But this Piso refused to permit, saying the murder of the Emperor, however evil he might be, would be an outrage against the laws of hospitality and the gods who protected it, and would arouse disgust.

The deed were better done in Rome, in that hateful palace which had been built with the loot extracted from Roman citizens. Or, since they were acting for the public good, let it be in some public place. This was Piso's ostensible reason. Privately, however, he feared the rivalry of Lucius Silanus, whose high birth and education at the hands of Gaius Cassius might exalt him to the loftiest position, and bring him to the throne. This would readily be conceded to him by those not privy to the conspiracy, who might pity Nero and look on his assassination as a crime. Some, too, thought Piso had it in mind to prevent the consul Marcus Vestinus, a man of keen intelligence, from restoring the Republic, or from making it his task to select another Emperor. For indeed Vestinus was not one of the conspirators, although Nero used that charge to satisfy a long hatred he had borne against an innocent man.

53. At long last they decided to carry out their plans in the Circus, on the day sacred to Ceres. For Nero seldom left the privacy of his palace or gardens, but he was a frequent visitor to the Circus, and in its relaxed atmosphere there would be good opportunities of approaching him. They drew up a plan of action. Lateranus was to prostrate himself before Nero as though begging for a personal favor, then bring him down and hold him on the ground—for he was both resolute and of a powerful physique. Then as he lay prostrate and pinioned, the soldiers and centurions, and all the others who were sufficiently daring, should rush up and finish him. Scaevinus demanded a leading part. He had taken a dagger from the Temple of Safety in Etruria (or, as others say, from that of Fortune at Ferentinum) and wore it as an instrument dedicated to some good purpose. Meanwhile Piso would wait in the temple of Ceres until Faenius and the others could fetch him and escort him to the Praetorian barracks. Pliny relates that Antonia, daughter of the Emperor Claudius, was to accompany him to win popular favor. I feel that this story, whether true or false, ought not to be suppressed; yet it would seem ridiculous either for Antonia to stake her name and fortune on this desperate enterprise, or for Piso, notorious for his love of his wife, to have pledged himself to marry another woman—unless perhaps lust for power dominates all other human feelings.

54. Considering that the conspirators were of different family and rank, of both sexes and various ages, and included both rich and poor, it was remarkable how well the secret was kept. But it was betrayed at last, and from the house of Scaevinus. The day before the attempt, he had a long conversation with Antonius Natalis, and then went home and made his will. Then, drawing from its sheath the dagger which

I mentioned earlier, he complained that it was blunt with age, and ordered a freedman called Milichus to put it on the whetstone and see that it was sharpened to a point. Dinner that evening was more lavish than usual: his favorite slaves were given their freedom, while others got gifts of money. He himself was obviously depressed, and in a state of great anxiety of mind, although in outbursts of rambling talk he affected good spirits. Finally, he ordered this same Milichus to get ready bandages for wounds and styptics. Perhaps Milichus was in the secret of the conspiracy, and so far had been trustworthy; perhaps, as most accounts have it, he knew nothing of it, and this was when his suspicions were first aroused. At any rate, his slave's mind now began to think of the rewards of treachery, and to conjure up fantasies of unlimited wealth and power. Considerations of duty, of his patron's safety, and of the freedom he himself had been given, flew out of the window. Moreover, his wife contributed a typically feminine and sordid argument—that there were solid grounds for alarm already, for many slaves and freedmen had been present and had seen all that he had: one man's silence would be useless, and the rewards would go to the first to turn informer.

55. So, at daybreak, Milichus made his way to the Servilian Gardens.[29] At first he was denied entry, but by dint of repeating that he was the bearer of terrible and important news, he was admitted by the porters to the presence of Nero's freedman Epaphroditus, then by him to Nero. There he told of the danger, the formidable character of the conspirators, and everything else that he had heard or guessed. Finally he showed the dagger, as it had been prepared for the assassination, and demanded that Scaevinus should be arrested. This was done at once by soldiers. Scaevinus began his defense by saying that the dagger, which was produced as evidence against him, was in fact a family heirloom that was kept in his bedroom, and that it had been stolen by Milichus. As for making his will, that was a thing he often did, without taking any particular note of the day. He had often before given slaves money or their freedom; if he did it on a more lavish scale in the day in question, it was because his capital was dwindling, his creditors pressing, and he was afraid his will would not be allowed to stand. Lavish banquets were habitual with him: he led a life of pleasure and no doubt earned the disapproval of the strict. He had never ordered bandages for wounds; this item was the invention of Milichus, added to his denunciation because it could be made to rest on his own evidence, since all his other charges, and the facts on which they rested, were obviously nonsensical. His self-possession reinforced his argu-

ments. He assailed Milichus as a perjured scoundrel with such a tone and expression of conviction that the whole accusation was tottering. Then Milichus' wife reminded them that Antonius Natalis had had a long and secret interview with Scaevinus, and that they were both intimates of Gaius Piso.

56. So Natalis was produced, and they were questioned separately as to this interview and its object. Suspicion was aroused because their accounts did not tally, and they were cast in chains. When the instruments of torture were displayed, they collapsed at the threat, Natalis being the first to break down. He knew more of the conspiracy, and he was more skilled at making an accusation. First he denounced Gaius Piso, then Annaeus Seneca. This may have been because he was the go-between between him and Piso, or he may have been hoping to curry favor with Nero, who hated Seneca and employed every means to bring him down. When he was told of Natalis' evidence, Scaevinus too broke down in the same feeble way. Thinking, perhaps, that everything was now out and it would be useless to keep silence any longer, he gave the names of the rest of the conspirators. Of these, Lucan, Quintianus, and Senecio long maintained their innocence. Finally they were seduced by a promise of free pardon, and the reasons for their hesitation were clear. For Lucan named his own mother, Acilia, and Quintianus and Senecio their dearest friends, Glitius Gallus and Annius Pollio respectively.

57. Meanwhile, Nero suddenly remembered that Epicharis was under arrest on the denunciation of Volusius Proculus. He ordered her to be put to torture, thinking that no woman's body could bear the pain. But neither the lash nor the branding, nor the anger of the torturers as they increased her agony to prevent a woman defying them—none of this caused her to weaken in her denial. The first day of investigation had revealed nothing. On the next day, she was dragged out to face the same ordeals. Being carried in a litter (for her limbs had been dislocated and she could not stand), she tore off her breastband and looped it around the canopy of the litter. Then she slipped her neck into it, bore forward with all her weight, and choked out what little life she had left. A freedwoman, and brought to the extremes of agony, she had tried to protect men who were no kin of hers, and almost strangers. How much nobler this example than that of freeborn men, Roman knights and senators, who did not even wait for the torture to betray their nearest and dearest! For Lucan and Senecio and Quintianus did not shrink from wholesale denunciation of conspirators, and Nero grew ever more alarmed, although his guard had been strengthened many times.

THE TERROR

58. Now virtually the whole city was under arrest: the walls were manned, and the river and the coast blockaded. Infantry and cavalry units patrolled the city squares, private houses, even the countryside and the towns nearby; their ranks were stiffened by Germans, in whom Nero put particular trust because they were non-Romans. Long lines of men in chains were dragged along and dumped at the entry to the gardens. When they came to answer the charges against them, they found that a smile directed at one of the conspirators, a chance remark, a sudden encounter at a dinner party or a show, were being accepted as evidence. Besides the brutal interrogation of Nero and Tigellinus, they had to face the fierce hostility of Faenius Rufus. He had not yet been denounced by the witnesses, and thought that he could best demonstrate his innocence by harshness toward his own allies. Subrius Flavus was standing by him, and asked by signs whether he should draw his sword and perform the murder while an investigation was in progress. But Faenius shook his head and checked the impulse, as Subrius' hand was moving toward his sword.

59. Now that the conspiracy was betrayed, and while Milichus was being heard and Scaevinus was hesitating, there were some who begged Piso to go to the Praetorian barracks, or to mount the Rostra and try to win the allegiance of the troops and people. "If you rally the conspirators," they argued, "others will join; publicity will follow any move that is made, and that counts for most in revolutions! Nero has taken no precautions against this happening. Even resolute men are shaken by sudden developments; how much less likely that this stage-hero, with Tigellinus and his mistresses, would ever take up arms against you! Action can bring results that the idle would think impossible. Useless to hope for silence and loyalty when the minds and bodies of so many conspirators are involved; torture and bribery between them can dissolve all resistance. Your arrest is impending, and it will be followed by a shameful death. How much nobler to die in the service of your country, calling men to the aid of liberty! The soldiers may desert you and the people fail you, but if you must meet an early death, die in a way your ancestors and your posterity can be proud of!" Piso was not convinced. He made a brief public appearance, then shut himself up at home, and steeled himself to face the worst. Then a troop of soldiers appeared,

specially selected by Nero from recruits or men newly joined; he dared not trust the veterans as disposed to favor Piso. Piso died by opening the veins in his arms. His will was marked by base flattery of Nero, undertaken for the sake of his wife. She was of low birth, and had nothing to commend her but her beauty, and he had stolen her from her marriage to a friend. This woman's name was Satria Galla; her former husband was Domitius Silus. His complaisance and her shamelessness both disgraced Piso.

60. The next murder perpetrated by Nero was that of the consul-designate, Plautius Lateranus. This was so hasty that he was denied the opportunity to embrace his children, and even that brief respite to choose his death that was usually conceded. Dragged to a place commonly reserved for the execution of slaves, he was cut down at the hands of the tribune Statius. He maintained a steady silence, not even reproaching Statius with the fact that he, too, was privy to the plot.

THE MURDER OF SENECA

The murder of Seneca followed. This, above all others, rejoiced the Emperor's heart, not because he had found Seneca implicated in the conspiracy, but because he could now accomplish by the sword what poison had failed to do. The only tittle of evidence was that Natalis had said that he had been sent to Seneca when he was ill to complain that he was refusing to see Piso—and to say that it was much better for friends to meet as friends should. Seneca had replied that exchange of speech and frequent interviews would do neither of them any good, but that his well-being was bound up with the safety of Piso. Gavius Silvanus, an officer of the Praetorian Guard, was ordered to report this to Seneca and ask him if he admitted that such had been the words of Natalis, and his own reply. By chance or foresight, Seneca had that day returned from Campania and was staying at a suburban villa near the fourth milestone. The officer reached it as evening drew on, and posted troops around the house. Then, as Seneca was dining with his wife Paulina and two friends, he conveyed the Emperor's instructions.[30]

61. Seneca replied that Natalis had certainly paid him a visit and brought a complaint from Piso about not seeing him and that he had excused himself on the ground of ill-health and a love of retirement. He had no reason to prefer the safety of any private citizen to his own well-being, nor was he given

to flattery. No one knew that better than Nero, who found Seneca outspoken more often than servile. This was reported by the officer in the presence of Poppaea and Tigellinus, the boon companions of Nero's brutality. He asked whether Seneca was preparing for suicide. The officer answered no, he had shown no signs of fear, his speech had been confident and his countenance in no way downcast. The officer was ordered to return and bid him prepare for death. Fabius Rusticus says that he returned by a different route and went to see Faenius Rufus. To him he revealed Nero's instructions, and asked whether he should obey them. Faenius, with that fatal paralysis that gripped them all, replied that he should carry them out. For Silvanus had been one of the conspirators, and was now piling up the crimes he had taken an oath to avenge. But he could not bear to see or speak to Seneca, and he sent a centurion in to tell him that the hour of death was at hand.

62. Unmoved, Seneca asked for his will, but the centurions forbade it to be brought. Turning to his friends, he said, "I am forbidden to reward you according to your deserts. I leave you, then, a single legacy, but that the noblest of all—the example of my life. If you keep that in mind, you will win a reputation for virtuous accomplishments as a reward for your loyal friendship." Their tears he checked now by conversation, now by recalling them urgently to the need to play the man. "Where are all the doctrines of Stoicism?" he said; "or where those resolutions we formulated over the years against the evils which now threaten us? Was anyone unaware of Nero's cruelty? Clearly the man who had murdered his mother and brother could not stop before he had added the death of his tutor and the instructor of his youth."

63. These words were addressed to them all. Then, embracing his wife and relaxing his sternness a little before the terrors confronting her, he begged and prayed her to temper her grief, and not give way to it forever. Sorrow for her husband's loss could be honorably assuaged by the contemplation of a life that had been devoted to virtue. But she insisted that she had made up her mind to die, and demanded the stroke of the executioner. Seneca had no mind to deny her glory. Besides, there was his love for her, and the thought that he might be leaving the wife so cherished by him to ill-treatment. "I was trying," he said, "to show you how to make life tolerable; you prefer the glory of death, and I shall not grudge it to you to set the example. So let us show equal constancy in facing the end; yet your death will carry greater honor." After this, they both severed their veins with a single stroke. But Seneca's body was old, emaciated by long abstinence, and his blood

flowed slowly, so he also cut the veins in his ankles and behind his knees. Exhausted by severe convulsions, and alarmed lest his agony should break his wife's spirit—and lest he himself should lose his self-control at the sight of her sufferings—he persuaded her to leave him and go into another room. His eloquence did not desert him even in his dying moments. Summoning the shorthand writers, he dictated to them at length; what he said has been published, and I shall not try to paraphrase it here.

THE FATE OF PAULINA

64. Nero had no hostility to Paulina, and he ordered her death to be prevented, lest he should increase his reputation for ferocity. At the command of the soldiers, slaves and freedmen bound up her arms, probably as she was unconscious. The public have a taste for the more invidious account, and there are those who say that she sought the credit of dying with her husband only so long as she believed Nero to be implacable, and that when the hope of pardon was placed before her, she succumbed to the blandishments of life. She lived for a few years longer, devoted to her husband's memory, and clearly showing by the pallor of her face and limbs how much her vital energies had been drained. Meanwhile, Seneca's death was protracted and slow. He asked his physician, Statius Annaeus, a loyal friend of long standing and a skilled doctor, for a draught of the poison that had long been prepared. This was the poison formerly used to execute condemned criminals at Athens. It was brought and he drank it, but in vain. His limbs were cold, and his body impervious to the poison's action. Finally, he entered a bath of hot water, sprinkling a few drops on the slaves within reach and saying, "This water is a libation to Jupiter, the giver of freedom."[31] Then he was carried into the vapor bath and suffocated in its steam. His body was cremated without funeral rites and according to the instructions of his will, when at the height of his wealth and power he had made provision for his end.

65. Report had it that Subrius Flavus and the centurions had a secret plan, which was not unknown to Seneca. This was, that when Piso had killed Nero, he too should be killed, and the throne be given to Seneca—as though he were the candidate of all good men, by reason of his virtues. Indeed, a saying of Flavus was widely quoted: "So far as the disgrace goes, it

will be small gain if the tragic actor succeeds the lyre player!"
For Piso used to perform in a tragic actor's costume, as Nero
did in that of a lyre player.

66. But now the military conspiracy was fully revealed.
The witnesses were so angry that they betrayed Faenius Rufus,
finding him intolerable in the double role of conspirator and
inquisitor. So as Faenius stood over him and blustered,
Scaevinus smiled back scornfully and said that no one knew
more about the affair than he did, and that it was time for
him to do a good turn for his beloved Emperor. Faenius
found neither speech nor silence to counter this thrust, but his
stumbling words and his obvious panic gave him away. All the
other conspirators, especially the Roman knight Cervarius
Proculus, pressed for his conviction. At Nero's orders, he was
seized and bound by the soldier Cassius, who had been chosen
to stand guard because of his exceptional physical strength.

67. Next their evidence betrayed Subrius Flavus, an officer
of the Guard. He first tried to defend himself on the grounds
of character, arguing that he would never have associated
with civilians and perverts in a crime of this kind. Then, when
he was pressed further, he admitted his guilt and gloried in it.
Nero asked him why he had been led to forget his oath of
allegiance. "I hated you," was the reply, "though you never
had a more loyal officer, while you deserved loyalty. I began
to hate you when, after the murder of your mother and your
wife, you paraded yourself as a charioteer and an actor and
an incendiary!" I have given the words he actually used, though
they did not achieve the same publicity as the last words of
Seneca. But the soldier's words deserve to be known; they
were blunt, but to the point. Nothing in the whole conspiracy
came as more of a shock to Nero; ready as he was to commit
a crime, he was not used to being told that he had done so.
A fellow officer, Veianius Niger, was given the task of execut-
ing Flavus. He ordered a trench to be dug in the nearest field:
Flavus complained that it was neither deep enough nor wide
enough. To the soldiers standing by, he said, "Slovenly again,
as usual!" Then, commanded to stretch out his neck firmly,
he said, "I hope your stroke will be equally firm." But Veianius
Niger trembled so violently that he needed two strokes to sever
the head. Making a boast of his cruelty afterward to Nero, he
said, "I took off his head with a blow and a half!"

68. Sulpicius Asper, the centurion, was the next to show
how to die bravely. Nero asked him why he had conspired
to kill him, and got the reply that it was the only way to save
him from his crimes. Then he suffered the penalty. The other

centurions did not disgrace themselves in their last sufferings. But Faenius Rufus did not match their courage, for even in his will he lamented his fate.

Nero expected that the other consul, Julius Atticus Vestinus, would be implicated in the plot, for he was disaffected and given to violence. But the conspirators had had no dealings with Vestinus—some because of old quarrels, others because they thought him indiscreet and too self-centered. Nero hated him because of their very intimacy. For Vestinus knew through and through the utter worthlessness of the Emperor, and Nero in his turn feared this outspoken friend. He had often been the victim of his sarcastic humor, and when remarks of that kind come close to the bone, they leave a memory that smarts. An added cause for resentment was that Vestinus had just married Statilia Messalina, knowing that Nero had been among her lovers.

69. So, there was no charge and no prosecutor, and Nero could not very well play the part of judge. Assuming that of despot, he sent the officer Gerellanus with a squad of soldiers. Their orders were to frustrate the consul's plans, capture, as it were, his citadel, and overpower his guards (for Vestinus had a house close to the Forum, and his servants were hand-picked for youth and looks). He had discharged the consular duties of the day, and was at dinner, with no suspicions, or none that he revealed, when the soldiers broke in, and bade him see their officer. At once he rose from the table. All his arrangements were carried out at speed: he was locked in his bedroom, a doctor was at hand; his veins were cut; he was carried, still full of life, to the bath, and then plunged into hot water. Not a murmur of self-pity escaped him. All his dinner guests were arrested, nor were they released until the night was far advanced. Nero, picturing with amusement their terror, and their expectation of death after dinner, finally decided that they had been well punished for dining with the consul.

70. Next he ordered the murder of Lucan. As his blood flowed, and his feet and hands became cold, and sensation gradually left his extremities, Lucan retained a lively mind and a stout heart. Remembering that he had written some lines about a wounded soldier, who had died in this very way, he recited them aloud, and these were his dying words.[32]

Senecio, Quintianus, and Scaevinus showed none of their former effeminacy in the manner of their deaths. Soon the rest of the conspirators perished, but they neither said nor did anything memorable.

71. Now Rome was full of funerals, and the Capitol of

thanksgivings. Men who numbered a brother, a son, a kinsman, or a friend among the dead, thanked the gods, decked their houses with laurels, fell at Nero's feet, and rained kisses on his hand. Taking this as a sign of joy, he rewarded Antonius Natalis and Cervarius Proculus with a free pardon because of their promptness in turning informers. Milichus was richly rewarded, and took to himself as a sobriquet the word for "Savior"[33] in Greek. Of the officers, Gavius Silvanus, though acquitted, took his own life; Statius Proxumus also wasted the pardon he had received from Nero by an ostentatious suicide. . . . Pompeius, Cornelius Martialis, Flavius Nepos, Statius Domitius, were deprived of their rank, not so much for hating the Emperor as for being believed to do so. Novius Priscus (through friendship with Seneca), Glitius Gallus, and Annius Pollio were condemned to banishment, discredited rather than convicted. Artoria Flacilla, the wife of Priscus, went with her husband, and Egnatia Maximilla followed Gallus. This latter lady's great wealth was not at first confiscated: later it was; both facts did her credit. Advantage was taken of the conspiracy to exile Rufrius Crispinus, whom Nero hated because he was a former husband of Poppaea. Their honorable reputation, one as a professor of rhetoric, the second as professor of philosophy, drove out Verginius Flavus and Musonius Rufus. Cluvidienus Quietus, Julius Agrippa, Blitius Catulinus, Petronius Priscus, Julius Altinus—to continue this long and massive list—were allowed to live in islands in the Aegean. Scaevinus' wife Caedicia and Caesennius Maximus were banished from Italy; only on being told of their sentence did they learn they had been on trial. Neither pardoned nor punished, Acilia, mother of Lucan, was ignored.

72. When all these sentences had been carried out, Nero addressed the Guards. Each man in the ranks received a present of two thousand sesterces and the right to free grain—which they had previously bought at the market price. Then, as though to announce a successful campaign, he summoned the Senate, and conferred triumphal honors on Petronius Turpilianus, the ex-consul. Cocceius Nerva, praetor-designate,* and Tigellinus, commander of the Praetorian Guard. Besides these decorations, Tigellinus and Nerva were further honored by being granted statues among the winners of triumphs in the Forum, and also on the Palatine. Nymphidius Sabinus was granted the rank of a consul: as he now makes his first appearance, I will comment on him briefly; he will have his part to play in the annals of Roman disasters. His mother was a freedwoman of some attractions, who had peddled herself among the slaves and ex-

* The future Emperor.

slaves of Emperors. Nymphidius Sabinus used to boast that he was the illegitimate son of the Emperor Gaius. And, indeed, Sabinus himself was tall and grim of countenance, and Gaius had a taste for whores, so that it is not out of the question that the Emperor did amuse himself with Sabinus' mother. . . .

73. After his speech before the assembled Senate, Nero published an edict for the information of the people, setting on record the evidence and the confessions of the convicted. Widespread rumors were assailing him on the charge of having caused the death of eminent men through hatred or fear, although they were innocent. But the origins, growth, and suppression of the conspiracy are very well attested by good contemporary sources, and the same story is told by those who returned to Rome after Nero's death. But the senators were lavish in their congratulations, especially those who had most cause of sorrow. Thus Salienus Clemens attacked Junius Gallio, who was alarmed by the death of his brother Seneca and begging for his life. Salienus assailed him as a public enemy and a parricide, but the Senate forced him to drop the charge, refusing to permit public misfortunes to be abused for the purpose of a private vendetta, or any new outburst of terror to arise from what had been either finally settled or canceled by the Emperor's clemency.

74. Then thanks and offerings were decreed to the gods, especially to the Sun, who had an ancient temple in the Circus, where the conspiracy was planned to take place, and who played a part in bringing it to light by his divine powers. Extra horse races were added to the Circus Games of Ceres. The month of April was renamed in Nero's honor. A Temple of Safety was to be constructed in the place . . .* from which Scaevinus had taken his weapon. Nero himself dedicated this dagger on the Capitol to Jupiter the Avenger;[34] this passed unnoticed at the time, but was taken as a presage and portent of future vengeance when Julius Vindex took up arms. In the Senate minutes I find it recorded that the consul-designate Cerealis Anicius proposed the immediate building, at public expense, of a temple of Nero, as a god. This he proposed because Nero had already transcended the pinnacles attainable by mortals, and deserved the worship of the human race. But Nero vetoed the proposal, lest ill-disposed persons should turn it to an omen of his death. Divine honors are not paid to Emperors until they have transferred their activities from this earthly plane.

* See Section 53. There is probably a lacuna in the text at this point.

BOOK XVI

DIDO'S TREASURE

1. Now fortune played a trick on Nero, thanks to his own gullibility and the bogus promises of Caeselllius Bassus. This man was a Carthaginian and of unsound mind. Putting his trust in a dream, he sailed to Rome, bribed his way into the Emperor's presence, and told his story. This was that a huge cave had been discovered on his estates, containing a great quantity of gold—not minted coins, but ancient, unshaped bullion. Huge ingots lay about, in some places standing up like columns; hidden from remote antiquity, this reserve had now come to increase the felicity of the present age. His own theory, which he explained, was that these riches had been hidden by Dido when she came from Tyre and founded Carthage, lest her new nation should be corrupted by excessive wealth, or lest the kings of Numidia—hostile in any case—should be incited to war through desire of gold.

2. Nero took no steps whatever to check the credibility of the man and his story; nor did he send agents to report on its truth. Indeed, he inflated it in his own imagination, and sent an expedition to collect what he regarded as treasure lying to hand. Warships were detailed with picked crews to make better speed. Nothing else was talked of at the time: the populace showing complete credulity, the sensible more reserve. It so happened that the Five-Year Games were being held for the second time, and this provided the orators with a superb theme for their panegyrics on Nero. "The earth," they said, "now not

369

only furnishes her usual crops, or gold inconveniently placed in mines,[1] but teems with a new fertility! We have only to stretch our hands to the wealth the gods provide!" Uniting the highest flights of rhetoric and the lowest depths of adulation, they added other sycophantic remarks of the same kind, never doubting that Nero would be credulous enough to believe them.

3. Meanwhile, these empty hopes fostered new bouts of extravagance. Existing resources were eaten into, as though capital for many years of prodigality had been discovered. Indeed, Dido's treasure was already being drawn upon for largesses; and this prospect of treasure to come was one of the reasons for public impoverishment. For Bassus had made excavations on his own and neighboring estates, declaring now this place, now that, to be the site of the cave he had promised. Not merely soldiers, but the farm laborers of the district were conscripted to help. But now at last Bassus came to his senses. Protesting that his dreams had always turned out to be true before, and that this was the first time he had ever been wrong, he escaped from his disgrace and fear by suicide. (Other accounts say that he was arrested and later released, after his property had been confiscated to compensate for Dido's treasure.)

NERO ON THE STAGE

4. The time for the Five-Year Games was now at hand. To avoid disgrace, the Senate thought of offering the Emperor the first prize for song, with the addition of a garland for eloquence, as a decent cloak for the ill-repute of the stage. But Nero said he wanted a fair contest and no favors from the Senate: he would meet the competitors on level terms, and trust the judges to award the prize according to their conscience. First, he appeared on the stage and gave a recitation;[2] then, when there were clamorous demands from the public that "he should display all his accomplishments" (they went so far as to use those very words), he entered the theater and gave a meticulous display of harpist's etiquette. No sitting down when tired, no wiping away of sweat except with his gown, no visible moisture on nose or lip—finally, the bended knee, the gesture of respect to the audience, the pretense of trepidation as he waited for the announcement of the verdict. The Roman mob —a connoisseur of actors' gestures—applauded in rhythmic cadence. They sounded pleased; perhaps, having no sense of public outrage, they really were.

5. But there were some who came from remote country

towns, from backward districts of Italy where perhaps something of an older morality still lingered on,[3] or visitors from distant provinces on embassies or private business, who were unpracticed in loose conduct and found the spectacle intolerable. Their hands lacked the stamina for continuous clapping, and they were unequal to the dishonorable task. They broke the rhythm of the more sophisticated, and provoked blows from the guardsmen who were stationed along the rows of seats to prevent any disharmony, or unappreciative silence for so much as a minute. It is known that many of the knights were trampled to death as they tried to force their way out through the narrow gangways and the surging crowds. Others, who passed days and nights together in their seats, contracted fatal diseases. But they had worse to fear if they absented themselves altogether. There were many spies openly (and still more secretly) taking down names, noting expressions—who was attentive, who was bored. On their report, instant punishment was meted out to the humbler sort; in more important cases, resentment was concealed for the moment but brought to bear later. Thus Vespasian, who had nodded off, was reproached by the freedman Phoebus, and only with great difficulty reprieved at the entreaty of men of eminence: he did it again, but this time his high destiny was a shield against the danger in which he stood.[4]

DEATH OF POPPAEA

6. Poppaea's death followed the games. It was due to a passing fit of anger in Nero; she was pregnant and he kicked her in the stomach.[5] The suggestion of poison I disbelieve, though some writers make it; but they are under the sway of prejudice rather than veracity. Nero loved his wife passionately, and he wanted children. The Roman custom of cremation was not followed; her body was stuffed with spices and embalmed, as they do with Eastern kings, and then buried in the mausoleum of Augustus. There was, however, a public funeral, at which Nero himself pronounced the funeral oration. As a substitute for virtues he praised her beauty, the fact that she was the mother of an infant now deified, and other gifts of fortune.

MORE VICTIMS OF THE TERROR

7. Poppaea's death occasioned public mourning, but to those who reflected privately on her shamelessness and cruelty it was welcome. Disapproval of Nero's action was increased when he forbade Gaius Cassius Longinus to attend her funeral —the first sign of a calamity that was not long delayed. Silanus was involved with him. Their only offenses were the ancestral wealth and honorable character of the one, and the high birth and blameless youth of the other. In a brief to the Senate, Nero requested that both should be expelled from public affairs, alleging against Cassius that he kept among the busts of his ancestors one of the tyrannicide Cassius, with the inscription "To the Leader of the Cause." This was to plant the seed of civil wars, and defection from the house of the Caesars: but, to have something more than a single hated name to stir up discontent, he had recruited Lucius Silanus, high-born and headstrong, as a figurehead for the intended revolution.

8. Next he attacked Silanus in the same terms used earlier against his uncle Torquatus: he was preempting the arrangement of imperial business by appointing freedmen for the posts of secretary for correspondence, secretary for petitions, and finance officer.[6] These charges were idle and untrue, for Silanus was already on his guard, and the warning of his uncle's fate had caused him to be especially careful. Then informers became associated with the charge, urging against Lepida, Cassius' wife, accusations of incest with Silanus, her brother's son, and also of black magic. The senators Vulcacius Tullinus and Marcellus Cornelius, and the knight Calpurnius Fabatus, were named as accomplices. They avoided instant sentence by an appeal to Nero; when, later, he was preoccupied with more serious crimes, they were insignificant enough to get off altogether.

9. A decree of the Senate condemned Cassius and Silanus to exile; the case of Lepida was referred to the Emperor. Cassius was sent to Sardinia, where old age was left to do its work. Silanus was taken to Ostia as though for transshipment to Naxos, but later was imprisoned in a town of Apulia named Barium.[7] He bore his undeserved fate with a philosopher's resignation, and a centurion was sent to kill him. Ordered to open his veins, he replied that he was prepared for death, but would not excuse the assassin his noble duty. The centurion saw that, though unarmed, he was a strong man and in a mood of anger rather

than fear. He therefore ordered the soldiers to dispatch him. Silanus resisted, and even exchanged blows—so far as he could with his bare hands—until at last the centurion killed him with all his wounds in front, as though he had died in battle.

10. Lucius Vetus, his mother-in-law Sextia, and his daughter Pollitta met their ends with equal courage. Their very lives were a reproach to Nero for the murder of Rubellius Plautus, son-in-law of Lucius Vetus. It was the freedman Fortunatus who provided Nero with an opportunity for unmasking his ferocity against them. After robbing his patron, this man turned accuser, and produced a certain Claudius Demianus, whom Vetus as governor in Asia had imprisoned for his crimes, and whom Nero now freed as a reward for turning informer. When Vetus realized that he would have to contend with a freedman on equal terms, he withdrew to his estates at Formiae: there he was kept under secret guard by soldiers. His daughter accompanied him. Besides the deadly peril now threatening, her mind had long been embittered with sorrow since the time she had witnessed the murder of her husband Plautus. She had embraced his bleeding neck, she kept her blood-stained garments; uncorrupt in the unending sorrow of her widowhood, she ate barely enough to keep her alive. At her father's request she hastened to Neapolis; when she was forbidden to approach Nero, she lay in wait at his door, and begged him to hear the plea of an innocent man and not to abandon his former colleague in the consulship to a mere freedman—now with a woman's tears, now abandoning the ways of her sex and assailing him in the most bitter terms, until Nero's immobility showed that he was dead to prayers and reproaches alike.

11. She therefore bade her father abandon hope, and bow to necessity. At the same time came news of an impending senatorial inquiry, likely to end in a harsh verdict. Advice was not lacking that Vetus should leave the greater part of his estate to the Emperor, thus insuring that his heirs would at least inherit the remainder; but this he spurned. Most of his life had been passed in freedom, and he did not wish to stain its last few days in servility. The money he had with him was distributed to his slaves; they were also permitted to remove anything portable, leaving behind only three couches for the last scene. Then, in the same room, using the same weapon, all three of them opened their veins. Clad only in a single garment, worn for decency's sake, they were quickly carried to the bath. Then the father gazed at his daughter, the old woman at her grandchild, and the young woman at them both. Their prayers vied with each other—for a speedy end to their feeble lives, and for their dear ones to outlive them, though

doomed to death. Fate preserved the order of seniority: the two old people succumbed first, and then the young woman. They were in their graves when formally denounced, and condemned to the statutory punishment for treason. The Emperor intervened to allow them to choose their own manner of death, thus piling farce on murder.

12. The Roman knight, Publius Gallius, was deprived of fire and water as a confidant of Faenius Rufus and an acquaintance of Vetus. The freedman who had turned informer was granted a reserved seat at the theater among the attendants of the tribunes. There were changes in the names of the months. May, which followed the Neronian—formerly April!—now became the Claudian month. June took the name of Germanicus, for, as the mover of the proposal Cornelius Orfittus explained, it was necessary to abandon the name June as having been rendered ill-omened by the execution of the two Junii Torquati.

13. This year, so full of human crimes, was marked by heaven with tempest and plague. A hurricane devastated Campania: destroying farms, crops, and orchards over a wide area, it reached the neighborhood of Rome. The whole population of the city was then being ravaged by an epidemic, though no visible distemper of the heavens[8] could account for it. But lifeless corpses filled the houses, funerals crowded the streets; neither age nor sex was exempt. Slaves and freeborn died like flies, children and wives were often cremated on the very pyre by which they had sat down to mourn. There were numerous deaths of senators and knights, but they seemed less lamentable because in their case it seemed that in the general mortality they had circumvented the cruelty of the Emperor.

This same year the legions in Illyricum were brought up to strength by levies from Gallia Narbonensis, Africa, and Asia, to make up for the losses they had incurred from discharges on the grounds of age or disease. The terrible disaster at Lugdunum drew a grant of four million sesterces from the Emperor to repair the city: this was the exact sum that the citizens of Lugdunum had previously subscribed to the disaster fund for the fire at Rome.[9]

66 A.D. Consuls Gaius Suetonius and Luccius Telesinus

14. I mentioned earlier the exile of Antistius Sosianus for writing libelous poems about Nero. This man had marked the rewards paid to informers and the murderous disposition of the Emperor. Being himself of an adventurous turn of mind and quick to seize an opportunity, he made use of the similarity of their fortunes to win the friendship of a certain Pammenes, who was exiled in the same place. Pammenes was a famous astrologer, which brought him into intimate relationship with many men, and Sosianus observed that relays of messengers came to consult him, presumably for good reason. He had also learned that Publius Anteius paid him an annual retainer. Further, he knew that Nero hated Anteius for his affection for Agrippina, and that his wealth was of the kind particularly calculated to arouse the Emperor's greed—the cause of disaster to many. He therefore intercepted a letter from Anteius, and also filched from Pammenes' secret archives a memorandum giving his horoscope and destiny. There, too, he found notes on the birth and life of Ostorius Scapula. Next he wrote to the Emperor saying that he had important information to give, relating to his safety—if he were granted a few days' remission from his exile—for Anteius and Ostorius were studying their own horoscopes and the Emperor's, and were thus endangering the state. At once Sosianus was fetched by imperial galleys. Once their charges were known, Anteius and Ostorius were looked upon as condemned malefactors rather than persons accused. So much so, that no one came forward to witness Anteius' will until Tigellinus granted permission, having already warned Anteius that the matter would brook no delay. Anteius took poison, but finding its action too tardy, opened his veins to hasten death.

15. Ostorius was then on a distant estate on the boundaries of Liguria, and a centurion was sent to carry out his murder. The haste is explained by the fact that Ostorius had a dis-

tinguished military reputation, and had won a decoration for saving the life of a Roman citizen, when on service in Britain;[10] moreover, he was of gigantic physique and skilled in the handling of arms. All this led Nero to fear a personal assault; coward as he always was, he had become still more so since the discovery of the conspiracy. So the centurion arrived, blocked all the escape routes from the house, and gave Ostorius the Emperor's instructions. Ostorius had always shown bravery in the face of the enemy, and now he turned it upon himself. His veins, when opened, let the blood out slowly, and he told a slave, "Pick up a dagger, and just hold it firmly!" Then he grasped his right hand and brought it to his own throat.

16. Even if I were describing wars with a foreign foe, and deaths suffered for our country, the narration of so many incidents with so little variation would weary me and bore my readers. They might think such deaths of Roman citizens honorable enough, but wearisome and repetitious. But now such passive servility, such a prodigal effusion of blood in times of peace, paralyzes the mind and dulls the sense of pity. The only concession I would ask from my readers is that they permit me not to despise these inglorious victims. For surely what was manifest was heaven's anger against Rome[11]—and not of the kind shown in the defeat of armies or the capture of cities, which one can dispose of with a single mention and then pass on. These were famous men, and let us grant this concession to their memory: that as their funeral rites distinguish them from the common herd, so each shall have his own memorial in the narration of his end.

17. Within a few days and, as it were, in column of march, there perished Annaeus Mela, Cerialis Anicius, Rufrius Crispinus, and Gaius Petronius. Mela and Crispinus were Roman knights of senatorial dignity.[12] The latter had formerly been commander of the Praetorian Guard and an honorary consul, but had been exiled to Sardinia on a charge of conspiracy. Receiving sentence of death, he committed suicide. Mela, a brother of Gallio and Seneca, had not sought a public career because he had the absurd ambition of wielding a consul's powers while remaining a Roman knight; at the same time, he saw a shortcut to wealth by acting as agent in the Emperor's affairs. As Lucan's father, he greatly enhanced his reputation. But when Lucan was killed, he called in the debts owed him so harshly that one of the latter's friends, Fabius Romanus, denounced him on the charge that both father and son had been implicated in the plot. His evidence was a forged letter from Lucan: this Nero inspected, coveting his wealth, and sent it to Mela. Mela took the then fashionable course of

opening his veins, adding to his will a codicil in which the bulk
of his money went to Tigellinus and his son-in-law Cossutianus
Capito, in the hope that the rest would be spared. He also added
a postscript which protested against his unjust fate: he had not
deserved any punishment, yet Crispinus and Anicius Cerialis,
deadly enemies of the Emperor's, were still alive. These charges
were supposed to have been invented, in the case of Crispinus,
because he was dead, and of Cerialis, to kill him. And, indeed,
Cerialis did kill himself soon after; he aroused less sympathy
than did the other victims, for it was recalled that he had once
denounced a conspiracy to the Emperor Gaius.

CHARACTER OF PETRONIUS

18. For Gaius Petronius, a brief retrospect will be in
order.[13] His days he passed in sleep, his nights in the pleasure
and duties of life. The reputation that others acquire by energy,
he won by idleness. Others who waste their substance are
thought of as profligate or spendthrift; in Petronius it seemed
a refinement of luxury. His deeds and sayings bore the mark
of unconventionality and insouciance, and people were glad
to accept them as unstudied and sincere. Yet as governor of
Bithynia, and later as consul, he had shown himself active and
fully equal to his duties. Later, relapsing into vice, or into a
pretense of it, he gained admittance to the exclusive circle of
Nero's intimates in the capacity of Arbiter of Elegance. Nothing was thought smart or amusing unless it had Petronius' approval. Tigellinus grew to detest him as a rival, with a greater
expertise in vice. So he addressed himself to the Emperor's
cruelty—his dominant passion—and accused Petronius of
friendship with Scaevinus. A slave was found to denounce
him; most of his household were arrested, and he was given
no chance of defense.

19. Nero was then in Campania; Petronius had reached
Cumae when he was arrested. He could not tolerate the hopes
and fears of delay, though he made no headlong escape from
life. Severing his veins, he bound them up again as fancy took
him, and talked with his friends, but not on serious topics, nor
to win a reputation for stoicism. He heard them reciting, not
on the doctrines of the philosophers nor the immortality of the
soul, but flippant songs and light verse. Some of his slaves
were lavishly rewarded, others were whipped. He went in to
dinner, dozed off to sleep—his death might be forced, but he
wanted it to seem natural. Even his will, which so many dying

victims used to flatter Nero or Tigellinus or some other powerful person, was handled in his individual manner. For he wrote
out a long account of the Emperor's perversions, naming all
his bedfellows, male and female, and categorizing the speciality
of each, and sent it under seal to Nero. He also destroyed his
signet ring to prevent its being used to incriminate anyone else.

20. Nero was at a loss to know how this detailed research
into his sexual refinements could have been compiled. Silia
seemed the leak: her marriage to a senator made her a person
of note, she had been Nero's partner in every lubricity, and was
also an intimate of Petronius. She was sent into exile for not
keeping quiet about what she had seen and known, and so
Nero paid off his own score. But he sacrificed to Tigellinus'
rivalries the ex-praetor Minucius Thermus; a freedman had
denounced him; he paid for it with torture, his patron with
an undeserved death.

THE ASSAULT ON "VIRTUE"

21. After the butchery of so many distinguished men, Nero
at last conceived the idea of exterminating Virtue herself by
the deaths of Thrasea Paetus and Barea Soranus.[14] He had long
hated them both, and Thrasea had given him fresh reasons for
hostility because he had left the Senate during the debate about
Agrippina, as I have said, and had not put in an appearance at
the Festival of Youth. This last offense was more keenly felt
because Thrasea had in fact played a tragic actor's part at
Patavium, his birthplace, at the festival founded by the Trojan
Antenor.

Moreover, on the day when the praetor Antistius was on
the point of receiving the death penalty for his libelous poem
on Nero, it was Thrasea who proposed and obtained a
lighter sentence. When divine honors were voted for Poppaea,
he had deliberately absented himself, and he was not present
at her funeral. Cossutianus Capito saw to it that none of this
was forgotten. He was eager for any criminal act, and he had
besides a grudge against Thrasea, who had once helped a delegation from Cilicia to get him condemned on a charge of
extortion.

22. He therefore cited further misdemeanors against
Thrasea. He had failed to take the oath of allegiance at the beginning of the year; though a member of the College of Fifteen,
he was not present when the national vow was taken; he had

offered no sacrifices for the Emperor's safety and for the well-being of his divine voice. For three years he had not entered the Senate House, where once he had been an enthusiastic and indefatigable member, taking part as proposer or opponent in even the most routine debates. Only recently, when there was general rivalry to suppress Silanus and Vetus, he had preferred to leave himself free to attend to his clients' affairs. This amounted to secession, to party strife, and, if many followed so bold a course, to civil war. "Rome is given to factions, Nero," he said, "and men now speak of you and Thrasea as they once spoke of Julius Caesar and Cato. He has his followers —or should they be called courtiers? They do not yet match his contumacious opinions, but they have copied his expression and his dress, they are gloomy and fanatical, a reproach to your geniality. He is the only man who cares nothing for your well-being, who despises your talents. He hates to see his Emperor happy! Even your griefs and losses do not satisfy him: to deny the divinity of Poppaea shows the same spirit as to refuse to ratify the acts of the deified Augustus and the deified Julius. He attacks religion, he brings the law into contempt. The official gazette of the Roman people is carefully read, in every province and every army, to see what Thrasea has *not* done. Either we must adopt their principles—if they are better —or we must take away from these agitators their leader and champion. This is the soil which bred men like Quintus Aelius Tubero and Marcus Favonius—ill-omened names, even in the old Republic. They attack the imperial government in the name of liberty: once they have overthrown it, they will attack liberty as well. It will avail you nothing to have struck down a Cassius, if you let these rivals of Brutus survive and flourish. However, do not brief us about Thrasea—let the Senate be the judge of the affair." Nero inflamed still further Cossutianus' angry purpose, and lent him the harsh but eloquent voice of Eprius Marcellus.

23. A Roman knight, Ostorius Sabinus, had already claimed for himself the prosecution of Barea Soranus on charges arising from his governorship of Asia. The energy and fairness he had shown in that office had added to his unpopularity with the Emperor. He had cleared the harbor at Ephesus, and refused to punish the city of Pergamum for resisting with violence an attempt by Acratus, Nero's freedman, to remove its pictures and statues. The actual charges, however, were friendship with Rubellius Plautus and an attempt to incite the provinces to revolutionary moves. Sentence was pronounced at a time carefully chosen—that of Tiridates' visit to receive the crown of

Armenia. This was to distract attention from an internal outrage to foreign affairs—or to display the imperial grandeur
by truly royal slaughter of eminent men.

24. All Rome turned out to welcome the Emperor and gaze
at the Armenian king. Thrasea was forbidden to attend, but
did not allow himself to be depressed. Instead, he sent a petition to Nero, asking for a list of the charges against him, and
saying he was certain he would be able to clear himself, if he
knew the case for the prosecution and had a chance to demolish
it. Nero perused it eagerly, hoping to find that Thrasea had
been frightened into writing something that would reflect glory
on the Emperor and damage his own reputation. In this he was
disappointed. Indeed, it was he who took alarm at Thrasea's
resolute air of independence and innocence. The Senate was
accordingly summoned to meet.

25. Then Thrasea consulted his closest friends as to whether
he should attempt to defend himself, or spurn the idea. They
gave contradictory advice. Some insisted that he should enter
the Senate House, since they knew his bravery could be depended on, and that he would say nothing but what would add
to his reputation. "A secret death," they proclaimed, "may suit
the indolent and fearful; let the people see how a brave man
encounters death: let the Senate hear words of more than
human inspiration! Perhaps there will be a miracle, and Nero
himself will be moved! But even if he persists in his cruel purpose, posterity will be able to note the contrast between a brave
death and the spiritless performance of those who have died
in silence!"

26. Another group thought he should wait at home. They
thought no less highly of Thrasea, but feared that insults and
humiliations awaited him; it would be better to withdraw out
of range of jeers and slanders. "Cossutianus and Eprius are not
the only criminals," they said. "Others too may not stop short
of criminal violence; and even good men may follow through
fear. Do not expose the Senate, which you have adorned all
your life, to a scandal of this kind: let it be left uncertain
what would have been their verdict on Thrasea, had he been
present to hear it. Useless to hope that Nero will ever be
ashamed of his crimes—the real anxiety is lest his cruelty will
reach out to your wife, your daughter, and your other dear
ones. In a word, you must die unassailed, unpolluted, meeting
a glorious death as nobly as those by whose example and precepts you have lived!" Rusticus Arulenus,[15] a young man of
high spirit, was present at the discussion. His thirst for glory
led him to suggest that he should, as tribune, veto the Senate's
decree. His enthusiasm was damped by Thrasea, who regarded

his suggestion as futile—unlikely to help his defense, and fatal to its originator. "I have lived my life," he said, "and I shall not now abandon the path I have trod for so long. You are just beginning your public career, and have not compromised your future. In times like these, you must consider very carefully what political course you intend to chart." He then decided to make a personal decision as to whether it was proper for him to attend the meeting of the Senate.

27. Next day, two battalions of the Guard in full equipment occupied the temple of Venus Genetrix. Others, in civilian dress but openly displaying their swords, guarded the approach to the Senate House. Troops were also posted in all the main squares and public buildings. Beneath these threatening glares, the senators entered the House. A quaestor read the Emperor's address. No names were mentioned, but the senators were rebuked for neglecting their public duties and for encouraging the equestrian order to a like idleness: no wonder men from distant provinces failed to present themselves, when so many ex-consuls and priests devoted the better part of their talents to the embellishment of their private gardens. This gave the prosecution a weapon which they were quick to seize.

28. Cossutianus spoke first, followed, in more violent terms, by Eprius Marcellus. "This is a matter of the highest public importance," he declared. "The contumacy of a few individuals is hindering the Emperor's indulgence. So far, the Senate has been much too easygoing, allowing itself to be made a mockery of by the insolence of Thrasea, by the no less infatuated Helvidius Priscus (his son-in-law), and also by Paconius Agrippinus (who inherits anti-imperial sentiments from his father) and the slanderous poems of Curtius Montanus. I insist that an ex-consul should attend the Senate; a priest, the national vows; a citizen, the oath of allegiance! Or has Thrasea already declared himself a traitor, and the avowed enemy of our ancestral rites and institutions? Let this man who protects the Emperor's critics truly play a senator's part and show himself: let him declare in this Senate what reforms and changes he wants. We should find it much easier to endure his detailed criticisms than the general condemnation his silence implies! Are worldwide peace, or the bloodless victories of Roman armies, something he finds objectionable? He grieves over public triumphs, regards the forums, temples, and theaters of Rome as so many deserts, and threatens to send himself into exile! A strange ambition—do not gratify it! The decrees of the Senate, the holders of public office, the very city of Rome, mean nothing to him. Let him withdraw his existence from a country that he has long ceased to love, and now no longer sees!"

29. Throughout this whole speech of Marcellus, grim and bullying, delivered with a fierceness of expression, voice, and mien, the Senate felt little pity. They had grown too familiar with the perils he stood for. But the weapons of the soldiers did arouse in them a novel and more penetrating fear. Then, too, the venerable figure of Thrasea passed before their minds, and some pitied Helvidius, so soon to die for an innocent relationship. What could be urged against Agrippinus but his father's unhappy fate—an earlier victim of cruelty under Tiberius? As for Montanus, he was an excellent young man, no libelous satirist at all: only the proof of his talents was sending him to exile.

30. By now Ostorius Sabinus, the prosecutor of Barea Soranus, had entered the Senate House. He began with his friendship with Rubellius Plautus, and then passed to his period as governor of Asia, a post which he had treated as a field for the display of his own talents rather than for the public good: he had actually fostered the rebellious tendencies of the Asian cities. These were old charges, but he added a new one which involved Barea's daughter in her father's peril. She was alleged to have spent large sums of money on magic rites, and indeed she had done so. But in the case of Servilia—that was the young woman's name—it was no more than filial piety, love for her father, and youthful indiscretion. All she had sought to know was whether her family would survive, whether Nero would relent, whether the Senate would refuse to pass the extreme penalty. So she was brought into the Senate House. Facing each other before the consul's dais stood the two defendants, the venerable father and the daughter, a young wife still in her teens, but a widow and isolated by the recent exile of her husband Annius Pollio, unable to look at her father because she thought she had added to his dangers.

31. Then the accuser asked her whether she had sold her wedding dress and her necklace to raise money for magic rites. She flung herself on the ground, weeping, and said nothing. Then she clasped the altar and its approach and cried, "I have never invoked forbidden gods, nor used black magic! My prayers have been unlucky, but all they asked were that you, Caesar, and you, members of the Senate, should spare my beloved father. I gave them my jewels and my dresses and other things that a lady of rank has, and I would have given my blood and my life if they had asked for it! I never saw the magicians before—they must answer for their own arts and reputation! I never mentioned the Emperor, except as a god. And my poor father knew nothing about it; if a crime has been committed, it is my fault."

32. Then her father took up her plea. "She did not accompany me to Asia," he said; "she is too young to have known Rubellius Plautus; she had no part in the misdeeds of her husband. You should take her case separately, since her only fault is an excess of filial devotion. As for me, I am ready to face any verdict." The girl ran to embrace him, and he started toward her, but the lictors interfered and dragged them apart. Then the witnesses were heard. If the cruelty of the prosecution had aroused sympathy, it was equaled by the anger induced by the witness Publius Egnatius. He was a dependent of Soranus, bribed for the occasion to bring his friend to death. He affected the gravity of the Stoic school, and in dress and countenance would have served as a model for that honorable company. Inwardly, however, he was treacherous and crafty, concealing both avarice and lust. The bribe unmasked him. He should serve as a warning that notorious evildoers and obvious deceivers are no worse than false philosophers and treacherous friends.[16]

33. But an honorable example was also brought forth by that day. It was that of Cassius Asclepiodotus, the wealthiest man in Bithynia, who had revered Soranus in his prosperity, and did not desert him in his fall. Losing his whole fortune and suffering exile, he proved that the gods do not distinguish good actions from bad. Thrasea, Soranus, and Servilia were allowed to choose their own deaths. Helvidius and Paconius were banished from Italy. Montanus was pardoned for his father's sake, but forbidden to take part in public life. The rewards to the prosecution were: Eprius and Cossutianus, 5,000,000 sesterces apiece, Ostorius, 1,200,000 and an honorary quaestorship.

THE DEATH OF THRASEA PAETUS

34. Thrasea was in his gardens when the consul's messenger came to him, and evening was drawing on. A gathering of distinguished men and women was in attendance, and he was listening with great earnestness to the Cynic philosopher Demetrius.[17] To judge from Thrasea's attentive expression, and a few words of the conversation that could be overheard, they were discussing the immortality of the soul, and the distinction between the body and the spirit. Then Domitius Caecilianus, one of his intimate friends, came to tell him the Senate decision.

As his friends wept and protested, Thrasea bade them go at

once, and not get involved in the danger of association with a condemned man. His wife Arria tried to share her husband's fate—and follow the example of her own mother[18]—but he persuaded her to live, and not deprive their daughter of her sole support.

35. Then he went into the colonnade, and there the quaestor found him. Having just heard that his son-in-law Helvidius Priscus had only been banished from Italy, he was closer to joy than sorrow. When the Senate's verdict had been delivered, he took Helvidius and Demetrius into his bedroom. He offered the veins of both his arms, and when the blood began to flow he sprinkled the ground. Calling on the quaestor, he said, "Let us pour a libation to Jupiter the Liberator. You had better watch, young man—for you have been born (may heaven avert the omen!) into an age when you may need the support of an example of fortitude." Then, in torment at his lingering death, he turned to Demetrius . . .

(At this point the manuscript of the *Annals* breaks off. We are thus deprived of the narrative of the remaining events of the year 66, and those of 67 and 68. They will have included the arrival of Tiridates in Rome, the ceremony at the conferring of the crown of Armenia, Nero's visit to Greece, the great rebellion in Judaea, the beginning of the rebellion of Vindex in Gaul, the advance to power of Galba, and the flight and death of Nero [June 9, 68]. It is not known on what scale these important events were treated by Tacitus. The *Histories* continue the story from the death of Nero to the death of Domitian in 96. The surviving books deal only with the civil wars [68–70].)

NOTES

BOOK I

1. The first words of the *Annals* echo Sallust, and the language of the first chapter is archaic and simple.

Dates of the events referred to: 753 B.C., foundation of Rome by Romulus; 510 B.C., expulsion of kings by Lucius Brutus; 451 B.C., Decemviri; 87–84 B.C., consulships of Cinna; 82–79 B.C., dictatorship of Sulla; 60–53 B.C., triumvirate of Pompey, Crassus, and Caesar; 49–44 B.C., dictatorship of Julius Caesar; 43–32 B.C., triumvirate of Octavian (later Augustus), Antony, and Lepidus; 23 B.C., final establishment of the principate of Augustus.

2. A famous claim. The problem of its justification must exercise all students of Tacitus.

3. The *annona*, or supply of cheap grain to the citizens of Rome, began with Gaius Gracchus (123–122 B.C.). What Augustus did was to improve the supply, especially from Egypt, and to organize special distribution in emergency.

4. Those organized by Octavian, Lepidus, and Antony in 43–42 B.C.

5. This is the "young Marcellus" whose early death is commemorated in Virgil. (*Aeneid* VI: 860ff.)

6. In the disaster at the hands of Arminius in 9 A.D. This—the worst Roman disaster in Germany—annihilated three legions and put an end to Augustus' plans of conquest in Germany.

7. The total amount of the legacies bequeathed by Augustus may be reckoned at about $6,000,000 of our money. He had received more than $30,000,000 in legacies, according to his account in the *Res Gestae*.

8.   The great Mausoleum of Augustus still survives. The *ustrinum,* or crematorium, is close by.

9.   Officially, temples to Augustus were permitted only in the provinces, and in association with the cult of Rome, during his lifetime. But there is ample evidence of local cults existing in Italy.

10.   Augustus deposited three documents with his will: (1) the comprehensive account of the Empire here mentioned, (2) instructions for his funeral, and (3) the draft of an inscription for the mausoleum, the original of the surviving *Res Gestae divi Augusti.*

11.   Livia was adopted into the Julian house under the will of Augustus. She bore the title of "Julia Augusta." In this translation she is called "the Empress Livia."

12.   The *praetor peregrinus* was first appointed c. 244 B.C. His decisions, recorded in the annual edicts, were of major importance in the development of Roman law.

13.   The three legions involved in the revolt were VIII Augusta, IX Hispana, and XV. The location of the summer camp is not known, but the reference to Nauportus (Vrhnika) suggests that it was somewhere in western Pannonia between the rivers Sava and Drava. Their permanent winter bases (*hiberna*) were Poetovio (Ptuj), Siscia (?), which is Sisak near Zagreb, and Emona (Ljubljana).

14.   These claques in the Roman theater often caused rioting. Cf. those of the opera house of Naples (and elsewhere) in the eighteenth century.

15.   I.e., though nominally discharged, the men are kept with the colors (*vexillarii*) on a full round of duties.

16.   The complaint about land grants seems to be specific and local. No veteran settlement had taken place in Pannonia under Augustus, but an inscription records the founding of a *colonia* at Emona in the first year of Tiberius, the time of the revolt. Emona lies beneath the buildings of the modern Ljubljana. To the north lie the foothills of the Karawanken Mountains; on the south side of the Sava plain begins the notorious limestone Karst plateau—a waterless, uncultivatable scrubland. Much of the plain itself is a forbidding swamp, and even modern attempts to drain it have had little effect.

After twenty years of grueling warfare, these Italian legionaries faced the prospect of eking out an existence on the swamps of Emona (modern *Ljubljanskdo Barje,* "sea of Ljubljana") or on the fringes of the barren Karst.

17.   There were at this time sixteen *asses* to the *denarius:* the soldiers were thus asking for a 60 percent increase in pay. Insofar as modern equivalents ever can be given, they were asking for a raise from, say, twenty cents to thirty-two cents a day.

18.   Augustus had employed a German bodyguard, but it had been disbanded after the disaster of Varus. Evidently it was by now restored.

19.   According to Roman law, the sons of a *familia* were not possessed of legal rights. The expression is used derisively.

20.   I.e., designations such as "Germanicus."

21.   The first known instance of provincials taking the oath of allegiance.

22.   The Chatti lived in what is now Hesse, and the Cherusci, their enemies, farther to the northeast. Arminius and Segestes were of the royal house of the Cherusci.

23.   This altar to Rome and Augustus would have been served by a priesthood of loyal and distinguished German chieftains, and the cult would have been a focus for the romanization of the province. Similar cults existed at Lugdunum in Gaul and (later) Camulodunum in Britain (cf. *Annals* XIV: 31).

24.   (Presumably) in the part of Germany first conquered.

25.   We do not know what this fate was.

26.   Now part of the Zuider Zee (now known as the IJsselmeer).

27.   According to Suetonius, Germanicus himself took a part in the collecting of the bodies. It was pollution for members of the priestly colleges to touch (perhaps even to see) a corpse.

28.   The site of this great causeway over the morass is not known.

29.   The *Bella Germaniae* of the elder Pliny is lost.

30.   The troops are now at the mouth of the Ems and are to march along the coast to the Rhine.

31.   Full triumphs were by now reserved for members of the imperial house.

32.   An old maxim of Roman law.

33.   The military treasury had been set up by Augustus.

34.   See VI: 27.

BOOK II

1.   Four Parthian princes were sent to Rome by Phraates in 10 B.C. They were not hostages.

2.   A Scythian people, living between the Caspian Sea and the Oxus River. Their name is thought to survive in the modern Daghestan.

3.   Marriage between brother and sister was also known in the dynasty of the Ptolemies in Egypt.

4.   The modern Waal.

5.   Tacitus says nothing of the journey from the Ems to the Weser.

6.   Perhaps near Minden.

7.   I.e., a pine forest.

8.   A Roman defeat may be read between the lines.

9.   The description suggests one of the great North Sea surges, like that of February, 1953, which caused immense damage and loss of life along the coasts of Holland and East Anglia.

   The surge of 16 A.D. is described in a splendid fragment of the poem of Albinovanus Pedo, who was on the expedition of Germanicus (quoted in Seneca the Elder, *Suasoriae,* I: 14).

10.   I.e., Libo could answer each charge as it was made.

11.   At the funeral of a Roman noble, persons wearing the masks of his ancestors took part in the funeral procession. A similar prohibition was enforced against the effigies of Brutus and Cassius.

12.   The appointed place of execution, near the present Porta Maggiore.

13.   See II: 3 and 4.

14.   After the capture of Rome by the Gauls (? 387 B.C.). His grandson was a more distinguished general than his son: Tacitus may have confused them.

15.   Germanicus' command entitled him to twelve lictors. To take only one—as Antony had done earlier—was a compliment to Athens.

16.   This famous oracle was in decline in the time of Augustus; it revived later in the first century A.D.

17.   I.e., Media Atropatene, the modern Azerbaijan.

18.   While the Roman government did not fail to exploit the financial resources of Cappadocia, the military advantages it might offer were signally neglected. See *Cambridge Ancient History,* Vol. X, pp. 745f.

19.   The chronology here seems faulty, and it seems that 59–61 should follow 67.

20.   It has been suggested that this action of Germanicus in Egypt precipitated the crisis in the grain supply of Rome mentioned in II: 87.

21.   As described by Livy (XXIX: 19.11).

22.   Egypt controls the sea routes from the Mediterranean to the Indian Ocean, and the land routes from Asia to Africa. At this period, Alexandria was the greatest port in the world.

23.   I.e., Ramses II (1324–1258 B.C.). The Egyptian Empire actually reached its maximum extent under Thothmosis III (1515–1460 B.C.).

24.   A key passage for the dating of the *Annals.* It was Trajan's conquests of 115 A.D. that pushed the Roman Empire to the Persian Gulf. These new acquisitions were renounced in 117 A.D.

25.   He should, from the Stoic view, have committed suicide.

26.   In the Forum of Augustus.

27.   A formal renunciation of friendship, whether between individuals or states, was in accord with ancient Roman custom.

28.   The comparison is strained and unconvincing.

29.   Such action before the praetor had "received the names" of the defendants was irregular.

30.   The famous ancient hymn, mentioned by Horace as no longer intelligible. The name of Augustus had also been added to it.

31.   See I: 72.

32.   They would have access to the *Acta Senatus,* the official gazette of Senate proceedings.

BOOK III

1.   The *Acta Diurna,* the nearest approach in Rome to a daily newspaper, was started by Julius Caesar. Tacitus refers to it only occasionally.

2.   In 9 B.C. Nero Drusus died from an accident while campaigning in Germany.

3.   The Megalesian games began on April 4. Agrippina reached Rome early in January, but public mourning began in December, and had thus lasted four months.

4.   Tacitus here uses innuendo with such refinement that it is not at all certain what he means to imply.

5.   The road from Rome to the Adriatic at Fanum, leaving the city by the Porta Flaminia, now the Porta del Populo.

6.   The words "of the previous summer," here and at the beginning of Section 20, seem to be an interpolation.

7.   A notably cool and impartial speech, of which Tacitus seems to disapprove.

8.   Here there is a gap in the text.

9.   The Gemonian Stairs led from the Capitol to the Forum. Here the bodies of executed criminals were displayed.

10.   Note the apparent candor with which this unverifiable evidence is produced.

11.   These words are a restoration to fill a lacuna in the text.

12.   Normally the senior consul would preside.

13.   Ronald Syme (in *Tacitus* [Oxford, 1958], p. 2) points out that in Tacitus' own times another Emperor was kept in reserve by fortune behind the scenes—Nerva.

14.   On May 28.

15.   See footnote 6, above.

16.   As governor of Africa.

17.   At least fifteen years earlier.

18.   I.e., had he intended acquittal, which would have been popular, Drusus would have got up to propose it.

19.   I.e., in the Theater of Pompeius, the first permanent theater in Rome (55 B.C.).

20.   The sentence was more severe than usual.

21.   The elder Julia and her daughter.

22.   The whole of this digression on the origins of civil law is in the manner of Sallust. See Syme (*op. cit.,* Appendix 53). It draws heavily on Stoic ideas of early man and the Law of Nature.

23.   E.g., in Parthia.

24.   The chief legislator of the (traditional) kings.

25.   I.e., the last piece of legislation to spring from the general consent of the community—all later legislation being the product of party strife or personal ambition.

26.   E.g., the attacks on Scipio Africanus, etc.

27.   Either Marcus Livius Drusus (tribune 122 B.C.) or, more

probably, his son of the same name (tribune 91 B.C.). See *Oxford Classical Dictionary*, "Drusus" (1) and (2).

28.   27 B.C. Note that the dictatorship of Julius Caesar and the period of the triumvirate are included in the twenty years of anarchy.

29.   I.e., an unmarried person would lose the right of inheritance, which would pass to the state.

30.   A group of minor magistrates.

31.   I.e., Augustus would thus be less involved than Tiberius.

32.   This is the only direct mention of Sallust by Tacitus.

33.   The territory of the Treveri was in the valley of the Moselle, and their chief city Augusta Treverorum, the modern Trèves. The powerful tribe of the Aedui had their capital at Augustodunum (Autun).

34.   The legions were now largely recruited from provincials.

35.   The Andecavi have left their name in Angers and Anjou, and the Turoni in Tours and Touraine.

36.   This, the most famous school in Gaul, was still in existence three hundred years later.

37.   From a Celtic word whose precise meaning is unknown.

38.   Tacitus here gives only the gist of a sagacious and well-reasoned communication, the original of which would have been recorded in the *Acta Senatus*.

39.   Tacitus' own family was of this kind.

40.   *Flamen Dialis*. In republican times the three *flamines*—of Jupiter, Mars, and Quirinus—were not allowed to leave Rome.

41.   Dionysus is here equated with the old Italian god Liber.

42.   Diana Trivia.

43.   The Roman name for the Persian Anaitis.

44.   One of Tacitus' most explicit statements of his view of history.

45.   This was the family of Augustus' mother.

46.   The Basilica Pauli stood in the Forum Romanum. It was completed and dedicated by Paulus' son, Paulus Aemilius Lepidus, in 34 B.C.

BOOK IV

1.   The phrases that introduce Aelius Sejanus have Sallustian echoes, evoking Catilina (see Syme, *op. cit.*, 353).

2.   The Castra Praetoria, on a site still used as a barracks by the Italian army.

3.   So in Dio Cassius 58: 4. 3, with the addition that "he often called him 'my Sejanus.'"

4.   This passage is an interesting example of Tacitus' social prejudices.

5.   I.e., before the conquests of Trajan in Dacia and in the East. The passage is of prime importance for the military history of the early Empire.

6. The Cantabrian conquests of Augustus (19 B.C.) mark the last stages of the pacification of Spain.

7. I.e., the colonies in Italy proper. Later, recruitment to the Praetorian Guard was extended, first to all Italians, then to provincials.

8. The notorious *publicani*.

9. These were the *procuratores fisci*.

10. This refers to the projected marriage between Sejanus' daughter and the son of Claudius.

11. A personal servant of Drusus, who may have been his "taster" (*praegustator*).

12. She was eighty.

13. Tacitus' critical methods are well displayed in this passage.

14. Cos was the center of one of the great medical schools of the Greek world, under the patronage of Aesculapius.

15. They were brought back by Gaius (Caligula).

16. 6 B.C.–2 A.D.

17. The temple of Mars Ultor in the Forum of Augustus became a kind of Hall of Fame, where statues of all the *triumphatores* were displayed.

18. Tacitus will have found the speech in the *Acta Senatus*.

19. This custom of marriage by *confarreatio* was confined to the patricians. Divorce for such marriages was highly complicated. The name is derived from the rite of offering a wheatcake (*panis farreus*) to Jupiter before witnesses.

20. In Roman law a woman was never (in theory) *sui iuris*, but always under the control, first of her father, then of her husband.

21. Tiberius had used the words of the "supreme decree" of the Senate, proclaiming martial law.

22. A technical term meaning, in effect, banishment from Italy.

23. The gangs of slaves on these great ranches had always provided combustible material for slave rebellions.

24. To be beaten with rods, then sewn up into a sack with a dog, a cock, a viper, and a monkey, and thrown into the sea.

25. This is a key passage for Tacitus' view of history.

26. The Pompeiani were the enemies of the Juliani in the civil war of 48 B.C.

27. Four poems of Catullus (29, 54, 57, 95) lampoon Caesar.

28. I.e., from the verdict of history.

29. According to Dio, they had failed to complete a temple to Augustus.

30. We have, presumably, a recasting by Tacitus of the actual words of Tiberius as recorded in the *Acta Senatus* (cf. III: 53).

31. What can have been Tacitus' source for this highly confidential letter, and the reply?

32. Which carried lighter penalties.

33. Both city and temple claimed to have been founded by Aeneas, ancestor of the imperial house.

34. The reference is to a *cause célèbre* of 94 B.C.

35. Tacitus here confuses the younger with the elder sister.

36.   Crossing the upper Elbe, in Bohemia, in 2 B.C.

37.   See Section 19.

38.   The story is also told by Suetonius. The source of the quotation is not known, though a similar saying is attributed to Jason of Pherae.

39.   The derivation of "Etrusci" from the name of Tyrrhenus is not obvious; the connection is clearer in the alternate Roman name for the Etruscans, Tyrrheni.

40.   Herodotus calls Pelops a Phrygian; Pindar and Pausanias, a Lydian.

41.   In 195 B.C.

42.   Note Tacitus' contempt for these Greek intellectuals.

43.   *Spelunca* means "cave"; the name survives as Sperlonga. Archaeology has strikingly confirmed Tacitus—or so it would seem. In 1957 the Italian archaeologist Iacopi excavated a large cave near the sea at Sperlonga. He found enormous quantities of statuary, and an inscription by a certain Faustinus explaining how the cave was adorned with sculpture for the imperial pleasure (see G. Iacopi, *I ritrovamenti dell' antro cosidetto "di Tiberio" a Sperlonga,* Rome, 1958).

44.   The words echo Sallust (H. 2. 23. i).

45.   Suetonius says 20,000 were killed. The casualty figures seem impossibly high. The Colosseum itself only held 50,000 at the most.

46.   In the great eruption of 79 A.D., which buried Pompeii and Herculaneum.

47.   Presumably twelve former villas were included in the estate of Tiberius.

48.   Referring to the custom of making New Year offerings to the gods. Dio has a story of how Sabinus' dog refused to leave his master's body.

49.   Granddaughter of Augustus, the younger Julia was as notorious as her mother. The exile of Ovid to the Black Sea is thought to be connected with her.

50.   The modern Friesland preserves their name.

51.   The urus, the great wild ox of Germany, now extinct. These cattle were said by Caesar to be "as big as elephants."

52.   Site unknown. A war goddess?

BOOK V

1.   Dio says she was eighty-six, Pliny eighty-two. The former seems more probable.

2.   In 39 B.C.

3.   Inscriptions refer to a *curator actorum senatus.* Rusticus may have been only a clerk, and not a member of the Senate.

BOOK VI

1.   The theme is thought to be the punishment of Livilla for her part in the poisoning of Drusus.

2.   This incomplete speech is by an unknown supporter of Sejanus, probably to a group of his friends.

3.   "Connection by marriage"—i.e., because of the proposed betrothal to Livilla.

4.   Blaesus, uncle of Sejanus, presumably put to death in the first purge of his followers.

5.   This was the *aerarium militare,* or military treasury.

6.   I.e., became responsible for their custody.

7.   Sejanus had three children by Apicata; the eldest had already fallen a victim to the purge.

8.   She was eleven.

9.   Their motives are hard to discern, and this has led some translators to take *Caesaris* as referring to Drusus and not to Tiberius.

10.   These were the gardens bequeathed by Caesar to the Roman people: the site is in the modern Trastevere.

11.   Both his names attest his Gallic origin. Syme notes the "ferocious irony" which Tiberius brings to bear on his silly proposal (*op. cit.,* 284, 563).

12.   IV: 68.

13.   I.e., Socrates, probably in Plato. (*Gorgias,* 524 E.)

14.   I.e., while the consuls were away from Rome during the yearly festival on the Monte Cavo.

15.   Revised once by Augustus (see I: 76), but apocryphal versions kept recurring.

16.   Before the time of Augustus, a quorum was 400.

17.   But the Capitol was actually burned in the civil war (83 B.C.), not the Social War. Tacitus gives the correct version in *Hist.* III: 72.

18.   Macro had engineered the fall of Sejanus, and succeeded him as commander of the Praetorian Guard.

19.   There seems to be a gap. Suetonius added the clause "and that debtors should immediately repay the same proportion of their debts."

20.   The Epicureans.

21.   The Stoics. Cf. Seneca, *Nat Quaest,* II: 36.

22.   I.e., as with Arruntius (in the next paragraph), he was not allowed to go to his province.

23.   Syme (*op. cit.,* 472) raises the question whether a phoenix appeared in 117 A.D. Certainly its image figured on the coinage of Hadrian. He notes that this is "the solitary digression of an exotic nature in all the *Annals.*"

24.   The dates of the reign of "Sesosis" are uncertain. "Amasis" belongs to the sixth century B.C. Ptolemy III Euergetes died 222 B.C.

25.   According to Dio, its subject was Atreus: Suetonius says Agamemnon—both explosive themes. Cf. Queen Elizabeth's dislike of the play *Richard the Second*.

26.   Cf. II: 58 and 68.

27.   Thus implying the recovery of Syria and Asia from the Roman Empire.

28.   The modern Pass of Dariel.

29.   The road along the west coast of the Caspian Sea.

30.   Ancient geographers gave highly colored accounts of the effect of the "etesian winds" of this locality (Pliny, *N.H.* II: 47. 127).

31.   I.e., the rebellion of 6–9 A.D.

32.   In Greek, "between the rivers."

33.   Thus making his property liable to confiscation.

34.   In a lost passage.

35.   The hereditary title of the commander-in-chief of the Parthian army.

36.   The *scaena* was only a restoration after a fire.

37.   I.e., incest.

38.   I.e., he pretended to kiss it.

39.   Similar measures were taken at the deaths of Augustus (I: 5) and Claudius (XII: 68).

40.   Cf. the rumors of macabre scenes at the deathbed of Stalin.

41.   This section—one of the best-known in Tacitus—is the culminating point of his attack on Tiberius. Purporting to give a balanced assessment, it shows how step by step all the mitigating or restraining influences were removed until in the end his character stood out in all its fundamental evil.

BOOK XI

1.   On the Pincian Hill.

2.   Originally passed in 204 B.C., and revived by Augustus.

3.   Gotarzes, Artabanus, and Vardanes were sons of the Parthian king Artabanus III, mentioned in Books II and VI.

4.   The secular games were held at intervals of 100 (or 110) years, so that no one would see them twice. Claudius based his calculations on the foundation of Rome in 753 B.C., the eight hundredth anniversary of which fell in 47 A.D. But this was only sixty-four years after the games held by Augustus in 17 B.C., and Claudius incurred ridicule because some of the spectators—and even some of the actors—had been present on the earlier occasion. (See Suetonius, *Claudius*, 21.) Tacitus dealt with the problem in a lost section of the *Histories*.

5.   In 88 A.D.

6.   A traditional cavalry display.

7.   E.g., the infancy of Hercules.

8.   One of his plays was on the theme of Aeneas. None survive.

9.   This was the Aqua Claudia, which enters Rome by the Porta Maggiore. The Simbruine Hills are near Subiaco.

10.   The three new letters were ⅃ for the consonant *v*, ⊢ for the sound of *y* (similar to the French *u* or German *ü*, occurring in words from Greek), ⊐ for *bs*, *ps*. They are found on Claudian inscriptions, but did not last. Syme (*op. cit.*, 515) points out that this digression on the origins of the alphabet reads like a parody of the pedantry of Claudius.

11.   As a result, the shameful truth is unknown. This is (perhaps) the Q. Curtius Rufus who wrote on Alexander the Great.

12.   Gallia Comata—the three northern and western provinces of Gaul.

13.   They were granted citizenship by Julius Caesar in 49 B.C.

14.   Under Vercingetorix (52 B.C.).

15.   On this passage Syme remarks, "Anger and pathos are helped out (it happens often) by the appeal to race or history, with arguments crude, feeble, or spurious. So Tacitus intended. He made them up to refute them majestically" (*op cit.* p. 624).

16.   Since Claudius' actual oration survives on a bronze tablet at Lyons (ILS 212), we have here an unusual opportunity of comparing a speech in Tacitus with its original. While preserving the general style, Tacitus alters, adds, and deletes freely.

17.   At the Battle of the Caudine Forks in 321 B.C.

18.   They received this title in 121 B.C., and still proudly claimed it in the third century A.D.

19.   Including, presumably, the wives and children of citizens.

BOOK XII

1.   Tacitus gives us here a set debate as if at a meeting of the *concilium principis*—the privy council of the Emperor. Note the prominence of freedmen, a feature of the reign of Claudius.

2.   What follows is a parody of Vitellius' bland manner.

3.   This is the younger Seneca, philosopher and tragedian; he had been banished by Claudius in 41 A.D.

4.   The name survives in Mt. Sanbulah, a spur of the Zagros Mountains. Hercules is identified with Nin, the god of hunting.

5.   About $100,000.

6.   Augustus had ruled that senators must not travel outside Italy without permission. He had made an exception, however, in the case of senators with property in Sicily who wished to visit their estates.

7.   The *pomerium* was the sacred furrow, ritually traced to mark the bounds of the city. This is one of the key passages for its original course and later enlargements. Claudius extended it by reasons of his conquests in Britain, Thrace, and Mauretania.

8.   *Cippi* (inscribed stones) show that his extensions were in the Campus Martius and on the Aventine.

9.   The founder of the gens Claudia who came to Rome from the Sabine territory in 504 B.C.

10.   P. Pomponius Secundus, already mentioned as a writer in XI:13.

11.   The Roman flotilla patrolling the Danube was an important part of the defense of the Danube frontier. Another flotilla operated on the Drava.

12.   This passage follows the reading "cunctaque cis Trisantonam et Sabrinam fluvios cohibere parat"—an emendation to one of the most disputed passages in Tacitus.

13.   Site unknown.

14.   In northeast Wales. For the territory of this and and the other tribes see the map of Roman Britian, p. 418.

15.   Son of Cunobelinus. Defeated by Aulus Plautius in 43 A.D., he had gone to Wales to continue resistance. The spelling "Caractacus" is a common error.

16.   Site unknown, but probably in the upper Severn valley west of Welshpool.

17.   The famous "tortoise" formation used in assaults on defended positions, illustrated on Trajan's Column.

18.   I.e., from the invasion of 43 A.D., using the Roman style of reckoning, which counts the first year as well as the last. It was 51 A.D. our style. See also note 23.

19.   The triumphs of Scipio Africanus (201 B.C.) and Aemilius Paulus (167 B.C.) were the most glorious of the old Republic. They were also notable for their display of clemency to a beaten enemy, which is why they were compared with Claudius' clemency to Caratacus. Tacitus conceals this point.

20.   By Tiberius in 8 B.C.

21.   Probably the Second Legion operating from Gloucester.

22.   This reference is lost.

23.   Actually, from 47 to 58 A.D., the longest of such continuous accounts in the *Annals*.

24.   The *toga virilis*, the token of adult status, was usually assumed at the age of fifteen. Nero was thirteen.

25.   Born in Gallia Narbonensis, Burrus was the protégé of Agrippina. He rose to high power under Nero.

26.   Actually, the privilege of using the *carpentum* had been granted to both Livia and Messalina.

27.   Great advances in siegecraft were made in the Hellenistic period. The Romans, in fact, added little new, but even so had a great superiority over the barbarians.

28.   Cf. the widespread belief in the ties of "blood-brotherhood."

29.   A striking exposition of *Realpolitik*.

30.   The project of draining the Fucine Lake was first mooted by Caesar, but attempts by Claudius, Trajan, and Hadrian all fell short of success. It was finally accomplished in the nineteenth century.

31.   A notable example of skepticism in the face of the Trojan legend, the cherished myth of the Julio-Claudian house.

32.   The chapter is a parody of Claudius' antiquarian learning.

Xenophon, the doctor mentioned, was later an accomplice in the poisoning of Claudius.

33. Tacitus is wrong—the lady was the daughter of the *elder* Antonia.

34. These gangs of slaves worked the great ranches of Apulia and Calabria.

35. There has been much discussion as to the species of mushroom served on this famous occasion.

BOOK XIII

1. An ominous beginning: so the reign of Tiberius had begun with the murder of Agrippa Postumus (I: 6).

2. Her portrait appeared on the coinage. See insert—coins of Gaius and Claudius.

3. The implication is that these artistic accomplishments were all very well, but Nero had pursued them at the expense of the training in oratory proper for a Roman.

4. I.e., on leaving office, when a magistrate, in the presence of his supporters, solemnly avowed his innocence. But the freedman, Pallas, had been able to insist that there should be no investigations.

5. The great December festival (17th–19th), a time of general indulgence. At this same festival Seneca had produced his witty and ungracious *Ludus de morte Claudii* (*Skit on the Death of Claudius*).

6. Suetonius says that previous experiments had tested it on a kid (which lived for five hours), and, in a more concentrated form, on a small pig, which died immediately.

7. So contemporary authorities are quoted for the death of Claudius (XII: 67).

8. A striking insight into feminine psychology!

9. This passage is important evidence for Tacitus' use of his sources.

10. This duty fell to the Emperor as Pontifex Maximus.

11. This passage has been used to support the view that Tacitus was of patrician origin. Syme (*op. cit.*, 612f.) points out that these disparaging remarks occur in a discussion.

12. An illuminating comment on the dignity of history.

13. In 47 A.D., recorded presumably in a lost section of Book XI.

14. In the Third Mithridatic War (74–63 B.C.).

15. The Celtic kingdom of Galatia was a great recruiting ground for the Roman army. It became a province in 25 A.D.

16. Corbulo's base was probably near Erzerum.

17. E.g., the annihilation of Crassus' army at Carrhae in 53 B.C.

18. Site unknown.

19. And thus expose themselves to the famous "Parthian tactics" —the feigned withdrawal followed by a devastating attack on troops sent out in pursuit.

20. See XI: 5 and note 3.

21. He was exiled in 37 A.D. for adultery with Germanicus' daughter Julia.

22.   Dio (but not Tacitus) says that his exorbitant rates of interest prompted the rebellion of Boudicca in Britain.

23.   A tribune's person was sacrosanct while he held office.

24.   The future Empress. Her portrait is very carefully drawn.

25.   See the similar comment on Petronius (XVI: 18).

26.   See VI: 43, 44

27.   A distinguished senator and Stoic.

28.   The reading here is *senatores;* another reading, *seniores,* would imply that the proposal was rejected at a meeting of the Emperor's council.

29.   Paulinus in Lower, Antistius in Upper Germany.

30.   This province stretched from the Seine to the Rhine.

31.   I.e., as pasture lands.

32.   Suetonius (who places the event in the reign of Claudius) says these were ambassadors from Parthia and Armenia.

33.   Their name survives in the River Ems.

34.   The tribe is mentioned in the fourth century A.D., so they were not exterminated.

35.   Whatever the process, Tacitus obviously does not understand it.

36.   This would seem to be a description of a peat fire.

37.   Cologne.

38.   When they were suckled by the wolf.

BOOK XIV

1.   Nero's banquets frequently began at midday.

2.   This command was usually given to a knight, but other freedmen are known to have held it.

3.   March 19–23.

4.   I.e., the sea had nothing to do with it.

5.   Dio adds the words "Because it bore Nero!"

6.   For the coin of Nero as "Apollo Citharoedus" see insert—coins of Claudius and Nero.

7.   This is the Circus of Gaius (or Nero) now covered by St. Peter's. Its survivor is the obelisk standing on the Piazza San Pietro.

8.   Dio gives such names as the Fabii, Furii, Porcii, etc.

9.   Presumably Stoics and Cynics.

10.   Died 96 B.C.: Cyrene became a province in 74 B.C.

11.   The Theater of Pompeius (55 B.C.), was the first permanent theater in Rome.

12.   The narrative of Eastern affairs is resumed from XIII:41, and covers the events of 59 and 60 A.D.

13.   The Roman soldier disliked meat and preferred a grain diet.

14.   But foundations of the older type were known under Trajan. See Syme, *op. cit.,* 447.

15.   Tacitus seems to have conflated the events of two years: the rebellion of Boudicca will have begun in 60 A.D. See Syme, *op cit.,* Appendix 69.

16.   Notable for his conquests in Mauretania in 43 A.D., since when he had held no command.

17.   The Druids stood for a pan-Celtic, anti-Roman nationalism. Anglesey was their chief center in Britain. A famous archaeological find—the treasure of Llyn Cerrig Bach—attests their wide influence over the British tribes.

18.   The temple of Claudius was constructed on an elaborate classical plan unique in Roman Britain. Its podium still survives under the (Norman) castle of Colchester.

19.   The base of the Ninth Legion was *Lindum* (Lincoln), and the battle must have taken place on the fen margins.

20.   This is the first reference to London in history.

21.   St. Albans, twenty miles from London.

22.   The site of this battle is unknown, but it must have been on the line of Watling Street, northwest of Towcester—perhaps near Nuneaton?

23.   Probably at Glevum (Gloucester). He had disobeyed an order to meet Suetonius on his march to London.

24.   "The real hero of the Boudicca rebellion" (Collingwood). His tombstone is in the British Museum.

25.   Tacitus is notoriously unfair to the nonmilitary governors of Britain. Under Turpilianus and his successors the romanization of the province made great strides.

26.   Sallustian echoes set the tone of these old-fashioned sentiments.

27.   Suetonius retails the poisoning story as fact.

28.   What can have been Tacitus' sources for this private interview?

29.   Stoic philosopher, and teacher of Epictetus.

30.   Nero's words, lost from the text of Tacitus, are supplied by Dio.

31.   Here there is a gap in the text.

32.   The text of this passage is corrupt.

BOOK XV

1.   The narrative is resumed from XIV:26.

2.   I.e., equal (presumably) to the rest of the force.

3.   Accepted by Suetonius, but not by Dio.

4.   In his *Memoirs,* used by both Tacitus and Pliny.

5.   See XIII:41.

6.   To suggest that supplies were plentiful.

7.   It is uncertain what this subsidy was. It may have been expenditure from the imperial treasury on the *annona*: it may have been the amount by which the total expenditure of the imperial exceeded that of the public treasury.

8.   The whole attitude to the provincials is significant, coming as it does from a senator of probity.

9.   According to Seneca, this earthquake took place on February

5, 63 A.D., sixteen years before the great eruption of Vesuvius which destroyed Pompeii and Herculaneum.

10.   Held at Nicopolis.

11.   I.e., a seat at the ceremonial *lectisternium,* or banquet of the gods.

12.   According to Pliny, as a Magian he must not travel by sea.

13.   By the *Lex Gabinia* of 67 B.C.

14.   For the opening of the campaign.

15.   One hundred thirty-two years.

16.   As beneath the dignity of history.

17.   The *stagnum Agrippae* was presumably close to the Pantheon, in the Campus Martius. See note 18 below.

18.   The buildings of Agrippa were the Pantheon and the adjacent thermae and colonnades.

19.   These estates are said to have been where the later Forum of Trajan was built.

20.   The Regia and the Atrium Vestae stood in the Forum Romanum.

21.   This refers to the destruction of the Palatine Library, founded by Augustus.

22.   It had been calculated that 418 years, plus 418 months, plus 418 days had elapsed since the capture of Rome by the Gauls.

23.   The famous *Domus Aurea,* or Golden House of Nero, which was never completed.

24.   The name first appears at Antioch about 45 A.D.

25.   By reason of the supposed cannibalism (in the Eucharist), infanticide, incest, and other charges brought against the early Christians.

26.   An instance of Tacitus' detestation of the Roman mob.

27.   I.e., the slave rising of 73–71 B.C.

28.   Now Piacenza.

29.   Site uncertain.

30.   Tacitus' authority here was probably Fabius Rusticus, who could have been present at this banquet.

31.   At the end of a banquet, the Greeks offered a libation to Zeus, "the giver of freedom."

32.   Perhaps *Pharsalia* III:635–646.

33.   Tacitus does not care to quote Greek.

34.   Jupiter Vindex.

BOOK XVI

1.   This was no mere rhetoric. Pliny (N.H. XXXIII:4. 21) mentions the discovery of a rich outcrop of gold, close to the surface, in Dalmatia during Nero's reign.

2.   According to Dio, part of his own poem on the Trojan War.

3.   Many contemporaries contrast the simple life of the Italian towns with the *dolce vita* of the capital. It is well seen in the letters of Pliny.

4.   Suetonius and Dio place this *contretemps* during Nero's visit to Greece. It is of course possible that the future Emperor Vespasian failed to keep awake at more than one of these recitals!

5.   Because, says Suetonius (*Nero,* 35), she reproached him for coming home late from the Circus.

6.   See XV:35.

7.   The modern Bari.

8.   The belief of a "blight in the air" as the cause of epidemics persisted until the nineteenth century.

9.   Both the date and the nature of this disaster at Lyons are uncertain.

10.   See XII:31. This is Marcus Ostorius, son of Ostorius Scapula, the second governor of Britian.

11.   "Ira illa numinum in res Romanas fuit"; cf. "Deum ira in rem Romanam"—"the anger of the gods against Rome" (IV:1): these are perhaps the most striking expressions of Tacitus' settled pessimism.

12.   I.e., they had the property qualifications of a senator.

13.   This is one of the most famous of Tacitus' character studies. The Petronius of this passage is (almost certainly) the author of that splendid picaresque novel, the *Satyricon.*

14.   These two men were the leaders of the "Stoic opposition" to Nero. For the whole movement, with its cult of the tyrannicides Brutus and Cassius, and its Stoic and Cynic sympathies, see *Cambridge Ancient History,* Vol. X, p. 730, and H. H. Scullard, *From the Gracchi to Nero,* p. 322.

15.   Later to suffer death under Domitian for writing the biography of Thrasea.

16.   This scandalous betrayal of a patron by a client, of a "pupil" by his "master," is stigmatized by Juvenal (III:116ff.)

17.   Praised by Seneca, the Cynic Demetrius was active in Rome under Nero and Vespasian.

18.   Arria's mother committed suicide with her husband in 42 A.D.

A NOTE ON THE
ROMAN ARMY

The army of the first century A.D. was the army as re-organized by Augustus. There were two great divisions, the *legions,* recruited from Roman citizens, and the *auxilia,* from provincials who were not citizens.

The legions were still the main fighting strength of the army. Each legion was of a nominal strength of six thousand men—in practice, usually about five thousand—under the command of a *legatus* of senatorial rank. Attached to his staff were the *tribuni* (military tribunes), young men of senatorial or knightly rank performing the military service which was the prelude to a political career. But the hard core of the officers was the sixty centurions, six in each of the ten cohorts into which the legion was divided. On these tough professional soldiers the discipline and fighting spirit of the legion depended. Each cohort was divided into six centuries, under the command of a centurion. The common soldier (*legionarius miles*) served at first for sixteen, later for twenty years; there was a further period of four to five years on reserve (*sub vexillo*). Recruitment to the legions in the time of Augustus was from Italy, Gallia Narbonensis, and Baetica; later it was extended to other provinces. On discharge, the legionary soldier received a grant of land in a Roman *colonia.* The legions, whose numbers varied from twenty-eight to thirty during the period, were stationed in large fortified bases (*castra*) on the frontiers. There was no strategic reserve. For the distribution of the legions see Book IV of the *Annals.*

The auxiliaries (*auxilia*) were originally recruited as supporting troops, especially cavalry, from the allies. Their units bore tribal or geographical names, but later recruiting was often done from the province in which the unit served. They comprised (1) *alae,* or cavalry squadrons, (2) *cohortes,* infantry units, of either one thousand or five hundred men, under the command of a *praefectus* who might be an ally or a Roman citizen of knightly rank. Thrace, Galatia, the German provinces, and the less romanized parts of Gaul and Spain were the main sources of recruitment. Their pay was less and their period of service (twenty-five years) longer than that of the legionary; they received Roman citizenship for themselves and their descendants on discharge. They thus played a very important part in the romanization of the provinces.

The total strength of legions and *auxilia* was about 300,000 men: a small force for the defense of so huge an Empire. The careful attention paid to weapons, training, tactics, communications, and the siting and construction of forts did something to make up for this deficiency in manpower. Throughout the first century, Roman troops, fit for battle and well led, were more than a match for any possible opponent. The real weakness of the system became apparent in the second century A.D.

Principal Place and Tribal Names and Their Modern Equivalents

ANCIENT	MODERN
Aedui (tribe)	Near Autun
Alba Longa	Castel Gandolfo
Albani (tribe)	Azerbaijan (U.S.S.R.)
Alesia	Alise St. Reine
Aliso	Near river Lippe
Ancona	Ancona
Andecavi (tribe)	Near Angers
Angrivarii	Near river Weser
Antioch	Antakyia (Syria)
Antium	Anzio
Aorsi	S.E. of river Don
Aquitania	S.W. France
Arduinna Silva	Forest of Ardennes
Armenia, Lesser	N.E. Turkey
Artaxata	Artashat
Augustodunum	Autun
Avernus, Lake	Averno
Baiae	Baia
Barium	Bari
Bastarnae (tribe)	Western Ukraine
Batavi, Island of the	Rhine Delta
Belgica, Gallia	N.E. France and Belgium
Bithynia	N.W. Anatolia
Bosporus, Cimmerian	Kerch
Brigantes (tribe)	N. of Humber-Mersey
Brundisium	Brindisi
Byzantium	Istanbul
Calabria	Southern Apulia
Camulodunum	Colchester

Cappadocia	E. Anatolia
Capreae	Capri
Carmania	S. Persia
Carrhae	Haran
Caspian Pass	Dariel Pass (Georgian Military Road)
Caudian Forks	Campania
Celenderis	Cilindire
Chatti (tribe)	Upper Weser
Chauci (tribe)	Lower "
Cherusci (tribe)	Middle "
Cirta	Constantine
Colchis	W. Georgia
Colonia Agrippina	Cologne
Corcyra	Corfu
Ctresiphon	Kut el Amara
Cumae	Cuma
Dalae	Turmenistan
Degeangi (or Decangi) (tribe)	N.E. Wales
Delos	Delos
Delphi	Delphi
Ecbatana	Hamadan
Edessa	Urfa
Elephantine	Asswan
Emona	Ljubljana
Ephesus	Selcuk
Fidenae	Castel Giubileo
Flevum, Lake	Zuyder Zee
Florentia	Florence
Forum Julii	Frejus
Frisii (tribe)	Friesland
Fucinus, Lake	Fucino
Galatia	Central Anatolia
Garamantes	Fezzan
Getae	Rumania
Gotones (tribe)	N. Poland
Gyaros	Gyaros
Halicarnassus	Bodrun
Hyrcania	N.E. Persia
Iberia	Georgia

Iceni (tribe)	Norfolk-Suffolk
Idistaviso	(?) near Minden
Ilium	Troy
Jazyges (tribe)	Between rivers Bug and Dnieper
Langobardi	Weser-Elbe
Leptis Minor	Lamta
Londinium	London
Lugdunum	Lyons
Maeander, River	River Menderes
Marcomanni (tribe)	Bohemer Wald
Marsi (tribe)	Ruhr
Massilia	Marseilles
Mauretania	W. Algeria and Morocco
Media	Ustan (Persia)
Media Atropatene	Azerbaijan (Persia)
Mesopotamia	N. Iraq
Moesia	E. Yugoslavia and N. Bulgaria
Mona	Anglesey
Musulamii	Sahara
Nabataei	Jordan-Saudi Arabia border
Nauportus	Vrhnika
Neapolis	Naples
Nineveh	Mospila
Ordovices (tribe)	N. Wales
Pamphylia	S. Anatolia
Pannonia	N. Yugoslavia, W. Hungary
Patavium	Padua
Pergamum	Borgamo
Perusia	Perugia
Pontus	W. Anatolia
Propontis	Sea of Marmora
Puteoli	Pozzuoli
Quadi (tribe)	N. of Danube in Bohemia
Raetia	Switzerland
Salamis	Famagusta (Cyprus)
Sanbulus, Mt.	(?) Sunbula, Mt.

Scythae	S. Russia
Seleucia-on-the-Tigris	Near Kut el Amara
Senonea	Near Sens
Silures (tribe)	S.E. Wales
Smyrna	Izmir
Surrentum	Sorrento
Taurus	Crimea
Teutoburg Forest	Weser-Ems
Thebes (Egypt)	Luxor
Tibur	Tivoli
Trinobantes (tribe)	Essex
Troy	Hissarlik
Ubii (tribe)	Around Cologne
Vangiones (tribe)	Around Mainz
Verulamium	St. Albans
Volandum	(?) Igdir
Vulsinii	Bolsena
Zeugma	Balkis

Kings of Parthia

Phraates I, also styled Arsaces			XV	38–2 B.C.
Phraataces	"	"	"	XVI
Orodes II	"	"	"	XVII	2 B.C.–5 A.D.
Vonones I	"	"	"	XVIII	5–16 A.D.
Artabanus III	"	"	"	XIX	16–42 A.D.
Gotarzes	"	"	"	XX	42
Vardanes I	"	"	"	XXI	42–46
Gotarzes (restored)	"	"	"	XX	46–51
Vonones II	"	"	"	XXII	51
Vologeses I	"	"	"	XXIII	51–78

Kings of Armenia

Vonones	c.11–c.16 A.D.
Artaxias	c.18–c.34
Arsaces	34–36
Mithridates	36–51
Radamistus	51
Tiridates	51–60
Tigranes V	60–62
Tiridates (restored)	63—crowned by Nero 66

FAMILY OF THE JULIO-CLAUDIAN EMPERORS

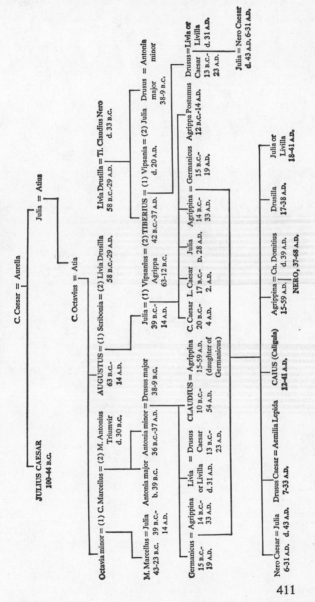

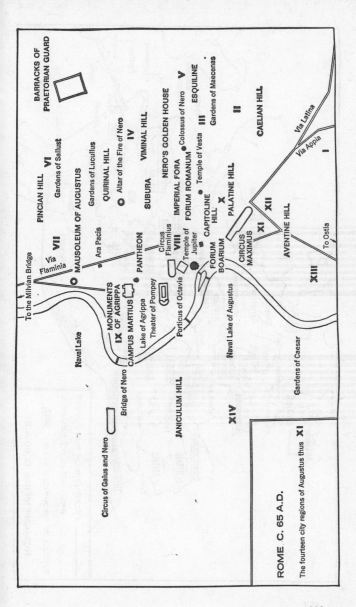

ROME. C. 65 A.D.

The fourteen city regions of Augustus thus **XI**

BARRACKS OF PRAETORIAN GUARD

Gardens of Sallust

PINCIAN HILL **VI**

Gardens of Lucullus

QUIRINAL HILL **IV**

VIMINAL HILL

Altar of the Fire of Nero

NERO'S GOLDEN HOUSE

SUBURA

Colossus of Nero

ESQUILINE **V**

Gardens of Maecenas

MAUSOLEUM OF AUGUSTUS

III

IMPERIAL FORA

FORUM ROMANUM

Temple of Vesta

II

CAELIAN HILL

Via Latina

Via Appia

I

Ara Pacis

Via Flaminia

VII

PANTHEON

Circus Flaminius

VIII

CAPITOLINE HILL

PALATINE HILL

X

Temple of Jupiter

To the Milvian Bridge

MONUMENTS OF AGRIPPA

IX CAMPUS MARTIUS

Lake of Agrippa

Theater of Pompey

Porticus of Octavia

FORUM BOARIUM

CIRCUS MAXIMUS

XI

XII

AVENTINE HILL

To Ostia

XIII

Naval Lake

Bridge of Nero

Naval Lake of Augustus

JANICULUM HILL

XIV

Gardens of Caesar

Circus of Galus and Nero

413

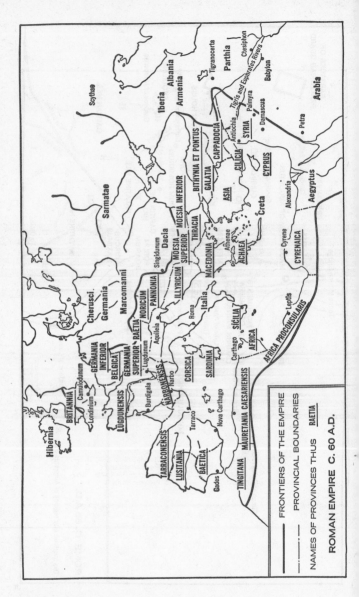

ROMAN EMPIRE C. 60 A.D.

FRONTIERS OF THE EMPIRE
PROVINCIAL BOUNDARIES
NAMES OF PROVINCES THUS **RAETIA**

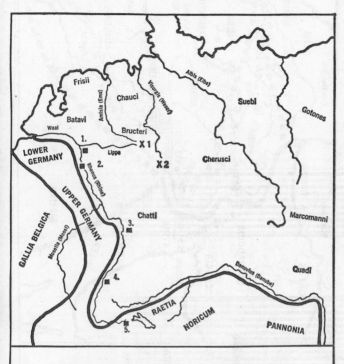

THE RHINE-UPPER DANUBE FRONTIER — TIBERIUS TO NERO ·

Roman Provinces **RAETIA**	1. Vetera (Xanten)
Tribal Names Chatti	2. Oppidum Ubiorum (Cologne)
X 1 ? Defeat of Varus 9 A.D.	3. Moguntiacum (Mainz)
X 2 ? Battle of Idistaviso 16 A.D.	4. Argentorate (Strasbourg)
Rhine Legionary Bases ■	5. Vindonissa (Windisch)

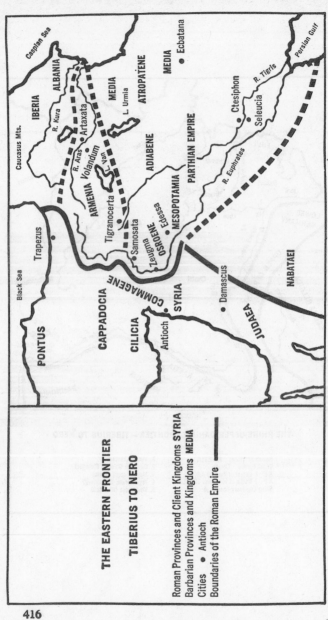

THE EASTERN FRONTIER

TIBERIUS TO NERO

Roman Provinces and Client Kingdoms SYRIA
Barbarian Provinces and Kingdoms MEDIA
Cities • Antioch
Boundaries of the Roman Empire

BRITAIN IN THE REIGNS OF CLAUDIUS AND NERO

Tribal Name **TRINOBANTES**
Cities ● *Camulodunum*
Legionary Bases ■ Viroconium
X1   ? Defeat of Caratacus 50 A.D.
X2   ? Defeat of Boudicca 60 A.D.

Index

421